CULTURE ON THE MARGINS

CULTURE ON THE MARGINS

THE BLACK SPIRITUAL AND THE
RISE OF AMERICAN
CULTURAL INTERPRETATION

Jon Cruz

PRINCETON UNIVERSITY PRESS

PRINCETON, NEW JERSEY

COPYRIGHT © 1999 BY PRINCETON UNIVERSITY PRESS

PUBLISHED BY PRINCETON UNIVERSITY PRESS, 41 WILLIAM STREET,

PRINCETON, NEW JERSEY 08540

IN THE UNITED KINGDOM: PRINCETON UNIVERSITY PRESS,

CHICHESTER, WEST SUSSEX

LIBRARY OF CONGRESS CATALOGING-IN-PUBLICATION DATA

CRUZ, JON.

CULTURE ON THE MARGINS : THE BLACK SPIRITUAL AND THE RISE OF

AMERICAN CULTURAL INTERPRETATION / JON CRUZ.

P.   CM.

INCLUDES BIBLIOGRAPHICAL REFERENCES AND INDEX.

ISBN 0-691-00473-0 (CLOTH : ALK. PAPER).

ISBN 0-691-00474-9 (PBK. : ALK. PAPER)

1. SPIRITUALS (SONGS)—SOCIAL ASPECTS. 2. AFRO-AMERICANS—MUSIC—SOCIAL

ASPECTS. 3. CULTURE—RESEARCH—UNITED STATES—HISTORY. I. TITLE.

ML 3556.C78 1999

782.25′3—DC21   98-43567

THIS BOOK HAS BEEN COMPOSED IN SABON TYPEFACE

THE PAPER USED IN THIS PUBLICATION MEETS THE MINIMUM REQUIREMENTS

OF ANSI/NISO Z39.48-1992 (R1997) *(PERMANENCE OF PAPER)*

HTTP://PUP.PRINCETON.EDU

PRINTED IN THE UNITED STATES OF AMERICA

1 3 5 7 9 10 8 6 4 2

1 3 5 7 9 10 8 6 4 2

(PBK.)

FOR HANNAH WHO ALWAYS MAKES ME SMILE,

JESSE WHO REMINDS ME THAT EVERY DAY

IS TO BE CHERISHED,

TESS WHO BRINGS GENTLE BALANCE TO CHAOS.

CONTENTS

ACKNOWLEDGMENTS

WRITING may be a solitary act, but the ideas that writing gives form to invariably contain influences from events, experiences, and certainly other people. In writing this book I have benefited from conversations and communiqués with Avery Gordon, George Lipsitz, Roger Friedland, Richard Flax, and Elizabeth Long. They read earlier drafts, shared their enthusiasm for what I was trying to accomplish, and sharpened my thoughts with their acumen. They also helped me to see things that I perhaps would have slighted, and to say things better.

A book in progress can often become an albatross. Thanks to friends Keith Osajima, Sara Schoonmaker, Eldon Vail, Lew Friedland, and Bob Dunn for intellectual, political, and moral camaraderie. In their own unique ways they helped give me buoyancy.

At different stages of this project I received endorsement in some cases direct, in other cases indirect, from Herman Gray, Charles Lemert, Pertti Alasuttari, John Mohr, John Sutton, Howard Becker, and Michael Denning. Dwight Reynolds and Richard Peterson read and gave helpful suggestions for chapter 5.

Todd Gitlin, Troy Duster, and Ronald Takaki helped me in the earliest launch of this study. For propelling me along the way I owe special thanks to Gerald Platt, Ed Driver, Archie Schepp, Douglas Daniels, Dan Clawson, Robert Faulkner, and Randall Stokes.

Some of my ideas, early research opportunities, and chances to try out notions and arguments were facilitated by my involvement with the Institute for Advanced Study in the Humanities at the University of Massachusetts, Amherst, and through fellowships through the Humanities Research Center at the University of California, Irvine, and the Interdisciplinary Humanities Center at the University of California at Santa Barbara. For these opportunities I thank Judith Fryer, Mark Rose, and Simon Williams. My gratitude for Hazel Hull, Marie Vierra, Michelle Wakin, Jonathan Cordero, and Sylvia Curtis who helped me troubleshoot and to locate materials during the research.

The sociologist C. Wright Mills insisted that history is the necessary shank for sociology, and that sociology without history is a blueprint for intellectual drift and default to managerialism. I take few disciplinary maxims seriously, but this is one that I do. My historically informed sociological horizons owe much to the work of Ronald Takaki, Lawrence Levine, Dena Epstein, Sterling Stuckey, Eugene Genovese, Eric Foner, and George Fredrickson.

Mary Murrell, my editor at Princeton University Press, supported this project from its inception to its completion. Her unflagging belief that I had a book of value remained even during a time when I felt its completion was being snatched away by circumstances I could not control. Fortunate I was to have the ever so careful skills of copy editor Cindy Crumrine.

Finally, I am especially grateful to William Bielby, Sucheng Chan, Don Zimmerman, Julius Zelmanowitz, and particularly Chris Allen and Sally Foxen for their human touch. They provided institutional support though a medical leave in the darkest year of my and my family's life. Without their institutional support, and the support of so many of my colleagues at Santa Barbara, this book surely would have withered along with my ties to the academy.

CULTURE ON THE MARGINS

INTRODUCTION

WHEN FREDERICK DOUGLASS published his autobiography in 1845 he asked his readers to pause and listen to the songs of slaves. In their "songs of sorrow," as he called them, we would hear their "tale of woe," for "every tone was a testimony against slavery." Douglass's invitation was heeded. By the eve of the Civil War, abolitionists were more than ready to hear the "spirituals"; black religious song making was even enlisted as cultural weaponry in the symbolic arsenal against slavery. Among the abolitionists a small number of individuals took the discovery of black songs quite seriously and set about finding and collecting examples of spirituals, which they transcribed and published. In their hands the religious aspects of black oral culture were transformed into written texts.

This "discovery" and the new attention it brought to black song making was unprecedented. It broke from the earlier frameworks in which black song making was heard as alien noise, and it created a critical humanistic interest in the music of African Americans. More important, this interest marked a major turning point in American intellectual development—it helped install the modern hermeneutical orientation toward cultural practices and laid the groundwork for a scientist and objectivist treatment of black music. Douglass had called for an interpretive ethos of pathos. The new mode of hearing that he helped champion required an attentive and refined sensibility, one that sought out the inner world that was presumably reflected in the expressions of slaves. Their songs were to be grasped as testimonies to their lives, as indices of their sense of social fate.

Amplified by the abolitionist movement, Douglass's invitation rode the much larger and more powerful cultural current of what I call *ethnosympathy*. Ethnosympathy—the new humanitarian pursuit of the inner world of distinctive and collectively classifiable subjects—marshaled the interest in slave-based cultural practices. The new ethnosympathy embodied as well as fostered the importance of such practices as windows into the lives of people. This cultural orientation, which grew from the new value placed upon the inner world of the slaves, also had roots in the earlier endeavors to provide religious instruction to slaves. During the second half of the eighteenth and the early-nineteenth century, increased emphasis was placed upon extending religious teachings to slaves. By proselytizing the slaves, clergymen, owners, and overseers not only acknowledged that slaves had souls; they set in motion a cultural process that recognized slaves as potentially practicing Christians. Though slaves remained objects of property, proselytization granted them a new subjectivity. In essence, through proselytization owners gave slaves a religious franchise. The budding spirit of ethnosympathy, which hinged on these religious developments, enabled slaves to adapt and modify for their own needs this new cultural arena, and it allowed sympathetic whites, particularly abolitionists, to further reconceptualize slaves as culturally expressive subjects.

As I shall argue, Douglass's call in the middle of the nineteenth century for listeners to hear black song making with new, sympathetic ears epitomized the rise of a new mode of interpreting the culture of people who inhabited the social and racial margins within American society. Between the time of Douglass's request and the early-twentieth century, black music had not only been discovered; it had also passed under a series of major interpretive lenses. During the Civil War the "Negro spiritual" emerged as a clearly recognizable cultural form; it was then grasped as a distinct, observable, and knowable element of black culture. Indeed, white moral and cultural entrepreneurs found it to be their *preferred* cultural expression by blacks. This preference had important implications for the interpretation of black expressivity, especially as the interest in the spiritual continued to grow beyond its earlier defining moment in slavery and beyond its status as a testimony to the evils of the "peculiar institution."

Ethnosympathetic interest proceeded along two entwined paths. The first path was opened by critical abolitionists whose romantic antimodernist and humanitarian reformist sensibilities were shaped in part by a view that modernity was corrosive to human nature. Henry David Thoreau's diatribes against the rapidly encroaching marketplace captured well this nexus of antimodern disenchantment. For socially critical Protestants like Thoreau, both capitalism and slavery were detrimental to the social and spiritual well-being of those who lived under these social systems. Cultural intellectuals—certainly not all, but a significant number of them—who were influenced by a new Christian radicalism and who felt disenchanted with the rise of market society were able to *use* their new notion of black culture; the Negro spiritual could be conveniently juxtaposed with their sense of a modernity that increasingly eclipsed both spirituality and human nature. The other path that developed after the 1860s was more rationalistic, scientistic, and modern, though it shared some of the sensibilities inherited from its romantic parentage. The emerging rationalism produced a more studied approach to the Negro spiritual, and it anticipated as well as fed into the early development of professional social science, particularly the study of folklore and what we would recognize as early cultural sociology. Yet the romantic-humanistic and the social-scientific paths were not mutually exclusive; indeed, there was sig-

nificant overlap. Both, after all, were cultural adjustments to and in dialogue with modernity. I hope to illustrate how romantic antimodernism
and rational social science converge and intersect the discovery of the
Negro spiritual. Put another way, the discovery of the Negro spiritual
refracted (as did many developments at the time) these two powerful and
modernizing currents.

The juncture at which black culture—or what has come to be known
as "slave culture"—was "discovered" as *culture* represents a turning
point in the rise of modern cultural interpretation. More specifically, this
juncture brought the new cultural inquiry into relationship with the racial
and cultural margins within American society. Opening the racial margins to cultural interpretation involved several important and interlocking developments. First, the new ethnosympathy and its interpretive impulse not only coincided with abolitionism but helped adjudicate intense
conflicts and profoundly important struggles that were emerging within
the core ethics of American Protestantism. The rise of what many scholars
of American religious history have called "social gospel" had its roots in
Protestant reactions to modern industrialization and market society. The
victims of the new order, particularly laborers, women, and slaves, became important subjects for socially critical Protestants, who saw that
"wage slavery," a central feature of industrialization, trapped white
workers. The women's movement, which challenged the assumption of
female subservience to patriarchy, also drew upon the lessons of slavery.
Rooted in religious debates, these criticisms of society spurred social
movements. At the forefront of these social movements were influential
ministers who were affiliated with the radical edges of Unitarianism and
Transcendentalism. Critical Unitarians and Transcendentalists not only
distanced themselves from a waning Calvinism; they also registered the
emerging sense of alienation that resulted from the unstoppable forces of
industrialization and market society. Both religious frameworks also provided theological, philosophical, and political views that helped both crit-
ics and reformers redefine an ethics suitable to confront modernity. As an
important font for the critique of a modernity that had forced a rapidly
changing society onto the horizon of Christian reflection, these orientations were greatly responsible for the ethnosympathetic discovery of the
spiritual.

In a similar fashion, and through their literary narratives, slaves themselves had launched a Christian-inflected critique of the religious justification of slavery. The critical interrogation of Christian ethics that emerged
out of the slave narratives fed into the antislavery movement in the North.
What makes ethnosympathy and the emerging interest in black culture,
particularly the spirituals, so efficacious is the way in which these two
cultural currents—the religious proselytization of slaves in the South and

Unitarian Transcendentalist Protestant disenchantment in the North—become intertwined. These currents were grounded in the Garrisonian wing of the antislavery movement in which Frederick Douglass was an early and key participant. The writings of William Lloyd Garrison and Frederick Douglass emblematize this new cultural conjuncture, and each found the other useful in promoting the antislavery movement during the two decades prior to the Civil War. Through his abolitionist publication the *Liberator*, Garrison helped bring slave narratives to a larger audience. Douglass brought the "songs of sorrow" into public view. It was in this context that the Negro spiritual developed—or, we might say, was invested with—a peculiar cultural gravity that attracted the small but highly significant number of collectors who, in turn, functioned as protoethnographers and protofolklorists. During and after the Civil War, white ministers, teachers, and volunteers who went to work among recently emancipated slaves continued the important task of discovering and transforming black oral culture into written forms.

When black and white intellectuals began to embrace the new sense of black subjectivity, they forged links between a humanitarian reformist redemption politics of abolitionism and a quest for cultural authenticity. Douglass had embodied the cultural and ethnosympathetic turn—he demonstrated a newly visible black authenticity. And for the first time, black subjectivity and authenticity became fathomable, accessible, and decipherable, and could be drawn into new circuits of familiarity. Authenticity could be formulated—hence, known—in ways that brought the listener closer to the meanings and intentions of the makers of black music. Indeed, the interest in the slave narratives helped prepare the ground for the sympathetic reception of black music, beginning with the spirituals.

Though rooted in a profound social critique, the cultural discovery of black music and the search for cultural authenticity soon began to pivot upon a particular cultural aestheticization of black practices that, in turn, highlighted black religious music over black political and literary voicings. As black culture became aestheticized, a separation emerged between black political claims for a greater social and political inclusion within American civil society and a more acceptable spiritual (and eventually cultural) place for blacks in the hearts and minds of northerners who were championing the new mode of benevolent cultural reception. In essence, a peculiar kind of culturalism triumphed through a cultural eclipse of politics. Interest in the interpretation of culture at the racial margins and the emerging modes of reception had roots in this particular nexus.

Black cultural practices, which had hitherto been misunderstood as well as scorned, derogated, and dismissed, were now discovered, objectified, and edified by critical abolitionists. Their desire to transcribe black song making, particularly the Negro spiritual, reflected a tendency that extolled the virtues of a preferred and idealized notion of the culturally expressive and performing subject—in this case the spiritual-singing Negro. This perspective had a dual function: it provided the recognition and admission of a specifiable black culture, and it granted black culture admission into the larger and certainly contentious domain of "American" culture. Muted, indeed eclipsed, in the process were the argumentative, critical, and elaborate black voices that had already emerged in the slave narratives. These voices had preceded the discovery of the Negro spiritual, but were overshadowed by the larger, newer, aesthetic appreciation of the *preferred* black culture.

The accomplishments of the interpretive turn toward the margins were numerous and important. The new ethnosympathy enabled the discoverers to seek an underlying authenticity of subjects through their cultural practices. It promoted a schema of interpreting the inner culture of individuals and groups. It established a scaffolding for an inquiry that was protoethnographic and prescient (prescientific as it was) of future analytical refinements. It highlighted cultural performances, practices, goods, and objects that could be studied in order to uncover a posited deeper reality. Cultural authenticity was the key to subject authenticity. Both, furthermore, could be studied as complementary parts of the interpretive vision that attempted to bring society into better focus.

But these accomplishments also propelled the ethnosympathetic spirit along a path of increased rationalization, where the epistemological desires of modern science could be accommodated. And this accommodation also involved attempts to reframe and tame the older romantic and reformist impulses. The result was (and remains today) an inexpungable tension between hermeneutic and objectivistic orientations toward cultural analysis in general and the study of cultural forms in particular. With regard to a sociology of black music making and its place within the rise of modern American cultural interpretation, none of these forms of emergent knowledge is visible if one stays within the comfort of received knowledge—whether it be of religiously inflected perspectives focusing on the essential virtues of fixed cultural objects or of the dehistoricized scientistic objectivism that lacks the reflexivity to recognize its own hand in the making of the "objective" world.

The challenge is to grasp sociologically the discovery of the spiritual. There are, of course, numerous ways to do this. In this study I try to show how the discovery was part of a larger cultural confluence in which black music making played a central role in the rise of modern modes of cultural interpretation. This angle requires that we shift our attention from treating black song making as an essential feature of an ethnic-specific group and instead move toward understanding the spiritual as a culminating point upon a sociohistorical map. I treat black song making as a cultural site, an intersection, where we see social interests and social struggles coincide and entwine as we go through the process of discovering and mapping black culture. The discovery, I argue, was crucial in helping us weave part of the intellectual fabric of modern cultural interpretation.

Approaching cultural discovery from this angle thus differs from more familiar approaches. I do not begin by adopting the Negro spiritual at face value, as if "it" were a fixed, ready-made cultural object, whether simply an ethnicized genre of religious song, a symbol of an underlying and essential black existentialism, or the eloquent and sacrosanct signature of an autonomous and transcendental spirit world traversed by, but ultimately exempt from, the dirty hands of history and human interests. Nor do I begin by investing it with already defined aesthetic features, or what we might recognize as institutionally established identity markers that have come to be accepted as knowledge about cultural forms and practices. Such markers are well known and quite valuable; indeed, they constitute much of the interest in culture as an "objective" realm of modern social science. They also function as abstracted musicological parameters, as systems of classification, and as technical scripts. Such approaches can just as easily render music as merely another problem of anatomy amenable to dissection, where its deciphered components can be arrayed through transcription and where they can be captured and catalogued as would be any specimen. Such capturing and cataloguing does come with expediency—at best it does "catch" cultural things and institutionalizes the knowledge of such things; at worst it reifies the notion of culture. And such *knowledge* leaves the problem of culture seemingly resolved as a system of elements grasped and organized in the spirit of scientistic atomism.

Let us ask instead: what kind of interest in black American culture was present and significant *before* the rise of modern professional social science? We can get at part of the answer by grasping the discovery of the spiritual from the vantage point of a sociology of knowledge. This requires that we push "it" back into the social processes in which it is embedded as a cultural form, back into what Norbert Elias calls "social figurations." Sociology, according to Elias, ought to involve a study of social figurations. As he put it, "How and why people are bound together to form specific dynamic figurations is one of the central questions, perhaps even *the* central question, of sociology."[1] But to grasp such figurations also involves understanding the conjunctures that give them their historically specific shape. Elias's suggestion draws upon a methodological debt to Max Weber, a debt he acknowledged. But Elias's notion of social figuration also shares some of the analytical framework that char-

acterizes the work of historian Fernand Braudel, and these links deserve
to be noted.

For Weber, "interpretive sociology considers the individual and his
action as the basic unit, as its 'atom'—if the disputable comparison for
once may be permitted. In this approach, the individual is also the upper
limit and the sole carrier of meaningful conduct. . . . In general, for sociology, such concepts as 'state,' 'association,' 'feudalism,' and the like,
designate certain categories of human interaction. Hence it is the task of
sociology to reduce these concepts to 'understandable' action, that is,
without exception to the actions of participating individual men [and
women]".[2] Although Weber used the term *atom,* his vision of sociology
was certainly not at all kindred to atomism. The micro dimensions of
everyday life—the level of personhood, identity, ideas, interests, beliefs,
and so forth—were always mediated by larger societal forces. Elias's approach to cultural questions—through his concept of social figurations
and his desire to view social practices as both emblematic and constitutive of historically shifting social structures—bears Weber's stamp. Elias,
however, did not draw upon Fernand Braudel, but his notion of social
figuration is conceptually quite similar to Braudel's notion of *conjuncture.* Rather than viewing society and history operating in linear cause-
and-effect fashion, we ought, Braudel suggests, to grasp instead historical change as conditioned by conjunctures. Here, the plurality of
sociohistorical components that constitute the meaning of the term is
crucial. To talk of conjunctures in history is to acknowledge the complexity of autonomous spheres of development that, at certain times and
certain places, become linked and condition one another. The forms, the
tensions, the strategies thus open to societies, institutions, cultures,
classes, group life, and individuals are thus shaped by economic and
noneconomic conjunctures:

> Conjunctural analysis, even when it is pursued on several levels, cannot pro-
> vide the total undisputed truth. It is however one of the necessary means of
> historical explanation and as such a useful formulation of the problem. We
> have the problem of classifying on the one hand the economic conjunctures
> and on the other the non-economic conjunctures. The latter can be measured
> and situated according to their length in time: comparable, let us say, to the
> secular trend are long-term demographic movements, the changing dimen-
> sions of states and empires (the geographical conjuncture as it might be
> called), the presence or absence of social mobility in a given society, the
> intensity of industrial growth; parallel to the medium-term economic trend
> are rates of industrialization, the fluctuations of state finances and wars. A
> conjunctural scaffolding helps to construct a better house of history.[3]

The cultural material that enables us to build interpretively toward a
sociological grasp of social figurations has to be grounded or contextual-

ized within the social relations of particular individuals, social groups, collective practices, and ideological and cultural texts. These various empirical domains serve as the units of sociological analysis. Assessing such domains in their social embeddedness and historical development enables us to clarify the social operations of cultural forms by identifying the conditions of their emergence, perpetuation, and modification. I try to retain this kind of theoretical and sociological orientation throughout this study.

To treat the interest in the spiritual in the context of abolitionism, and to view abolitionism, in turn, as an expressive nexus of a number of social, political, cultural, and economic forces, is to treat the problem of culture and the discovery of black music making as a *social figuration*. This approach, however, positions, such cultural discovery in the context of economic, institutional, political, and ideological forces. These aspects are in turn intersected by class, racial, and gender factors. Such analytical endeavors are thus always selective rather than comprehensive, and in the process certain emphases and distinct analytical accents arise. In order to make the discovery process more visible, I probe not so much the content of cultural practices but their social and cultural forms and structures. I thus emphasize the emergence and development of the cultural and ideological dispositions that intellectuals—intellectuals both black and white, "traditional" and "organic"—had toward black music. The distinction between traditional and organic is Antonio Gramsci's.[4]

This study also underscores the great difficulty one encounters in working with the distinction between traditional and organic intellectuals. As I shall argue, the modern spirit of cultural interpretation can be seen in the way in which the Negro spiritual is discovered as hermeneutic practice and made into a distinct cultural entity. This discovery, which has come to be associated with the discovery of organic, or "authentic," culture, has roots in the crisis marked by the rise of nineteenth-century ethnosympathy. But is ethnosympathy the work of traditional or organic intellectuals? The question breaches the problematic dichotomy. Where does the traditional end and the organic begin? These are not at all neat categories, especially when so-called organic cultural forms appear to draw their lifeblood from deep engagements with traditional cultural schemas. After all, such was certainly the case in the religiously constituted slave narratives that used traditional teachings of Christianity to underscore the illegitimacy of the so-called Christian practices of slavery.

Rather than proceed with the received distinction between what is traditional and organic, or what is artificial or authentic I examine how such intellectual formations come to be. I present here the origins of how black music in the American context began to be *re-cognized* within an emerging modern humanistic orientation that allowed its purveyors to pursue the notion that cultural practices had their own intrinsically meaningful domain. I focus on the sensibilities that abolitionists brought to bear upon black song making as they struggled to comprehend and grasp black music as something more than alien and barbaric noise. My interest is thus not in music as a discrete and autonomous cultural entity, but rather in the intellectual schemas that viewed and appropriated black music.

In essence, this is a study in the vicissitudes of cultural appropriation. In taking up a lead suggested by Raymond Williams, I concern myself with how the appropriation of black music engendered interpretive formations that gave shape to institutionalizing forces. This angle, I believe, allows us to see from a developmental perspective how institutionalization serves the articulation of larger social formations.[5]

It is important to distinguish the makers of songs from the users of songs. Makers are of course users, but not all users are makers. Nonetheless, in the larger historical context in which the social production of musical practices took place, it is not possible to reduce "black" music to black producers and white consumers (though this distinction is at times worthwhile). Consider a slave who is forced to sing: Who is *producing* music? To even begin to unpack such a question requires understanding how and why the various actors and groups involved are enmeshed in what Antonio Gramsci called the "ensemble of social relations." Moreover, the appropriations of black music involved many accompanying interests that had little or nothing to do with that music. It is precisely this kind of cultural complexity that contributed to black music's function as a stage upon which other nonmusic—social, political, and cultural — struggles could be enacted. The songs of blacks, particularly the spirituals, were appropriated by people who did not produce them (in the immediate sense), yet the appropriators' relationship to the music had enormous consequences. They helped shape the cultural ground upon which black music was heard and produced.

The way in which black music making was discovered, put to use, and interpreted conceals, I believe, a not so obvious confluence of historical forces that intersected and shaped the sensibilities, interests, and logics of cultural intellectuals, black and white. This confluence, I argue, enabled the spiritual to emerge as an apprehendable cultural object within a discursive field of meanings that surrounded and shaped its multiple social functions. But there is more at stake than smoking out a discursive field and pursuing a deconstructive angle simply for its own sake. What is important is that the black and white abolitionists that brought the spiritual into visibility also set into motion a form of cultural interpretation that was contextually unique and also symptomatically modern. This orientation hinged on interpreters comprehending and making use of black song making while bringing a new focus upon the cultural and racial margins within American society. Emerging from this interest in the discovery of meanings at the cultural margins were modern features of ethnographic interpretation. In the American context, the abolitionist juncture nurtured the orientation toward the study of what we today call "subcultures." Ethnic studies and women's studies have roots in the connection studied here. Our contemporary debts to this cultural convergence are as great as they are seemingly obscure.

In chapter 1 I open the study by posing a number of related issues as well as questions. I begin with some reflective comments on the important and contemporary concern to retrieve the lost or buried cultures of people, cultures omitted by the modern professionalization of cultural knowledge. A common contemporary perspective is that cultural analysis, or what is sometimes refered to as the "cultural turn," is quite recent, and more specifically associated with revisionist history and historically informed social science. However, much of the contemporary interest in cultural study appears to be a return—to the vibrant currents of a critical ethnosympathy that began to take its interpretive forms in the middle of the nineteenth century. With this in mind, I ask: What does "cultural authenticity" mean when applied to black music? I argue that this notion has been inherited, and its origins deserve to be probed. To illustrate how authenticity has been framed, I draw on examples from nineteenth-century white commentators (Francis Kemble and Mary Boykin Chestnut) and early-twentieth-century black intellectuals (W. E. B. Du Bois and Alain Locke). I present the problem of authenticity by discussing the way in which the spiritual might flow over time, how it is ceaselessly appropriated, modified, and pressed into servicing many different interests.

In chapter 2 I address the question of where authenticity comes from with regard to how owners and overseers, and radical abolitionists heard black (slave) music. I consider examples of the earliest statements regarding black music—before such music was "discovered" as "authentic" as well as emblematic of the inner lives of slaves. I suggest a way to chart how the evolution of hearing shifted from "noise" to "meaningful" sounds in ways that helped prepare for a more modern hermeneutic orientation.

Chapter 3 examines how religious proselytization helped nurture the early modern shift in the way in which black song making was heard. Proselytization made possible the social and cultural context in which whites could hear black song making as a font of meaning. Coinciding with proselytization was the early admission that slaves had a subjectivity. This crucial institutional development integrated the recognition of spiritual subjectivity with its most acceptable expression: religious hymnology. Providing religious teachings to slaves may have been part mission and part social management, but it also engendered slave rebellion and revolt. Writers of slave narratives were particular adept at using the lessons of Christian ethics to reveal the hypocrisy of slavery as a social system. Religious singing also enabled slaves to express their despair over their status as chattel. But it was the spirituals rather than the more elaborate social and institutional critiques penned in the slave narratives that antislavery sympathizers tended to hear.

In chapter 4 I consolidate the themes in the previous chapters by looking specifically at how the abolitionist movement began to rally around, absorb, and organize the new ethnosympathetic mode of hearing black song making. Fueled by the antislavery crusade, the new patterns of hearing began to highlight the idea that the songs represented a hitherto buried, but now deeply significant, human (black) subjectivity. The gateway to discovering this new human subject was through cultural expressions. Frederick Douglass's insistence that white abolitionists slow down and hear the inner voices of slaves through their "songs of sorrow" was crucial in helping promote this view. Douglass's autobiography was unique in that it was the first slave narrative to point with great care to the hermeneutic dimension of slave songs.

Chapter 5 looks at how the Civil War provided the context in which the various cultural strands emerged around recognizing black song making. The discovery of "Go Down Moses," the first spiritual put into print, not only signaled the emerging cultural interest in black religious music; it also served as a template for what sympathetic white abolitionists should be looking for in their reception of the preferred new Negro. What resulted was an explosion of interest in the discovery and collection of spirituals. At this juncture the religious ideologies that helped fuel Unitarianism and Transcendentalism also helped nurture a protoethnographic turn toward fieldwork. Two important discoverers and collectors of black religious singing, Thomas Wentworth Higginson and William Frances Allen, exemplify the new orientation. Both were former Unitarian ministers, and they played a crucial role in transforming the orally based spirituals into written form through musical transcription. Making good on Frederick Douglass's invitation for study, their work launched black religious singing on its way to becoming a distinct object for modern cultural analysis.

In chapter 6 I argue that the longer history of the discovery of black music culminated in a modern and often contentious blend of humanistic as well as scientist approaches to studying the culture of African Americans. Abolitionists had highlighted religious song making. But after the war, the transformation of the spiritual into an analytical object was continued by the fledgling black schools and colleges such as Fisk, Hampton, and Tuskegee, which were launched shortly after the abolition of slavery. These schools continued to champion the work of retrieving cultural practices that were perceived to be on the verge of dying out. Their endeavors were eventually overtaken by the emerging professional folklorists.

In chapter 7 and the epilogue I offer a summary of the implications of the discovery of black song making and the interpretation that opened up a modern formation that pivoted on the study of cultural practices on the racial margins. On the one hand, the new interpretive disposition drew upon older humanistic and romantic orientations that viewed cultural practices as testimonies to the intersection of lived experience and social structures. On the other hand it embraced and cultivated the modern scientific orientation in which the inner lives of people were less important than the classification and examination of their cultural expressions, practices, and artifacts. This orientation stressed a taxonomic and cataloguing spirit in the pursuit of cultural objects. These blended sensibilities, one in pursuit of testimonies, the other in pursuit of artifacts, coexist in tension and are fundamental to the modern interpretation of culture.

What comes into focus in this study is an opportunity to reconsider some of the historical and cultural roots of what we today know as folklore, ethnography, cultural anthropology, cultural sociology, cultural studies, and ethnic studies. From the perspective suggested here, ethnic studies appears not as political constructions wrought in the ferment of the 1960s, but as histories that stem from the very marrow of modern American intellectual formations. This statement may be rather obvious to some, but the perception of the latter as being a recent, hence problematic, enterprise reflects a peculiar, even dangerous, kind of amnesia. Related to this amnesia is the fact that the historically informed sociological contours sketched in this study are not readily recognized within the contemporary paradigms of the study of culture. *Culture on the Margins* seeks to restore these historical ties to modern cultural analysis.

I explore the formation rather than inhabit the outcomes of the analytical consensus that emerged during the second half of the nineteenth century. The angle and manner in which I discuss black music will undoubtedly not ring familiar to readers who have come to expect that a study on music ought to always treat the intrinsic meaning of music as the primary object. This viewpoint is particularly prevalent in much of the scholarship on music treated under the larger lens of subcultural analysis. But this interpretive sensibility and corresponding expectation is precisely one of the historical frameworks I try to unpack in this study. My discussion weaves in and out of the *topic* of black music as I attempt to get at how music is framed by social actors. This requires taking important leave from what we recognize as the domain of music proper. To the reader who might peruse these pages anticipating a discussion of the deeply canonized singing voice, this study will appear like a sky emptied of stars. Unlike lyric-centered studies, this book offers no lengthy discussions of lyrics, where I tell the reader what they *really* mean. The reader who prefers the important account about agency couched in the triumph of subculture, or who thumbs through these pages looking for familiar subjects made popular by a longer history of the edifiers of "popular culture," will find a well-tuned paradigm already available with many other studies to satisfy.

This study focuses on the unpopular behind so-called popular culture. I provide a chart without musical stars because this is a work that focuses on social activity presumably external to what we ordinarily consider as music—in this case important patterns among listeners who attempt to interpret and draw cultural usage from the musical soundings of slaves. Just as there are no musical stars in these pages, there is no sustained treatment of greatest hits, and no lineage of progress that culminates in the testimonies of singing subjects and genre celebration no *Hit Parade,* no *American Bandstand,* no *Soul Train,* no *American Music Awards,* no "resistance through rituals," and no musical appreciation course. Yet, in changing the sociological key, I hope this study engenders a different kind of appreciation, one that considers how central and indispensable the music of early African Americans was in the rise of modern cultural interpretation. This angle of appreciation is meant to complement the progressive and revisionist consensus associated with subject-centered studies concerned with "the popular."

The music making stars who have taken their worthy places in the sky of human deeds—the great men and women of all hues who have achieved the status as cultural heroes and icons, who tell the(ir) story right, and the intellectual and interpretive constellations in which they have been placed and thus recognized— are themselves an expression of important cultural epistemologies. They shine in their aesthetic beauty, human art, and the force of personas and persistence. But they are also indicators of a power and knowledge formation, an interpretive formation, that operates like a force field shaping the very idea that culture and culture-making people harbor many things, including authenticity and truth. The human stars of early black musical history are well known (especially after black music was annexed by market forces in the early 1920s). They and the many who follow have waded in the historical rivers of popular memory and have given, as Du Bois said, a priceless gift to the world. Music's humanizing voice articulates the dreams and dreads that overpower language and gives visions and aspirations a voice that can sometimes nudge the world into a bit more suppleness. In order to understand black music, with its sedimented histories that archive a world of meanings that the larger society perpetually falters at fathoming, we have to rely on the interpreters who spell out the stakes of song making and who tell us just how music taps the fate of black people and people in general. Along with the music makers, the interpreters too give their gifts to the world, gifts that are continuously given. The analysis of what slaves accomplished by creating music, how they produced music that was their only property, what it meant to them, and how their swift and deep rivers of cultural symbols and meanings operated as culture is of great importance. To such insights we turn tirelessly to W. E. B. Du Bois, Carter Woodson, John Work, Alain Locke, Langston Hughes, Harold Courlander, James Weldon Johnson, Zora Neale Hurston, John Lovell, Eugene Genovese, Lawrence Levine, Dena Epstein, Tony Heilbut, Amiri Baraka, Angela Davis, Sterling Stuckey, and many more—with more to come.

But rather than occupy this important interpretive terrain, I seek to broaden and complement it by asking about the relationship between this now expansive modern terrain and its sociohistorical antecedents. My concern is thus not with pinpointing cultural authenticity with the precision that economistic Marxists sought not long ago when they pursued the ever-fleeting "point of production." For modern scholars, finding authenticity in the construct of "folk" was, of course, a major problem in the nineteenth century, and such categories are important for what they are—strategic social constructions that also yield powerful institutional effects.

Nor is it authenticity as a thing in itself that I pursue here, but rather how authenticity enters on the historical horizon as idea and as quest; and this in turn brings up concerns of a quite different order. The authenticity and truth associated with the self-penned slave narratives and spirituals were such cases. Such notions of authenticity, however, were never simply tied to the black subjects, but to black subjects' credibility to testify to an even greater and graver social problem: slavery and the invidious fate of blacks who succeeded slavery's demise.

As Lawrence Levine has argued, "If the cultural categories we utilize are the product of a specific historical moment . . . then the immediate question is less whether we should employ hierarchical categories than whether we should employ *frozen* categories ripped out of the contexts in which they were created. The only way to decide this is to learn more about the categories and their development."[6] This is good advice, and it is advice that is particularly complementary to treating the rise of cultural interpretation within the framework of a sociology of knowledge. I hope this study brings into visibility the social dynamics behind the discovery of African American culture, dynamics that I believe have been somewhat obscured by the culturalism that was produced by the discovery process itself. In taking this angle I hope to show how the phenomenon of slave culture—black culture in general and the Negro spiritual in particular— was central at the crossroads of the two larger cultural developments of American hermeneuticism and cultural scientism. What these crossroads produced was a modern orientation that tried (and continues to try) to embrace the older politics of hermeneuticism (the problem of meaning within embedded lives) and the scientistic impulse (the problem of objectification). By tracing the rise of this tension between these two modern orientations, we witness, I believe, the beginnings of the American analysis of culture on the margins and the rationalization of nineteenth-century ethnosympathy.

How might we convene a sociological interpretation of the interpreters and of the formation of interpretations? How ought we to chart the sociological development of cultural developments? It is not aesthetics, authenticity, or truth that this study seeks, but rather the socially constructed force fields that helped to make this kind of interpretive knowledge possible and powerful. This study, then, is about historically constituted cultural force fields that bequeath ways of seeing. To talk of force fields is thus not an account of "common people," however justly concerned such work is with retrieving a hidden or lost popular culture (and perhaps even a sense of a lost populism), or of restoring historical and sociological accuracy to the constitution of society—though it is about how subjects emerge and get "found." It is not a "cultural resistance" story—though it helps account for the rise of an interpretive formation that has enabled people to become mapped, to struggle over existing maps, and to become reflexive mappers themselves. Nor is it a kind of "spirit work," the attempt to conjure the immutable essence of identity traceable through the transcendental vernaculars of people—although it is certainly concerned with tracing the social forces and ensuing implications that prompt those who take up the important work of discovering and pursuing the vernaculars of others.

The interpretive forms that come into place in the late-nineteenth century are partly traceable to what happened, and what failed to happen, with regard to the slave narrative and the Negro spiritual within American culture. To talk of cultural force fields may also appear somewhat hyperbolic in that the white radicals and abolitionists who were able to read black authors and hear black music with new ears were small in number. They were certainly not part of a mass movement. Indeed, the radical abolitionists who were also hunters for the quintessential Negro spiritual were fringe figures. And while there were numerous individuals interested in the spirituals, only a few actually collected and published samples of black songs by 1870. But the perspectives they used to speak of black songs and the grammars that were being forged in the context of change set modern cultural interpretation on one of its major courses. The number of individuals who were central to the positive discoveries of black music was small. But, as I shall argue, they set into motion big results in their paradigm-establishing interpretive enterprise.

How cultural interpretation worked the issues of race, culture, and modernity, is, of course, much broader than I sketch here.[7] My intention is to highlight in the American context the importance of the discovery of black culture in this nexus. Although it has long been an object of American cultural interpretation, the central role that black music played in the rise of American cultural interpretation has not been adequately acknowledged. If the social contours that enabled modern interpreters to turn to the cultural and racial margins come a bit more into view, I have succeeded. So if the phenomenological stars and what they illuminate are not in this analytical sky, if the romance that has come to be expected when dealing with music and popular culture in general is not sung, it is because I wish to bring into view something else: the lines of cultural influence that surround, bring into focus, and propel in their trajectories ideas and orientations, and that bestow upon our knowledge-forms their power to ascribe, to value, to place, and to stake purposes within the sites of culture on the margins. Just what it is that makes such stellar interests so down to earth deserves some sociological reflection.

ONE

THE CONUNDRUM OF AUTHENTICITY

WERE FREDERICK DOUGLASS alive today he would certainly wonder about the career of the slave songs that he implored white abolitionists to hear. He might wonder as well about the professional folkloristic studies of black cultural expressions that were being produced in the late-nineteenth and early-twentieth centuries. We might wonder how he would ponder the dilemma presented by an era that produced a vibrant intellectual interest in black folk culture, but that placed a much greater emphasis upon methodological and taxonomic sophistication as it abandoned the pathos he had tried to bring to the songs of sorrow. What would he make of the growing deafness that greeted the black intellectuals who continued to seek, as did he, the larger ideals of a genuinely egalitarian society? And if he were interested in historicizing the cultural turn that he himself helped shape at the height of the antislavery crusade, how would he respond to what has become a central problem within the modern enterprise of cultural interpretation: How does one begin to study the historical formation of modern modes of interpretation if his or her conceptual framework is itself a product or symptom of that history?

Douglass's unavailability, of course, precludes answers to these questions. The last question goes more to the heart of social science, however, and for it there is no pat answer, because all constructs within the social sciences are fated with what Anthony Giddens referred to as the "double hermeneutic."[1] Our knowledge constructions are shaped by the very social world that such constructions attempt to comprehend. In this regard, the double hermeneutic applies to, as well as complicates, the question. The double hermeneutic comes with the terrain of this study. And it makes the challenge in this study twofold. On the one hand this book is an endeavor of interpretive social science; on the other it also interrogates the frameworks in which we do our interpretive work by considering the scaffolding upon which we stand and by examining the contours of familiar assumptions.

How in the American context did the interest in questions of culture at the racial margins come about? More specifically, how and why did the songs of sorrow come to be understood as a particular aspect of African American—and American—culture? The problem of interpreting the "discovery" of African American music in the years surrounding the Civil War is complicated by its own endowment. The discovery, as I shall argue, helped to shape the rise of modern American ethnoscience. Unpacking this important cultural development is the task of this study.

One immediate issue I want to raise has to do with the cultural status of the Negro spiritual. A great deal of reflection upon this particular cultural form has found its way into print since the late-nineteenth century. What seems incontrovertible is the fact that black religious song making, as with all other forms of music making, served multiple functions under slavery. It is a well established fact that music was one of the primary means by which slaves cultivated collective knowledge and solidarity. Music making helped create as well as maintain fledgling and fragile black public spheres. This aspect of culture has not been lost upon scholars of American history and culture, and it remains a lesson that deserves to be continually underscored. From gospel to blues to soul and to rap and hip-hop (and certainly more forms will follow), black music making remains part of an enormously important as well as a sprawling black cultural public sphere.

It was in the context of slavery that black music emerged as a distinct analytical object. Particular interpretive schemas developed from this interest, and they helped launch the concern for what black religious singing might mean to those who produced it. This interest, given form by moral and political entrepreneurs who remained outside of the most fundamental practices of blacks themselves, was certainly linked to black music's functions within historically embedded social and cultural negotiations. But it cannot be reduced to any cultural essence attributed to music. To probe this problem we must try to disentangle the *appropriation* of black music as a distinct social dimension in its own right.

We can begin by posing some questions. What ought we to make of the received notion that the spirituals have a peculiar, indeed essential, quality? Where did this quality come from? What skills or shifts in cultural orientation were required in order to allow appropriators to hear and grasp black song making within more modern aesthetic frames? Aesthetic appreciation, after all, presupposes the objectification of cultural forms that, in turn, appear (only because they have become defined to do so) as distinct, comprehendible, accessible, and meaningful. What "cultural forms" correspond to the consideration that black music was worth fathoming? How did the new orientations toward black music yield the modern pathos-oriented mode of hearing that enabled white and black commentators to elevate the spirituals to such new interpretive heights and to invest in them such interpretive depth? Why were the spirituals consumed by those who did not produce them? Did the consumers (if we wish to use such a modern, market-determined term) reshape both the producers and the product?

These questions invite reflection upon the social forces that intersect all domains of culture. When we probe the various ideas of what is considered "genuine" and "authentic" black music, strange shadows appear that come not from the music itself but from the extramusical interests that surround it. These invariably involve social movements, struggles, conflicts, and histories that were invoked and played out for those who discovered black music. It is therefore important to open up the issue of cultural authenticity as it became attributed and attached to black music making in the middle of the nineteenth century. The notions of authenticity that were applied to black music, especially to the spirituals, have their own historically embedded roots. How this modern attribution unfolded and what implications this historical conjuncture has had upon modern notions of cultural interpretation will take on greater importance throughout the study as I revisit the problem within a series of elliptical and analytical steps.

In this chapter I pose and probe three problematics, each of which helps to unravel the knotty conundrum of cultural authenticity as a historically attenuated construct. First, I look at the idea of black cultural authenticity as a cultural good that fell into crisis as a result of the ways in which black music was tapped, appropriated, and assimilated by the larger, dominant culture. Viewed within the framework of cultural erosion, and even as a symptom of cultural theft, this crisis has been a salient narrative within modern cultural criticism. I open this issue through a discussion surrounding key statements on music from three of the most important black intellectuals in American history: former slave Frederick Douglass, the sociologist W. E. B. Du Bois, and Harlem Renaissance era cultural critic Alain Locke. The statements I select are, I believe, symptomatic of the larger concern with the erosion of black authenticity within the sphere of black music. Together the statements mark the important contours of black authenticity as a kind of socially rooted aesthetic that is challenged incessantly by profane pressures.

The concept of authenticity under siege or as the marker of cultural loss, along with themes of erosion and theft, is certainly not unique within modern reflections upon African American music. It is, I believe, part of a much larger intellectual trope that measures the down side of modernity. Such criticism reaches back to Jean-Jacques Rousseau and forward to the Frankfurt School, and is echoed even in recent laments over Hollywood's abandonment of traditional American "family values" (each critique, of course, has its own historically specific and politically distinct features). I glean by the cultural criticism of Douglass, Du Bois, and Locke that the concerns expressed are not hermetically sealed in some kind of black exceptionalism; they have their specificity, but they also reveal a much more pervasive attempt within the West to adjudicate perceptions shaped in the clash of modernity and social change.

Second, I turn to statements about black music by important white observers who express significantly different yet complementary modes of fondness for black music. In the statements of Frances Kemble and Mary Boykin Chestnut, both of whom witnessed American slavery, and of the earl of Shaftesbury, who hosted the Fisk Jubilee Singers during their European tour in 1875, I identify an aspect of cultural interpretation that I think is emblematic of a deeper cultural logic that operates behind the discovery process of black music and the career of that process in the second half of the nineteenth century. Kemble, Chestnut, and Shaftesbury help us to see ways in which cultural aesthetics becomes separated from the larger social, political, and economic contexts in which the culture being observed has taken shape. I call this sensibility *disengaged engagement*. As I introduce here, and shall argue more fully in later chapters, the career of the discovery of the spiritual is characterized by a peculiar engagement with black music that also disengages aesthetic and culturalist interest in black music from the plight of blacks during the decades after the Civil War. The role of "culture" as an interpretive enterprise thus appears to have had a rather decisive impact on how the spiritual was transposed from its status as a moral item or testimony to that of an abstract object or artifact, precisely through being defined as a genuine and quintessential feature of black authenticity. By "role of culture" I do not refer to things found outside the mind (e.g., material culture, objective practices, etc.), but rather to the historically specific form of finding, and to how such intellectual conceptualization operates as a social orientation, a mode of apprehending and appropriating, and an interpretive sensibility. I explore this finding, appropriating, and interpreting orientation insofar as it offers us a case in which aesthetic cultural discovery became edified in ways that eclipsed the much more important problem—the social fate of African Americans and other racialized peoples after the Civil War. As I will argue, the process of discovering black music from a sympathetic perspective coincided with the notion of salvaging a black cultural authenticity. The angle I take does not reject the arguments about "cultural theft." The modern history of white musicians and entrepreneurs drawing heavily upon black musical culture and obtaining great economic rewards at the expense of black musicians and the black communities that generate such cultural forms is an important dimension of the relationship that black music has had within the larger culture of popular music. However, it is not theft or appropriation but the origins of social definitions of cultural authenticity that I wish to chart. One mea-

sure of this modern cultural turn toward the end of the nineteenth century
was the corresponding inability of those who participated in the transformation to hear the political voices that attempted to speak not of black
spiritual virtues but of race relations in an egalitarian civil society.

Third, I attempt to show how music is so easily reified and treated as
a fixed cultural good. I try to explode such a perspective by tracing what
we assume to be a distinct and discrete musical form or practice—such as
a slave singing—across social, cultural, and historical terrain. I argue for
a different perspective, one informed by the sociology of knowledge and
the goal of grasping music in terms of how it is embedded within larger
historical flows.

Taken together, these three problems—the emergence of authenticity
and its ensuing crisis, the tendency to separate sympathetic cultural observation from social life, and the proclivity to reify music—help illustrate
the need to consider the social and historical roots of modern cultural
interpretation, and how it took shape through an objectification of interests at the racial margins. These interpretive roots are sunk deep into
inherited ground. Where did this inheritance come from? How might we
understand the historical influences that link cultural interpretation to the
formative moments of such development? Assessing these problems puts
us in a position to see how abolitionism engendered new sensibilities that
produced the turn toward analyzing culture at the racial margins. As I
shall argue throughout the study, the spiritual played a central role in this
turn.

Sacred Music on Profane Ground

In 1845, Frederick Douglass brought to the attention of abolitionists the
importance of the songs that slaves had long sung. He was the first to
write in penetrating detail about the social significance of the music of
slaves, and he did so from a slave's perspective. In his *Narrative of the
Life of Frederick Douglass, An American Slave*, Douglass wrote about
the slaves' "wild" and "rude and apparently incoherent songs." The
songs, according to Douglass, "told a tale of woe which was then altogether beyond my feeble comprehension; they were tones loud, long, and
deep, they breathed the prayer and complaint of souls boiling over with
the bitterest anguish. Every tone was testimony against slavery, and a
prayer to God for deliverance from chains."[2] Reflecting on his first recollection of the songs of sorrow, Douglass noted that he "did not, when a
slave, understand the deep meaning of those rude and apparently incoherent songs." He could not understand and appreciate them because he
was too close; he was "within the circle" and "neither saw nor heard as

those without might see and hear."[3] Douglass's narrative was a work written in contribution to the ascending abolitionist movement, the most important social movement in the nineteenth century. It was part of social movement literature. By inviting his readers to study black music, he aimed to broaden their understanding of slaves as well as their commitment to abolitionism. Though the music Douglass introduced was largely alien to white abolitionists, it was to be understood as harboring an authenticity that was hidden and misunderstood. The songs of sorrow were to be unveiled, and behind the veil was the black social subject.

Shortly after the turn of the century, W. E. B. Du Bois commented on black songs and reiterated Douglass's call. Du Bois asked the "gentle readers" of his day—or those among a cultural and literary bourgeoisie who might still possess some of the humanistic pathos now ebbing after the dismantling of slavery, the collapse of Reconstruction, and the rise of social Darwinism—to return to the spirituals of black Americans and to the cultural expressions of other groups as well. In the closing lines to the first chapter in *The Souls of Black Folk* Du Bois wrote:

> there is no true American music but the wild sweet melodies of the Negro slave; the American fairy tales and folklore are Indian and African; and, all in all, we black men seem the sole oasis of simple faith and reverence in a dusty desert of dollars and smartness. Will America be poorer if she replace her brutal dyspeptic blundering with light-hearted but determined Negro humility? or her coarse and cruel wit with loving jovial good-humor? or her vulgar music with the soul of the Sorrow Songs?[4]

In the last chapter, titled "Of the Sorrow Songs," Du Bois returned to these analytical sentiments. Bearing the stamp of the new social scientific consciousness, and influenced by the relatively recent folkloristic orientation, his writing focused upon the spirituals to take note of an important crossroad in the history of black music. He posed the problem of how "the songs of white America . . . distinctly influenced by the slave songs" had incorporated "whole phrases of Negro melody, as 'Swanee River' and 'Old Black Joe.'" To Du Bois, this signified "debasements and imitations" of black music; it was the result of a blending of gospel hymns with minstrelsy and "coon songs" that produced "a mass of music in which the novice may easily lose himself and never find the real Negro melodies."[5] Black music was no longer the distinct testimony of black collective fate; it had been pulled into association with other musical styles and genres.

Like many writers at the turn of the century, Du Bois was signaling one of modernity's most lamented cultural casualties: authenticity. But what had pushed such authenticity into trouble? Had Douglass's call to heed the spirituals gone too far or opened the door too wide? Was black music the victim of too much attention? The wrong kind of attention? We should ask as well: Was there ever that special place of cultural purity in a world of social danger where the songs that both Douglass and Du Bois identified remained free from the gravitational pulls of symbolic and cultural miscegenation?

The problem that Du Bois flagged in 1903 escalated as the new century churned on. New and unforeseen relations between black music and the marketplace began to expand as the entire field of popular music mushroomed in the age of the recording industry. Sound recording was just emerging at the turn of the century. By 1920 black demographics and market-savvy entrepreneurs converged in the grooves of black shellac as the "race record" industry was launched. Two decades later, black renaissance cultural critic Alain Locke attempted to take stock of the new problems of black music's historical trajectory and its now morally questionable social career. In 1939, almost a full century after Frederick Douglass had asked readers to take a privileged peek behind the racial veil, Locke published *The Negro and His Music*. In this book Locke complained vehemently that "one of the handicaps of Negro music today is that it is too popular." Black music, Locke insisted, had become "tarnished with commercialism and the dust of the market-place."[6] It had lost its authenticity.

The road that black music took thus began with a hard-won struggle to create and maintain a system of collective meanings under tremendous adversity, only to succumb to the pressures of a popular culture industry that reduced creativity to cliché and commodification. Black music had once mapped the desire of people to escape the "jaws of slavery"; now that very music fell into the jaws of the cash nexus. This story of innocence, fall, and perpetual pursuit of redemption remains central to the critique of modernity and mass culture, what Adorno calls "culture criticism."[7]

Selected for their provocative concerns rather than their representational qualities, these statements on black music from three very important intellectuals map a larger argument. Du Bois's concern with the way black songs were being appropriated, developed from Douglass's view of black music as a key to slave phenomenology, and Locke's lament over the vulgar forces of the popular market are the narrative of *cultural theft*. This narrative charts a history of black music as its genuine voice emerges, which in turn, commandeered, pulled into circuits of profitability, and tarnished (some might say perverted), as black musicians and black communities relinquished both cultural and economic control. As it has been put, it moves from "black roots" to "white fruits."[8]

Douglass, Du Bois, and Locke thus chart a line of cultural development. Slaves had produced a cultural gift, their music, which was squandered under centuries of ignorant ears that could afford to hear their sounds only as noise. But as the antislavery movement grew, black music emerged more autonomous (that is, appreciably and appreciatively perceptible to white listeners) by taking on new political significance for abolitionists. Douglass was instrumental in positioning slave music making upon the central stage of the political crisis that grew and resulted in the dismantling of slavery. Ensuing market forces, however, annexed, mimicked, and caricaturized the deeper aesthetic dialogue between black cultural forms and American social history. And the half-romantic, half-earnest outreached hands of politically marginalized white Americans in search of cultural goods to satiate the hunger for a world of deeper connectedness further expanded the cultural draw of (and upon) black music. Each of these phases is complex.

These cultural passages, and the narrative of the fall of black culture to capitalism (Locke's particular critique of black culture under modernity), signify specific relations of both black cultural production and the complex conditions surrounding its appropriation. These relations, which come to an apex during the 1920s, were contradictory as well as productive, and certainly historically contingent. Moreover, they underscore the importance of music as part of the vast cultural miscegenation so fundamental to American history.

Yet, as a trajectory, this story of black music's fate in the hands of appropriators harbors additional fundamental cultural processes that are obscured by the moral patina of the cultural theft narrative because that narrative starts with what I believe to be a highly complicated as well as problematic notion of cultural authenticity. This very knot is one that I hope to unravel in the following chapters. Consider for now these passages as surface markers of a much more fundamental process, that of a deeper dialogue involving a more profound set of cultural exchanges and a more intimate nexus of interdependencies and borrowings; this dialogue renders problematic from the very beginning the attempt to reduce arguments of authenticity to some kind of kernel or original point of identity.

But let us acknowledge that the perspective of cultural theft has a particular relevance as well as a theoretical attractiveness. It is consistent with a Marxian framework in which the commodification of black culture carried out through economic exploitation coincides with surplus extraction—black production, white appropriation. In the process, an innocent "species being" in the form of an original black authenticity gave way to the external pressures of racialized alienation. As an expression of an essential authenticity, black culture was, in this case, wrenched away from its initial producers and expropriated by another class as well as another race.

But this perspective is insufficient. While it has great moral and political purchase, it cannot grasp the origins of the interpretive formation in which authenticity itself was generated as a cultural object, value, and good. Authenticity did not spring out of the air; it was a sociohistorical construction. As I shall argue in a later chapter, the notion of authenticity was rooted much more firmly in religious rather than economic constructs. While this remains to be assessed, we can, for now, consider a working proposition. Beneath the modern "cultural criticism" of black cultural authenticity is a more fundamental cultural point at which two interlocking developments took place. First emerged a cultural struggle in which slaves were able to express a subjectivity forged from within the religious frameworks built by early proselytization. A second factor involved the emergence of a rather small number of black and white reformists who helped construct an interpretive framework that enabled slaves to be seen as social subjects. As I shall argue more fully in chapter 3, slaves did not have to wait for the discovers of their song in order to achieve a critical subjectivity. I refer here only to the issue of how the appropriators of black music emphasized slave subjectivity. This cultural conjuncture coincided with the abolitionist movement of the mid-nineteenth century, and one of its most important cultural legacies was the development of a humanistically oriented interpretive interest in the racial and cultural margins within American society. It was in the context of the abolitionist movement that the issue of cultural authenticity with regard to slaves and free blacks was developed and from there further refined.

Disengaged Cultural Engagement

Let us turn to another cultural trajectory that spins from an appreciation of black music. I believe it is central to how the cultural turn to the racial margins generated a modern mode of interpreting the intersection of race, culture, and modernity; and it directs us into the remaining chapters. The white voices discussed below, like Douglass, Du Bois, and Locke, saw (through hearing) something of importance in black music, and they saw and heard it in the cultural conjuncture in which black authenticity emerged. Let us back up historically and cross the racial divide, but in strides of loose historical parallel to the observations of Douglass, Du Bois, and Locke.

Frances Kemble, an English actress-abolitionist married to a slave owner, expressed the entrepreneurial spirit that had already begun to draw upon slave music for profit, a relationship that would eventually culminate in the transformation of black folk culture into marketed entertainment and the cornerstone of American popular music. Reflecting on her experiences of living on a Georgia plantation between 1838 and 1839, Kemble anticipated cultural possibilities of a black music that later troubled both Du Bois and Locke. In one of her many journal entries that described slave music Kemble wrote:

> I thought I could trace distinctly some popular national melody with which I was familiar in almost all their songs; but I have been quite at a loss to discover any such foundation for many that I have heard lately, and which have appeared to me extraordinarily wild and unaccountable. . . . The high voices all in unison, and the admirable time and true accent with which their responses are made, always make me wish that some great musical composer could hear these semi-savage performances. With a very little skillful adaptation and instrumentation, I think one or two barbaric chants and choruses might be evoked from them that would make the fortune of an opera.[9]

Of course the "skillful adaptation and instrumentation" based upon actual musical themes from black Americans—or based upon preferred aesthetic selectivity and racial caricaturization—was already institutionalized through "blackface," the codifications of a panicky racialized humor that encoded the everyday epistemology of race relations so central to the cultural and symbolic work of minstrelsy. Minstrelsy, it should be noted, was by the 1840s one of the most pervasive forms of American popular culture. As a cultural practice, minstrelsy provided a framework for "understanding" African Americans, and this understanding, in turn, was central to the way whites imaged their own shifting and contentious notions of whiteness. In its appeal to different yet overlapping cultural sensibilities, minstrelsy charted race relations in several contradictory ways. Through its caricaturization of slaves as childlike, docile, and happy, it legitimated and reinforced slavery as a necessary system for supervising black subjects who were either incapable of taking care of themselves or who represented a threatening populace. Minstrelsy thus functioned as a cultural mechanism of social control and as a system of totemic representations that addressed the physiognomy of racial hierarchy.[10] Yet, as a representation of the social relations of race and slavery, minstrelsy also provided images that joined with arguments to block slavery's expansion into the western territories. In the North, minstrelsy endorsed the racial divisions between white workers and free blacks. Like many forms of popular culture, minstrelsy was more than a mode of entertainment; it served also as a social and cultural epistemology, a form of knowledge and knowledge making that brokered the meanings of race, ethnicity, and class throughout the nineteenth century.[11]

Insofar as Kemble's notion of an opera based on black music, many years would pass before the European composer Antonin Dvořák would come to the United States, heaping praise upon the beauty of black spirituals and prodding the fledgling American composers to turn to the racial and cultural margins as the overlooked font of an authenticity that qualified as distinctly American and that emerging nationalist highbrows were intensely seeking. In 1895, Dvořák wrote in *Harper's* magazine,

> The most potent as well as the most beautiful (among America songs) . . . according to my estimation are certain of the so-called plantation melodies and slave songs, all of which are distinguished by unusual and subtle harmonies, the like of which I have found in no other song but those of old Scotland and Ireland. . . . The music of the people is like a rare and lovely flower growing amidst encroaching weeds. Thousands pass it, while others trample it under foot, and thus the chances are that it will perish before it is seen by the one discriminating spirit who will prize it above all else. The fact that no one has as yet arisen to make the most of it does not prove that nothing is there.[12]

Dvořák gave the green light to the European-influenced American composers to mine their own backyard, where race and romance commingled.

Frances Kemble's statement, however, represented one approach to black music, albeit one that expressed a desire to absorb, tame, uplift, and refine. Her vision foresaw the separation of the civilized wheat from the barbaric chaff, and imagined black musical elements suitably refined for *zivilization's* annexation of the cultural margins.[13]

Mary Boykin Chestnut got close to black music in a quite different way. Chestnut, a white woman with abolitionist leanings, and also the wife of a slave-owning husband, recalls her close experience with what Douglass called the inner circle when she visited a black religious gathering. After attending a service at a Negro church located on her husband's family's plantation near Camden, South Carolina, Chestnut wrote in her diary on October 13, 1861, the following recollection:

> [There was] a very large black congregation. . . . Jim Nelson, the driver . . . a full-blooded African, was asked to lead in prayer. He became wildly excited, on his knees, facing us with his eyes shut. He clapped his hands at the end of every sentence, and his voice rose to the pitch of a shrill shriek, yet was strangely clear and musical, occasionally in a plaintive minor key that went to your heart. Sometimes it rang out like a trumpet. I wept bitterly. It was all sound, however, and emotional pathos. . . . The words had no meaning at all.

Words with no meaning at all—yet Mary Boykin Chestnut "wept bitterly." Her diary entry continues describing the emotionally ladened service, and it is clear that the session is full of meaning for her. "Suddenly, as I sat wondering what next, they broke out into one of the soul-stirring

Negro camp-meeting hymns. To me this is the saddest of all earthly music, weird and depressing beyond my powers to describe."[14]

Meaninglessness does not engender such deep pathos. Profoundly meaningful emotions, however, are difficult to render into words, for meaning encompasses language but is not reducible to it.[15] Chestnut is the classic southern abolitionist caught between the ideology of antislavery and the comfort of her upper-class status that removed her far from the lowest caste. Through marriage into a slave-owning family, this white woman of the South is pulled into the orbit of black musical soundings. Although she is not one of the many protoethnographers who intentionally sought out black musical practices (though her published diaries were read for their musical insights by many scholars in the years after the Civil War), she is, like many before her, an incidental rather than an intentional listener. Her emotional connections to an event that was ostensibly meaningless appear abrupt; her emotions erupt as if they were accidental, or certainly unanticipated. Encircled by slavery and writing at the beginning of a massive war to end it, she leaves no doubt that the observations were personally difficult ones to witness, let along adjudicate.

Five months later she appears to have reached a resolution in how to cope with the emotional and familial intimacy with "Negroes": "The best way to take Negroes to your heart is to get as far away from them as possible."[16] Distance could make the heart grow fond. Chestnut's solution was characteristic of one major strategy with which abolitionists coped with coming close to actual black populations—through the psychic retreat of romanticism and sentimentalism. Sentimentalism helped broker the conflict between the commitment to end slavery and the reticence to encounter former slaves, work with them, and aid in their equitable incorporation into civil society. Sentimentalism sustained the generality of antislavery values and propped up "the slave" as a rhetorical or literary abstraction. Many in the North could ply their ethnosympathy by engaging in a kind of literary ethnotourism afforded through the works unleashed by the antislavery publishing industry. Such works included actual narratives penned by slaves, as well as Harriet Beecher Stowe's enormously popular *Uncle Tom's Cabin*, and a host of "parlor" or "gift" books that were imagined slave stories written by sentimental white northerners.[17]

There was, of course, a popular market of sorts for these stories of America's most unwanted. Disengaged engagement provided a safe distance from the immediacy of flesh-and-blood social trauma; it dislocated one from personal implication, from the pressures of reflecting on one's responsibility to a raging crisis. Sentimentalism allowed social crises to metamorphose through a series of symbolic substitutions that would allow one, with ease of conscience, to vehemently oppose slavery yet have no concrete sense of a slave as a human being with a face, a name, a voice. Chestnut, found it more agreeable to ponder fond thoughts for those on the other side of the chasm of the color line than to weep bitterly with slaves in their inner circle and to take up the dirty work of confronting politically and institutionally the sources of anguish in the hard, protracted work of social, political, and economic rectification. As was the case with so many antislavery northerners and Republican Free-Soilers, Chestnut's psychic move still allowed for a critical disapproval of the institution of slavery without need for her to confront, negotiate, and even dwell among actual black subjects.[18]

Taken to extremes, sentimentality offers a spectacular plunge into soppy disingenuousness. In 1875 the famed Fisk Jubilee Singers from Fisk University in Tennessee were at the height of their popularity. While on tour in Europe, they were hosted in London by the earl of Shaftesbury, who, after hearing their concert, exclaimed: "When I find these young people, gifted to an extent that does not often fall to the lot of man, coming here in such a spirit, I don't want them to become white, but I have a strong disposition myself to become black. If I thought color was anything—if it brought with it their truth, piety, and talent, I would willingly exchange my complexion to-morrow."[19] Shaftesbury's remark—which certainly beats Normal Mailer's quest for the "white Negro" to the punch by almost a full century—signifies a much larger romanticization and exoticization of blacks and other marginalized groups whose positive identifications can be traced to Rousseau's notion of the "noble savage."[20]

Woven into all three of these commentaries is a deeper cultural sensibility that functions as a strategy of comprehension and appropriation. In each there is an aspiration toward an aestheticism that has peculiarly attractive and transcendental powers; it embraces the subject (by which I mean the "topic") of black music but not the black subjects from whom this music comes. It is an aestheticism that effectively disengages from any reflection on the social. Beauty eclipses fate and tragedy, while aesthetic pleasure serves as a blind spot to pain. Whether it is Kemble's recipe for cleaning up black song to make it aesthetically, economically, and morally marketable; or Chestnut's fondness secured only by the distance of disengaged engagement; or Shaftesbury's will to pave a one-way avenue to accommodate cultural travel—the desire of a white voyage into blackness,[21] but not a black journey from the other direction—is in its own way a strategy that separates moral reflection from politics. As a mode of disengaged engagement, aesthetic appreciation divorced from the artist's life functions as a denial of that life. In the context of intertwined black and white lives, this scenario bears an uncanny resemblance to the social problem of sex under slavery. The public secret of sex and the "tragic mulatto" offspring under slavery belonged also in the realm of symbolic exchange: cultural miscegenation was desirable but only if and when it could be controlled and regulated.

Certainly there is a strain of romanticism in operation with these passages. Romanticism's seductiveness, however, is not only a historical phenomenon of the past. It is also always present because modernity cannot banish it; modernity continually produces it. Romanticism serves not as an outdated historical and premodern epoch, but as a tireless countersensibility to a modernity that constantly threatens increasingly fragile notions of identity and authenticity. It serves even those who are critical of the ways in which racial categories can be so entrapping. Few turn-of-the-century intellectuals were as carefully reflective on the matter of race as a culturally and politically constructed legacy as was W. E. B. Du Bois. Yet Du Bois was beholden to romantic tropes, and beyond doubt sincere, when he asserted that "like all primitive folk, the slave stood near to Nature's heart." Commenting interpretively on selected lines from the spirituals, which he called the "sorrow songs," he concluded in the spirit of the romantic poets that "the soul-hunger is there, the restlessness of the savage, the wail of the wanderer, and the plaint is put in one little phrase: 'My soul wants something that's new, that's new.' "[22] Such desires to find in groups, peoples, or subcultures an authenticity that juxtaposes the virtue of everyday life against the crushing steamroller of modernity are actually quite routine. It is a sensibility that points to the larger, older, and pervasive struggle with regard to how groups are conceptualized by strategic elites,[23] usually in connection with tension or crisis, in ways that enable these elites to grasp and talk about the otherwise abstract forces of modernity and society. In other words, such tropes are not so much fads that mark a lamenting sensibility, but elements of a more fundamental feature of how the always present modern sense of social crisis is instantiated and actuated through our use of concrete social categories of distinct people and of particular subjects in crisis.

But let me provide one more fragment in this black and white mixing of accounts, this time from the white jazz musician Milton "Mezz" Mezzrow. Mezzrow was a contemporary of Alain Locke. Along with his "teenage refugees from the sunny suburbs," he sought in jazz an "honest and self-inspired language." Jazz offered a way for disenchanted whites to distance themselves from a suffocating conformity. In Mezzrow's words, playing jazz was tantamount to "a collectively improvised nose-thumbing at all pillars of all communities, one big syncopated Bronx cheer for the righteous squares everywhere."[24] Mary Boykin Chestnut sought distance from Negroes in order to appreciate them; Mezz Mezzrow and fellow white bohemians sought closeness to blacks in order to achieve a desired distance from the dominant white society in which they held their troubled membership.

These groups of quotes from black and white observers contain two interrelated scenarios that have been part of the more recent critiques of the history of black music in America. One concerns cultural theft. The other revolves around the motives of white individuals who were highly attracted to black music and appropriated it for reasons that were more complex and certainly not reducible to any ostensible economic interest. This second case, which is not about cultural theft, taps into a larger and subtler set of relations toward black music in which it is sometimes used to help whites negotiate aspects of their own society that they find stifling and repressive. These complex relations run the gamut—from accusations of racial fraternizing, slumming, and voyeurism to initiating the search for ways to deepen social critique, pursue creative cultural inspiration, and envision radical social renewal.

Du Bois and Locke flagged concern for the fate of a black music that had been discovered for its authenticity, but was also being plunged into a crisis for having lost its presumed autonomy and authenticity. We ought, then, to wonder about the career of music, and the overwhelming dispositions toward "it," as if "it" possessed some hidden, rare, and valuable essence. In a way this is one of the fates of the discovery process of the Negro spiritual. In being edified as the bastion of authenticity—a construction shared and cultivated by intellectuals both black and white from Douglass's first revelation to the present—there was another cultural logic at work, cultivating what I referred to as disengaged engagement. Slavery, fate, and the future of social relations evaporate in the forward-looking imagination of Kemble's proposed opera, in Chestnut's move away from blacks and into the emotional geography of sentimentalism, and in Shaftesbury's nascent blueprint for an ethnotourism that worked the Lévi-Straussian border of culture and nature while celebrating cultural difference *and* segregation simultaneously.

As we shall see, disengaged engagement took its most paradigmatically modern form in the hands of the radical abolitionist discoverers of the Negro spiritual. As I shall argue later, the interpretive paradigm took shape in the entwined endeavors that grew from Frederick Douglass's invitation and culminated in writings published by Thomas Wentworth Higginson and William Frances Allen shortly after the end of the Civil War. Higginson came upon black song making when he commanded the first all-black Union Army regiment composed of recently freed slaves. Allen helped mobilize the efforts behind the publication of the first massive collection and musical transcription of black songs.[25] Higginson's romantic and Allen's scientific assessments of black music helped launch it as an object of modern cultural analysis. They worked in tandem to herald the coming of black cultural authenticity as an American intellectual construct. The new cultural welcome that came from these two musically sensitive abolitionists, schooled in the Unitarian corridors of

Harvard moral philosophy, laid the groundwork for the intellectual humanitarians who pursued the retrieval and study of black culture. Black subjectivity and authenticity had emerged, but were filtered through the treatment of selected black expressions.

Culturalism and national politics now joined in a new, important way. The radical recognition of and the newly minted intellectual accommodation to black subjectivity, black authenticity, and black culture took place just as the experiment of Reconstruction was being scuttled in the South. The tragedy behind the discovery process, which I suspect is a real rather than a so-called public secret, is this: the new knowledge in service of inner refinement (*kultur*), which was partly motivated by the search for culture as a good in itself, actually eclipsed from view the machinations of politics and stunted in the process the development of a critical grammar among the most humanistically driven white cultural intelligentsia. Ironically, the new cultural liberalism that sprang from the discovery of the Negro spiritual also promoted a kind of arrested development. The most liberal wings of the intelligentsia, however, had constructed a workable appeasement. The aesthetic cleanliness and redemptive spirit of "culture" shielded them from the dirty hands of politics. What culminated was a restricted notion of progress (*zivilization*) that joined their willingness to abandon the recently freed black population in the South to the resurgence of states' rights.[26] The development of culture as benevolent and inclusive knowledge helped paper over the postwar redrawing of what Du Bois would later call the "color line." With slavery dismantled, a laissez-faire Republican virtue could triumph unfettered. For the new cultural experts, Negro authenticity was alive and well as part of the wellsprings of new national culture. Cultural modernity had given birth to new subjectivities, new authenticities, even new ethnicities on the margins. This transformation is incorporated in the discovery of black spirituals.

Tracing Music through the Sociohistorical Body

To approach music sociologically requires avoiding treating it as if it were an entity unto itself. Such treatment is entirely appropriate for a strict musicological approach that might emphasize the technical and material rather than the social dimensions of cultural practices. However, as a sociological problem, music must first be pushed back into the social frameworks in which it is produced and used.[27]

In thinking of how music fits into this schema, I find it helpful to introduce the complexity of the problem with an analogy. There is a particular diagnostic technique in the microscopic dimensions of medicine that involves applying a chemical dye to specific cell tissue or injecting directly into the bloodstream. The dye or chemical can then be observed as it comes into contact with particular cells or can be traced as it passes through the entire circulation system and various organs of the body. This technique enables the physician to observe a number of things: metabolic activity, structural regularities as well as irregularities, and—if I may use the term—communicative pathways or mediations along which the dye or chemical can be seen to move. Reactions to them can be observed as they are absorbed, metabolized, and altered in being taken in by the body.[28]

As a sociologist, I find this diagnostic technique quite intriguing when applied to cultural processes and to questions of cultural interpretation. What if we thought about this diagnostic procedure in metaphoric rather than medical terms, and as a framework for sociological, cultural, and historical analysis?[29] What if instead of dye or chemicals we substituted a specifiable cultural practice like the singing of a spiritual? What if we were to follow the particular musical practice, object, artifact, or symbol—or an ensemble of such practices and "things"—through certain aspects of its social circulation over time? Which social cells and cultural forms would music illuminate? Which individuals, groups, economic classes, or institutions would we encounter? Which relations of power would come into view? Which ideological configurations would be important? Which among the range of developments would be more prevalent?

Given that social practices unfold in time, which social configurations would we find the most salient? And when do things salient become crucial to social relationships? For how long? And why? Furthermore, what happens to things we thought we had such a keen concept of at the beginning? Does the music remain unaltered—like a coin passing through a long sequence of hands and transactions? Or does the music itself become transformed and transmuted? Which configurations come and go? Which last? How would we describe transformations and changes? By what criteria would we mark things "significant"? How are effects to be judged as possibly profound? What becomes a period, and how do we specify its parameters? At what point does music reveal larger crises? What gets changed forever—or are there unintended consequences of importance—because of the introduction and circulation of the music?

We can contextualize the problem in all of its sprawling complexity—which is sprawling precisely because we have returned the issue of cultural practice to social history—by emphasizing the shifting and unstable milieus in which music was produced and launched into social circulation. Let us begin with a simple construct: a solitary slave sings. The singing is heard as enigmatic noise by an overseer on the ship at sea moving somewhere along the middle passage; or heard by a young and enslaved

Frederick Douglass, and *remembered* (differently in the process of reflection and critical interpretation) as he composes his memoirs; or heard by the white abolitionist whose own sense of pathos guides him or her to anticipate that this experience will be repeated again and again; the slave's song is captured as a fleeting specimen fitting some mid-nineteenth-century protoethnographic schema of "natural history"; or it is heard by the man of scientific training who now knows that it has a proper place within a taxonomy of ethnologically conceived folkways.

In its earliest registration, the sounding was already more than a discrete practice. It was a recognized and collectively fabricated form—as an expression of forced production to ready the slave for the auction block, or as part of a clandestine gathering in the piney words or "hush arbors" where slaves assembled presumably beyond the vision and earshot of overseers, or as fulfillment of the request from a missionary teacher who had deemed such a song a "personal favorite." While the singing emanates from an individual or a group, it is never reducible to only the sound of a singing subject. In breaking the air, it punctuates an existing history and ruptures into the present. Certainly it hails a past just as much as it marks its own movement. As a cultural form, the song further extends an already extended cultural passage, just as it also begins passages that will cover new cultural terrain. It may be an isolated cry, but more often than not it is *heard* and appropriated by those for whom it is intended—an interpretive community of fellow slaves. But it may be a coerced sound, the product of an overseer's insistence that the sound be part of the labor process or the evening entertainment at the big house. Even when expressed "freely," it is often also heard by others for whom it was not meant. Whether it is appropriated by fellow slaves who bring to it a cultural memory or by others, it enters a social circulation that quickly leaves the immediate arena of the singer or singers. It is appropriated by owners as well as fellow slaves, for quite different purposes. It can register upon deeply kindred and sympathetic listeners like Frederick Douglass and others who are composing their slave narratives and memoirs. But through Douglass, it is then also launched into a circulation for which it was not initially intended. White abolitionists from the North in the 1850s and 1860s learn from Frederick Douglass's autobiography. Through transcription it leaves the confines of orality and becomes decontextualized, only to be recontextualized as a literary text. Its status as cultural object is transformed. It becomes the object of a new set of appropriations that are also practices, practices that are productively embedded in different cultural forms, practices that are themselves articulations of entirely different sensibilities governed by different needs of individuals and groups who have different social locations than those of slaves or even freed African Americans. It is distributed, exchanged, read, interpreted, rewritten, and resung—and, in each context, reused, redeployed, reinscribed, and re-encoded. All the while it is subjected to multiple reproductions. And it proliferates. It is modified. Its modifications proliferate. "It"—or part of it—in some semblance, facsimile, or rendition, is reobjectified and recontextualized again and again. We can trace it to an abolitionist political tract, to a quote in a speech, to the lines on the page of a visitor's diary, to an item in a travel narrative, to a feature story in a northern highbrow magazine or newspaper.

After the Civil War the song becomes part of a series of collections, a unit among others of its same class or category, in a text among a class of similar texts. Soon it takes on newly ascribed properties—that is, it takes on attributes that enable it to be objectified within externally imposed systems of classification: "spirichils," "sorrow songs," "folklore." Meanwhile it has been learned by white missionaries, then retaught to the children of former slaves. It is, in turn, rehearsed along with others by black singing groups, some of which are groomed to raise money in northern cities at home and European cities abroad in support of the fledgling black colleges established during and immediately after the Civil War. Audiences of former slaves as well as of European royalty hear what has been irrefutably defined as the true heart and soul of the American Negro.

The words—or their derivations—move on, propelled by new social currents; and they are revalued as parts of new cultural currencies that become enmeshed with political, moral, and economic forces, each with different institutional affiliations, each endowing the words or the practices of the music itself with particular investments of symbolic capital, and each spending or exchanging those words and practices for something else. Thus it becomes part of the folklorist's catch, a specimen or artifact filling out a larger taxonomy, an ethnological map, and a symbolic infrastructure that coincides with the making of a new intellectual discipline such as professional folklore. Highbrow classical music composers find it worthy enough to mine its elements, capture its phrasings, and incorporate it into new compositions. Under the reign of a new set of aesthetics it is straightened up and uplifted while being praised as the "wellspring" of an authentic Americana. Its once sung melismatic notes, broken upon a highly rationalized chromatic scale, are transmuted to enable it to enter as the raw material of refined art. As art it is struggled over, reclaimed again by African American intellectuals of the Harlem Renaissance. Through strategies of cultural recuperation it is subjected to a series of revisionings: it is again remembered, retrieved, reinstated, redefined as popular memory, and repositioned as the material for present and future aesthetic battles. It is also found by the white cultural bohemians of the lost generation of the 1920s. And in this decade, we hear traces of it turning up for the first time on recordings, played now on new talking machines and windup Victrolas, filling the black southern sharecropper's and the northern urban domestic worker's homes with the sound of cultural memories. This time the new markets of popular culture have captured it, its words and sounds etched in the grooves of black shellac. It is of course fully commodified—but as a material commodity it becomes a new element in an emerging cultural archive. It is now largely underwritten by the economic relations of the market. With the help of new technologies of cultural representation, it is launched into vast social orbits where it can be heard far beyond the immediate contexts in which it was initially produced. As a record it is simultaneously part of a cultural archive, held as frozen sound to be heard again and again by an endless number of increasingly modern appropriators. It can be heard in the context of domestic privacy. It is reworked into new forms and styles by emerging blues and gospel singers eager to record their versions, and it is also there to be covered by white recording artists.

As we follow it into the era of the Great Depression, the song is again rediscovered and recovered, this time by the liberal welfare state, and through a National Recovery Act that has developed a nationally defined interest in seeking out and transcribing the memories of the last of the living former slaves. It has already been fully absorbed in the hymnbooks and continues to be sung within the hundreds of black churches, their choirs, and congregations. But it moves beyond the churches to the streets and jails throughout the 1950s and 1960s. The words are now punctuated by the snarls of police dogs and the thump of truncheons. It becomes part of one of the largest social spectacles and public spheres ever formed and electronically transmitted through the mass media in the history of the United States. In the late-twentieth century we moderns can hear traces of it treated with dutiful pathos in televised documentaries aired on the Public Broadcasting System during Black History Month.

There is thus a quite extensive gamut along which the reception and social uses of black music runs—from its being least understood (as alien noise), to its place in mid-nineteenth-century intellectual as well as popular culture, to its thorough integration with the process of modern capitalist commodification, and its culmination as one of the important events in the annals of American history.

Cultural Interpretation and the Sociology of Knowledge

Social science, however, seems to stand somewhat perplexed (if not dumbfounded) in the face of the multidimensional flow I have sketched. There are two general reasons for this. First, consider the analogy given. At any single point along the way we (and the music) are confronted with quite different sets of social interests and widely varying modes of recognition and usage. This is always the case, even as we attempt to isolate something as ostensibly empirical as a singing subject, a cultural object, or a cultural practice. The work of social science goes more smoothly when the objects of the social world are not volatile, and when they are measurable and discrete.[30]

The "it" which I've been invoking (not as *thing*, but as a way of marking a more nebulous *cultural process*) in the above discussion is of course highly problematic: there is no unified "it" or "thing"—unless we are willing to accept things outside of their social and historical contexts. But as C. Wright Mills put it, to do this is to abandon the historical shank of sociology.[31] If we focus on *cultural movement* and *cultural formations*, rather than on the dehistoricized notion of music or practice, we are compelled to envision a long and sprawling cultural field that stretches over historical periods, and that takes on discernable yet shifting shapes through a series of distinct social processes, all of which span outward from the presumed starting point of what could be identified as an empirical and traceable cultural form (e.g., the singer, the hearer, the "spiritual," etc.).[32]

The second reason for the difficulty in analyzing such cultural flow has to do with the origins of the interpretive schemas of the social sciences themselves, and it is thus a problem of a peculiar order. Those branches of the social sciences most concerned with cultural interpretation were configured within the historical processes that shaped the emerging discovery of "culture" in the context of modernity (a historically specific conjuncture in which the double hermeneutic takes its modern root). The interpretive sciences, to which sociology is core, are thus subject to the double hermeneutic. The concepts at our disposal, which we rely upon to give us better accounts of the social world, are generated by that social world.[33]

The problem of interpreting culture thus entails a problem of interpreting the rise of the modern interpretive constructs themselves. The domain within sociology that has tried to address and embrace this conundrum is the sociology of knowledge. As Karl Mannheim suggested, critical social thought must attempt to account for its forms and the logic of its content as part of a deeper dialogue with the social and historical conditions that enable its very emergence.[34] This requires that we conceptualize cultural transformations as inextricably interlocked with material and social transformations. But rather than hinge cultural analysis on some nebulous notion of weltanschauung, as did Mannheim, these dimensions need to be grasped as human relationships.

The process that I have just sketched is enormous and sprawling. My study touches but a brief moment within this longer history of intertwined musical forms and social relations. But it is precisely in this brief period that the modern mode of cultural interpretation emerges, and where it becomes intertwined with sympathetic, benevolent, and managerial impulses and becomes progressively rationalized as an ethnoscience

of and at the racial margins. This emergent recognition not only preceded
modern social science; it helped prepare some of the important cultural
and institutional ground upon which modern social scientific orientations
toward cultural interpretation unfold. Indeed in the American context,
cultural interpretation was prefigured in early-nineteenth-century travel
narratives penned by white visitors to the South, in the slave narratives
that offered an inner black (slave) phenomenology that spoke simultaneously to social structures, in the protoethnographic and romantically
tinged advocacy of the abolitionists during the 1860s, and in the early
modern folklorists who come into being in the last decade of the nineteenth century. These developments paved the way for ensuing cultural
sociologists and kindred social scientists who, among other things,
refined and championed (in an on again–off again pattern) what we today
refer to as "ethnic studies." It was not social science that discovered cultural practices such as the slave narratives or the Negro spirituals of the
nineteenth century. Rather, modern social science—especially the
branches concerned with cultural, racial, and ethnic interpretation—inherited the ground upon which the various cultural discoveries were
made. As I suggest throughout this study, a significant dimension of modern American cultural analysis, especially with regard to how racialized
groups were culturally conceptualized, took shape in tandem with the
discovery and assessment of African American song making. In this regard, the professional study of folklore and the ethnic-oriented reaches of
early-twentieth-century American sociology and anthropology were late-
comers. They also carry the imprint of earlier political as well as institutional struggles involving the emergence of and the societal reaction to
ethnic and racial groups. Such institutional struggles were partially constituted through the rise of cultural interpretations.[35]

· · · · ·

The problems of authenticity, erosion, and cultural theft provide important assessments of the history of black music. And disengaged cultural
engagement also explains some of the cultural ways in which sympathetic
listeners negotiate the color line. Likewise, views resting upon the reification of culture are always present and seductively convenient. Each of
these problematics offers tempting starting points that spring from not-
well-understood outcomes of forms of cultural domination that were and
continue to be facilitated by the force and power of modern institutions
of cultural production. However, to assess the *interest* in black music
sociologically requires that we resist beginning the analysis with received
notions and reified forms.

The challenge is to understand the cultural templates that came into
place in the nineteenth century and that gave form to the interpretation of

black music. When it comes to black music in American history, the prob-lem is complicated from the very beginning. The easiest solution, one that I do not embrace, is to adopt the received notion of "natives" versus "observers." It is important to distinguish the makers of songs from the users of songs. However, given the larger historical context in which the social production of musical practices took place, the issue cannot be easily reduced to black producers and white consumers. Slave owners forcing slaves to sing makes slave owners part of the productive process. The music that results is enmeshed in social relations. Moreover, when owners, overseers, ministers, and critical abolitionists began to appropri-ate black song making, they brought many different interests with them, and many of these interests had little, if absolutely nothing, to do with black music per se. Black music under slavery (as well as today) certainly afforded a stage upon which other nonmusic—social, political, and cul-tural—struggles could be enacted.

But what do we do about the fact that the "insiders," who are the analytical object of the "outsiders," carry out their cultural practices upon cultural terrain prepared largely by outsiders? What do we do with cultural practices that have already developed a mixture of elements from the outside? Where is this line between inside and outside, natives and observers, producers and consumers?

Antonio Gramsci suggested, I believe, a helpful framework. Com-menting on the limitations involved in rigid distinctions between "intel-lectuals" and "nonintellectuals," he argued that "the most widespread error of method seems to me that of having looked for this criterion of distinction in the intrinsic nature of intellectual activities, rather than in the *ensemble of the system of relations* in which these activities (and therefore the intellectual groups who personify them) have their place within the general complex of social relations."[36] Gramsci's attempt to problematize the distinction between intellectuals and nonintellectuals also needs to be pushed further. For Gramsci, "traditional" intellectuals operate as cultural maintenance workers who, in their intellectual duties, wittingly or inadvertently carry out the normative requisites of a hege-monic formation. "Organic" intellectuals, on the other hand, are viewed as marginalized by institutional systems of social management, and are by definition members of subaltern classes who challenge the normative order and cultivate leadership in tension with or in opposition to tradi-tionalism. However, the distinction between traditional and organic is not at all simple. Traditional intellectuals can become transformed and invested in modes of opposition to hegemony; organic intellectuals can also become transformed and incorporated into new functionary roles beneficial to hegemony. Making sense of the distinction between tradi-tional and organic intellectuals thus had to proceed, Gramsci insisted, not with a priori proclamations based on a presumed identity reducible to a crude and ahistorical social typology, but rather within the framework of careful historical study. In this regard, the study of politics and culture is inextricably a problem of social figurations and conjunctures in the context of a society full of shifting identities and social alliances. As we shall see, the line between traditional and organic is difficult to see— for what do we make of an author of a slave narrative such as Frederick Douglass, who not only introduces the inner (and organic) facet of black song making, but does so within a form of writing and a religious ideology that embraces what could arguably be called the most core values and ethics of Christianity? Is this the work of a traditional or an organic intellectual?

Received and reified notions of intrinsic values attributed to presumably autonomous and distinct groups and their cultural practices, generate valuable perspectives. However, the challenge is to understand the way in which cultural practices and the interpretation of such are always embedded within historically contingent social relations. The problem of authenticity and the desire to conjure it, locate it, and capture it is much more complicated than Pierre Bourdieu seems to suggest when he wrote that "the purely ethical pursuit of 'authenticity' is the privilege of those who have the leisure to think and can afford to dispense with the economy of thought that 'inauthentic' conduct allows."[37] By examining the discovery and appropriation of black music in the nineteenth century, I hope to illuminate a much larger issue—the rise and development of a major and effective *interpretive formation* that was put into place at the intersection of racial, class, and cultural politics. This interpretive formation is, I believe, one of the ways that we have come to understand the intersection between modernity and cultural life.

We have come to appreciate the recent rejuvenated interest in cultural study and the problem of meaning because they contribute to the restoration of culture as central to a broader understanding of history and society. Yet this interpretive development reflects a rather complex move, one that hinges on the bestowal of subjectivity as well as of cultural value upon groups that hitherto had not been attributed such value. How this development of subjectivization emerged, how it engendered a new phenomenological turn, and how it opened up a modern mode of cultural interpretation deserves a closer look. Thus, rather than work within this modern interpretive formation, let us try to get beneath it.[38] In order to do this with regard to the discovery of black music we must back up to an earlier problem that predates the emergence of black subjectivity, selfhood, and cultural authenticity. We need to look at the way in which black music—black soundings—was heard before the emergence of modern ethnosympathy. This takes us to the problem of *meaningless noise*.

TWO

SOUND BARRIERS AND SOUND MANAGEMENT

Slaves are generally expected to sing as well as to work. A silent
slave is not liked by masters or overseers. "Make a noise,
make a noise," and "bear a hand," are the words usually
addressed to the slaves when there is
silence amongst them.
(Frederick Douglass, 1845)

HOW DID the captors, owners, and overseers of slaves hear black
music prior to the rise of the abolitionist movement? What did
they hear? And how did they respond to or act on what they
heard? Prior to the mid-nineteenth century black music appears to have
been heard by captors and overseers primarily as *noise*—that is, as
strange, unfathomable, and incomprehensible. However, with the rise of
the abolitionist movement, black song making became considered increasingly as a font of black *meanings*. Today we recognize this new,
mode of hearing, with its emphasis upon the meanings of culture producers, as fundamental to the modern phenomenological and hermeneutic
dimensions of cultural interpretation within the social sciences and the
humanities.

To comprehend the shift of reception from noise to meaningful sound,
we must first sketch the features of earlier modes of hearing. Three distinct modes of hearing black music can be identified: incidental hearing,
instrumental hearing, and pathos-oriented hearing. Considering these
modes allows us to assess the different ways in which black music making
was not just heard but was actually appropriated. By incidental hearing
I refer to the kind of accounts logged by white observers who did not
intend to hear black music, but who instead stumbled upon it. Their responses reflected little of what we today would acknowledge as sympathetic comprehension. Instrumental hearing, on the other hand, involved
attempts by overseers to use music for nonmusical objectives. Owners
could induce slaves to sing quick-paced songs to speed up the labor process, or could force them to make sheer sounds as a way to monitor them,
or could draw upon a slave's musical skills to augment his or her market
value. In contrast, pathos-oriented hearing, as I shall argue, marks the
modern humanistic turn; it champions black song making as a window

on the inner lives of slaves. Pathos-oriented hearing is thus the most important cultural development that I trace in this study.

The earliest modes of hearing need to be understood insofar as they provide the basic framework out of which the new ethnosympathetic mode of cultural interpretation emerged. Surveying them allows us to see what had to be challenged in order for a modern mode of meaning-centered interpretation to develop. To hear slave music as noise is an extremely limited interpretation and shaped entirely by slavery. Yet as a restricted cultural framework, "noise" offers, I believe, an analytical base-line from which other modes of hearing black music develop. As a cultural construct, noise enables us to see how ensuing changes in hearing grew from this earlier and most simple yet imperial orientation. Noise, however, is not just sound without meaning. Noise and meaningful sound are opposites, and together they are part of a broader and deeper social construct, a cultural logic, that enables and puts into motion some of the most basic boundary-mapping interpretations of meaning available to those who work with these categories.

In order to bring this logic into focus, I treat noise as an ideal-type against which other modes of hearing can be assessed. The changing schemas of interpreting black music also provide us with an important vantage point from which to view conflicting lines of social and institutional power that intersect the developing interests in the cultural expressions of people on the margins of society. As we shall see, early perceptions of black music as noise do not disappear in the wake of more culturally probing and reflexive modes of interpretation. Nevertheless, the most intense sense of bewilderment and the most strident tones of revulsion were over time muted, absorbed, modified, and recast under the humanitarian reformist impulses of the mid-nineteenth century and the ensuing professionalization of cultural analysis that developed in the latter decades of the century. It is against the early backdrop of noise, however, that we are able to gauge the more elaborate and complex orientations that emerge as new modes of cultural analysis and interpretation.

To explore these issues I shift the emphasis from "black producers" of music to "white consumers" of black music. This allows us to examine how hearing music, not from the perspective of a maker or producer, but from the perspective of an outside observer, is also a cultural practice—the *practice of hearing* the practices of others. This shift is required, I believe, if we are to rethink and reassess the rise and development of modern forms of cultural interpretation, especially in relationship to how new forms of social knowledge were generated within the dominant culture and were applied to the understanding of culture on the racial margins of American society. As I argue throughout the study, the development of such knowledge constituted an important intellectual juncture that has had a significant impact upon our sense of modern cultural interpretation.

Emotional Noise

Noise governs the interpretive schemas of the early preabolitionist era.[1] In most cases, when slave traders, owners, overseers, and other listeners heard black music, they heard noise. Earlier, preabolitionist descriptions of slave music characterize its qualities as impenetrable, incomprehensible, and unfathomable. Though scant prior to the nineteenth century, the early observations of black music tend to evoke two interpretive poles. On the one hand observers readily admit an inability, even failure, to understand slave music, often due to language barriers. On the other, they display an emerging comprehension of the meanings attributed to the feelings of the black individuals or groups in whose singing they hear fairly well defined emotions and offer interpretations of what these emotions might mean. Slave singing is interpreted as "doleful," "mournful," "melancholy," "monotonous" and "sad." But of the two sets of attributes, it is *noise* that overrides the nascent perception of emotional noise.

The first published account of European slave traders that logged observations of African music confronted the language barrier. In 1445, Portuguese slave traders reported that they "could not understand the words of their language." Yet "the sound" they heard from captured blacks "right well accorded with the measure of their sadness."[2] Testifying in 1791 before the British House of Commons investigations of the slave trade, carpenter James Towne described how the slaves on ship were forced under whip to sing and dance. "Have you ever heard the Slaves singing, and have you been acquainted with the subject of their song? I have. I never found it any thing joyous, but lamentations." Towne, unlike most, claimed to have fathomed their language, and reported that the slaves sang "complaints for having been taken away from their friends and relations."[3] Ship surgeon Alexander Falconbridge, who witnessed slaves forced to sing and dance on the slave ships, noted their song making as being "generally, as may naturally be expected, melancholy lamentations of their exile."[4] Other early observations gathered from slave ships describe slave singing as a "wild yell," as "[making] merry, when their heart was sad," and in a "plaintive tone, when left to themselves." Terms like "rude and uncouth," "strange," "wild," and "devoid of all softness" indicate a dominant sensibility with regard to black music and tend to place it on the farthest margins of social value, at the borders of culture and civilization. Perceived as fundamentally incoherent and without distinct meaning, black music was simply defined consistently within the dehumanizing social classifications of blacks as chattel. This, of course, fit within a culture that endorsed the idea that "in seventeenth century Virginia a master could not murder a slave. He might cause his death, but he could not legally murder him."[5]

As black music began to be appraised with increasing sympathy, it also became more comprehensible. Yet even among sympathizers, black music remained enigmatic. Frederick Law Olmsted, who traveled extensively in the South as a journalist in the mid-1850s and who was critical of slavery, described slaves singing during a black funeral procession he witnessed in Washington, D.C., in 1853 as

> a wild kind of chant. . . . [A]n old negro . . . raised a hymn, which soon became a confused chant—the leader singing a few words alone, and the company then either repeating them after him or making a response to them, in the manner of sailors heaving at the windlass. I could understand but very few of the words. The music was wild and barbarous, but not without a plaintive melody.[6]

Reminiscent of many earlier accounts, Olmsted's description remained ensconced within what we might call the "barbarous-plaintive" dichotomy. These two interpretive dispositions—one standing in perplexity at the barrier of language and culture, the other signaling a presumed insight into the window of human emotions—continues well into the nineteenth century.

References to the emotions of slaves increased in frequency and in descriptive elaboration during the abolitionist period, and became a salient feature of what came to be associated with the Negro spiritual. The division, however, between intellectual incomprehensibility and irrepressible emotional knowledge continued as well. During the Civil War, Elizabeth Coxe witnessed a "negro prayer meeting" on her father's South Carolina plantation. "I remember a slight thrill of alarm one night that winter when D. and I heard very wild singing at their church. . . . [It was a] scene of barbaric frenzy that I have since thought the howling Dervishes reminded me of."[7] Coxe did not make the same empathic reach that Mary Boykin Chestnut did when the latter attended a Negro church gathering during which she was exposed to words that had "no meaning at all," though she "wept bitterly" in response.

The combination of unfathomable noise and fathomable emotions signals a peculiar disposition toward black music and a capacity to hear what we might call *emotional noise*. This double-dimensional hearing that coupled a sense of meaninglessness with a sense of meaning marks, I believe, the beginning of an important cultural and interpretive renegotiation in the hearing process that eventually yielded a more subjectivistic orientation toward black music, one that became increasingly attuned to the meanings of black subjects. As an early recognition of emotions it was an incipient as well as feeble sensibility, but it grew in importance and developed most rapidly in the early-nineteenth century, when it was aided in critically important ways by the publication of the slave narratives, which coincided with the emergence of humanistic modes of cultural reception. With the slave narratives (which I discuss in a later chapter), the inner dimensions of black lives were opened up for the first time to white readers, and black and white abolitionists were able to begin mining emotional noise. And they did so by bringing to it accounts that were more reflexively refined, accounts that also resulted in a new as well as a major reinterpretation of black music. I will return later to this important issue of emotional recognition, which was only nascent in the earliest accounts but which reached a quite sophisticated stage by the Civil War.

Noise as Ideal Type

Noise is, by definition, a messy problem. However, it is helpful to treat noise conceptually as an ideal-type. This requires creating a construct that is something of an analytical fiction—for as Max Weber has argued, in social science there are no "pure" or "ideal" ideas in themselves, but constructs that are indispensable as "heuristic" devices. The concept of "ideal-type" is Weber's astute contribution to confronting the human and socially constructed dimension of all analytical ideas or conceptual formations. The ideal-type works this way: We confront a myriad of statements, observations, examples, cases, practices, or procedures and sift for lines of thematic continuity. We then attempt to extract or distill from the variation at hand a narrow set of features that might highlight or accentuate the features of the social pieces of what we wish to comprehend. The intellectual construct itself, derived from attempts to pull the features (which are ultimately analytical ideas) into relationship, is an ideal-type. We then attempt to bring the social pieces of concern into approximate closeness or distance with the constructed ideal-type.

To treat noise in an ideal-typical manner requires isolating and highlighting the notion of noise in order to ascertain its narrowest conceptual meaning. Basically, noise is sound out of order. It is sound that lacks—and even defies—organization. As such it cannot be grasped because the schemas with which it is to be comprehended lack the categories for processing it along lines of order. Noise simply evades. It eludes culturally normative categories of cognition because it does not fit them; it is rejected sound that spills out of, or flows over, the preferred channels along which known, accepted, and regulated sounds occur. Sound that cannot be meaningfully placed is aberrant sound, sound out of place. Noise defined as such is difficult to fathom; it is resistant to capture—for to capture it would be tantamount to transforming noise into sound, to securing noise a place, to granting it its own grammar, or to allowing it to enter into a recognized grammar. In giving it such logic, such significance, noise would cease to be noise, and would be transmogrified into meaningful sound.

When applied to the reception of black music, the problem of pure noise is never really found. But to treat it as an ideal-type allows us to generate and assess the distinctions and variations with regard to how hearing patterns approximate or diverge from noise. As we move closer to the ideal-type of black music as sheer noise, there is room only for an increasingly restricted and one-sided view of black music as incomprehensible and with alien qualities that place it outside of any kind of recognition. Such views are authorized interpretive angles from *above* and *outside* of black music making. The problem of meaning and point of view thus becomes a stark contrast in black and white. The ear is thus involved in seeing, and such views appear to have no investment whatsoever in the sensuous cultural work of music insofar as the meaning making of slaves is of importance. The slave's inner world remains eclipsed.

Yet as the long history of scholarship on slave music has shown, the production of music and other cultural forms enabled slaves to collectively exercise symbolic control. Song making helped them comprehend their fate and wrest from their conditions some sense of order. But to hear only noise is to operate from outside of what Frederick Douglass called the "inner circle"; it is tantamount to being oblivious to the structures of meaning that anchored sounding to the hermeneutic world of the slaves. To perceive only noise is to remain removed from how slave soundings probed their circumstances and cultivated histories and memories, even though the enterprise of music making was continually made fragile by the ever-present threat of social dislocation and violence. The most ideal-typical and simpleminded notion of noise thus approximates the dominant society's cultural incapacity to grasp how slaves created, cultivated, and maintained shared cognitive maps. As an interpretive schema, noise is simply a din that prevents the powerful from perceiving the collective symbolic enterprise of the dominated, those very practices that twentieth-century scholars would come to call "slave culture." This deeper, vibrant, subterranean culture and the meanings that it entailed could only be, at best, a feeble hunch to the managers of chattel, even when they were able to muster a sympathetic recognition of black emotions behind the otherwise "crude," "uncouth," and "rough" noise made by slaves.

But pure, unfathomable noise (like a pure idea) did not really exist. Far too many of the accounts of owners and overseers that describe black noise also contain a deeper unraveling of noise—an unraveling toward the irrepressible acknowledgment of meaningful emotions. Time after time, observers attribute meaningful emotions that crop up in descriptions of black songs. The recognition of emotions that were latent from the outset becomes increasingly manifest, and erupts with great and irreversible importance in the early-nineteenth century to become one of the most central shanks of modern social and cultural interpretation.

Hearing of course always takes place within cultural settings. It is a social and cultural act whose functions cannot be separated from social, cultural, and historical forces; it is situated perception. When captors, owners, and overseers heard black song making in the context of slavery, they were hearing not just unrecognizable sounds; they heard *within* slavery. This is just as much the case for the northerners, black as well as white, from free states who traveled or lived for some time in the South and heard slave music. At the height of the discovery of the Negro spiritual during the Civil War, William Allen, who assembled the first major collection of such songs, stated the working assumption of many abolitionists when he compared "negro music" that was "*civilized* in its character" because of the "influence of association with the whites," to music that was "intrinsically barbaric."[8] Songs of the "barbaric element" fell beyond the civilized boundary marked by the Christian spiritual, and could be heard only as unrecognized and unapproved noise. From the time of the earliest observation through most of the nineteenth century there remained a considerable body of black song making that was not readily accessible even to those whites whose interest in humanitarian reformism carried them to the racial and cultural margins.

Even the black abolitionist Charlotte Forten Grimke, grand-daughter of the prominent black Philadelphian sailmaker Charles Forten, carried deeply ingrained presumptions of slaves, presumptions circumscribed by slavery. Grimke was invited in 1862 to aid in helping the recently freed slaves residing on St. Helena Island off the coast of South Carolina. She noted in her journal on January 31, 1863: "We had a lovely row [to Beaufort] across,—at noon—in the brightest sunlight. But neither going nor coming did the boatman sing, which disappointed me much. The Sergeant said these were not singers—*that* is most surprising. I thought *everybody* sang down here. Certainly every boat crew *ought*."[9] Slaves evidently were all supposed to be singing subjects, especially when they labored to serve others. Grimke too, though herself a free black from the North, heard within slavery. Her presumptions were also shaped by a deeper, older, cultural ideology rooted in a proslavery apologetics that was inherited, adopted, and readapted by well-intentioned romanticist and reformist entrepreneurs. Grimke's presumptions were part of an interpretive schema that was endorsed by prominent radical white abolitionists who worked with an already deeply routinized link between blacks and music—of blacks as singing people. Such hearing, structured as it was by the peculiar institution, was neither innocent nor exempt from the context in which it took place. Slavery comprised as well as compromised both the social nature of soundings made by slaves and the ears of even the most sympathetic nonslaves who heard them.

As would be expected, comprehension and understanding of black song making became somewhat more sophisticated by the nineteenth century. As slaves developed an ease with the English language they could continue melding remnants of Africanisms that they managed to retain ("survivals") with new cultural practices, especially those made available to them through Christian proselytization.[10] But even well after slaves developed a facility with spoken English and had internalized aspects of Christian teachings into their cultural practices, the persistent view was that black music making that was not religious singing was alien and incomprehensible.

The Work of Music

Black music did not have to be fathomed and understood to be pulled into service by the planter and overseer classes. That they would not understand the slave as a human, a subject, did not matter; nor did they need to understand their music (at least until the concern for extending Christian teachings began to take on importance in the early-nineteenth century). Along with the laboring body of the slave came the music of slaves, and both were harnessed. Overseers and owners were quick to use music. Even on the slave ships music was coerced out of slaves as they were forced to exercise in order to look lively on the auction blocks.

Whether they were coerced or acted by their own will, slaves put music to work. To slaves, music was cultural work—the work of solidarity. Through music slaves were able to ease the harshness of their lot while exercising one of the few options available for a collective black voice. For overseers, music aided in the management of work as well as the management of slaves. Music was thoroughly incorporated into the labor process and became a common adjunct to carrying out work, though its performance usually meant different things to slaves and overseers. Slaves with musical skills were also pressed into service to entertain the planter class. Sometimes this entertainment overlapped with the function of dissipating or syphoning off deep social tensions, which were put aside during harvest festivals and holidays, when both owners and the owned celebrated together. Thus a slave's musical skills and competencies were often valued, and musical attributes increased a slave's worth both domestically and as a marketable commodity. These forms of musical usage, which I will discuss, reflect not so much a listener's understanding of black music, but rather an instrumentalist orientation that enabled masters and overseers to pull music into a larger sphere of slave surveillance and management. In this regard, owners and overseers did not understand black soundings in a phenomenological sense—this only came about with the aid of black cultural instructions and interpretive guidance in narratives penned by former slaves—but they nonetheless imposed their own limited comprehension upon the music by treating it as a resource to be cultivated, manipulated, and exploited, and linked it to strategies of chattel management and social control.

As noted, from the very earliest moments of capture aboard slave ships, slaves were forced to make sounds, to move, and to jump in their chains. Slavers called this "exercise," and its purpose was to stave off the depression and lethargy of their dispirited human cargo, for many slaves died in passage. Exercising the slaves was ostensibly aimed at preparing them to appear vigorous and vital, and in some cases at simply keeping them alive. Getting the slaves to move about on deck usually required physical inducement such as whipping them with the "cat" (cat-o'-nine-tails). West Indian planter John Riland provided an account of his experiences on a slave ship, and of these required bouts of "exercise" that appear to have been standard operating procedures in transporting slaves across the Middle Passage:

> The captain wanted the slaves to dance; but they did not seem disposed to comply with his wish. He began to dance himself, by way of setting them an example; but they shewed no inclination to follow it, till the *cat* was called for. Then, indeed, they began to sing and skip about. A few, however, were content to have the *cat* smartly applied across their shoulders several times, before they would so much belie their feelings as to make merry, when their heart was sad. . . . An air of dejection appeared in the faces of most of them. . . . They were very averse to any kind of exercise; and, when they danced, their whole aim seemed to be to make noise enough to please the captain.[11]

The terms "singing" and "dancing" that have come to be commonly used in the early literature appear just as much to be euphemisms for forced soundings and the pain-induced rapid motion of slaves in shackles. Of course slaves were quite capable of singing and dancing, these being fundamental dimensions of deep cultural value to most peoples of the world. But it is not likely that individuals ripped from their homes and families, shackled by strangers, and forced upon ships and whipped would break into spontaneous song and dance in ways that are usually signified by these terms (that is, ritual and celebration). From the onset music emerged in a profoundly coercive context where its progressive incorporation into the entire system of slave management was launched.

Proper Music and the Rate of Work

Frederick Douglass's recollection of how overseers distrusted the "silent slave" and insisted that slaves "make a noise" during working suggests that sound making was a requisite to appease the discomfort of owners who preferred to know that whatever occupied the slave's mind was not inimical to the well-being of overseers. Overseers, however, often viewed slaves as having plenty of inimical qualities of mind. As Frederick Douglass recalled, there were many ways in which a slave's presumed demeanor could elicit retribution.

> Does a slave look dissatisfied? It is said, he has the devil in him, and it must be whipped out. Does he speak loudly when spoken to by his master? Then he is getting high-minded, and should be taken down a button-hole lower. Does he forget to pull off his hat at the approach of a white person? Then he is wanting in reverence, and should be whipped for it. Does he venture to vindicate his conduct when censured for it? Then he is guilty of impudence,—one of the greatest crimes of which a slave can be guilty. Does he ever venture to suggest a different mode of doing things from that pointed out by his master? He is indeed presumptuous, and getting above himself; and nothing less than flogging will do for him. If slaves were discouraged from talking, their silence was at times just as likely to elicit retribution.[12]

Overseers could easily monitor slaves who were forced to sing just to make noise; they could also limit as well as monitor what kind of auditory exchanges slaves could carry out. Coerced soundings checked silence as well as ordinary dialogue. In this regard singing from the perspective of the owner was not meant to be a means of communication; on the contrary, it was supposed to trim or shut down slave communication. Of course the studies that reveal the opposite are now quite numerous. As former slave Harriet Tubman observed, singing was a way to displace talk. "Slaves," wrote Tubman, "must not be seen talking together," but they could sing. Singing thus filled in where everyday discourse was prevented: "And so it came about that their communication was often made by singing."[13]

But any singing? Not according to Frances Anne Kemble, an English actress and wife of an American slave owner. According to Kemble, it was "cheerful" music that overseers preferred.

> Many masters and overseers on these plantations prohibit melancholy tunes or words and encourage nothing but cheerful music . . . deprecating the effect of sadder strains upon the slaves whose peculiar musical sensibilities might be expected to make them especially excitable by any songs of a plaintive character, having any reference to their particular hardships.[14]

Cheerful songs presumably blocked the slaves from singing songs that reflected their "particular hardships." By making such distinctions between "cheerful" and "sadder strains," and by preferring the emotive expressions of the former, owners and overseers displayed their capacity to grasp (correctly it seems) the emotional investments slaves placed in songs. Embedded in this distinction is the latent issue of whether slaves possibly had subjectivity. As we shall see in later chapters, when the abolitionists discover black music, they reverse this emotive valuation almost to a tune: plaintive and sad strains become much more credible than secular and presumably light, frivolous, and even happy music associated with minstrelsy. Both of these problems—whether blacks had subjectivity and what the abolitionist's strategies of appropriation were—are issues to which we shall return. The interest in, and intervention into, music went beyond the mere preference for soundings free of sad or plaintive strains. By the middle of the nineteenth century music had already become recognized as a feature of the pace of labor itself. Along with bodies, muscles, and limbs, music was integrated into the labor process.[15]

Evidence that the reflection upon music had evolved into a more rationalized mode of appropriation appeared in the pages of *De Bow's Review* in 1855. An article entitled "Management of Negroes" suggested that slaves should not be allowed to sing "drawling tunes" that might slow work down, and recommended instead labor-appropriate music such as "whistling or signing some lively tune."[16] Commenting on overseers' attempts to regulate the pace of work by manipulating tempo, Eugene Genovese notes that slave masters "encouraged quick-time singing among their field slaves" as an aid to increase output. Quick songs induced the speedup of the labor process. Slaves, however, sometimes "proved themselves masters of slowing down the songs and the work."[17]

Music was by no means the entire expression of coercion and labor. Though music was often forced from them, slaves also relied heavily upon music as one of the few symbolic forms in which they could collectively indulge. Music making was also a refuge where a great deal of important communication could take place, and became especially crucial, fragile, and precious when mere talk among slaves was strongly discouraged or when talk itself was not enough to meet their collective need to work out the pain of slavery. In 1862, James Miller McKim, a former Presbyterian minister and early founding member of the Anti-Slavery Society, visited the Sea Islands of South Carolina, where he observed slaves working. Intrigued by the frequent combination of song with work, he asked where the songs came from. The answer:

> "Dey make em, sah." "How do they make them?" After a pause, evidently casting about for an explanation, he said, "I'll tell you; it's dis way. My master call me up and order me a short peck of corn and a hundred lash. My friends see it and is sorry for me. When dey come to de praise meeting dat night dey sing about it. Some's very good singers and know how; and dey work it in, work it in, you know; till dey get it right; and dat's de way."[18]

Song making helped broker the conditions of work, but it also eased the aftermath of brutal punishment, stretching even further the social functions of music. Such recourse to music also served to absorb and hide pain from the overseer. Blues musician Booker T. White recalled stories told him by a 110-year-old black woman, herself a former slave. While working in the fields, the slaves would actually cry the songs out: "sing[ing] them songs so pitiful, and so long. . . . "[W]hen they see the boss coming they would make like a gnat got in their eye. 'Cos you know, the boss didn't want them to feel that-a-way, you know, they had to be cool, play it cool, you know."[19]

William Allen, one of the key compilers of black religious songs, recalled observing the continuous singing of stevedores loading and unloading ships at the wharves in Philadelphia and Baltimore: "I have stood for more than an hour, often, listening to them, as they hoisted and lowered the hogsheads and boxes of their cargoes; one man taking the burden of the song (and the slack of the rope) and the others striking in with the chorus. They would sing in this way more than a dozen different songs in an hour."[20] Allen gives no indication that the stevedores are being forced to sing. On the contrary, Allen suggests that the black workers who produced the music might have been developing their own therapeutic response to the drudgery of labor.

Yet the historical roots of the incorporation of music making in the labor process can also lead to the conflation of the two as an essential racial trait. Such would be expected from those who defended slavery. But northern abolitionists were influenced as well by racialized cultural mores that pervaded the culture, and these mores shaped their conceptions of social nature. Few white abolitionists had the sensitivity toward blacks of the former Unitarian minister Thomas Wentworth Higginson, who commanded an all-Negro regiment for the Union Army during the

Civil War. Higginson, however, in his romantic descriptions of the black troops under his supervision, also conflated historical pressures with natural essences.

> Never have I beheld such a *jolly scene of labor*. Tugging these wet boards over a bridge of boats ashore, then across the slimy beach at low tide, then up a steep bank, and all in one great uproar of merriment for two hours. Running most of the time, chattering all the time, snatching the boards from each other's backs as if they were some coveted treasure, getting up eager rivalries between different companies, pouring great choruses of ridicule on the heads of all shirkers, they made the whole scene so enlivening that I gladly stayed out in the moonlight for the whole time to watch it. And all this without any urging or any promised reward, but simply as *the most natural way of doing the thing*. The steamboat captain declared that they unloaded the ten thousand feet of boards quicker than any white gang could have done it; and they felt it so little, that, when, later in the night, I reproached one whom I found sitting by a campfire, cooking a surreptitious opossum, telling him that he ought to be asleep after such a job of work, he answered, with the broadest grin,—
>
> "O no, Cunnel, da's no work at all, Cunnel; dat only jess enough for stretch we."[21]

Higginson might have indulged in another conflation, that the boards hauled by the black soldiers were the spoils of a raid they had just completed in "rebel" country. The troops had carried out a successful strike against the hated Slave Power. The glee of carrying on their backs the booty of war might just as likely explain their gusto.

Well after slavery was abolished, the link between labor and song remained, as if tied firmly to the cultural anchor of slavery. Even at the end of the century the tradition of incorporating and rewarding the role of music in the labor process was still observable. The American Folk-Lore Society reported that in the "canning industry establishments in Baltimore . . . the leading singers are actually paid more by their employers, showing that their leading has a distinct money value from the capitalist's point of view."[22] The article offers no indication that singing increased the productivity of labor, but only that the singing laborer was preferred to the one "who merely did his work and kept still."

> Testimony from several persons present tended to show that the singing of the slaves at work was regarded by their masters as almost indispensable to the quick and proper performance of the labor, and that the leaders of the singing were often excused from work that they might the better attend to their part of the business. The statement was also made that on the Missis-

sippi in the old days, the wharf laborers were selected and retained largely because of their ability as singers, a good singer being regarded as worth more on the wharves than a laborer who merely did his work and kept still about it.[23]

Booker T. Washington noted the music-labor linkage as well: "Often-times in slavery, as to-day in certain parts of the South, some man or woman with an exceptional voice was paid to lead the singing, the idea being to increase the amount of labor by such singing."[24] Charles Peabody provided an account in 1903 of work songs being performed by Negro laborers who were assisting in an excavation of a mound for the Harvard Peabody Museum. Acknowledging the link between song and the labor process, Peabody wrote:

> Most of the human noise of the township was caused by our men, nine to fifteen in number, at their work. On their beginning a trench at the surface, the woods for a day would echo their yelling with faithfulness. The next day or two these artists being, like the Bayreuth orchestra, sunk out of sight, there would arise from behind the dump heap a not unwholesome murmur as of the quiescent Furies. Of course this singing assisted the physical labor in the way as that of sailors tugging ropes or of soldiers invited to march by drum and band. They tell, in fact, of a famous singer besought by his co-workers not to sing a particular song, for it made them work too hard, and a singer of good voice and endurance is sometimes hired for the very purpose of arousing and keeping up the energy of labor.[25]

Well into the twentieth century, music historian Newman White observed the preference that employers had for the musical skills of black workers: "I myself have seen gangs of Negro laborers in North Carolina and Alabama working to songs started by a song-leader, and have been told by several men who have been in charge of construction gangs in various Southern states that it is a common practice to give the leader extra pay."[26]

These examples do more than just connect blacks and labor in the context of slavery. Such descriptions cut a deeper common trail across the great cultural divide. Slave owners drew their own linkages between slave labor and the perpetually happy singing subject and used them as a defense of slavery. Antislavery northerners drew such linkages as well, not in defense of slavery but in support of a subtler, more modern, and incorporative notion of labor and racial dispositions. Even in the protoethnographic accounts by abolitionists like William Allen, James McKim, and Thomas Wentworth Higginson, the interpretive framework linking work and the disposition for it with song was still in operation. As we shall see, these cultural attitudes toward black music tended to smooth fate's rough edge. Slaves may have made music in order to negotiate their social location, but the new discoverers turned toward cultural appreciation as a way to buffer themselves from the social pain of a deeply embedded color line. This adjudicating sensibility echoes across many of the modern end-of-century accounts of folklorists and social scientists.

Musical Leisure beyond the Pleasure Principle

Music also had value to owners and overseers beyond the day-to-day labor process. Slaves provided a major source for the entertainment needs of masters, especially during holidays, harvest times, and other special occasions. On such special days, musical talents were often given free reign. Slaves with musical skills were considered valuable, and musical attributes not only distinguished a slave; they enhanced the slave as a commodity. An exceptionally good musician was also more mobile, fulfilling requests from other owners for the use of his or her services.

Advertisements in colonial newspapers reveal among other things the qualities, skills, and attributes that owners valued in slaves. According to Eileen Southern, slave advertisements generally fell into three categories: "those offering slaves for sale; those offering slaves 'for hire' by the day, week, month, or even year; and those giving notice of runaway slaves. If a slave possessed special skills, the advertisement emphasized this, for a skilled craftsman or a musician commanded a better price than a field hand."[27] Solomon Northup, an excellent fiddler, wrote in his narrative how fortunate he was to have such sought-after musical skills, for his fiddling presented opportunities that he would not otherwise have had.[28]

> Alas! had it not been for my beloved violin, I scarcely can conceive how I could have endured the long years of bondage. It introduced me to great houses—relieved me of many days' labor in the field—supplied me with conveniences for my cabin—with pipes and tobacco, and extra pairs of shoes. . . . It heralded my name round the country—made me friends, who, otherwise would not have noticed me—gave me an honored seat at the yearly feasts, and secured the loudest and heartiest welcome of them all at the Christmas dance.[29]

Such celebratory occasions at which a fortunate musician like Northup might play were high points that punctuated the long year of arduous labor. As Eugene Genovese notes, former slaves frequently recalled corn shuckings as their best times.[30] But on such occasions the function of music served more than the coercive whims of masters; it was pulled into dimensions of master-slave relations in ways that were special only to such rare moments of collective celebration. Seasonal corn husking and certain other types of labor, for example, turned into events that allowed slaves as well as whites to associate on more convivial but inevitably fleeting terms, circumscribed by the specific occasion. Lewis Paine, a white native of Providence, Rhode Island, provides an important observation of how slaves and whites sometimes shared harvest time festivities: "Log-rollings and [corn] shuckings are always participated in by the whites. These sports are episodes in their lives. They are like oases to the weary traveler of the desert; they help to enliven the sad journey of life; they are faint rays that shine over the dark voyage."[31] Paine's description of black and white participation indicates that the event provided not just entertainment, but also a particular kind of temporary release for both groups from the norms and mores of everyday life under slavery.

> They generally so arrange matters, as to get [the work] done before night, when they take up their line of march for the house; and, on arriving there, take a drink all round. Then commence their gymnastic exercises. They wrestle, jump, and run foot-races. Black and white all take part in the sport, and he who comes off victorious has an extra sip of the "white eye." After indulging in these exercises as long as they wish, some one calls for a fiddle-but if one is not to be found, some one "pats juber." This is done by placing one foot a little in advance of the other, raising the ball of the foot from the ground, and striking it in regular time, while, in connection, the hands are struck slightly together, and then upon the thighs. In this way they make the most curious noise, yet in such perfect order, it furnishes music to dance by. *All indulge in the dance*. The slaves, as they become excited, use the most extravagant gestures—the music increases in speed—and the Whites soon find it impossible to sustain their parts, and they retire. This is just what the slaves wish, and they send up a general shout, which is returned by the Whites, acknowledging the victory.[32]

This ritual of collective play and conviviality capping a season's work suggests a rare concession on the part of the slaveholding class. A fleeting and momentary equality arising in the brief suspension of master-slave relations takes place in the sphere of play where whites and blacks participate on an equal basis. But after the dancing escalates, the whites, according to Paine's description, acknowledge the superior dancing skills of the slaves and retreat as audience. Paine notes a victory conceded to the slaves. With the whites out of the dance, "[the slaves] all sing out, 'Now show de white man what we can do!' And with heart and soul they dive into the sport, until they fairly exceed themselves. It is really astonishing to witness the rapidity of their motions, their accurate time, and the precision of their music and dance. I have never seen it equalized in my life."[33] Paine's observation of the festive incident indicates no coercion. Rather, it reflects how Paine and others of his class were somewhat captured by the "curious noise" and the "extravagant gestures" of the slaves as they watched both whites and blacks interact in singing and dancing. But it also demonstrates how even in the rigid social relations of slavery there could occur a transitory event (in the sphere of play) during which roles of winners and losers could be reversed.[34] That slaves could at times express happiness was seized upon by defenders of slavery. Such images of contented slaves were strongly cultivated in minstrelsy, the most widespread form of popular culture in the two decades before the Civil War, and the views of slaves as singing subjects pervaded the North.

Nevertheless the legacy of noise ran deep and wide. Despite barriers to comprehension, owners and overseers attempted to harness black noise and manage black music making much as they did any other exploitable attribute of one's property. The utilitarian linkage between music and forced labor drew upon the deep cultural orientation through which owners and overseers heard black music as noise; it cultivated as well the notion of a black essence naturally yoked to forced labor. This linkage was the cultural underpinning of the dominant mode of conceptualizing and appropriating black music, and it grew out of the predominantly utilitarian orientation toward slave music. It was this cultural anchorage that offended the most radical sensibilities of the abolitionists and the one that they tried to dislodge.

Three Modes of Hearing

I can now identify three modes of hearing that make up the significant orientations toward black music: *incidental hearing*, *instrumental hearing*, and *pathos-oriented hearing*. They are not rigid categories; indeed, they shade into one another and overlap in operations. Each mode, however, involves interests, intentions, and investments (attending to the expressions of others is never a neutral act), but these also vary greatly. Owners, overseers, and free white northerners who visited the South logged observations of music that reveal important insights into what they heard, how they heard, and why they heard, and into the context in which they heard black music. Furthermore, their accounts tell us about how they reacted to or acted upon the music of slaves.

Orientations, like dispositions, are not just sensibilities; they are cultural logics informed by ideas, interests, intentions, and actions.[35] These vary in complexity as they develop and differ from the most basic ideal-type notion of black music as unintelligible noise. Incidental hearing represents perhaps the most analytically simple relationship to black music, for it is the least encumbered by any overt interest in music. In a sense, incidental hearing is often accidental hearing. Music is happened upon, and this can take many forms: a visitor is present at a plantation where slaves are witnessed working or celebrating; or happens to be at a seaport where slaves are loading or unloading cargo; or is in the town where slaves are being auctioned; or encounters a black religious gathering. He or she does not intend to hear music, and being in those places was not motivated by an a priori desire to hear black song making. But hearing music happens anyway, for incidental hearing is fundamentally inadvertent.

Yet when observers recorded and published their inadvertent observations, these were pulled into a much broader context in which struggles over the definitions of black music took place. A written record of incidental observations could have and, in many cases, did have important cultural consequences. In some cases, such writings were the first installments of critical insight into the more complicated place of black music in antebellum America. The journal entries, travel narratives, and memoirs of Frances Kemble, Fredrika Bremer, and Frederick Law Olmsted contain many accounts of slave music.[36] These particular writings and others like them were important not only to white readers of their own period. They have also taken on important archival status since their publication, and virtually every major historian and social scientist interested in antebellum black culture has combed through their pages. These early observers were not motivated by a distinct interest in identifying, pursuing, and capturing knowledge of black music. Nonetheless, their writings can be read as prescient examples of what would later become known elements of formal ethnographic work, as individuals extracted a more refined notion of *ethnos* from the socially exploratory frameworks of travel narratives, formal literary narratives, and natural history writing. Most important, others who were passionate about fathoming black music as a cultural entity in its own right read their observations and drew upon the knowledge and insights of these incidental hearers had presented.

But not all incidental hearing was of this caliber. Observing the large gatherings of slaves that took place on Sundays at "Congo Square" in New Orleans led architect Benjamin Latrobe to write in the early-nineteenth century of practices he found detestable. "The allowed amusements of Sunday have, it seems, perpetuated here those of Africa among its inhabitants. I have never seen anything more brutally savage, and at the same time dull & stupid, than this whole exhibition."[37] There are also many observations made by Protestant ministers who heard the collective singing of slaves as noisy expressions of heathenism and who began introducing slaves to Christian teachings. Incidental hearing thus can produce morally incensed responses that run the gamut from sociological insight, to disgust, to abolitionist-tinged sympathy and sentimentalism. Even the most sympathetic incidental hearers made a mixed and ambivalent sense of black music and questioned whether it was noise or meaningful sound. Most important, incidental hearing is not based on an attempt to harness and make use of black music, and its reactions can take many forms. It is the unintentional orientation toward music, the lack of a central preoccupation with music, that is the characteristic feature behind this kind of hearing.

Making use of black music is precisely what the instrumentalist and the pathos-oriented modes of hearing attempt. Both spring from motivations to appropriate black music. Instrumental hearing, however, is fundamentally utilitarian. It treats music as one of many available resources within a slave. Like strength, fertility, youth, and so forth, musical ability is an attribute that can be exploited—all within the goal-oriented considerations of achieving outcomes that rest fundamentally upon, and firmly within, the maintenance of slavery as an institution. Thus a seller goads his slaves to sing and dance to increase their appearance as valuable commodities on the auction block; an overseer forces song from the workers to increase the pace of labor or to monitor them within earshot; a master sets time aside for the slaves to sing for his guests or to sing among themselves as a way of discharging tensions; a minister insists that certain hymns be sung with words that endorse the religious interpretation of subservience and duty to God's order of things. In short, the instrumentalist mode of hearing tends to be strong on noise and comparatively weak on meaning, for the listener has no overriding incentive to fathom the hermeneutic dimensions of black expressions. The opposite is the case: the meanings generated by slaves must be disavowed, repressed, or interpreted in ways that continually legitimate slavery—such is the case even when "noise" is primarily heard by listeners who nonetheless feel compelled to note the existence of human emotions or when the explanation of slave singing in general is considered a testimony to the benevolence of the peculiar institution. The extent to which repression cannot be carried out requires that indomitable expressions be harnessed as best as possible toward the maintenance of slavery.

The pathos-oriented mode of hearing breaks significantly from both incidental and instrumental hearing. It is fundamentally the antislavery sensibility that makes it possible as an emergent social form of cultural perception and classification. And it is the kind of hearing that coincides with and undergirds the interest of the abolitionists (black as well as white) who are the first to take a keen and strategic interest in—and who in a sense "discover"—black music as a font of meaning. The shift from noise to meaning is accomplished by the emergence of the pathos unleashed by nineteenth-century humanitarian reformism, out of which the antislavery movement developed. This mode of hearing elevates meaning over noise, but still retains traces of the latter within its schemas of interpretation, an indication of the persistent legacy of the earlier orientations centered on noise, which revealed broader cultural strategies of racial distinctions. While both incidental and pathos-oriented modes of hearing allow listeners to express sympathy, it is the latter that carries this sensibility the farthest toward a modern transformation of interpretive modalities expressed by the reformist spirit of black and white abolitionists. They amplify and expand the modern ascription of subjectivity (which emerges first as a religious construct), champion the rhetorical as well as political energies to salvage and exonerate black subjects buried by slavery, and unleash the protoethnographic incursions into the cultural margins—all of which herald the coming of modern subject-centered cultural interpretation in the American context. All three modes of hearing bring some kind of interest and investment to the perception of black song making, and all are shaped by the social and institutional forces through which slavery and its aftermath operate.

Incidental and instrumental modes of hearing were the primary ways black music was comprehended and appropriated prior to the abolitionist movement. Yet, as we have noted, those who heard black soundings from within these frameworks often displayed an incipient desire to view slaves with some acknowledgement of their human qualities. By acknowledging human emotions, sensibilities, and feelings, overseers sometimes extended in their incidental and instrumental interpretations a reach toward an admission of a slave's nascent human subjectivity. Such admissions, however, remained only fleeting during much of the antebellum period.

By the mid-nineteenth century the interpretive framework shifted considerably in ways that not only enabled white observers to expand and showcase their sympathetic recognition of slaves as having deeper feelings, but also made it possible for them to link black meanings to black cultural expressions. This new framework was able to sustain the emerging interpretive orientations toward both black meanings and black cultural practices. By drawing upon the larger ideologies of romanticism, new interpreters began to fathom black meanings along with recognizing and acting upon their own newly acknowledged sympathy. That is, the emerging cultural interpreters began to recognize their own sympathetic consciousness as a moral virtue. As Charles Taylor suggests, the romantic reorientation toward the concept of a human inner goodness began to merge with a modern notion of "nature as an inner source"—finding this inner nature was tantamount to rediscovering and reclaiming one's spiritual authenticity. An individual attuned to the goodness of inner nature could follow "an inner voice or impulse" that led, in turn, to "the truth within us, and in particular our feelings—these were the crucial justifying concepts of the Romantic rebellion in its various forms. They were indispensable to it."[38]

As we shall see, it was within this early modern protoethnographic framework that the new idea of *cultural practice* emerged as a domain worthy of attention and analysis.[39] Through the activities of culture the observer could get "inside" the heads of slaves and fathom their representations of, as well as their meanings and organized orientations toward, the world. This (posited) inner, hermeneutic world to be ascertained through pathos-oriented hearing, was precisely what was to be re-(dis)covered and interpretively retrieved by the critical abolitionists.

Noise and Deep Culture Revisited

The view of music making as noise is much more than an aesthetic orientation. The concept opens up music as a site of important societal tension. On this point, Jacques Attali provides us with a provocative thesis that is worth extending to the case of black music making under slavery. In his book *Noise: The Political Economy of Music*, Attali attempts to reassess the function of music within the context of social change. Music, according to Attali, can function as socially disruptive noise. When it does, it carries the seeds of social transformation. As noise, music is socially disruptive because it makes "audible the new world that will gradually become visible" even to the established ways of seeing. In this capacity, music has the potential to "impose itself and regulate the order of things; it is not only the image of things, but the transcending of the everyday, the herald of the future." This makes music "prophetic" in that it "explores much faster than material reality can, the entire range of possibilities in a given code."[40]

This view of music as noise suggests that there are important links between music, society, and social change. It also requires that we shift our notions of music from viewing it as a predominantly emotional, aesthetic, leisurely, or technical domain to viewing it as a social site intersected by conflicting social interests. From this perspective music is not an autonomous essence or self-enclosed entity; it is never able to fully transcend or leave the social spheres out of which it is constitutively shaped. As culture, music is not a thing—it is a social field of relations that engender historically distinct forms through the continual interplay of social processes, practices, and productions. Music takes shape within social and institutional struggles.

Attali's thesis of noise must be subjected to additional critical qualifications. Certainly not all music is noise. And music is not intrinsically prophetic. A slave owner might celebrate his birthday with singing among his immediate family. Song in this context differs dramatically from that of the night woods, where slaves, presumably out of their master's earshot, commence to sing in their "hush arbors," and knowingly indulge in forbidden activity. Music becomes noise the more so when it unfolds upon, invokes, negotiates, and thus renders transparent social tensions.

As a cultural site music can foster the formation and expression of important sensibilities and even enable people to confront and negotiate the present and anticipate a future. Frederick Douglass's slave narrative, published a decade and a half before slavery was abolished, describes how the "songs of sorrow" carried out the subtle cultural work of slaves anticipating the overcoming of slavery. What enslaved singing subjects imaged, history managed to deliver. But while this example might qualify in Attali's perspective as a case of music's "prophetic" potential, I do not think that music is intrinsically prophetic. What music envisions carries no inexorable guarantees that any of its visions will be realized. Realization that turns desires into reality also involves politics. What we see by way of social desire is not necessarily what we get. The extent to which music can be called prophetic is actually a historical and empirical problem: music is prophetic only in post hoc accounts, by after-the-fact outcomes that appear to validate human desires and anticipation. In such cases it is not music but the social movements upon which music rides that matter. (How lyrical content and its particular meaning and spirit can be attributed to its makers is very important, but the quest for authorship and the notions of cultural authenticity that come with this quest tend to emphasize only one sociological slice. As the passages from Douglass's narrative indicate, song making under slavery is steeped in an already complex set of social relations that force upon music a host of cultural complications.) Nor would I endorse the idea that the problem of music and social transformation is best captured in whether or not the cultural content of music manages to "herald the future" by working its way into some kind of resolution true to its imagery. It is not music's "prophetic" capacities that warrant examination, but rather the complex processes by which social relations and social disruption are sounded and heard through music's noisiness.

Music nonetheless allows people to chart histories, to cast and recast recollections, to remember (as well as forget) the past; it helps anchor daily emotions from the simplest to the most anguishing and complex; it helps broker fears, anxieties, and notions of loss and threat just as it facilitates aspirations, hopes, dreams, and fantasies; it helps human beings mourn worlds gone by, probe worlds that trap, anticipate worlds not yet born. And if, in all of this, music happens to delight and enlighten, it can just as well be an obnoxious or even a frightening din for some. If music can do all of this, then it does amount to a great source of psychic as well as cultural noise, for in a complex society, all of these functions invariably entail at some point conflicts with other groups. Attali's thesis highlights these problems. "Even when officially recognized, [music and musicians] are dangerous, disturbing, and subversive," and it is thus "impossible to separate their history from that of repression and surveillance."

However, the repression of music results not in its annihilation, but in its transmogrification. In the context of slavery, this meant the formation of symbolic alternatives, overcodings, semiotic masquerades, and the like, where music was permitted but always under a watchful eye. The complexities noted above resonate with much of what is known of black music under slavery in the United States. Considered from this framework, black music takes its place in the constellation of historically and socially embedded forms. Attempts to reduce it to an essential domain of identity (e.g., "black music" as a thing in itself) untouched and uncontaminated by the larger forces of history become problematic. Such endeavors are fruitful in generating political solidarities; strategic self and group definitions help not only define membership, but engender among members a sense of social boundaries fundamental to a sense of autonomy and authenticity. But such well intentioned reductionism transforms identity from a constitutive practice into a font of essential origins. The resulting identity takes shape through, while eclipsing from view, the field of social relations that tie such domains of cultural life to a much wider network of social and historical forces. In understanding the initial framework of black music as noise, the entire problem of the production of culture in general, and the production of black music in particular, takes on a new social complexity. As a social construct, the framework of music as noise restores our critical grasp of the connections between cultural practices and social struggles. It is this cultural complexity that needs to be grasped.

. . . . .

Hearing black music as noise continued well into the nineteenth century (and arguably much longer, even to the present), but it was not the predominant orientation.[41] The managerial strategies to control and use black noise were renegotiated in important ways in the early-nineteenth century, and along lines of complex compromises with black musical producers. Slaves made use of opportunities to indulge in collective forms of expression that arose from the sheer psychic struggle for a sense of place and the need for cognitive maps to show them how to survive and negotiate everyday life. Through proselytization slaves were given religious instruction and were allowed to practice Christianity under the watchful eyes of overseers. These privileges amounted to being given a *religious franchise*—the granting by clergy in the dominant culture of an opportunity for slaves, who were deemed to have teachable and savable souls, and were thus eligible to have limited membership as subjects with the larger ideology of Christian thought. This franchise was not uniformly accepted or respected, and differed greatly across the various Protestant denominations. Though policed, black religion flourished, and in the process slaves gained relative cultural autonomy. This helped slaves expand and amplify their collective strategies. How this process worked will be discussed below. Slaves gained and cultivated cultural ground by extending their music making and enlarging a distinctly black musical public sphere. This sphere, too, became a recognizable dimension of American cultural life in the late-nineteenth and early-twentieth century. Still another line of development came as the preempathic notion of noise was progressively outgrown by the abolitionist's new emphasis on the cultural expressions of slaves. As we shall see, the interpretive assistance provided by black abolitionists was crucial. The narratives written by former slaves provided early field maps that guided white sympathizers into the hitherto mysterious and noisy domain of black culture. The older orientation toward black soundings as meaningless noise did not lose its grip, but it was challenged on the margins by the new white cultural workers who detested slavery. Their feelings of relative disenchantment with modernity and market society enabled them to begin to explore what black sounds might actually mean to slaves. The results of this hermeneutic turn toward black expression, regardless of whether or not white listeners ever actually "understood" black vernaculars with a comprehension equal to the slave's own consciousness, is of course open to debate. My concern is with the formation of the new forms of knowledge that were shaped in this very cultural conjuncture. The hermeneutic turn championed by the new reflexivity of both black and white observers opened the doors to the increasingly recognized appreciation and study of "black culture" and paved the way for protoethnographic probes into American subcultures. It is to these important developments that I now turn.

THREE

FROM OBJECTS TO SUBJECTS

The greatest obstruction is, the masters themselves do not
consider enough, the obligation which lies upon them, to have
their slaves instructed. Some have been so weak as to argue, the
Negroes had no souls; others, that they grew worse by being
taught, and made Christians.
(David Humphreys, 1730)

PRIOR TO THE nineteenth century the music produced by slaves
appeared to have little value other than meeting the managerial
needs of owners and overseers. But by the outbreak of the Civil
War a profoundly important cultural change had taken place. The antislavery sentiment, which had existed since the early-eighteenth century,
had matured to become the most powerful social movement in American
society. A large body of antislavery literature had emerged, including important autobiographical narratives written by former slaves. These writings were unprecedented. Through the "slave narratives," deeply personal accounts of what it meant to live the life of a slave made their way
to critical reading publics in the North. Their cultural and literary significance has been considered a "germinating influence on American letters in the 1850s and 1860s."[1]

Abolitionism reshaped the reception of black music making. The writings of Frances Kemble, Fredrika Bremer, Frederick Olmsted, and others
included new, detailed, and descriptive accounts of slave music that were
much more analytically nuanced than the older descriptions of "barbarous noise." More important were the small number of important articles
on black music that appeared in highbrow journals and magazines, some
of which published transcriptions of black lyrics. The new cultural accounts and reportage prefigured ethnographic and folkloristic interests
by offering probing commentary and insightful cultural interpretation.
For the first time the song making of slaves was being reproduced in literary form. As the war raged on, more important works emerged, works
that not only retrieved and sought to preserve black lyrics, but also provided a sympathetic comprehension of black expressions as culture.[2]

As noted above, music making played host to incidental as well as
instrumental listeners, and the latter, in their attempt to harness it, were
particularly demanding. However, for slaves, music making was funda-

mental to collective expression because it offered one of the few cultural sites in which slaves were relatively free to cultivate a shared voice. Song making served also as a clandestine sphere in which slaves tried to temper the harshness of their lives; it gave form to struggles over meaning that were meant to elude their overseers.

The war only intensified musical practices. As the antislavery sentiment merged with war, black song making became the object of new interest among northern intellectuals, for some quite consuming and passionate. But it was not black music in general that was catching the ears of more and more white observers; it was the Negro spiritual. The spiritual seemed to have acquired a magnetism peculiar to its new status as a distinct cultural object. Black religious music had become *meaningful* music. Slaves, of course, had long produced music for virtually every occasion. But in the years surrounding the Civil War, music that resembled Christian hymnology was able to bridge the chasm that separated black noise from meanings relevant to white listeners. Religious singing enabled black sounds to cross the barrier. Plenty of music remained that did not fit the new schemas of appreciation, and music that was not deemed religious remained black noise. The spirituals, however, were depicted as unique in their emotive intensity. Abolitionists comprehended them as credible and honest testimonies, and they served as evidence to the newly admitted idea that slaves were possessors of spiritual depth, and authors and makers of meanings. And what slaves expressed by way of their narratives and song making could be examined more carefully for something that was also recoverable—the existence of an underlying and authentic *slave culture* there to be uncovered and appreciated. How did this interest in black writings and black songs come about? What brought these two black cultural forms into the appreciative perceptual reach of abolitionists? Where did this new spirit—which was rapidly becoming a new field of cultural interpretation—come from?

This discovery of slave culture (as it eventually came to be called) was rooted, I argue, in a more general religious reorientation that involved both the expansion of proselytization among slaves and a deepening and broadening of antislavery sentiments. In the eyes of the most radical abolitionists, blacks were being transformed (ethnosympathetically) from chattel objects to human subjects. And in this reorientation, black music could be appreciated as a meaningful and meaning-driven expression. Black music making could now be approached from another cultural framework of interpretation that competed with the older perspective of alien noise. The discovery involved the transformation of interpretive schemas that were emerging in the second half of the eighteenth century, schemas that would reach a high point during the Civil War. Focusing on the development of the orientation toward the cultural and racial margins involves examining both the distinct activities of slaveholding classes as well as the activities of a smaller but significant number of countercultural workers in the abolitionist movement, black and white, who attempted to reinterpret black expressions.

Slave owners and radical abolitionists had obviously different orientations toward slavery; they are rightly understood as worlds apart. Nonetheless, they shared a deeper linkage, a profound cultural development that redefined slaves as persons with a subjectivity grounded (contentiously) in religious orientations. The interest in authenticity and subjectivity also shared ties with larger changes in the modern notion of western subjectivity. Slaveholders and abolitionists differed in their roles in helping bring this cultural turn about. As I shall discuss more fully, the Church of England, and later Baptists and Methodists, pressured slave owners to allow ministers, initially white and then black, to tend to the religious instruction of their slaves. Some owners acquiesced willingly, some reluctantly, and some rejected the obligation. Their individual reactions were shaped by the complicated role that religious proselytization and instruction played in larger problems of slave management and control. Yet religious proselytization, I shall argue, actually helped inaugurate a new slave subjectivity, an inadvertent consequence that grew out of attributing savable souls to slaves. This new subjectivity engendered, in turn, a resonating black voice among former slaves in the form of the slave narratives and the Negro spiritual. These two cultural modes of black expressions were, in turn, seized upon by radical abolitionists during the last few decades of the antislavery movement.

To proceed, we need to examine some of the central cultural issues and tensions involved in the extension of Christian teachings to slaves. After this we can turn to the slave narratives and offer a cultural account of their place against the backdrop of the crisis in which religious principles were used by slaves to amplify the critical emergence of slave subjectivity and selfhood. These steps provide a way of seeing how culturally and historically specific quests for authenticity were introduced and came to warrant interpretive attention. This path takes us not into the back door of the slave's clandestine cultural sphere or into the hermeneutic details of what James Scott has called the "hidden transcripts" of peoples struggling to find and preserve a voice under conditions of enormous repression.[3] Such a vein of analysis is certainly valuable; indeed, it is the one that most investigators have chosen, and for good reason. But the path I suggest instead takes us through the back door of the discovery process at work; it brings into view the emergent cultural schemas in the making by looking at the cultural developments that enabled critical abolitionists to pronounce the revelations of lived culture (as did Frederick Douglass) and to pursue such discoveries as part of a critically emerging ethnosympathy.

Extending the Religious Franchise

When church officials proposed giving religious rights to slaves (I refer to this as the "religious franchise"), they introduced a cultural process that was fraught with tensions and conflicts. But its importance is due to the fact that it was a first and fundamental step leading to the birth of the modern interpretive attention to the cultural expressions of slaves. Proselytization engendered significant cultural complications; among other things, it fostered a deep logic among slaves to justify the revolt against slavery. Yet once set into motion, the extension of religious instruction and the cultural contradictions that ensued were irreversible. And this was especially so during the conjuncture in which competing Protestant sects were in ascendancy in the late-eighteenth and early-nineteenth centuries. The religious populism that emerged through the Great Awakenings was a crucial development. Led by Baptists and Methodists, the popular-religion drives into the spiritual as well as the racial frontier impacted the entire sphere of slave management in the South and reinforced the already existing but piecemeal efforts to extend the religious (Protestant) franchise to blacks. The religious franchise had multiple purposes; it reflected sheer concerns for proselytization as a duty and obligation in its own right, but it also overlapped with concerns for controlling slaves and to a need to corral rebellions. As I shall discuss, this was certainly the case after the infamous and bloody revolt of 1831 led by Nat Turner. The extension of the religious franchise also led to the inadvertent expansion of black cultural and symbolic spheres within which slave expressivity grew. This, in turn, fed into the production of an elaborate social criticism that was articulated through the slave narratives and an increasingly refined mode of religious singing that fostered an emergent black public sphere. Both of these developments are inconceivable outside of the deep contradictions of Protestant ideology superimposed over the social system of slavery. Embedded within the cultural contradictions of slavery (e.g., slaves as subjects and as chattel), these developments involved social and institutional processes by which slaves began to be recognized initially as soul possessors, and then as modern social and political subjects as well as cultural selves.

Religious instruction for slaves hinged on attributing souls to them; souls, in turn, warranted ministerial guidance. The process turned, in part, on the way in which ideology operates as a cultural system of instantiating and beckoning subjects. As Louis Althusser argues, ideologies "call," "hail," or "interpellate" subjects.[4] But this proposition, while a valuable theoretical abstraction, can be meaningful only in very specific and concrete terms. Interpellation is always a very grounded and *personal* process precisely because interpellation must speak to distinct, flesh-and-blood subjects, who are simultaneously called into being through culturally dominant modes of address. Ideologies, of course, do not exist in themselves, nor do they speak from the sky; they do not surround people like ether. People surround people, and this takes place through language and socially constructed institutions; people—with power, ideas, and interests, which are always already embedded socially and institutionally—are the ones to call their fellow beings. All ideologies have to be instantiated through discursive regimes, but the "work" is performed most efficaciously at ground zero, and through intimate social relations.

Under slavery, slaves were, by definition, "called" first as property and as labor to serve a worldly master. The language of law backed by force and violence convened this call. But with religious proselytization, slaves were exposed to an additional mode of address that was overlaid upon the discourse of slavery. This address acknowledged that a slave possessed a soul, and indicated a cultural investment in black subjects through religious incorporation, even though this investment was largely overshadowed by slavery. Slaves were eligible for spiritual identity along with their identification as material objects of property. The disposition toward proselytization as well as subjectification is rooted deeply within Christian eschatology, for each soul has to be singly salvaged by transformation from a fallen to an uplifted state. Salvation through conversion can take place only through the transformation of one's earthly spiritual condition; it can be carried out only during one's earthly incarnation in the flesh.

The ramifications unleashed by extending the religious franchise to slaves were profound, and the propositions regarding whether blacks had souls and were worthy candidates for proselytization engendered wrenching debate. What we shall trace is how the religious franchise, which posited a spiritual place, even for slaves, within the broader cultural system of religion, was simultaneously an important turning point for the rise of modern ethnosymathy and cultural interpretation.

In the early-eighteenth century, Congregational clergyman Cotton Mather insisted that Negroes were equal to slaveholders, and that it was proper for ministers to acknowledge the slave's humanity. This acknowledgment, however, ventured on what planters saw as dangerous ground. To make urgent the slave's humanity was one thing; to declare his "'equal Right with other Men, to the Exercises and Privileges *of Religion*' was another."[5] Conversion, after all, is not something that comes about on the basis of wish or self-will; it is based upon and carried out through proper Bible instruction. Religious pedagogy was required—and this was precisely the rub. Religious instruction could proceed only upon the premise that slaves, like their masters, had souls. Beneath the hue of one's skin, beneath the manmade institutional layers of racial hierarchies, beneath the artifice of worldly laws was the essence of what one was in a fundamental and radical sense—a soul. All souls were to be taken seriously, and, in a transcendental world they were essential epiphenomena as well as essentially equal.

But the transcendent and the earthly were not equal. Cotton Mather's advice may have included the premise that blacks were equal to whites in the eyes of God, but Mather also argued a distinction between the rules of heaven and the rules of earth—in essence, different rules for different worldly orders. The existence of souls in black bodies could coincide consistently with slavery. Thus, in Mather we find the quintessential explanation of a Christian theology that rationalized antebellum race relations and clarified the view that slavery could be maintained and justified—even as black souls were being admitted, ministered to, and saved. Slavery, argued Mather, was not a contradiction to Christianity; it was meant to coexist with the Christianization of slaves. Indeed it was one's duty to extend Christian teachings to the slaves. By doing so, he told owners, "Your *Negroes* are immediately Raised unto an astonishing Felicity, when you have *Christianized* them. . . . Tho' they remain your *Servants*, yet they are the *Children* of God. Tho' they are to enjoy no *Earthly Goods*, but the small Allowance that your Justice and Bounty shall see proper for them, yet they become *Heirs* of God, and *joint-Heirs* with the Lord Jesus Christ."[6] In other words, righteous slaveholders could have their cake and eat it too. In essence, slavery as a worldly institution was permissible, shored up by law, and acknowledged in the Bible. But what was not permissible was an owner's dereliction in failing to extend Christianity to slaves. Owners, overseers, and most of all the clergy were morally obliged to open to the slaves the ideologies of egalitarianism in the spiritual (but not the worldly) realm. The religious franchise thus inadvertently presented the opportunity for black selfhood to emerge as a culturally specific attribute (recognized from above) and as a self-attribution (generated from "inside"). The great importance of religion as a cultural force that saved slaves from the most profoundly dehumanizing pressures of slavery has been well argued. Religion as a cultural force certainly had its roots in proselytization and in the day-to-day cultivation of a black religious public sphere that grew from the emergence of semisanctioned as well as clandestine religious practices during the antebellum era.[7] As will be noted below, the classic slave narratives express this cultural force in profoundly important ways.

As abolitionism developed from a moral sensibility to a powerful social movement, the recognition of slaves as injured but retrievable social subjects grew reciprocally as blacks began to deepen and give expression to their own critical subjectivity and selfhood. These two intertwined developments—antislavery and black subjectivity—took on their most important profile in the slave narratives. The captured self wrote (in retrospect) of his or her experiences as a slave. While the new self-expressions of individual black subjects were meant to be understood as personal testimony and statements engendered from a single slave's life, they were also meant to be taken as black collective representations and comments on the social and institutional structures of slavery. As writings on both black selfhood and slavery, the narratives profiled the larger interlocking problems of black fate in general.

The authors of the slave narratives drew deeply from the framework of the religious franchise. Many of the self-penned narratives displayed a subtle grasp of, as well as a firm conviction in, the ideals harbored in Christian teleology, and the authors "worked" the rhetorical forms to establish a framework for the intense cognitive dissonance expressed in the slave narratives. Former slave authors revealed the schism that existed between the deepest and most universal Christian principles and the institutional practices of slavery; they disclosed the problem of agency and structure through the crisis-ridden lens of slave-based interpretation. In this manner, the religious framework that the narratives frequently embraced engendered profound unintended consequences as black intellectuals-writers began publishing scathing and insightful indictments of a morally bankrupt social system that had begun to attend only begrudgingly to the spiritual well-being of all peoples yet stiff-armed those whose skin color warranted their exclusion from the rights and privileges of civil society.[8] Christian teachings had long been used to justify the "peculiar institution," but now that the objects upon which slavery rested, the slaves themselves, had become religious subjects, these new subjects used Christianity to condemn slavery as a social system.[9] The expansion of religious instruction to slaves engendered a major cultural transformation by inaugurating from above a new classification of slaves as subjects, and inadvertently engendered from below a powerful answer in the narratives that reclassified as fraudulent and hypocritical the official orthodoxy of Christian teachings.

Ironically, the endeavors to provide religious instruction to the slaves were designed as much if not more for purposes of social control than for spiritual edification. The irony was not lost on the slaves. But beyond irony, the intertwining of proselytization and new critical voices, both of which were predicated on a mode of religious expansion that privileged the inner life, had an additional consequence. When applied to slaves, the cultural expansion based upon the inner turn toward subjectivity helped cultivate an emerging form of cultural interpretation that sought and targeted the modern idea of *cultural authenticity*. As we shall see, it was this dynamic that brought the Negro spiritual into the sights of the critical abolitionists in the years surrounding the Civil War. There were, of course, lots of "abolitionists." Many who opposed slavery did so because it was a major obstacle for capitalism and market society. But, by "critical abolitionists" I refer to a rather small minority of agitators and moral and political entrepreneurs at the fringes of the antislavery movement who were deeply skeptical of market society, the industrialization of life, and the pulverizing impact these modern forces had upon the individual, the community, and the society at large. Their criticisms were also religiously rooted in the troubled tensions between Protestantism, shifting notions of human nature, and modernity. As I discuss more fully in chapter 5, the critical abolitionists tended to be represented by the radical edges of Unitarianism and Transcendentalism. Furthermore, this interpretive path led into the wider arena of late-nineteenth-century ethnosympathy that further nurtured the idea that the cultural practices on the racial margins of American society were to be retrieved as cultural objects and goods in themselves. In essence, the discovery of the Negro spiritual was a prescient development; it drew on the convergence of romantic and reformist strains in response to modernity, but also pointed forward as a part of the progressive rationalization of cultural interpretation that would later crystallize in the more modern forms of professional folklore and ethnic studies.

When considered from the cultural logic outlined above, the discovery of the spiritual appears as a cultural development that was framed within a historically embedded sociocultural complex rather than as an expression of an essential spiritualism or as an autonomous practice "in itself" where a simple (musical) cultural object (as well as a quasi-romanticized spectacle) could be apprehended by the neutral mechanisms of a modern cultural or social science. However, to get at the discovery of the spiritual requires that we relax our grip on music as if it were a thing in itself and shift our attention instead toward an appreciation of the cultural-interpretive scaffolding that helped bring the notion of such cultural goods (and ethnopractices) as having an intrinsic value into view. Both developments—tending to souls and the ensuing production of slave narratives—were central in extending, expanding, and deepening the processes of attributing subjectivity to slaves and former slaves, and they constituted key interpretive structures that helped culturally to produce the Negro spiritual and make it simultaneously discoverable. And this process, in turn, yielded the important preferred representation of "authentic" black culture during the years surrounding the Civil War.

The Nervous Obligations of Proselytization

As dehumanized objects and property, slaves could certainly have traits, quirks, distinguishing features and other distinctive markings, as could any distinct object. But as long as their status as human beings was a contested issue, they were not eligible to have bestowed upon them the attributes considered emblematic of modern selfhood, even as such cultural developments were taking place within the West in general and American society in particular.[10] But once they were considered candidates for ministerial attention, blacks could be more readily conceptualized as human subjects, as individuals with souls, and as persons who possessed the self-interior structures of meaning that came with the modern notion of selfhood.

Prior to the nineteenth century, instruction of the slaves in matters of religion was not a high priority. But by the 1830s proselytization had developed as part of cultural management. It developed in an important crossroads that included a recent history of significant slave revolts, expansionist drives to extend slavery into the newly acquired western states, and the growing fervor of abolitionists. But in the early-eighteenth century, proselytization was only in its beginning stages. When it did emerge, it did so as a rather feeble dispensation from abroad. In 1701 the Church of England had established the Society for the Propagation of the Gospel in Foreign Parts, an organization devoted to ministerial expansion in areas that were under England's sphere of political, economic, and cultural influence. Blacks and Indians in the colonies were not initially considered targets for conversion, but they fell under the moral obligation where possible.[11] The society's appointed ministers to the American colonies were quick to point out this responsibility, as did Cotton Mather, but they were confronted with slave owners who were largely uninterested in, reluctant about, or even vehemently opposed to the idea.

Owners and ministers had obviously different relationships to slaves, and the efforts of ministers were frequently thwarted by owners.[12] The Reverend Samuel Thomas, who was appointed minister by the Society to the Province of Carolina in 1702, noted the presence of a "multitude of ignorant persons to instruct," which included "many Negroes" and "Indians," and he requested that Bibles and Books of Common Prayer be given to "the poor Negroes."[13] Thomas also surmised that at least 80 percent of the slaves spoke enough English, in his opinion, to receive oral religious instruction, and that many were "desirous of Christian knowledge."[14] The obstacle, however, was with the owners: "It is indeed much to be lamented that the generality of our Planters are no great friends to the design of giving their slaves Christian instructions."[15] The bishop of

London, another representative of the Church of England, noted in 1724 the uncooperative stance of owners regarding his efforts to establish instruction to slaves.

> I have several times exhorted their Masters to send such of them as could speak English to Church to be catechised but they would not. . . . The Negroes . . . cannot . . . be said to be of any Religion for as there is no law of the Colony obliging their Masters or Owners to instruct them in the principles of Christianity. . . . The poor creatures generally live and die without it.[16]

The society, wrote David Humphreys in 1730, acting in keeping with its responsibility for converting the Negroes, had instructed, baptized, and admitted to Communion

> some hundreds. . . . But alas! what is the instruction of a few hundreds, in several years, with respect to the many thousands uninstructed, unconverted, living, dying, utter Pagans. . . . The greatest obstruction is, the masters themselves do not consider enough, the obligation which lies upon them, to have their slaves instructed. Some have been so weak as to argue, the Negroes had no souls; others, that they grew worse by being taught, and made Christians.[17]

Indeed, from the point of view of chattel management, religion could serve as an obstacle rather than an aid. Florida slave owner Zephaniah Kingsley complained that his slaves' "natural and rational happiness" was destroyed by religious instruction. His slaves once danced in merriment according to "their own manner." But after a "man, calling himself a minister, got among them . . . [i]t was now sinful to dance, work their corn or catch fish, on a Sunday." Kingsley indicted the ministerial effect: "I cannot help regretting that honest well meaning men, with so much ability to do good . . . should so misapply their talents as to . . . render our species miserable."[18]

Furthermore, religious instruction was intrinsically counterproductive. Slaves, after all were tools to be used for work; why should they be given tools for their minds? Christian teachings, which in some cases included literacy instruction supplied the slaves with new cultural tools, ones that would not necessarily serve their immediate masters. Indeed, these implements could be used beyond the master's sphere.[19]

Owner Reluctance and Slave Revolts

Nothing fueled planter and overseer anxiety about religion among the slaves more forcefully than did the slave revolts that took place in the first three decades of the nineteenth century. Slave unrest was a social problem, but so was distributive religion and the ideology that promoted proselytization. As Mechal Sobel put it, "Whites feared the revolutionary equality preached by Baptists and Methodists, as well as the opportunity for fellowship and conspiracy afforded by religious meetings."[20] Religion was indeed a major cultural factor in the revolts. Exposure to Christian teachings, however, was not a simple causal factor or a cultural prerequisite in slave opposition to domination. As Herbert Aptheker has shown, slaves resisted and revolted against slavery long before white ministers attempted proselytization. Nonetheless, the availability of religion deepened the cognitive and ideological framework of revolt.[21]

The planned but foiled insurrection in 1800 led by Gabriel Prosser in Richmond, Virginia, led white owners to blame Sunday worship gatherings for their role in cultivating rebellious sentiment. Prosser himself cited biblical sources for his actions. Also discovered and thwarted in advance was the Bible-quoting Denmark Vesey, who had planned to carry out his revolt in 1822 in Charleston, South Carolina. The Vesey conspiracy resulted in 139 arrests and 47 executions. Among those executed as conspirators were members of the African Methodist Church in Charleston.[22] In 1831, Nat Turner, a lay preacher, planned and carried out a slave revolt in Southampton County, Virginia. Sixty whites and more than a hundred slaves were killed before it ended. Sixteen blacks, three of whom were free, were executed after the revolt.[23] Baptist and Methodist ministers, white as well as black (but particularly black ministers), were blamed for the souring of slave-planter relations.

The Vesey conspiracy brought about a concerted effort to bring the religious activity of slaves under white supervision, and black preaching was strongly discouraged. According to one outraged Charleston resident, the missionaries brought more than just religion to the slaves; they were also "fire-brands of discord and destruction" who "secretly disperse[d] among [the] Negro Population the seeds of discontent and sedition." Through such teachings, "a powerful agency was put into operation by the dispersion among our Negroes of religious magazines, news paper paragraphs, and insulated texts of scripture." Religion had brought "a spirit of dissatisfaction and revolt" that was inimical to social control.[24] Black preachers who practiced without strict supervision and who exhorted "in words of their own" bore the brunt of blame for the planned insurrection. Intense debate ensued as to whether religion in general or the irresponsible Baptist and Methodist sects in particular fostered an incendiary streak among slaves. Prior to the Vesey conspiracy, masters had been more indifferent than resistant to religious instruction. As Freehling notes, some slaves had already learned to read—a requirement for Bible study—had held religious meetings in white churches, and even had formed black congregations. Literacy, however, was not as significant among slave populations as was the oral tradition that produced and maintained black cultural memory. Literacy and orality aside,

Vesey's conspiracy "demonstrated that churches could be centers of intrigue and that slaves could acquire what seemed to Carolinians the most erroneous religious notions. As a result, class meetings and Negro churches were disbanded. A long debate ensued over the matter of reading the Bible."[25] Planters had come to deeply distrust preachers and teachers, and their instincts were well grounded. "No other group in South Carolina—or in the nation—criticized slavery so severely" as did the clergy and their supporters.[26]

In the socially charged environment following the Vesey incident, planters frowned upon even oral instruction. The withdrawal of white engagement left only slave preachers to continue the process of religious cultivation. But not all Protestant sects were viewed as fomenters of insurrection. In defense of proper religion, white leaders argued that black Episcopal preachers were noticeably not involved in the slave unrest because they were allowed to base their ministerial deliveries only on prescribed passages from the Book of Common Prayer rather than on "words of their own."[27] Throughout the 1830s piecemeal religious instruction reappeared but with strict limits upon content. When it did take place, religious instruction had to be carried out in lessons that promoted the orthodoxy of slavery, and only through oral means.

The Turner conspiracy of 1831 resulted in a significant loss of black and white lives and a flurry of repressive measures.[28] Black preachers, suspected of fomenting unrest, were the targets of these measures. In some areas, blacks were banned from preaching. Where blacks continued to preach, laws were passed requiring the presence of white supervision during black religious gatherings. Even singing was grounds for extreme retribution. Lydia Maria Child, who published her important book *An Appeal in Favor of that Class of Americans Called Africans* five years after the Turner conspiracy, interviewed a slave by the name of Charity Bowery about the aftermath. Bowery described the repression that ensued.

> The brightest and best men were killed in Nat's time. Such ones are always suspected. All the colored folks were afraid to pray in the time of old Prophet Nat. There was no law about it; but the whites reported it round among themselves that, if a note was heard, we should have some dreadful punishment; and after that, the low whites would fall upon any slaves they heard praying, or singing a hymn, and often killed them before their masters or mistresses could get to them.

Child asked Bowery for an example of the type of hymn. Bowery sang:

> A few more beatings of the wind and rain,
> Ere the winter will be over—

Glory, Hallelujah!
Some friends has gone before me,—
I must try to go and meet them—
Glory, Hallelujah!
A few more risings and settings of the sun,
Ere the winter will be over—
Glory, Hallelujah!
There's a better day a coming—
There's a better day a coming—
Oh, Glory, Hallelujah!

With a very arch expression, she looked up, as she concluded, and said, "They wouldn't let us sing that. They wouldn't let us sing that. They thought we was going to *rise*, because we sung 'better days are coming.' "[29]

Virginia's governor had expressed the same concerns that had been raised after the Vesey plot. Preachers, he insisted, provided the channel "through which the inflammatory pamphlets and papers [were] brought . . . [and] circulated among the slaves." Behind the "ostensible purpose of religious worship" were more sinister motivations. "The public interest requires that the negro preachers be silenced."[30]

The white recoil against slave religion in Virginia, however, was short-lived. Religion was irrepressible; it was, after all, the foundation of virtually all social orthodoxy. But it was emerging as the penultimate cultural contradiction of slavery. As William Freehling notes, many white South Carolinians were so unsettled by the Vesey conspiracy that they temporarily suppressed their own religious practices as well as repressing those of blacks, because they "preferred to risk their salvation rather than their necks."[31] But repressing religion was not the long-range solution. The bloodletting of the Turner revolt appears to have forced a struggle over the control rather than the eradication of religion. Rather than leave religion to the politics of neglect and default, clergy, owners, and overseers intervened more forcefully into black religion. As Genovese notes, proselytizing efforts were soon intensified. Slaveholders had long distrusted slaves with religion, but after the Turner event "they feared slaves without religion even more," and Christianity was seen no longer as an impediment to social control but now "primarily as a means of social control."[32] Religion was too important, too fundamental to the shifting social imaginary; it had to be made safe for the planter aristocracy.

But perhaps the planter class had little choice in turning toward religion as an indispensable mode of social control. The Vesey and Turner affairs signaled the tip of an iceberg; beneath was a growing legitimation crisis that was being brokered into critical consciousness within—not outside—the framework of religion. Vesey was a member of the African

Methodist Church; Turner was a self-appointed Baptist preacher. Sheer repression could cut out individual renegades once they were detected; individuals could be punished or purged by whatever means. But the soul-granting, subject-granting denominations unleashed by Evangelical populism had now multiplied in their infectious patterns. The viruslike spread of the subjectivizing process could not be expunged, for that system's very organic host was the deepest principles of the religious franchise. Slaves had been hailed as souls, and there was no reversing the process.

As we consider the political and economic conjuncture, it appears that the cultural compromise made by the slave-owning class in their decision to continue steps to expand the religious franchise was actually a fortuitous if not shrewd decision. In this conjuncture slavery advocates were pushing for the expansion of the peculiar institution at the same time a more vibrant and radical antislavery movement was in the making. Slaves had already developed a critical sensitivity over the ideals of Christian teachings in relationship to the actual practices of slavery. In effect, the planter class's pretensions to moral authority based on scripture were in the process of being deconstructed by an emergent and highly articulate consortium of black as well as white antislavery advocates. For religious-minded slaves, the choice of which interpretive version of slavery they prefered to believe in—that proposed by slaveholders or that by abolitionists—was not a difficult decision. It was not religion in itself; it was its appropriation that mattered. By and large slaves chose Christian political idealism while the planter class hoped that the expansion of religious instruction within a repressive and supervisory framework would keep slavery intact. Cotton production and the market for cotton were both expanding, bringing pressure to extend slavery westward in pursuit of arable land. Moreover, the antislavery movement was picking up quickly—Turner's revolt and the debut of William Lloyd Garrison's abolitionist paper the *Liberator* both occurred in 1831. Two years later the American Anti-Slavery Society was launched.

Given this set of circumstances, planters relied even more upon, rather than tried to repress, religious instruction. A more reformist and humanistic orientation toward black religion emerged, though there remained among all the major denominations in the South an opposition to independent black church formation. The slave revolts changed the owner's views on the functions as well as appropriateness of religious instruction. Prior to the rebellions of the 1820s and 1830s, owners tolerated their slaves learning religion and indulging in autonomous religious practices. After the Vesey and Turner rebellions, slaveholders adjusted their earlier, laxer attitude, and brought slave religion under much closer scrutiny. This cycle of on again–off again, relative tolerance–vehement repression appears to recur but with varying intensity from the late-eighteenth century up to the Civil War. Yet against this history a consistent and progressive institutionalization and rationalization of black Christianity emerged out of the religious franchise. Black religion was augmented by the unanticipated cultural power of the Evangelical movement, the Great Awakenings, and the increasingly secular thrust of mid-nineteenth-century humanitarian reformism that championed a new vision of political morality.

Souls on the Racial Frontier

The revivalist movements associated with the First and Second Great Awakenings brought slaves into Methodist and Baptist folds. The first took place in the 1740s; a second series of revivals occurred between 1800 and the mid-1840s. Evangelicalism moved into the South through large camp meetings and made an even greater concerted effort to bring denominational church structure to the plantations.[33] Following these two major revivals was a third that took place around 1857–58, distinguished by a progressive theology that fueled the takeoff of modern humanitarian reformism.[34]

Of the religious movements, the Second Great Awakening, which hosted the massive tent-meeting revivals, was perhaps the most significant demographically. As neo-Calvinist orthodoxy and Congregationalism waned, Protestant denominations, particularly Methodist and Baptist, flourished. By 1855, Methodists and Baptists dwarfed all other Protestant denominations with memberships of 1,577,014 and 1,105,546, respectively. Presbyterians, the third largest denomination, trailed with 495,715. Congregationalists and Evangelical Lutherans each had approximately 200,000.[35]

Mainstream Protestantism was being challenged on two important fronts, and both of these had important implications for black expressivity and the emergent interpretive scaffolding upon which black culture would soon be viewed. In the Upper South and western states a highly emotional Evangelicalism was underway. In the North, Unitarianism emerged as a major break from the Calvinist legacy. Frontier revivalism and the critical wing of New England Unitarianism both pressed in different ways their disenchantment with dominant institutions. Revivalism opened its wide gates to poor whites, immigrants, and in some cases even to blacks. The Great Awakening's passionate revivals fostered well-attended camp meetings in the white and black hinterlands, and emphasized the necessity of individuals taking the first steps to Christian salvation and perfection by *immediate* conversion. The Methodist and Baptists sects received their boost in the Evangelical movements and expanded the piecemeal efforts of soul-tending made by southern overseers, a process that expanded the extension of the religious franchise to slaves.[36] *Immediatism*—the doctrine of immediate transformation of the soul based on erasing through repentance one's flawed spiritual history and starting anew—had its societal corollaries in utopian community formation and, of course, abolitionism.[37] Northern Unitarianism's antiinstitutionalism took the form of a disenchantment with runaway capitalism, market society, urban disorder, and "wage slavery." The most critical wings of Unitarianism fostered the radical antislavery movement. Eventually these two streams of antiinstitutional disenchantment converged in the form of sanctified and Christianized Negroes indicting the system of slavery (from the vantage point of their authentic experience as chattel) and of northern abolitionists championing their cause (from the perspective of the morally incensed outsider). As we shall see, these two streams converge as well in the protoethnographic search for the black singing subject who takes on the peculiar and momentary romantic role of representing the noble savage converted into the ideal Transcendentalist.

The Great Awakenings were just as much an indication of the waning grip of Calvinist theology as they were struggles to rejuvenate a spiritual realm in the midst of demographic, geographic, economic, and cultural transformations. Unlike the neo-Calvinist Anglican and Congregational denominations, which were largely the bastions of cultural and economic elites, the new Evangelical populism spoke to and from new social formations peopled by a sprawling white lower and middle class, but reached downward also to its social and cultural base among poor white ethnic immigrants and free as well as enslaved blacks. This was a Protestantism in the process of shedding an older skin and growing a new one that reflected different class and ethnic profiles, and a religion in the process changing its racial hue.[38]

While the South's cultural overseers vacillated between religious repression and reformism, Evangelicalism, with its revivals, spectacular camp meetings, and brazen disregard for most established ("worldly") institutions, worked entirely against the sensibilities of many southern elites. Southerners continued to press their local ministers to circumscribe black religious gatherings, tighten strict white supervision over them, and instill in their slaves a solemn and passive approach to religious conduct. The evangelical revivalists, however, held huge gatherings that defied such close and repressive scrutiny; the culture of religious populism that swept the Upper South and western states called such emotional expressivity forth. The emotionally charged camp meetings left no room for lulling acquiescence in the context of soul-searching worship. Evangelical revivalists were boisterous precisely because they trusted human emotions. For Evangelicals, emotion was the language of the soul; establishment religion, with its rigid, unspontaneous, and staid approach to worship, reflected alienation from God. Such expressive and spontaneous emotionalism, or unsanctioned autonomous "exhortation," was what the South's planter-minister power structure attempted to purge from black religious practices. The irony in the Evangelical incursions into traditional Protestantism is that many white leaders in the South, and in the North as well, had long viewed unbridled emotionality as a Negro (as well as female) trait; this emotionally insurgent religious revisionism was largely a white phenomenon that was marginally open to blacks.[39]

Slaves had long relied on cultural forms that were collective, interactive, and emotionally expressive. Even when black congregations emerged as recognized and legitimate extensions of major Baptist and Methodist denominations, they retained such forms in their modes of worship while the mainstream, predominantly white sectors shed the emotionalism that had been crucial in their great takeoff period. The tensions between black and white norms of practice remained, however, and consistent with the larger concern that black culture had to be broken and eradicated was the view that slave obedience was tied to proper religious instruction. What was proper? The simplest definition was behavioral and could be defined operationally: proper instruction produced docility and subservience, but no troublesome outcomes. As mentioned, proper was the Episcopal example of supervision of black ministers, with its strict adherence to selected textual use and ready disapproval for autonomous exhortation. The Reverend Charles Colcock Jones spoke for many clergy and owners who sought to rid slave culture of its Africanist practices. As Jones put it, "The public worship of God should be conducted with reverence and stillness on the part of the congregation." And by this Jones meant no "demonstrations of approbation or disapprobation, or exclamations, or responses, or noises, or outcries of any kind during the progress of divine worship; nor boisterous singing immediately at its close." Such behaviors, Jones noted, were "not confined to one denomination, but appear to some extent in all."[40]

The ability of slaves to construct their own religious songs with expressive forms of worship, which included dancing along with singing, clashed with the traditional Protestant disdain for celebration and boisterous activity. Norms of Protestant worship required that parishioners refrain from any combination of excitement with religious ceremony. White churchmen had long attempted to discourage slaves from creating their own "spirituals," and were especially outraged over the religious dance that frequently accompanied song. Such dancing, cited frequently in many accounts, consisted of "clapping and striking of the thighs and legs."[41] Alarmed at the deviance of these "negro spirituals," Philadelphian Methodist John F. Watson claimed: "We have too, a growing evil, in the practice of singing in our places of public and society worship, *merry* airs, adapted from old *songs*, to hymns of our composing: often miserable as poetry, and senseless as matter, and most frequently composed and first sung by the illiterate *blacks* of the society."[42] According to Eileen Southern, Watson's attack was aimed at the Methodist's Society, the dominant black Methodists in the Philadelphia Conference at the time.[43] Black Methodists had split off from the white Methodist hegemony, which opened up greater possibilities for blacks to modify solemn religious hymns and construct their own expressive material. Whites' loss of control over both black subjects and Christian practices aggravated already existing unease with the autonomy of black religious practices, whether they were related or not to denominational influences. Watson's charges against the "merry airs" also suggest that it was not only black slaves who indulged in such deviance; some whites seem also to have been attracted to the religious practices of blacks:

> [The songs] are sung in the merry chorus-manner of the southern harvest field, or husking-frolic method, of the slave blacks; and also very greatly like the Indian dances. With every word so sung, they have a sinking of one or other leg of the body alternately; producing an audible sound of the feet at every step, and as manifest as the steps of actual negro dancing in Virginia, &c. If some, in the meantime sit, they strike the sounds alternately on each thigh. What in the name of religion, can countenance or tolerate such gross perversions of true religion! But the evil is only occasionally condemned, and the example has already visibly affected the religious manners of some whites.[44]

Watson's alarm sounded three sins: excessive emotion, dancing, and black influence on fellow whites. The ongoing busywork of fixing the weak links in traditional Protestantism's great chain of emotional repression was never near completion. In the context of declining Calvinism, the chains seemed beyond repair. That blacks and whites might be indulging in emotionally satisfying but unsanctioned cultural miscegenation was part of a much larger problem.

Unintended Cultural Expansion through Social Control

The alterations that Evangelicalism and the Great Awakenings brought to Protestantism represented important cultural opportunities for slaves. The new religious populism actually expanded and intensified the religious franchise to slaves and enhanced the cultural ground for black subjectivity. Under the irrepressible influences of the revivals, southern cultural gatekeepers were forced to take religion seriously. As noted, they could ignore the growing demand created by the religious franchise, and risk losing control of its content and its consequences; they could repress black religion, and hasten the already deepening legitimation crisis. This left the only other option: to continue and expand religious instruction. And this solution only hastened the institutionalization of an already emergent formal black church structure and black congregations serviced by a growing number of black ministers.

By forcing black religious practices into public, planters were presumably able to continue to oversee black collective practices, even those sanctioned and given quasi-legitimacy by formal denominations. Allowing black religion to expand would help monitor black cultural expressivity, and this was preferable to leaving black cultural practices to their dreaded Africanist autonomy and thus beyond institutional surveillance. As George Rawick, Sterling Stuckey, Albert Raboteau, and Mechal Sobel have shown, Africanist practices, particularly the "ring shout" and the clandestine gatherings in "hush arbors," were quite widespread, and slaveholders went to great lengths to curtail such practices.[45] Even if the circumstances took on the game of white capture and black evasion, religious expansion nonetheless signaled the newly emerging sensitivity displayed by owners and overseers on behalf of their long recognized but tension provoking obligation to extend religious teachings. And manifest as this obligation was, owners employed a latent strategy of crisis management with the hopes of securing social control. The situation escalated religious cultural production.

Masters were correct when they sensed that slaves "grew worse by being taught" religion. As Freehling notes, "most [South Carolinian] lowcountry gentlemen believed that 'their slaves who professed to be followers of Christ, were generally the most negligent in their duty and the most difficult to manage.'"[46] The problem, of course, was much more serious than that of an owner's negligence or managerial difficulties. Teaching the same Transcendental principles of Christianity to slaves, the same ones that supposedly were to govern slave owners and overseers as well, was fraught with contradictions. As Levine noted, "The dilemma that white ministers faced was simple to grasp but not to resolve: the doctrine they were attempting to inculcate could easily subvert the institution of slavery—and both they and the slaves realized it. These tensions and contractions were inevitable."[47]

Behind Zephaniah Kingsley's complaint that religion destroyed his slaves' "natural and rational happiness" was a more troubled and troublesome truth—a new and public black voice that spoke in the literary form of the critical slave narrative.[48] The former slave Charles Ball wrote, "They fear the slaves, by attending meetings, and listening to the preachers, may imbibe the morality they teach, the notions of equality and liberty contained in the gospel."[49] From a managerial perspective, an attitude like Ball's was bad business. Worse, the religious franchise was expanding the range of cultural fronts available to slaves, and these could only augment the emergence of slave subjectivity. And such subjectivity was being cultivated from above, by the religious franchise, and from inside, by slaves increasingly cultivating a voice informed by religious principles that were ostensibly universal.

Although the extension of the religious franchise took place on embattled terrain, slaves greatly benefited. These benefits were not likely the ones that masters and ministers would list, but for slaves (and for the rise of modern forms of cultural interpretation) they mattered significantly. Religious instruction inadvertently enhanced the cultural sphere of slaves. Slaves acquired new symbolic tools, increased their psychical as well as physical mobility through the Evangelical ferment and the camp meetings, and gained important exposure to the core principles of the dominant ideology. The camp meetings were, after all, the first mass form of collective exposure slaves had to Christianity, and these experiences constituted a stark contrast to the shrunken and pulverized realms of daily plantation life.

As with any worldly religion, Christianity was rich in symbolic devices for imparting deep moral lessons. Bible instruction and teachings gave slaves a new set of symbolic constructs in the form of parables, principles, maxims, and metaphors, which could be drawn upon and used in ways that slaves saw fit—sometimes with quite critical consequences: both Denmark Vesey and Nat Turner were remembered for their references to the bondage of the Israelites and their struggle to flee from Egyptian slavery. Hymns, as they were learned and sung, added to an existing body of collective forms. Though designed just as much for purposes of social control, religious instruction inadvertently fostered what it was supposed to eradicate—the expansion of relatively autonomous forms of black cultural activity.[50]

The new modes of assembly that the Evangelical movements made available for prayer, singing, and worship were collective rather than solitary practices. Combined with the formation of congregations and churches, those collective practices helped to expand black public spheres. Evangelical revivals gave slaves license to cultivate and deepen emotive avenues, collective bonds, the presentation of spiritual selfhood, and ensuing social criticisms. Though they were usually segregated affairs, the camp meetings sometimes brought whites and blacks together for common worship. The underlying but largely ignored principles of equality appeared in luminescent moments. As Sobel notes of the revivals, the "excitements became formalized and ritualized in the second quarter of the nineteenth century. . . . Blacks were assigned a formal area in which to sit: white women were to the right (facing the speaker's stand), white men to the left, and blacks behind the stand." Sobel also points out that "excitement often led to joint experience, and it became a tradition to pull down tall barriers on the last day for a union ceremony."[51]

Christian practices also protected slaves against masters and others. Slaves were able to use Christianity as a shield against a social system that aimed at nothing less than pulverizing them into docile, compliant bodies. As Eugene Genovese argues, "The religion practiced in the quarters gave the slaves the one thing they absolutely had to have if they were to resist being transformed into the Sambos they had been programmed to become. It fired them with a sense of their own worth before God and man. It enabled them to prove to themselves, and to a world that never ceased to need reminding, that no man's will can become that of another unless he himself wills it—that the ideal of slavery cannot be realized, no matter how badly the body is broken and the spirit tormented."[52] The spiritual emancipation of the individual presaged the capacity for the social development of collectivity. This was the psychosocial reach—from soul to social-collective representation, from object to social subject— that the extension of the religious franchise enabled slaves to begin to envision while they were still slaves.

And this leads to the last major implication of the religious franchise. The franchise provided slaves with with the keys to the dominant ideology. It is this benefit that produced the deeply pensive interrogation of slavery and Christian ethics that surfaced in the slave narratives written prior to the Civil War. If religious instruction gave slaves new tools (as disgruntled masters insinuated), these were not just any tools. Religion provided the sharpest minds with the core principles, the universals of the dominant culture and its hegemonic ideals. Ideals, values, and principles are not facts in themselves; they have to be beckoned, instantiated, and brokered by daily grammar; people must work to cultivate them practically, and must activate them continually through interpretation. The most radical appropriation of an ideal is to bring it as close as it can be toward being realized—that is, to make it real insofar as it can be grasped as material practices (as the young Marx would say).[53]

And here was the unceasing rub: slave owners relied on one set of interpretations for justifying the material manifestations of slavery by focusing on biblical passages that stressed subservience and duty to the Lord, who happened to be represented by the masters. Slaves, on the other hand, emphasized the themes that made their lives and slavery's operations transparently incompatible: narratives of Hebrew bondage and escape from slavery (which became crucial analogues to black slavery), the tenets that souls were principally equal under the eyes of God, and the ideas of radical individualist egalitarianism, which emphasized that no person had the dispensation to be another's person's master. By the 1830s, a growing number of antislavery sympathizers had also emerged who sided with the view of many budding black abolitionists that slavery was an abomination, a profound sin, and a worldly evil.[54]

The Cultural Work of the Slave Narrative

According to Marion Wilson Starling, there were at least one hundred abolition societies operating in the 1820s.[55] In this cultural conjuncture American slaves began to press their own subjectivizing claims as self-presenting and socially representative subjects. The most eloquent crystallization of the unintended consequence was the slave narratives. Black authors benefited from the growing receptivity of the antislavery movement. They were able to take advantage of the new ideological privileges of subjectivity and selfhood to stake claims to an experientially based self-authenticity, and to testify from a personal experience and to a social movement.

The rise of radical abolitionism and a shift in the subject matter of the slave narratives appear to have developed reciprocally. As Starling notes, prior to the mid-1830s, narratives tended to be written in the "adventurous" mold, whereas those after 1830 were much more likely to be engaged in the work of abolitionism. This shift, according to Starling, was due to the development of the abolitionist press, which seized upon the writing of slaves. In the fervor of a rising social movement, all forms of writing, regardless of source, appear to have been of value as long as they provided treatments critical of slavery. However, those deemed most authentic—composed by former slaves themselves—were the most valued. The personal was political, as long as genuineness was rooted in experience. Experience carried unimpeachable credibility.

In essence, the extension of the religious franchise, as it culminated in the nineteenth-century slave narratives, was transformed into a cultural license authorizing black authors to practice as modern selves and to present critical observations based on their lives. And this is precisely the kind of phenomenologically based thick description that the critical slave narratives achieved (and without their authors having read a word from Descartes or Locke.) Slaves had internalized and cultivated the religious ideologies only to have them checked and disregarded by the very masters who purported to live by them, and this engendered a profoundly contradictory cultural location. What could clash more than religion and slavery? Conversion, after all, provided an avenue for admission into subjecthood (an unintended consequence). Conversion, however, was irrelevant to the legal force of slavery. Converted or not, slaves by civil law were property; they were objects, not subjects. This contradiction funneled religious teaching toward a criticism of everything existing as slavery; in essence, religion became, as Marx saw it, "the *expression* of real suffering and a *protest* against real suffering."[56] Religious practices churned up a deeper understanding of what the core teachings *meant*, and an understanding of the societal conditions that thwarted the realization of Christian teachings and changed that awareness into a potential powder keg.

One of the earliest slave narratives published illustrated precisely this concern. In 1789, former slave Gustavus Vassa struck at the heart of Christian morality when he wrote: "O, ye nominal Christians! might not an African ask you, 'learned you this from your God, who says unto you, Do unto all men as you would men should do unto you?'"[57] Vassa worked the cultural crossroads where ethics and practices collided. Many narrative authors after Vassa addressed the same tension. Free Negro David Walker published in 1829 what was, according to John Hope Franklin, a bellwether narrative and one of the most vehement attacks on slavery to appear in print in the United States.[58] Walker's *Appeal in Four Articles, Together with a Preamble to the Coloured Citizens of the World, But in Particular, and very Expressly, to those of the United States of America* posed the notion of the universalism inherent in the concept of justice, and took aim at the hypocrisy of slaveholding:

> Is not God a God of justice to *all* his creatures? Do you say he is? Then if he gives peace and tranquility to tyrants, and permits them to keep our fathers, our mothers, ourselves and our children in eternal ignorance and wretchedness, to support them and their families, would he be to us a God of *justice*? I ask, O ye *Christians*!!! who hold us and our children in the most abject ignorance and degradation, that ever a people were afflicted with since the world began—I say, if God gives you peace and tranquility, and suffers you thus to go on afflicting us, and our children, who have never given you the least provocation—would he be to us a *God of justice*? If you will allow that we are MEN, who feel for each other, does not the blood of our fathers and of us their children, cry aloud to the Lord of Sabaoth [*sic*] against you, for the cruelties and murders with which you have, and do continue to afflict us.[59]

Walker's *Appeal* was as much an appeal to a critical religious consciousness as it was a critique of dominant religious practices, and reflected general tenets of abolitionism. In one year, Walker's *Appeal* went through three editions.[60] Its popularity could not be ignored, and it was indicted as a political text that provoked slave insurrection; it was certainly an incendiary statement. But in the historical context, any articulate statement against slavery was automatically seditious. The slave insurrection led by Nat Turner took place the following year.[61] And on the heels of these two major cultural events was the launching in 1831 of William Lloyd Garrison's scathing and emotionally ardent publication, the *Liberator*, which enabled the Garrisonians to stake out the high moral ground and take their place as front-runners in publishing the most vehement critiques of slavery.[62] During its first year, 400 of the 450 subscribers were Negroes. By 1834, the *Liberator* had over 2,300 subscribers. Garrison's publication played a major role in distributing black accounts of slavery.[63] Nearly three hundred of these accounts of varying lengths, written by slaves themselves, appeared in the paper. They were "undressed" texts, distinct from idealized "parlor" or "gift book" versions written by white abolitionists. Such ideal narratives were written with an affected intimacy that allowed both author and reader the moral opportunity of vicarious consumption by "imaginatively [involving] themselves with persons they had never really known and the like of whose besetting problems they had never even seen."[64] In 1836, there were at least eleven journals devoted to the abolition of slavery, with a combined subscribership of 1,095,000.[65]

By the time of the Civil War the slave narrative literature offered as routine criticism the well honed perspective that embraced Christian principles while it denounced slave owners, flagrant abrogation of these tenets. Former slave Harriet Jacobs put the matter in terms of the failure of missionaries to convert the slaveholders themselves:

> They send the Bible to heathen abroad, and neglect the heathen at home. I am glad that missionaries go out to the dark corners of the earth; but I ask them not to overlook the dark corners at home. Talk to American slaveholders as you talk to savages in Africa. Tell *them* it was wrong to traffic in men. Tell them it is sinful to sell their own children, and atrocious to violate their own daughters. Tell them that all men are brethren, and that man has no right to shut out the light of knowledge from his brother. Tell them they are answerable to God for sealing up the Fountain of Life from souls that are thirsting for it.[66]

What stands out in the earliest recognition of the slave narratives is the distinct accent that radical white abolitionists placed on the authenticity and truthfulness of these accounts and on the power of legitimacy they contained. The Reverend Ephriam Peabody, presiding over the Anglican-turned-Unitarian King's Chapel in Boston, wrote a review in 1849 in which he emphasized his belief in how the slave narratives could "exert a very wide influence on public opinion" because "they contain the victim's account" of the workings of slavery.[67] An editorial comment printed in 1853 in the *Chronotype*, an abolitionist publication, was insistent in its conviction that the new literary works written by slaves would usher in slavery's rapid demise. "We defy any man to think with patience or tolerance of slavery after reading [Henry] Bibb's narrative, unless he is one of those infidels to nature who float on the race as monsters, from it, but not of it. Put a dozen copies of this book into every school, district, or neighborhood in the free states, and you might sweep the whole north on a thoroughgoing liberty platform for abolishing slavery, everywhere and everyhow."[68]

However tied the interpretive power of the slave narratives are to a black subjectivity coming of age, they also point to a rather remarkable engagement with modernity. The narratives perform a fundamentally modern kind of cultural and ideological deconstruction through the lens of critical social subjectivity. Yet upon a closer look, they exemplify the very efficacy of hegemonic ideals. Their insights are not revolutionary and they do not reject Christianity. Indeed, they embrace the core ideologies of Christianity. Charles Ball, David Walker, Frederick Douglass, Harriet Jacobs, and many other authors actually argue for particular *meanings* of the dominant ideology that enabled them to challenge the interpretations of masters. Interestingly, when William Lloyd Garrison argued that the Constitution should be dismissed because it was so flawed as to permit slavery, Frederick Douglass objected by insisting that the Constitution ought to be embraced, and read as a document that repudiated slavery.[69]

Even the titles of slave narratives that began to emerge in the 1840s indicated that the author's words were there to claim a subjective truth and to witness a reality. Many titles included references to the author's life—as in "From His Own Mouth," "The Life of . . ." or "My Life . . ." These titles suggested the indisputability of experience; truth was framed in the account of who lived it. Titles like Wilson Armistead's *A Tribute to the Negro: Being a Vindication of the Moral, Intellectual and Religious Capabilities of the Colored Portion of Mankind with Particular Reference to the African Race* (1848) and Lewis Clarke and Milton Clarke's *Narratives of the Sufferings of Lewis and Milton Clarke, Sons of a Soldier of the Revolution during a Captivity of More than Twenty Years Among Slaveholders of Kentucky, One of the So-Called Christian States of North American, Dictated by Themselves* (1846) reflected the critique of slavery as an institution purportedly erected on Christian foundations. Frederick Douglass's address in 1852 to a white audience that gathered to celebrate Independence Day in the city of Rochester, New York, captured well the way in which former slaves challenged the Christianity of slave apologists by drawing upon the biblical accounts of Hebrew bondage and emancipation and linking them to the contemporary plight of American slaves.

> By the rivers of Babylon, there we sat down. Yea! we wept when we remembered Zion. We hanged our harps upon the willows in the midst thereof. For there, they that carried us away captive, required of us a song; and they who wasted us required of us mirth, saying, Sing us one of the songs of Zion. How can we sing the Lord's song in a strange land? If I forget thee, O Jerusalem, let my right hand forget her cunning. If I do not remember thee, let my tongue cleave to the roof of my mouth.[70]

What these early black writers were presenting were not rejections of the dominant ideology of Christianity. These writings were not aberrant, external, or alien cultural texts. Rather, these writers shared in the conviction that religion harbored the keys to emancipation. It was the struggle over the *meaning* of the dominant ideology of Christianity, not its rejection; it was the struggle over cultural interpretation. In presenting their radical challenges to those who condoned slavery from a religious perspective, the authors of the narratives offered another path to get at the "truth" of both Christianity and the aberration of slavery.[71] In the process, black intellectuals made the hermeneutic claim to have gotten at this "deeper truth" better than those in power who guarded and dispensed the official reality. In this regard, the illuminating break engendered through the religious franchise produced a social critique that was fundamentally modern in its capacity to render the social into a transparent object.[72]

Public Travels into the Black Domestic Frontier

As public literature, the slave narratives were, arguably, well fitted to the literary tastes of many inquisitive (if not liberal) white Americans in the North. The self-penned narratives shared similarities with travel narratives, a popular genre in the nineteenth century. Travel narratives entailed visits to strange and distant places; they provided reportage of voyages to places hitherto unexperienced; and they mapped new experience. They brought the reader to the foreign, the distant, the exotic. Their authority resided in the narrator as the central and trustworthy source of statements of authentic experience.

One might think an eighteenth- or nineteenth-century travel narrative and a slave narrative would be worlds apart. But the slave narratives are frequently about inner, psychic movement, of coming into a realization about the social forces that have moved (and moved through) one's life; their narrators recall being shackled, having nowhere to go except psychically inward and morally outward. Their travel covers moral and emotional geography rather than physical geography. The recently acquired soul (an internalized attribution that coincides with institutional pressures) merges with the expressive authenticity of one's newly acquired status as redeemable social subject (expressive authenticity) in the form of the modern subject. The ports, terrain, and horizons toured for the reader are alien, distant, and foreign as well as morally repugnant. Yet the moral, emotional, and psychic geographies are inescapably familiar, domestic, homely. They are American, and, for the very sympathetic reader, much too close for comfort.

Nineteenth-century travel narratives, of course, come in many forms. But there is a particular kind that we have come to associate with certain refinements of descriptive precision—emergent conventions—that bear the mark of modern systematic observation. Examples of these developments might be Alexis de Tocqueville's *Democracy in America*, Charles Darwin's *Voyage of the Beagle*, or Richard Henry Dana's *Two Years before the Mast*. Tocqueville gathered his observations in the United States between 1825 and 1831; Darwin's journal entries, which served as the basis for *The Voyage of the Beagle*, were logged in the mid-1830s, and Dana's narrative was composed in the 1840s—thus they coincide with the emergence of the slave narratives. These examples, all well known and indicative of modern styles of highly refined and even critical reportage, also bear the stamp of composition aimed at a readership that is not merely after the pulp fiction adventure. Tocqueville's travel narrative doubles as a search for new political forms, to be contrasted with the crumbling establishment of late-eighteenth-century postmonarchic French politics. The treatment of the context of American civil and political society is shadowed by the souring European pretext. Tocqueville's travel narrative prefigures the modern interest in *comparative institutions*. Darwin's journal entries are also modern in that they illustrate the maturation of the travel narrative's assimilation of natural history, especially in his skillful, almost photographic, presentation of the technical minutia of landscapes, geological formation, and flora and fauna. (Only on occasion does Darwin's flat and staid prose break with incensed emotionality, when he observes cruel human actions. The pages flare with his moral indignation as he witnesses slavery.) The modern imprint on Dana's travel narrative is indisputably that of nineteenth-century humanitarian reformism. Dana wished to dislodge Amercans' romance with maritime life, which was fostered by an imagery shaped by officers themselves. Dana's interventionist and reformist text illustrated the magnitude of mistreatment, the rapacious, capricious, and arbitrary cruelty experienced by the common seaman laboring in a floating institution that offered no reprieve.

Tocqueville and Darwin both register sympathy for the recipients of cruelty and degradation. But Dana's travel narrative (abundantly sprinkled with racialized commentary)[73] contains some rather interesting parallels with many of the slave narratives. It is most clearly a proto-muckraking presentation, and a negative ethnography, penned from a morally indignant insider's privileged view. With its reportage of undesirable experiences, it, too, is a book of revelation and is meant to be read as such. Consider some words from the preface to *Two Years before the Mast*:

> There has not been a book written, professing to give [the common seaman's] life and experiences, by one who has been of them, and can know what their life really is. A *voice from the forecastle* has hardly yet been heard. . . . I design to give an accurate and authentic narrative of a little more than two years spent as a common sailor, before the mast, in the American merchant service.

And in the spirit of the times, he closes the preface with a reformist twist:

> If it shall interest the general reader, and call more attention to the welfare of seamen, or give any information as to their real condition, which may serve to raise them in the rank of beings, and to promote in any measure their religious and moral improvement, and diminish the hardships of their daily life, the end of its publication will be answered.

Now let us compare some opening remarks printed in 1835 from Charles Ball's slave narrative:

> These pages . . . will present . . . a faithful view of the opinions and feelings of the colored population. . . . [The reader] will here see portrayed in the language of truth, by an eye witness and a slave, the sufferings, the hardships, and the evils which are inflicted upon the millions of human beings, in the name of the law of the land and of the Constitution of the United States.

With the important exception of the interiorization of racial experience, there are many uncanny similarities.[74]

The slave narrative, then, can be understood to operate like a travel narrative turned inward, an interiorization that displays an exterior and overwhelming negative ethnography of domination. Moreover, the slave narratives are kin to the emerging form of literary muckraking and to the discovery of "social problems" that fed the larger culture of an ascending humanitarian reformism. But their epistemological ground is in their function as representations of the historically bequeathed new cultural-interpretive complex that unfolded along a specifiable sequence of cultural transformations—of soul recognized and salvaged, then transformed into a redeemable subject, then acquiring authenticity as a modern self, and then transmogrifying into a spokesperson for a larger collective subject.[75]

The ties to the Enlightenment and the political contextualization of the slave narratives deserve to be acknowledged. However, I do not think that the narratives can be classified as simply a species of Enlightenment politics; we need not rely on some distant philosophical rupture to account for how enslaved humans might draw upon religion to express their grievances with their fate or the social order in which they were caught. Yet both Enlightenment thought and slave writings engage in a radical struggle over redemptive ideologies as well as ideologies of redemption. By invoking ties to Enlightenment, I do not want to argue that there is some grand sort of structuralism at work, and that the narratives were simply and mechanically performing Enlightenment-produced ventriloquism or mimesis. The conditions under which they were produced—of human suffering measured against a religiously framed moral outrage—cannot be reduced in this manner to some overarching framework. However, I do think that the connection between critical Enlightenment thought and the slave narratives lies in the broader cultural context in which the narratives were read by those who were beginning to be morally moved by the modern recognition of subjects seeking redemption from "traditional" social and political oppression and who found the statements of such subjects worthy of appropriation. It was within an "enlightened" turn that slave narratives were read by critical abolitionists from the new vantage point of an emerging ethnosympathy that had already been championed by Jean-Jacques Rousseau, who, along with others, emphasized the need to retrieve damaged subjectivity.

Black writers also embraced principles that could be considered part of the radical core of Enlightenment thought, including the desire to render power transparent, to critique all received forms of traditional authority (including political as well as religious authority lodged in established institutions), and to embrace the ideology of radical egalitarianism.[76] All three of these principles cut across a great many Enlightenment discourses, and they are found in the more significant and influential slave narratives because these narratives belong not only to the problem of racial specificity in the American context, but to the larger problem of social crisis and political representation unfolding in the western world. Thus to reduce the narratives to a racial trope, to a kind of essential blackspeak—or, for that matter, to an effect of humanitarian reformism, as if they were simply akin to a black floating rib taken from Adam's body to mark the eve of black subjectivity—does not enable us to grasp the interplay between the emergent racialized voices and the deeper currents of ideological crises in the West.[77]

The slave narratives thus provide a rather remarkable trip wire that grounds the immediacy of individual and personal subjectivity within the context of sociohistorical crisis, a theme consistent with many of the emergent political critiques of power that were endemic to Enlightenment thought. They facilitated emergent black subjects who pursued—and who were pursued by—the perspective that individual experience was the key to deeper truths, and that experience rendered transparent also rendered power transparent; both were new functions of truth. "Reader, be assured this narrative is no fiction. I am aware that some of my adventures may seem incredible; but they are nevertheless, strictly true." These are the words that open Harriet Jacob's *Incidents in the Life of a Slave Girl* (1861). Jacob's words are an oath: to tell the truth. And the truth is where self and social system, biography and history intersect.

> I do earnestly desire to arouse the women of the North to a realizing sense of the condition of two millions women, at the South, still in bondage, suffering what I suffered, and most of them far worse. I want to add my testimony to that of abler pens to convince the people of the Free States what Slavery really is. Only by *experience* can any one realize how deep, and dark, and foul is that pit of abominations. May the blessings of *God* rest on this imperfect effort in behalf of my persecuted people.[78]

The question of just where and with whom truth resided, and which subjects were most likely to dispense it, thus introduces an important cultural development. The idea that the former slave as writer be recognized as a subject in possession of a truth-telling capacity enabled abolitionism to throw wide open the door that had been nudged a bit by the extension of the religious franchise. But only at its most radical-humanist margins, where the slave narrative emerged, did the cultural energy take hold to champion the reconceptualization of chattel as individual selves and persons. Slaves, now recognized as authentic sources of observation, could be reclassified—from objects of property to authenticating subjects. Radical abolitionists, black and white, thus helped bring about a significant alteration in cultural perceptions of black expressions by introjecting a new element of humanness—selfhood—into the white accounts of blacks.

In the long run, Christian teachings had a profoundly unsettling impact. Slaves found their symbolic universe widened by the addition of cultural practices whose very forms—praying, congregating, singing—could feed into ongoing struggles, enabling them to carve out their own sphere of discourse and their collective engagement with one another.[79] It would be only a matter of time and refinement before the focus upon the self-reports from truth-through-experience tellers would shift to the focus upon the reports of investigators who would seek to get at that experience with their own accounts themselves—through the work of an ethnosympathetic social science. In confronting this new cultural-interpretive complex, reformers engendered nothing less than a new mode of culturally invested and investigative work at the subcultural margins. This was the new work of an ethnosympathy that emanated from within the abolitionist movement, and that heard black *and* white meanings in what was once only black noise.

.   .   .   .   .

The recognition of black subjectivity and its rapid expansion was an inadvertent outcome of proselytization. The slave's inner spiritual being was given a name, and called forth—this is what conversion at minimum must accomplish. Yet the process was invariably overlaid with strategies of social control and cultural repression. However, by the third decade of the nineteenth century, the "black subject," conceived in individual as well as collective terms, was no longer an inadvertent consequence; black subjectivity became a distinct political object (as well as an important analytic and interpretive cultural trope) useful in a variety of ways to the burgeoning antislavery movement. Slaves had fathomed the core values and principles of Christian teachings, and had taken them to heart. And they took them into the public sphere.

For disenchanted cultural elites who possessed humanitarian sympathies, who were increasingly compelled to confront their sense of cultural erosion, who worried about the coming of market society and the new men of industrial power, and who were questing after a fleeting authenticity with the ideological weapons of romanticism, what better place to find evidence of an indisputable self rooted in an indisputable experience than in a slave? What more convenient place to find such authenticity than on the cultural margins and in the domestic backyard of American civil society where the spiritual-singing *new* Negro was now found? And what better testimony could be found to help frame the disenchantment with the reigning modern ethos in the North and its ability to elevate the new captains of industry to the top of the heap of freedom that was burying a rapidly growing number of white workers in "wage slavery"? Such crises, which fueled as well as were fueled by the abolitionist movement, helped inaugurate the unprecedented cultural turn toward the plight of marginalized black subjects, went far beyond the evils of slavery.

Culture on the margins could speak to crises at the center. But this meant that culture had to be further defined, identified, specified, singled out, demarcated, and captured—and interpreted, of course, with an appropriate pathos. This is precisely what was in store for black song making, particularly the Negro spiritual. Such broadened use of black music contained the seeds of a new interpretive formation that would be soon launched, with the coming of the Civil War.

FOUR

FROM AUTHENTIC SUBJECTS TO

AUTHENTIC CULTURE

> I did not, when a slave, understand the deep meaning of those
> rude and apparently incoherent songs. I was myself within the
> circle; so that I neither saw nor heard as those without might
> see and hear. . . . If any one wishes to be impressed with the
> soul-killing effects of slavery, let him go to Colonel Lloyd's
> plantation on allowance-day, place himself in the deep pine
> woods, and there let him, in silence analyze the sounds that
> shall pass through the chambers of his soul,—and if he is not
> thus impressed it will only be because "there is no
> flesh in his obdurate heart."
> *(Frederick Douglass, 1845)*

AS THE SPIRITUAL emerged within the new order of recognition
and interpretation, it became immediately more than a category
of singing; it marked a *cultural complex* by functioning as a two-
dimensional testimony. On the one hand, it was most commonly recognized both as a testimony *of* black meanings, as a signifying system for the
psychological, spiritual, and collective subjectivity of slaves, and as a
symbol of the slaves' perseverance within a history of oppression. On the
other hand, it functioned as a testimony *for* the emerging critical perceptions of white northern progressives. Their recognition and use of the
Negro spiritual spoke, in part, to their sense of their role as partisans in
the opening of new critical horizons, and it aided in their attempts to
frame, criticize, and conceptualize their disenchantment with a new modern industrial society that challenged their once-taken-for-granted sense
of purpose and place.

These issues come into focus when we consider four interlocking developments. First, the new interest in the spiritual can be understood as
a staging ground for the cultural battle against slavery. Douglass's interpretation of black song making added to the abolitionist movement's
cultural arsenal against slavery. In his rallying call to northern Christian
abolitionists, Douglass invited "outsiders" to understand the cultural

strategies of slaves. He presented himself as a source of unimpeachable hermeneutic insight into the "inside" lives of slaves, and this "inside" could be glimpsed through the lens of their music. Thus I examine in this chapter the significance of Douglass's attempt to pinpoint and highlight black song making from the eyes of this former slave. Douglass was crucial in bridging the gap between a more diffuse ethnosympathy and black culture. The result of the conjuncture was a highly skewed mode of interpretation that centered upon the "Negro spiritual" as the penultimate cultural good generated by black subjective expressivity. The earlier emphasis that had been placed upon black religious performativity fed into and off of Douglass's important invitation to fathom the songs of slaves.

The process of selectivity narrowed the comprehension of black expressivity considerably. As the war commenced, the interest that critical abolitionist's had in black song making shifted from an ostensible recognition that the spirituals were about slavery to a more diffuse struggle over where the spirituals were to placed upon an emerging cultural and aesthetic map.[1] In the process black culture became the object of a new protoethnographic imagination, and the spiritual became the site of a new kind of investigation that examined the cultural products and practices of groups on the racial margins of American society. The spiritual, as I shall argue in this and the ensuing chapters, was transformed from a testimony to a cultural object or an artifact. As abolitionists began to analyze it, their encounters with black expressions helped shape this new interpretive mode. Thus, as the discovery of black song making progressed, the study of culture gravitated increasingly toward new modes of validation in which interpretation also became an intellectual value in and of itself. By the 1860s, when Unitarian abolitionists like William Allen, Lucy McKim, Charles Ware, and Thomas Wentworth Higginson were gathering sought-after "specimens," the interest in songs had increasingly less to do with social conditions and slavery. The interests had already begun to shift in response to accommodating the troubled notion of cultural authenticity and the new scientist impulse that would eventually take form as a modern mode of empirical description.

Second, the discovery called for entirely new schemas of recognition and new modes of appropriation. It required a pathos-oriented hearing and a view that such pathos was a modern and progressive virtue. Action upon this virtue was consistent with the larger ethos of humanitarian reformism of which abolitionism was a major expression. Third, the new hearing required actual engagement with, and intimate proximity to, black singing. Authenticity could not be fathomed from a distance, nor at second hand. It—more specifically, the people who embodied it—had to be witnessed, and its forms had to be captured; analysts had to engage subjects. This approach put a premium on what I have been calling the protoethnographic impulse (we today would recognize it as fieldwork). Fourth, the new orientation actually required the possession and cultivation of ethnosympathy, which fueled the new protoethnographic imagination. The object of this sensibility was twofold: it pursued the authenticity of singing subjects as well as the authenticity (or earnestness) of the seekers themselves, whose motivations were continually rationalized and justified in the process of hearing, defining, and accounting for black music. In this regard an externally sought after authenticity and an internally valued earnestness and purposiveness were combined to create a qualitatively new orientation toward culture at the racial margins.

The search for authenticity had a double dimension. Spiritual hunters sought authenticity *externally*—in the body of a genuine social subject such as an author of a slave narrative or the black singers of spirituals. And authenticity was sought *internally*—through a self-reflexive recognition and cultivation of one's genuine pathos, what I have called an *ethos of pathos*. This reflexivity, this internal recognition of the virtue of pathos, entailed the seeker's consciousness of his or her own moral compass, a sign of transcending the rigid, despiritualized dimensions of modernity. As a cultural process, the two dimensions—locating authenticity and possessing the new humanistic virtue of being able to perceive it—merged into a more general orientation. The pursuit of authenticity hinged on the new ethnosympathy, and the latter grounded itself in the recognition of an appropriate—that is, a deserving—social subject.[2] The discoverers of the spiritual were thus fully present in the process of authenticating their own notions of authenticity. In this regard, finding black authenticity was simultaneously a way in which the searchers for authenticity could pursue their own sense of social, cultural, and political legitimation.

This enterprise carried out missions of salvage and retrieval—the cultural retrieval of goods, meanings, practices, and artifacts of subjects who were either in the process of disappearing in the wake of social change or who were buried by other social forces. Such cultural goods or practices (along with the "host" subjects who produced them) could be retrieved as part of a larger moral responsibility. By pursuing black culture, moral and political entrepreneurs furthered an already developing form of ethnography that had begun to take shape by the mid-nineteenth century. What they aimed to capture was, by definition, authentic subjects who yielded authentic culture. Black expressivity thus emerged for the first time as a font of authentic cultural goods. By the end of the war the growing interest in black music making was firmly rooted, and at the apex of the newly discovered goodness were black religious singing and songs that were soon to be called "spirituals."

The discoverers of black music drew on earlier developments, but their forays into cultural retrieval also marked the beginning of an ensuing mode of cultural interpretation on the racial margins. Frederick Douglass's invitation to his readers to hear black song making exemplifies this transition. After Douglass, abolitionists not only turned their attention to the music of blacks and to the interpretation of the culture of slaves; they also began to explore the question of the meaning of *American* culture. As I shall discuss later, coupled with the search for black authenticity was a quest among elites for a larger American cultural authenticity. Elite interest in black culture was not only tied to the critique of slavery, but was related to an emerging project to discover and clarify an American cultural aesthetic.

As I shall introduce in this chapter, but shall argue more fully in chapter 5, Unitarianism and Transcendentalism represented the cutting ideological edges of the new social anxieties and social criticism. The key figures who aided and carried out the discovery and retrieval of black culture, especially by capturing into print the Negro spirituals, were predominantly Unitarians and Transcendentalists, who were prone to viewing modernity through a disenchanting lens. These issues lead directly to the problem of how the new reception of black music actually developed, and how critical white abolitionists' proclivity for spirituals worked as an interpretive scaffolding upon which their preferred or idealized Negroes could be viewed. This process was also deeply tied to the new religious orientations among the discoverers themselves. To accomplish this we will have to look at how the preference for spirituals over other forms of black expression developed out of pathos-oriented hearing, and how such cultural interpretation led to a form of cultural enclosure around the symbolic terrain upon which black subjectivity was emerging—that is, how black culture came to be selectively perceived, screened, and viewed as viable, authentic, and admissible to a small but highly significant number of cultural entrepreneurs. In essence, we need to look at how the broader notion of authenticity became conflated with religious orientations and symbolized by the spiritual, culminating in the production and institutionalization of what Raymond Williams calls a "selective tradition" for interpreting culture at the racial margins.[3]

Of course the humanitarian interest in black expressivity appears at this conjuncture as just another intense application of the benevolent arm of modern reformism, this time extending downward for the purpose of black uplift. And it certainly was this for a short time, at least until the abandonment of Reconstruction in the early 1870s. With the ending of Reconstruction, however, the plight of black populations was severed from the list of humanitarian reformist projects, and reformist energies and sympathies were funneled toward the disciplining, taming, and "uplifting" of under-Americanized urban white ethnics. By century's end, this redeployment of reformist and redemptive energies had transmogrified into more professional social scientific endeavors such as social work and urban sociology. Such trajectories are important. However, I want to focus on the more subterranean process of cultural legitimation, of how troubled elites gathered at the racial margins to hear, see, inquire, and probe black expressivity, and how they drew upon the tropes of a religiously inflected subjecthood in their recognition of the Negro spiritual.[4]

Cultivating Singing Subjects

The teaching of hymns had long been viewed as one of the most expedient ways to speed up the proselytization and conversion of slaves. By regulating and monitoring slave religion and the singing of Christian hymns, ministers and owners could guage the desired effects of social control. Clergy and owners' ability to manage religion provided a practical index for social stability. Anglican clergyman William Knox recognized in 1768 that teaching the Negroes to sing hymns was "the pleasantest way of instructing them, and bringing them speedily to offer praise to God."[5] Knox's method was cost effective: the easiest task would involve at a minimum the inculcation of rote mimicry, and this did not necessarily entail teaching to slaves the more reflexive knowledge of the dominant culture's deeper ideological principles, such as actual Christian ethics.[6] In 1784, Anglican Bishop Porteus continued by refining the same work order. The slaves already sang, Porteus noted; they had a "natural turn for music." But their "rude and artless" song making could be improved by turning this cultural propensity toward "purposes of devotion." He went on to suggest that clergy compose "short hymns . . . set to plain, easy, solemn psalm tunes, as nearly resembling their own simple melody as possible."[7]

As modern anthropology might put it, Porteus was suggesting a way of cutting a deal with the fact of cultural syncretism, the blending of cultural practices of different origins.[8] But in this case, the syncretic compromise was to be based on an unequal cultural exchange. The melodical shell of black song could be retained, but the semantic content was to be supplied for them, no doubt along with some lessons on "devotion." In this way, overseers presumed to extend their control over musical practice.[9] Slaves, of course, had taken up religious singing as one of the additional cultural resources allowed them, then had expanded this cultural terrain. Singing, even if tutored and policed from above, provided them with an opportunity to exercise their own collective voicings, and these opportunities were cultivated and broadened through the religious franchise. Slaves were thus able to modify hymns to fit their own symbolic needs in both public as well as clandestine cultural practices.

By the 1840s, Baptists and Methodists had made successful institutional incursions into the slave states. In 1842, the Reverend Charles Colcock Jones, a prominent figure in the missionary outreach to American slaves, argued that effective instruction ought to purge undesirable traits and practices. Teaching slaves "good psalms and hymns" would, he hoped, displace their "extravagant and nonsensical chants, and catches and hallelujah songs of their own composing; and when they sing, which is very often while about their business or of an evening in their houses, they will have something profitable to sing."[10] The kind of cultural profit Jones referred to might be put another way: what they should sing mattered when it came to social control. Interventions such as this helped to conflate what was socially inculcated with what was perceived as "natural." By the 1840s, the conflation appeared to be well established. William Cullen Bryant, who observed Richmond, Virginia, tobacco workers in 1843, noted that the slave's "taste is exclusively for sacred music; they will sing nothing else."[11] Bryant's observation was echoed by Swedish visitor Fredrika Bremer: "The slaves [in Richmond] were all Baptists, and sung only hymns."[12]

As noted, religious instruction engendered social and political risks in the form of Christianity-based slave revolts. But such risks were far outweighed by the belief that Christianity was the fundamental font as well as the cultural front of civilization. Fredrika Bremer expressed this belief in her observation of black music. During her travels in the South in the early 1850s, she logged her own comparative observations, which expressed the sentiments of many other whites. In comparing slaves in Cuba with those in the American South, Bremer was struck by "the beneficial influence of Anglo-American culture on the negro." In an analogue that one would expect from the popular natural-history travel narratives of the day, Bremer compared apples and Negroes: "The sour crab [apple] is not more unlike our noble, bright, Astrachan apple, than is the song of the wild African to the song of the Christian negro in the United States, whether it be hymns that he sings or gay negro songs that he has himself composed." Cuba's slaves were prone to "screeching improvisations," while in South Carolina slaves demonstrated "inspired and inspiring preaching of the Savior." Untouched by the civilizing process, Cuban slaves were stuck in their "low," "sensual," "lawless life"; but the American Negroes manifested a "spiritual intoxication in song and prayer, and religious joy, which is seen and heard at the religious festivals of the negro people here."[13] Of course, any form of black culture that fell outside the emerging religious enclosure—work songs, "secular" music, songs that accompanied dancing, and Africanist "shouts"—qualified immediately as "low," "sensual," and "lawless."

Aside from the kind of preferred Negro or slave that white observers imagined during the hearing of musical practices, it was the former slave Frederick Douglass who embodied both the efficacy and the cultural complexity of the religious franchise. Douglass connected the new phenomenon of black expressive subjectivity to the growing moral crisis that was brewing among the most critical white abolitionists. And it is through Douglass that the perception and discussion of black song making first take on the quality of ethnosympathetic revelation.

Breaking the Sound Barrier: Frederick Douglass's Revelations

Douglass's *Narrative of the Life of Frederick Douglass, An American Slave* has been recognized, rightly so, as an eloquent and powerful contribution to the ascending political power of the abolitionist movement. It is arguably the most important and widely read narrative prior to the Civil War.[14] But it was also his unprecedented hermeneutical turn toward music and the spotlight aimed at slave songs that distinguished Douglass's narrative from all other slave narratives. He brought slave music out from its subterranean and quasi-clandestine world and almost single handedly placed it upon the analytical table, where it could be probed by abolitionists. These steps were first taken within the pages of a slave narrative that was written as a personal contribution to the cultural arsenal of the political goals of the antislavery movement.

Douglass's autobiography provides a most valuable cultural indicator of how the slave narratives established an expressive black social subjectivity. Douglass did more than present an argument about hidden meanings; he demonstrated how a sympathetic attentiveness to songs could bring into focus the hitherto unappreciated collective consciousness of slaves. And this was new. Prior to the 1840s, slave owners, overseers, and visitors to the South logged numerous accounts and interpretations of the cultural, religious, and musical practices of slaves. Most of these observations were meanings imposed from the outside, and framed in the one-way power of interpretations from above. The narratives by Douglass and other free blacks, however, reversed this current of interpretation and opened up the *interior* sensibility of slaves to cultural analysis.[15] Charles Ball's slave narrative, published a decade before Douglass's, had put the problem of authenticity quite forcefully. Only "through the language of truth, by an eye witness and a slave," Ball argued, could one actually grasp the reality of slavery.[16] Douglass and other abolitionists, black and white, said much the same. Because he highlighted the "songs of sorrow" (he did not call them "spirituals"), slave songs became the most advantageous cultural terrain upon which slave authenticity in its compressed simplicity could be seen. Douglass broke the sound barrier; his insider's unimpeachable experience provided for the first time a blueprint for black cultural analysis.

In black songs Douglass heard slaves framing, representing, and managing their deepest feelings of collective suffering. In his words, the songs "told a tale of woe which was then altogether beyond my feeble comprehension; they were tones loud, long, and deep, they breathed the prayer and complaint of souls boiling over with the bitterest anguish. Every tone was testimony against slavery, and a prayer to God for deliverance from chains."[17] With novel tenderness Douglass wrote of how "hearing . . . those wild songs" always depressed his spirit, filling him "with ineffable sadness." He embodied pathos-oriented hearing:

> I have frequently found myself in tears while hearing them. The mere recurrence to those songs, even now, afflicts me; and while I am writing these lines, an expression of feeling has already found its way down my cheek. To those songs I trace my first glimmering conception of the dehumanizing character of slavery. I can never get rid of that conception. Those songs still follow me, to deepen my hatred of slavery, and quicken my sympathies for my brethren in bonds.[18]

So thoroughly were these songs embedded in the anguish of slavery that their makers even lacked the distance necessary to understand them: "I did not, when a slave, understand the deep meaning of those rude and apparently incoherent songs. I was myself within the circle; so that I neither saw nor heard as those without might see and hear."[19]

We have no reason to doubt Douglass's emotional realism and its purpose in linking truth and experience through self-based reportage. Driven by a critical empathy, such an account rested its power in its claim to witness at first hand the experiences being recorded. Moreover, the tie between experience and truth grounded in emotion had already been established; it was fundamental to the testimonial and experiential domain of American evangelical epistemology (Douglass, after all, was attracted to the Baptist denomination while still a slave) and was central to the larger currents of romanticism. Such emotionally powerful accounts of the dehumanizing experience of slavery warranted an equally emotional reception. This was precisely the reception that William Lloyd Garrison, the most influential abolitionist in the years between 1830 and the Civil

War, produced in the preface that he wrote for Douglass's autobiography.[20] With white abolitionist readers in mind, Garrison wrote:

> He who can peruse it without a tearful eye, a heaving breast, an afflicted spirit,—without being filled with an unutterable abhorrence of slavery and all its abettors, and animated with a determination to seek the immediate overthrow of that execrable system,—without trembling for the fate of his country in the hands of a righteous God, who is ever on the side of the oppressed, and whose arm is not shortened that it cannot save,—must have a flinty heart, and be qualified to act the part of a trafficker "in slaves and the souls of men." I am confident that it is essentially true in all its statements; that nothing has been set down in malice, nothing exaggerated, nothing drawn from the imagination; that it comes short of the reality, rather than overstates a single fact in regard to SLAVERY AS IT IS.[21]

Garrison's remarks do more than introduce another person; they introduce the new interpretive ethos of pathos, the new radical ethnosympathy. Garrison's comments were meant to address just as much the pathos that served as an indicator of a new kind of humanism as they were to introduce Douglass's personal account of slavery.[22]

But it was Douglass's claims about what was at stake in black song making that proved to be so analytically efficacious. If black songs were only grasped properly and truly understood, they would reveal how slaves brokered everyday life; they would provide a most valuable window through which abolitionists could see the souls of black folk through the singing subjects of slavery. Douglass told his readers just how to conduct the analysis, and even walked them through an example. In recalling an attempt of slaves to escape, he wrote:

> [A]s I now look back, I can see that we did many silly things, very well calculated to awaken suspicion. We were, at times, remarkably buoyant, singing hymns and making joyous exclamations, almost as triumphant in their tone as if we had reached a land of freedom and safety. A keen observer might have detected in our repeated singing of
>
> > "O Canaan, sweet Canaan,
> > I am bound for the land of Canaan,"
>
> something more than a hope of reaching heaven. We meant to reach the *north*—and the north was our Canaan.

Douglass continues with an interpretation of another song fragment:

> > "I thought I heard them say,
> > There were lions in the way,
> > I don't expect to stay

> Much longer here.
> Run to Jesus—shun the danger
> I don't expect to stay
> Much longer here."[23]

This "favorite air," Douglas notes, "had a double meaning." For some, it "meant the expectation of a speedy summons to a world of spirits, but in the lips of *our* company, it simply meant a speedy pilgrimage toward a free state, and deliverance from all the evils and dangers of slavery."[24] Songs were thus sung one way in the presence of the slave owners and overseers.

> "Yes, we shall be free,
> Yes, we shall be free,
> Yes, we shall be free,
> When the Lord shall appear."

One key line was altered, Douglass tells us, when slaves sung in the presence of one another:

> "Yes, we shall be free,
> When the *Yankee* shall appear."[25]

Is this one song but two meanings? Or two songs and two meanings? The lyrical structure is identical in both versions with the exception of the substitution of "Yankee" for "Lord." But the presence of either word is enough to shift the entire semantic key of the song's meaning. This also appears an example of two very different cultural practices, even if the empirical features—the structure of the song, its melody, its predominant lyrical content, its forms of performance, and its social and institutional settings within sanctioned assembly—are uniform.

In the above example, Douglass opened for observation the double coding of slave communications that was designed to pass meanings and messages in publicly observable forms and to evade surveillance. He showed how the double coding created by slaves enabled them to share a cultural form like a particular religious song. And such a song, which on the surface was useful to both whites and blacks, could serve as the site for deep cultural antagonisms. Slaves and their overseers might mutually embrace the surface forms of culture, but beneath the cultural form, claimed Douglass, waged a subterranean struggle over the representation of meanings that involved not just the control over symbolic practices, but ultimately the control of a captured population. Nat Turner used "Steal Away" to summon a clandestine meeting.[26] As Genovese points out, "When the meeting [of slaves] had to be held in secret, the slaves confronted a security problem. They would announce the event by such devices as that of singing 'Steal Away to Jesus' at work. To protect the meeting itself, they had a presumably infallible method; they would turn over a pot 'to catch the sound' and keep it in the cabin or immediate area of the woods."[27] Harriet Tubman used spirituals as codes to communicate with slaves. "Go Down, Moses" summoned those she was prepared to help escape through the underground railroad; "Wade in the Water" was used to warn slaves to confuse tracking bloodhounds. Douglass revealed how a presumably unifying cultural form could host two struggling social groups, slaveholders and slaves, who each made a quite different use of the same song and the same practice. Douglass thus exposed slave culture—which was not just black culture as a realm of autonomous practices, but rather the cultural relationship between blacks and whites through the larger social framework of slavery.[28] As we shall see, it is precisely the sensibility of this relationship that is lost as the position of the Negro spiritual advances from the earlier ethnosympathetically driven protoethnographic accounts to its place in modern professional and scientistically driven folklore.

Print revelations of the inner workings of slave culture would seem risky. Such intelligence could be used against the fledgling black public spheres. But owners and overseers already knew about the deep contradictions engendered through the religious franchise. They had been apprehensive from the outset about slaves learning religion. The religious dimensions of the slave revolts had already confirmed such concerns. Owners and overseers were not oblivious to the fact that slaves double coded their songs. Charity Bowery, a slave interviewed by Lydia Maria Child in the aftermath of the Turner revolt, had noted that slaves experienced brutal retribution when singing the line "There's a Better Day a Coming."[29] The publication of such secrets did not give owners new knowledge of public secrets.[30] Douglass's revelation did not produce what the Gestalt psychologists called "aha experiences," resulting from the new awareness of new figure/ground relations. What Douglass's inside information did accomplish, it would seem, was to create a new and different kind of cultural significance. It gave to white abolitionists a genuinely insightful as well as politically flattering knowledge: cultural interpretation sanctioned by an insider. And with this key, abolitionists could leap to the great presumption that they could apply their ethnosympathy with some shrewd intelligence. Having been given the inside scoop, they could grasp the inner meanings of the slave's song more accurately than could the slaves. The readers' advantage was their position outside the circle; they could be objective. After all, Douglass admitted the lack of detachment of a slave who sang songs that expressed his or her total engulfment within slavery: "I did not, when a slave, understand the deep meaning of those rude and apparently incoherent songs. I was myself within the circle; so that I neither saw nor heard as those without might see and hear." Singing slaves had only a limited knowledge of what their practices really meant; they were not able to see and appreciate the very authenticity that characterized their own song making. As chattel, slaves did not have the luxury of repositioning themselves to look in from the outside. Bondage precluded that, and violence held them in check. Presumably, sympathetic outsiders and former slaves were able to make that separation. Here, one of the meanings of authenticity comes into sharper focus: authenticity is an ascribed and appreciated dimension of cultural activity rather than an urgent and lived activity. Authenticity is thus observed, witnessed, caught by a spectator who recognizes the category of authenticity as an abstraction.

Yet the suggestion that slaves lacked a critical knowledge of their own song making seems preposterous. On the contrary, slaves were not caught by the immediacy of their own songs and thus were not blinded to their meanings. They knew the meaning of those "deep meanings" and the larger stakes involved precisely because they were insiders who spoke to fellow inhabitants inside the circle of slavery. Why else would slaves have gone to the trouble of forging elaborate codes underneath ostensibly restricted codes if they did not know the meanings of their own songs? Why would a people syphon off so much psychic and cultural energy toward the production and maintenance of the deeper river of collective meanings that fed such a well documented pool of clandestine cultural practices? If slaves were capable of revolting and rebelling, then they were certainly able to sing about the meaning of things and of the world they wished to change or leave. Meaning, not confusion, drives the strategies to convene, cultivate, and protect a clandestine sphere and the making of what James Scott has called "hidden transcripts." Meaning is both the *impetus* and the *outcome*; it is the hermeneutic circle of the process of such song making. Song making, after all, was central to the slaves' abilities to produce a discursive grasp of slavery, despite the fact that such collective activity and communal expression, such cultural work, operated within the context of surveillance and, in many cases, perpetual repression. Forging collective meanings and practices provided slaves with solidarity and enabled them to express things of common importance. This was always a delicate matter that took place through predominantly masked forms that enabled them to evade retribution.[31]

It would seem disingenuous that Douglass would attribute to himself the same kind of misunderstanding of black music that was pervasively characteristic of outsiders. For outsiders, black song making was primarily "rude and incoherent" (at least before Douglass demonstrated how slave songs were actually elaborate and coherent). Few whites actually understood black song making enough to cross the barriers that divided "noise" from meaningful sound. Given that singing was one of the few forms that enabled them to evade the surveillance of collective interactions, slaves had all the reason to map their social lives through making songs. They were making them far from blindly. To think otherwise, as Douglass suggested (to his white Northern readers), and with a sympathetic heart, was to adopt a view fitting to romantic rescuers who could for the first time find black song makers and their songs user friendly. That slaves might lack insight into their cultural practices actually tantalized the sympathetic outsider who was ready to aid in the proper and appreciative interpretation.

Such interpretive benevolence was an easy plank to add to the abolitionist platform and was well suited for a small but significant literary public willing to board. It was a cultural development that had plenty of additional support. In the two decades prior to the war a burgeoning market for all types of writings on slavery had emerged. With the rise of the antislavery movement and the proliferation of antislavery literature, former slaves like Douglass, were being launched on a national—or at least a northern—tour. Such cultural production quickly engendered a significant number of easy-chair readers who could vicariously consume the images of pathetic, emaciated slaves cringing under the whips of cruel masters. In the new antislavery literary field there was something for the sympathetic book-buying literary highbrow as well as for the sentimental middlebrow. The South and its enslaved inhabitants could be known intimately through the representations of a slave culture that became part of the symbolic arsenal of the abolitionist movement. Those who were not attracted to antislavery literature, and who did not find slavery offensive, could always find supportive representations of blacks, free or enslaved, in the racial caricature of minstrelsy.

But let us not lose sight of the fact that Douglass was a superb practitioner in the field of cultural politics. Though he was not an ethnographer, he was preparing the cultural ground upon which protoethnographic probes into black culture would soon take place. And he was not gripped by delusion or self-denial. Douglass, with his own fiery eloquence, was effective in agitating the antislavery sensibility, and quite good at mediating between the market for critical populist ideas and the moral structure of Christian sympathy. Douglass knew that dismantling slavery required significant support from whites in the North, and he worked successfully to garner that backing. After reading Douglass's narrative, the radical Unitarian minister Theodore Parker said of the new black literary genre: "all of the original romance of Americans is in them, not in the white man's novel."[32] In his widely read travel narrative, Frederick Law Olmsted had nothing but praise for Douglass: "All the statesmanship and kind mastership of the South have done less, in fifty years, to elevate and dignify the African race, than he in ten." Douglass and other blacks who had joined their voices to the antislavery cause were held in the highest esteem. As far as Olmsted was concerned, "There are no white men in the United States that display every attribute of strong and good soul better than some of the freed slaves."[33] Douglass exercised good political sense in providing the tools of cultural interpretation to fellow abolitionists. He pulled back the veil of slave culture. Along with the battery of Garrisonians and other radical abolitionists, he helped recruit sympathetic northerners to join the intensifying moral and cultural war against slavery.

Black music after Douglass was accessible black music—black noise transformed into sounds within a recognizable cultural and spiritual order. By decoding the encoding process he showed how these songs came about, discussed their content, and related their lyrics to psychic as well as social functions. When Douglass wrote about the songs of sorrow he was attempting to ground and deepen an already emergent pathos toward slaves. This he did. More important, in opening up black song making he helped fashion the emerging template for perceiving what kind of songs slaves sang, why they sang such songs, and how listeners were genuinely to hear them. And he commanded cultural authenticity; he was, after all, knowledgable about slavery, having been a slave. Now black song making could be keyed and examined with interpretive profit by outsiders. Douglass had inaugurated the sociology of black American music.

The new key, however, seemed to open particular doors of perception. As did many others, Fredrika Bremer singled out as representative the "spiritual intoxication in song and prayer, and religious joy, which is seen and heard at the religious festivals of the negro people." But what a contrast between Fredrika Bremer's account and that of Frederick Douglass. Nowhere in Douglass's narrative is there a description of the intoxicating religious joy that Bremer thought she heard. When he does describe being forced into religious practices by his master, he renders his behavior as sullen, resentful, and recalcitrant.[34] Indeed, the view that slaves sang because they were happy was a distortion that Douglass insisted on rectifying. Even in the North the appreciation for the music of slaves, which Douglass tried to cultivate in his narrative, was thwarted by a popular perspective equating the slave's music with a presumed state of happiness. Douglass was "utterly astonished . . . to find persons who could speak of the singing, among slaves, as evidence of their contentment and happiness."[35] Certainly, this perspective of happy slaves made more sense in the South. There, the practice of slavery was being challenged by a growing abolitionist movement, and the challenge was met by defenders who framed slavery as an appropriate and beneficent institution best able to provide for the blacks in their care. Slaves, argued proslavery spokespersons, were appreciative of this benevolence, and their habitual singing was interpreted as proof of their contentedness under slavery. But force, not surprisingly, managed such presumed consent. The English actress Frances Kemble, wife of an American slave owner, noted that owners and overseers attempted to cultivate what they considered a display of desired affect. This involved prohibiting "melancholy tunes or words" and encouraging instead "nothing but cheerful music and senseless words." In Kemble's assessment, owners disapproved of the "sadder strains" of emotional expressions or of "any reference to their particular hardships" because they affected the slaves in ways that made managing them more difficult.[36] As George Rawick notes in a discussion of the connection between racism and slavery,

> The more slavery was incorporated into the world capitalist market, and the more paternalism became obviously limited by great exploitation, the more the slave owners tended to withdraw from reality and to build up, even for themselves, the image of patriarchal, paternalistic relations. The less true in fact it was, the more the Southern master class believed that slavery was beneficent, the more they became systematically blind to its horrors, and the more they either turned its operations over to overseers or sold their slaves to new men who were hacking plantations out of the bottom lands of the Mississippi.[37]

But for Douglass it was "impossible to conceive of a greater mistake" than to associate happiness with the production of music. As Douglass said of himself: "I have often sung to drown my sorrow, but seldom to express my happiness. Crying for joy, and singing for joy, were alike uncommon to me while in the jaws of slavery."[38] Regardless of Douglass's accounts of what he thought were the predominant conditions under which singing functioned, the spiritual had emerged as a point of peculiar cultural gravity. Whether the songs were of joyful intoxication or of sorrow, their presumably isolatable religious content was what seemed to matter. By investing and attributing black expressions with religious value, abolitionists were able to hear black music in ways that were compatible with the emerging schemas of ethnosympathy. The modernization of cultural analysis had taken hold on the racial margins.

Cultural Quests and Spiritual Proclivities

Douglass had thematized the songs of sorrow for the new white reading public sympathetic to the antislavery crusade, and his insights were helpful in the ensuing efforts to mine the spirituals with the new pathos that

Douglass himself helped introduce and codify. Douglass, however, did not create the quest for authenticity; he merely strengthened the currents connecting it with black subjectivity. The new interpretive schemas of disenchanted cultural elites fused humanitarian reformist ideologies with the larger romantic quest for authenticity. Their pursuit was driven in part by the view that there were things of human value, things tangible as well as intangible, that had to be protected and preserved, even salvaged, from the damaging power of an already rampant modernity. The new ethnosympathetic hearing of black music was configured partly within this antimodern sensibility.

The first issue of the *Atlantic Monthly*, which appeared in November 1857, raised the connection between music, cultural authenticity, and the downside of modernity. An anonymous column entitled "Music" juxtaposed the specter of factories, railroads, mills, and profit-seeking "speculation" against the backdrop of the major economic depression that took place in 1857. Wild speculation had produced the collapse of railroad stocks and banking; northern manufacturing floundered. These developments instilled a "panic" that reverberated throughout the North. An uncontrollable economic machine was in turn contrasted with what the new powerful and runaway market society threatened—"Art." And art was the "ideal, feminine element of life." The article posed the questions:

> What will the Muses do in these hard times? Must they cease to hold court in opera-house and concert-room, because stocks fall, factories and banks stop, credit is paralyzed, and princely fortunes vanish away like bubbles on the swollen tide of speculation? Must Art, too, bear the merchant's penalties? [O]r shall not rather this ideal, feminine element of life, shall not Art, like woman, warm and inspire a sweeter, richer, more ideal, though it be a humbler home for us, with all the tender love and finer genius, now that man's enterprise is wrecked abroad? Shall we have no Music? ... Panic strangles life, and the money-making fever always tends to panic. Panic is the great evil now, and panic needs a panacea. What better one can we invent than music?[39]

Of course the music the essay referred to was not the music of slaves, but an imagined and idealized music that signified an as-yet-not-produced American high culture. In an ensuing volume, the *Atlantic Monthly's* music column expressed the desirability of a more distinct American cultural identity by arguing that trained and capable composers ought to develop "a national school of music."[40] Such music would aid the quest for an elite-based, autonomous (e.g., non-European) American cultural identity in the context of a rapidly changing society.[41] As an emergent highbrow magazine devoted to "literature, art, and politics," the *Atlantic Monthly* represented among the cultural bourgeoisie a growing desire to nurture the development of a distinctly American elite culture.

Many social and political currents fed into the quest for cultural nationalism,[42] but here it is important to note the relationship that Transcendentalism as a religious and philosophically based intellectual movement had with the critical abolitionist's interest in the black spirituals (a connection I explore more fully in chapter 5) and a more inchoate cultural and aesthetic nationalism that was taking shape around the mid-nineteenth century. It seems reasonable to view Transcendentalism as an important and perhaps primary forerunner to the mid-nineteenth-century quest for an Americanist (protonationalist) aesthetic. As Clarence Gohdes notes, Transcendentalism inspired a number of important periodicals that began publishing in the 1840s, such as the *Dial* and the *Radical.* These publications provided an early literary outlet for the expression of antimarket cultural criticism. As literary venues they were important forerunners to the coming of the more successful *Atlantic Monthly.*[43] As Alexander Kern points out, Transcendentalism drew upon the thinking of Unitarian ministers like Edward Everett, who called for an American literature, and William Ellery Channing, who held up the ideal of an American writing that should "do more than express the utilitarian side of American life." Transcendentalism helped express a "rebellion against the cultural dominance of Europe."[44]

The attempt to forge a distinctly American criticism of music as well as to prod composers to produce new music was being championed in the pages of the John Dwight's new journal, *Dwight's Journal of Music. Dwight's Journal,* which began publication in 1852 and continued to 1881, served as an independent periodical of musical scholarship and criticism aimed at edifying the role of music in American society, and it shaped and influenced the discourse on professional music during the years of its publication. The journal even devoted important discussion to the cultural significance of black American music and black musicians.[45] John S. Dwight, the journal's founder, was born in 1813, graduated from Harvard University in 1836, and settled on a career as a Unitarian minister. In 1840 he abandoned the ministry and devoted his time to performing, studying, and criticizing music. He followed Transcendentalism, was involved in Associationism, and was an active member of the alternative community of Brook Farm, which attracted many of the luminaries of the Transcendentalist and Christian socialist movements.

Transcendentalism had an important impact on the notion of authenticity that critical abolitionists sought in the black spirituals. The idea that nature harbored truth and that social conventions tended to obscure rather than reveal this truth was central to Transcendentalist thought. In the wake of romanticism, the concept of authenticity was no longer limited to the older hermeneutical argument based on the traditionalist forms of religious authority. Indeed, in their intellectual, political, and aesthetic response to early modernity, romantic thinkers fretted over the loss of authenticity and launched an early search for subjects who might represent the holdout of authenticity against the pressures of social change. The romantic response to modernity enabled some to detach authenticity from its older moorings in traditional religious thought, and this led to a search for authenticity among new as well as more worldly places—hence their interest in idealized subjects like "noble savages," innocent, Old World peasants, and in the American case, slaves.

For disenchanted intellectuals at the fringes of New England's cultural bourgeoisie, authenticity (nebulous as it was) was a precious good under attack by modernity, an attack that was particularly acute because it came through the unstoppable forces of capitalism, utilitarianism, and the tandem developments of industrialization and market society. Transcendentalists like Henry David Thoreau dreaded such progress. Transcendentalists thus placed emphasis on the individual's capacity to divine truths by transcending social as well as theosophical artifices. This orientation, of course, put a premium upon the authenticity-seeking self.

The interest in authenticity was thus not new to the critical-liberal wing of northern intellectuals, especially those affiliated with Unitarianism (or what has been called "Harvard moral philosophy") and Transcendentalism, Unitarianism's critical offshoot.[46] But their interest in black song making was new. In the hands of seekers after the inner truths of revealed religion—as were the most radical American Transcendentalists, who relied heavily upon Hindu religious thought in particular and upon a more diffuse notion of Orientalism in general—the truthful feelings attributed to black subjects represented an unimpeachable sentiment. The slave (as a humanistic abstraction) might even actually provide the most genuine case for that sought after essence of humanity.

All of these aspects—the romantic response to modernity, the loss of confidence in traditional theology and authority, the clamor for remaking society through reform, the quest for an elite-based, autonomous high culture distinct from European imitation and for a home grown authentic music found in the racial hinterlands of slavery—combined in the attitudes of the critical abolitionists who discovered and elevated the spirituals because they resonated with these aspects. It was not easy for the discoverers to find a romanticized, humanistic essence in a subject that was not contaminated by machines, the marketplace, and the worst of the now undesired European pretensions. Yet, the search for such waning as well as idealized causes—in nature, in the cultivation of critical consciousness, and in selected black subjects—occupied those along the most socially critical fringes of liberal Protestant thought. In keeping with romanticism, Transcendentalists wished not only to find authenticity among noble savages and noble theosophies beyond the boundaries of western civilization; authenticity was also to be discovered, salvaged, and rekindled domestically. Such desires fostered the good fit between the antimodern spiritual quest and the quest for the Negro spiritual. The interest that northerners brought to the new hearing of the spirituals thus refracted many of the tensions between moral, religious, and political perspectives shaped in the context of modernity.

Decades before the abolitionists went to the occupied South to garner song specimens from former slaves, the Transcendentalists had pointed toward a radical spiritual idealism conceived as an antidote to, as well as a therapeutic retreat from, industrial society. In his pursuit of an authentic consciousness unfettered by social institutions, Thoreau's self-willed social isolation in the cabin on the shores of Walden Pond embodied the most antisocial strains of antimodernism. Other disenchanted northerners attempted to establish utopian experimental communities in the hope of creating alternatives to the calculating business culture that surrounded and penetrated modern life.

But by the late 1840s, communitarian utopianism had waned, and the antislavery and women's rights movements had ascended in importance. The battle was to be fought within, not outside of civil society. And by 1860 the battle lines were drawn long and deep. Life had become irreversibly complicated; industrialization was not going to go away; and slavery remained firmly entrenched and even threatened to spread in the western territories. The fractures in American society would soon turn into civil war. In this context the spiritual, sung by a social subject untouched by modernity, found a peculiar cultural fit within the romantic sensibilities of northern radicals. Beneath the surface of a politically righteous hatred toward slavery and an antimodern melancholy, a newly emerging form of cultural interpretation caught spiritual-singing black subjects in its sights. Transcendentalism reflected an apprehensiveness toward the coming of industrialized market society, a sensibility important in the emergence of the turn to the cultural and racial margins.

But it was the radical abolitionists affiliated with Unitarianism and Transcendentalism who sought distinctly American aspects of culture and authenticity at these margins. They began to probe black music as part of a cultural structure that had a particular place within an Americanist framework. While there were other racialized groups, such as indigenous Indians throughout the continental land mass and Mexican occupants of lands annexed from Mexico during the war of 1848, only blacks were subjects of benevolent passions from the fringe of abolitionist authenticity seekers. Indians were resisting national expansion, and throughout most of the nineteenth century the relationship between the state and the indigenous tribes was bloodshed. The Mexicans of the Southwest region were in the process of being incorporated into the new polity and in many cases the government annexed their lands and re-defined their political place on the lowest rungs of the social hierarchy. Like Indians, Mexicans presented obstacles to the "legal" transfer of land ownership (after military annexation) to the hands of railroad magnates, mining companies, and the thousands of settlers streaming in from the East.[47] Prior to the Civil War the relations between the polity and the Indians and Mexicans precluded the development of the kind of popular romanticism toward them that shaped the new ethnosympathy toward shackled black Christians. Indians and Mexicans did not find themselves objects of the kind of northern critical literary imagination responsible for making Harriet Beecher Stowe's *Uncle Tom's Cabin* (1852) so successful.[48]

Unlike Indians and Mexicans, blacks had always been within the geographic bosom of America, not on its extremities; though as chattel they were denied political status, their central presence *as labor* had fueled the economy of the entire South, an economy that benefited many in the North. With their unique and intimate place within cultural hegemony, slaves at least appeared to echo the grace notes of Protestant proselytization—they sang spirituals. To radical abolitionists (though not necessarily to many slaveholders), their religious singing reflected sanctioned Christian content. The black singing subject thus fit rather well within the quest for a romantically engendered yet politically critical rediscovery of an American heritage.

The interest that northerners brought to the new hearing of the spirituals thus refracted many of the tensions between moral, religious, and political perspectives shaped in the context of modernity. In their new hearing the recently emancipated blacks in the South symbolized the salvaging process of humanitarian reformism in stark terms. Slaves had become candidates to be rescued from a most aberrant and perverse form of social power, and what slavery had long eclipsed could now come into view: the new Negro.[49] It was easy for sympathetic northerners to conclude that Negroes were prone to spontaneous bursts of religious expression. One would expect this view after the cultural ground had been altered by abolitionists like the Garrisonians, and especially by the political sentimentalism found in Harriet Beecher Stowe's enormously successful *Uncle Tom's Cabin*.[50]

As Epstein observed, the image of "the saintly pious slave" represented by Stowe's Uncle Tom had evolved by the second quarter of the nineteenth century."[51] As I suggest here, and will expand in the next chapter, the idea of the slave as a religious singing subject emerged as a cultural trope. This trope contained two interlocking meanings: on the one hand, it referred to the singing slave as a human subject, one who produced and performed, and on the other, to the new cultural subject matter of the black spiritual. Both meanings were linked to the newly exonerated black subject who was understood to display particular signs of cultural authenticity; these signs, seen in their most powerful, distilled, and compressed form, were those associated with the doubled meaning of the new *singing subject*. Nonetheless, the romanticized aspects of the pious slave, rather than the historically nuanced knowledge of religion as a foundation of cultural and ideological grammar, characterized the discovery process during the war years. The sentimentality of Stowe's popular novel was more consistent with critical and reformist populism than with the reflexive pathos-oriented hearing and experientially rooted political testimonies of a Frederick Douglass or a William Lloyd Garrison.

What Douglass had asked sensitive readers to consider was heeded. Not that his sympathetic white readers needed his authority or permission—the desire for the spiritual as the best handle on black subjectivity seemed to be in the air. After Stowe's impact, the thick description of black song making—which is what Douglass attempted to present—was increasingly reduced to clichéd summary statements extolling the black singer's "depth of feelings" or his or her manifestation of the "genuine Negro spirit." As if propelled by an unchecked cultural velocity, such descriptions carried in their wake all humanistic and sensitive comments, discussions, and studies of black music throughout the latter decades of the nineteenth century and early decades of the twentieth century.

Yet what self-flattery it was for abolitionists to think (after Douglass's contribution) that the souls of black folk could be had for the simple price of reading a transcribed song or witnessing a black religious assembly. Every pathos-oriented listener who understood that the spirituals were slavery-induced cries of anguish to God could be a full-fledged cultural interpreter, a reader of what had hitherto been the slave's secrets. Nonetheless, a critical path had been created for the well-intentioned voyeur of the black subject, who had been until recently only a literary enigma in the most tolerant circles of the North. Any sympathetic reader could be a seer and truth teller readily armed to do battle in the war against the Slave Power. Only some singing subjects upon whom to ground and ply this new knowledge were needed. As we shall see, spiritual singing former slaves provided this ground with the commencement of the war, and when the Union annexation of the islands off the coast of South Carolina brought Northerners and freed slaves face to face.

. . . . .

We can now recap the major lines of cultural transformation that helped shape and deliver the spiritual as a cultural object that could be appropriated by the abolitionists. And we can begin to point toward the key figures who took the first important steps in the 1860s to collect the spirituals, who transformed black oral culture into literary texts.

Slaves found the religious franchise a powerful cultural resource to augment their emergence as subjects. As noted earlier, struggles over the interpretation of religious precepts and worldly practices created social antagonisms. Quite logically, the franchise engendered social and political—as well as religious—transformations. As slaves become proselytized, overseers culturally categorized them as either possessing or lacking the rudiments of civilization. This process legitimated the proselytization policies of the moral and religious guardians of antebellum culture, but it also exacerbated cultural struggles. Proselytization, of course, cannot fully account for the rise of black subjectivity.

When abolitionists recognized that slaves possessed salvageable souls, it opened an important door from which nascent (and certainly radical) black subjectivity could emerge. White abolitionists most easily understood slaves as producers of acceptable cultural forms—religious song making. Religious practice was a measure abolitionists could understand—and religious practice that could be cultivated, monitored, and controlled was all the better. But it was religious singing that provided a key to interpret black culture; cultural practices could be defined and understood relative to their proximity to, or distance from, dominant religious norms. In essence, religious norms governed how black music was heard—as aberrant noise or as meaningful sound.

Having emerged through the religious franchise, the new system of cultural recognition rested tendentiously on the relative success of general surveillance—of extending religious instructions while policing black expressivity through rewards, repression, punishment, and violence. By the mid-nineteenth century, black song making under slavery had come to incorporate a long history of struggles of representation and social control, a history of tensions, conflicts, negotiations, and accommodations that were barely submerged in black institutionalized church structures (e.g., those affiliated with mainstream Baptist and Methodist denominations). These structures deepened and rationalized the ties to subject emergence through religion, and thus through "religious singing," as slaves built their relatively autonomous systems of cultural strength out of the long struggle over the *meaning* of the religious franchise.

While proslavery southerners construed religious practices and norms from the vantage point of protecting slavery, radical black and white abolitionists viewed the religious expressivity of slaves as a symbol of slavery's aberration from Christian principles. As a predominantly religious social movement, abolitionism centered upon religious antagonism. Indeed, abolitionism was an expression of it. What more powerful signifying system could radical abolitionists find to ground the notion of a religiously sanctioned inner authenticity than the spiritual (at least for a short while)? Most of the committed abolitionists, whose new cultural perceptions turned appreciatively toward the spirituals, viewed them as the penultimate signifiers of the essential value of new black Christian subjects. In this regard the white radical abolitionist's penchant for the spiritual echoed the more elaborate kind of cultural work that had already been carried out by slave narratives and their radical embrace of— or their embrace of radical—religious principles.

But lost in the echo were the sharper points that the slave narratives had articulated. The critique of the racial norms of civil society, the hypocrisy of racism maintained within a Christian profile, and the failure of slavery advocates to live up to the ethical standards of the most cherished core ideologies—insights and arguments so central to the literary work of black authors—were muted in the new turn toward the singing subjects. Cultural recognition came at the expense of the voices and presence of critical black writers and reading publics that chose not song making (the reception of which was rapidly being overtaken by romantic sentimentalism) but the written political discourses of black literary and political entrepreneurs. The long history of these works paralleled the critical collective function of song making, and both activities were nurtured by social repression. A complex cultural double bind emerged as the spiritual ascended into view, the social crisis of race relations began its eclipse, and the visions of new social ideals were obscured by the new romantic and scientistic glaucoma; as ethnosympathetic listeners increasingly heard the spiritual, a deafness to other grammars of discontent took hold.

As we shall examine more closely, in their penchant for the spirituals the abolitionists drew upon black culture to help them ground and articulate a minority and marginal Protestant struggle within a dominant hegemonic Protestant order. Black culture contributed to the new Protestant disenchantment with the effects that Protestantism itself had unleashed. On the religious front, slaves struggled against a social system of black bondage cloaked in Christianity. White radical abolitionists shared this critique, but they also distrusted the new directions that modern capitalism was taking, particularly the looming and dominant power of an increasingly machine-centered market society that was condoned by an establishment theology quick to equate capitalism with progress. The growing critiques of slavery and capitalism were entwined in ways that ushered in a profound sense of crisis at the edges of the Protestant hegemonic culture. This crisis began to reshape the tensions between race, culture, and modernity, and in its wake came the unprecedented attention to culture on the margins.

The new interpretive conjuncture was full of potentialities, yet it was also fragile. Critical abolitionists had an opportunity to employ a mode of interpretation that could have integrated the narratives and the spirituals, but the spirituals quickly were attributed with their newly recognized "simplicity" and "eloquence," and appear to have trumped the more elaborate insights of other forms of black expressivity. Abolitionists could have also used the new interpretive conjuncture to open, broaden, and deepen the more urgent grammar of egalitarian reform (which, of course, was supposedly one of the charges of the official business of Reconstruction). But what transpired instead was a loss of nerve in the interpretive conjuncture; the turn toward cultural interpretation downplayed such connections. In this process, Negro *religious performativity* was celebrated by the cultural discoverers at the expense of the black-authored dialogical contributions to the larger fate of American civil society. In their capture and embrace of the outer expressions of a black Protestant theology, the discoverers aided in the separations between the problem of everyday politics, the deepening racial conundrums of American institutions, and the new benevolent recognition of black performativity. What the discoverers mobilized on their cultural front was a pathos toward and acceptance of an idealized black theological subject and black cultural practices that corroborated their new cultural preference and their new preference for black culture.

The edification of black culture and the emphasis upon *intrinsic* authentic virtue thus began to carry out a peculiar kind of cultural work that served to eclipse the vital and cognitive connections between slave music, social context, and the desire of former slaves and radical abolitionists for even greater social and institutional transformation. The new cultural interest (its benevolent spirit notwithstanding) began to drive a wedge between black voicings and the social world that such voicings attempted to comprehend and interrogate. As I shall discuss in the next two chapters, this wedge had a romantic, sentimental side as well as a scientistic side. The new developments also readied the ground for an emergent intellectual autonomy that would take the form of *professional* cultural interpretation. And as this professionalism arose, it inherited the already established blind spots and cultivated new ones. As we shall see, professionalism carried its own legitimacy and championed its own institutionalizing forces that "looked for [its] criterion of distinction in the intrinsic nature of intellectual activities, rather than in the *ensemble of the system of relations* in which these activities (and therefore the intellectual groups who personify them) have their place within the general complex of social relations."[52]

By pursuing a scientism that championed a mode of cultural analysis on the racial margins as a relatively autonomous field in itself, professionalized analysis would paper over the social crises of black fate. How this came about in the important work of former Unitarian ministers like Thomas Wentworth Higginson, William Allen, and others, who, in the cultural ferment on the edges of northern Protestantism, produced the installing works that solidified the new cultural interpretation, is what we shall now examine.

FIVE

FROM TESTIMONIES TO ARTIFACTS

The musical capacity of the negro race has been recognized for
so many years that it is hard to explain why no systematic
effort has hitherto been made to collect and
preserve their melodies.
(William Frances Allen, 1867)

Often in the starlit evening . . . [I] have silently approached
some glimmering fire, round which the dusky figures moved in
the rhythmical barbaric dance the negroes call a "shout,"
chanting, often harshly, but always in the most perfect time
some monstrous refrain. Writing down in the darkness, as I
best could,—perhaps with my hand in the safe covert of my
pocket,—the words of the song, I have afterwards carried it to
my tent, like some captured bird or insect, and then, after
examination, put it by.
(Thomas Wentworth Higginson, 1870)

ON APRIL 14, 1861, the long-smoldering antagonisms between
the North and South finally broke out into war. Following the
surrender of Fort Sumter to the Confederate Army, the North,
in one of its first military responses, used the Union's combined army and
navy force to annex Port Royal, a major sea island off the coast of South
Carolina. Port Royal and environs gave the North a strategic foothold
between the major Atlantic ports of the Confederacy. A month after the
fall of Fort Sumter, the first wave of former slaves crossed Union lines at
Fortress Monroe, Virginia, on the Chesapeake Bay. Union Army officials
at Fortress Monroe began the policy of refusing to return refugee slaves
to their southern owners, calling them "contraband of war." As refugee
numbers grew, volunteer groups from the North responded by mobilizing
aid, and this philanthropic endeavor expanded rapidly in the early war
years. Through these efforts, the Port Royal experiment, the first major
program of federally supported Reconstruction in the South, was
launched.[1] A battery of military and volunteer philanthropic personnel
descended upon the recently freed slaves, zealously exercising for the first
time their chance to aid those black subjects who had been up to now
only literary voices, images, and representations within the cultural

arsenal of the North's antislavery propaganda. In the shadow of a major military occupational force, volunteers established a fledgling infrastructure of new institutions. Waves of teachers and ministers—some professional appointees, many exuberant volunteers—convened to operate schools and churches. Managerial teams worked to rekindle the domestic economies of the abandoned plantations. It was in this context of military occupation that northerners with distinct cultural interests in blacks were given the opportunity to pursue the Negro spiritual.

Northerners approached the recently freed blacks with a mixture of benevolent patronage and romantic zeal. And in the blended interests of ethnosympathy and ethnotourism, these visitors considered hearing blacks sing a spiritual an event not to be missed. As William Allen put it, their exposure to former slaves had sparked a "fresh interest" in slave songs. In this early phase of the war, black religious singing took on new cultural gravity. In his own account of his involvement in collecting black songs, Allen noted how the "agents of this mission were not long in discovering the rich vein of music that existed in these half-barbarous people." For visiting northerners, "there was nothing that seemed better worth their while than to see a 'shout' or hear the 'people' sing their 'spirichils.' "[2]

Black song making, which had hitherto been entirely an *oral* cultural form, was on the verge of being transformed into literary representation. The stage was set for the spiritual to surface as a new and distinct cultural discovery. Soon Thomas Wentworth Higginson, William Allen, and others would bring the spiritual into print, and launch black music on a new cultural trajectory. It was first viewed as a social and political testimony, but then rather quickly it was increasingly considered as a modern scientific artifact, a specimen fit for capture by the spreading nets of an emergent ethnoscience.

To assess the appropriation of black music by northern intellectuals requires that we examine important cultural developments that had little to do with black music, but that impacted the emerging forms of interpreting it. This inquiry takes us away from black music making in order to assess how new modes of cultural reception were repositioning it. This analytic route enables us to appreciate the productive effects of ethnosympathy upon this sphere of black expressivity. Though the new modes of interest in reception of and appropriation of black music were never able to fully annex black music, they nonetheless inaugurated a new cultural logic that informed and shaped the discovery, recognition, and assessment of black song making, situating it within the newly emerging ethnoscientific imagination.

Of the cultural forces in operation, new religious impulses deserve to be highlighted. As I shall argue, the ministerial activism associated with the more radical currents of Unitarianism and Transcendentalism appear to have been determinant. Radical Unitarianism and Transcendentalism were crucial in cultivating the growth of northern abolitionism and in launching important criticisms of modern society. As I shall argue, Unitarianism and Transcendentalism also played major roles in shaping the protoethnographic interests that Higginson, Allen, and others brought to the new cultural "field." Higginson's field was his opportunity to live with and command former slaves in Union Army uniform. Allen and others found their field in the opportunity afforded by the North's military incursions into the South, which enabled them to collect the spirituals. Higginson's observations in particular can be situated in relation to significant theological, intellectual, and cultural currents that were central to the ideological forms of Unitarianism and Transcendentalism. My excursion into shifting religious ideologies allows us to assess key developments that spawned theological activism within Unitarianism, and to trace how these in turn shaped social criticisms of modern society that arose from the social crises mapped at the critical edges of Protestantism. More importantly, it allows us to conceptualize abolitionism as a complex cultural conjuncture that contained ideological and religious impulses that further fueled the discovery-oriented cultural turn to the racial margins. Both Unitarianism and Transcendentalism were minority sects within the rapidly changing post-Calvinist Protestantism. Yet they were crucial in the development of the religious orientations of Higginson, Allen, and other figures who launched the enterprise of collecting black spirituals. These theological and philosophical orientations reflected disenchantment with capitalism and market society, and this disenchantment paved the way for the new ethnosympathy that informed the reception of black religious singing.

Contextualizing the interplay of romanticism and disenchantment that operated at the fringes of radical abolitionism allows us to broaden and develop further the argument that the manner in which the cultural discovery of the spiritual developed also eclipsed an aspect of black voicing that the writers of the slave narratives had tried to bring out. In their benevolent but narrow approach to black music, and in their unmitigated desire to overcode it primarily within a restricted religious framework, the critical abolitionists were able to use black music as a conduit to express their own disenchantment with market society. The cultural intellectuals who had emerged as the most sympathetic to the abolitionist movement and who displayed the most interest in the lives and expressive dimensions of slaves edified black culture for its preferred musical virtues. But in doing so they exacted a cost by muting the potential black public sphere and the larger dialogue over the fate of black Americans within civil society. In the process, blacks could be easily envisioned and heard

as spiritual performers (and later as "folk" culture performers and producers) but not as speakers and writers concerned with the larger American dilemma involving the transformation of American institutions
within civil society. What might have flourished was instead truncated.[3]

In understanding their turn away from politics and toward culture and
how they championed the spiritual and aesthetic dimensions of black
song making, we can see how radical northerners drew upon the new
ethnosympathy in ways that enabled them to frame the problem of race
within American civil society in a relatively safe manner, one that merged
cultural benevolence with sociocultural managerialism. In the process,
the new interpretation failed on one front while it succeeded on another.
It greatly expanded the recognition of and receptivity toward black culture. But it also failed to entail any serious commitment to institutional
transformations beyond the juridico-legal abolition of slavery. Rather,
the new culturalism continued to promote what I referred to earlier as
disengaged cultural engagement (see chapter 1). On one hand, it created
an ever-expanding opening for cultural study. On the other, it encouraged a mode of social and political enclosure; black expressivity was
screened, and the "spiritual" forms that were heard engendered intrigued
study as they were admitted into a new *cultural-interpretive reservation*.
In essence, the new interest in black culture was characterized by limited
recognition.

I use the term *reservation* in two of its possible meanings—as a form of
hesitation and as an enclosing tactic. In the first case, the meaning of
reservation involves limits upon reception and interpretation that
proceed hand in glove with preferences and predispositions. In the development being discussed here, the politics of reception demonstrated reservations; romantic and sentimental perspectives appear unable to accommodate social, political, and economic discourses, particularly those
associated with transforming the fate of former slaves (e.g., Reconstruction and substantial egalitarianism). In the second case, the notion of a
reservation invokes a cultural and even institutional parallel to the racial
reservations that were being constructed and maintained for Native
Americans. Native Americans, unlike slaves, were always defined as outside the polity, and beyond the borders of cultural and economic spheres.
Slaves, however, were chattel, a status that obviated total exclusion;
slaves were economic property and politically subordinated within
American civil society. The option to pursue biological exclusion for
slaves through "colonization" (the returning slaves to Africa) was considered by some abolitionists during the first three decades of the nineteenth
century, but free black opposition was intense, and northern radical abolitionists rejected the idea. Of course, the entire economy of the South
would have been in jeopardy had such steps actually been taken. Thus,

the process of black incorporation after slavery took place economically through the resurgent feudalism of sharecropping and debt peonage in the South and through bottom-entry positions of wage labor in the North.

The cultural turn, however, involved more than the creation of a symbolic reservation that admitted black expressivity through the religiously framed windows of selective reception. In mapping black song making, the new cultural intellectuals were taking the first modern steps toward installing the study of *subcultures* in the American context. Fronted by a critical and humanistically oriented cultural bourgeoisie, the new enclosure welcomed the spiritual while it expanded and intensified the benevolent interest in black culture. This interest took place within a small domain of American society, but one that had important knowledge-forming repercussions. Other possibilities of incorporating blacks—options that might have matched this ostensibly benevolent gesture, but within economic and political arenas—were simultaneously stiff-armed and held in abeyance.

As we shall see, an examination of some of the ideological currents behind Unitarianism and Transcendentalism helps bring into focus just how Thomas Wentworth Higginson—a member of New England's "natural aristocracy," a Harvard-educated minister, and a person with long and deep social ties to some of the most influential and important radicals, reformers, and intellectual luminaries in the North—could come to hear and to collect those "words of the song" that could be "carried . . . to [his] tent, like some captured bird or insect." We leave slavery and the spiritual in order to fathom the intellectual reorientations that were beginning to remap the meaning of slavery and slave expressions, and to assess some key dimensions of the discovery process and the cultural logic that operated within a mode of disengaged engagement.

Higginson and Allen are exceptional individuals to consider because of their central role in publishing and providing qualitatively new frameworks for interpreting black song making. Drawing upon the larger trope of natural history, Higginson, I argue, translated the already burgeoning development of ethnosympathy into a more reflexive relationship with black culture through what I call *protoethnography*. This he accomplished through his novel fieldwork. Allen, however, took the protoethnographic incursion a step further by subjecting black musical specimens to a new scientistic taxonomy. What these two key interpreters accomplished in the conjuncture was a synthesis of emergent sensibilities. They helped install a dialogue that blended romanticism with the scientistic quests into the cultural practices at the racial margins. In the process, black music continued to serve as testimony to lived lives, but it was also objectified and reclassified by the new scientistic interest in cultural artifacts. By century's end, the emphasis upon the more scientistic mode of interpretation took on greater institutional weight. Hence, the larger problem can be partially grasped as a shift from testimonies to artifacts.

First Transcriptions

When social crises rupture the normative order, one result is the compression of elaborate and complex cultural discourses into simpler and more urgent forms. The coming of the Civil War appears to have had such an effect upon the awareness, perception, and receptivity of black religious song making. War intensified the quest for additional cultural and ideological weapons against the evil of slavery. What better weapon against slavery than the spiritual, the quintessential expression of black Christians shackled by southern slaveholders?

As Dena Epstein points out, it was at Fortress Monroe where events led to the publication of the first Negro spiritual. The incident is worth noting because it illustrates the initial ties that the discovery process had to the great moral crisis of slavery and war. And as the war proceeded, so too did the discovery of the spiritual. When the Reverend Lewis C. Lockwood was sent by the Young Men's Christian Association of New York to aid the destitute contrabands at Fortress Monroe, he did not go with the intent to hear black music.[4] But he and many others did hear singing throughout the tent camps that sheltered the former slaves. As an incidental listener, Lockwood was deeply moved and impressed by a particular song he first heard on September 1, 1861. He transcribed the song and sent it along with a letter to the secretary of the YMCA, who, in turn, sent it and his own accompanying letter to the *New York Tribune*. The *Tribune* printed the lyrics, making "Go Down, Moses" the first publication of the complete text of a Negro spiritual.[5] The important abolitionist publication the *Anti-Slavery Standard* reprinted the song, and the American Missionary Association, which had sponsored Lockwood's excursion to Fortress Monroe, also offered the song with printed music for sale—"a sweet melody. Price 25 cents."[6] By March 1862 "Go Down, Moses" was available for purchase as sheet music through the Anti-Slavery Office in Philadelphia. The event appears to have stimulated the interests of others in acquiring the texts of spirituals.

The nascent commodification of the spiritual that is evident in these first publications is important in its own right.[7] What I want to highlight, however, is that "Go Down, Moses" was initially received as a song that testified unequivocally to the spiritual plight of the contrabands. It likened the slaves to the children of Israel, and it spoke of their deliverance from bondage. It was heard first and foremost as an *antislavery* song, and its reception marked an interpretive desire to connect song and social circumstance—the very connection between existence and social structure that Frederick Douglass had tried to launch sixteen years earlier.

Yet, it appears that soon after the Negro spiritual had been discovered as an indisputable testimony to slavery, a shift in interest emerged. This shift severed the spiritual from slavery, the social context in which it was produced. The result was that the initial moral connections that the spiritual had with slavery, the social and political tensions that had given the spiritual its initial grammar, withered by the late 1860s. By the time Thomas Wentworth Higginson, William Allen, and other affiliated black culture hunters arranged to print their accounts of black music, the specter of slavery had lost its framing and interpretive power; it was no longer part of the interpretive gestalt. How and why did this happen? If slavery was no longer a salient factor, what kind of interpretive framework was emerging? How might we understand the decontextualizing and recontextualizing developments in which the spiritual was being interpreted?

It could be argued that slavery had ended by the time Higginson and Allen were preparing their works for publication, and thus there was no compelling reason to view the spirituals through an antislavery lens. But this does not account for Higginson's frameworks, which were composed as journal entries during the war when slavery was still in operation. The shift was an interpretive one, and it appears to have moved quickly from one terrain of moral and social crisis to another—from a highly focused concern with slavery to a more nebulously refracted concern with modernity (and in the process it was becoming tied to a modern knowledge of cultural interpretation). This shift also marked the departure from the issues raised by Frederick Douglass; he had used the songs of sorrow explicitly to open a larger discourse on not just the testimonies of inner authenticity or on the evils of slavery, but also on the hopes and aspirations of blacks seeking an equitable inclusion in civil society. But in their pursuit of the spiritual, the abolitionists transformed the cultural ground upon which it was to be understood. Black song making became a site that hosted two general cultural fronts: it helped critical abolitionists to stage their anxieties of social transformations that were altering older modes of living (for both slaves as well as for the new pathos-oriented cultural bourgeoisie), and it hosted the new activities of a modern, ethnosympathetic mode of cultural interpretation. Abolitionists continued to hear religious song making as the sign of the civilizing process; they were, after all, clamoring to champion the latter. They operationalized this older recognition by reinforcing religious singing and repressing black noise, those forms of music that fell beyond recognized religious categories and that lacked the proper, or at least approximate, fit against the template of Protestant hymnology.

In essence (and perhaps in effect), the cultural turn developed in a peculiar direction, one that asked blacks to sing rather than to write about, talk about, or dream out loud their desire to open further the doors of Reconstruction and to probe the pressures that were pushing this door closed. The ending of slavery and the new benevolent reception authorized by a rather limited aesthetic seemed to be concession enough. What is striking about the new culturalism—which begins with the interest in the spiritual and becomes increasingly elaborated with the creation of professional folklore—is its reticence if not its incapacity to include and embrace any additional dialogue that might imagine alternatives to postslavery racial subordination. As I shall discuss here and in the next chapter, the new culturalism's withdrawal from the politics out of which it developed was coupled with the professionalization of cultural analysis.

Renegade Ministers in the Abolitionist Conjuncture

It makes sense to speak of an "abolitionist conjuncture" as a social figuration, one shaped by a number of developments that merge, make possible, and nurture the fledgling cultural turn toward the discovery of blacks as having practices worth fathoming. I have already noted several lines of development that stem from the culture of slavery: the emergence and rationalization of a critical selfhood for slaves, rooted partially in the external attribution of and the internal expansion of soul and subjecthood made possible by the religious franchise; the emergence of the slave narratives as symptomatic of a deeper crisis within religion and American society; and the reception of the spiritual as the preferred cultural practice—the "good culture" among black cultural goods—among slaves. As noted earlier, the slave narratives were certainly deeply grooved voicings within the *racialized* framework of western cultural and political crises. But they were more than a peculiar kind of blackspeak, more than a racial discourse. They spoke of, to, and from the core ideology of Christendom and to the much broader political ideologies of the Enlightenment as well. The cultural origins of the narratives and their sensibilities went deep into the marrow of political and ideological configurations, into the fateful marriage between New World Protestantism and American slavery. This, too, could be said about the cultural origins and sensibilities of their white radical abolitionist counterparts, who found the slave narratives and the Negro spiritual so useful in launching their social critique of an errant society.

Radical abolitionists also had ideological roots that linked them to a Jeffersonian pastoralism represented in the idealized, independent, and autonomous yeoman-farmer. This gentry class was, by the mid-nineteenth century, increasingly caught in the displacing forces of industrialization—and losing cultural ground.[8] The class erosion that members of the northern clergy were beginning to face in the early-eighteenth century had intensified by the early-nineteenth century. In the aftermath of the revolutionary war with England, New England Congregational ministers were already concerned about their social place. As Harry Stout argues, "For New England's clergy, the most frightening aspect of the internal revolution accompanying independence from England was a loss of mastery." At the end of the revolution, Congregational ministers remained the dominant voice in public opinion throughout New England and enjoyed state support, but their hold was precarious. "Belatedly they saw themselves threatened by other speakers in New England and in other 'states' who held very different beliefs about the compatibility of established religion and republican ideology." In the middle states no other established denominational structure possessed the kind of hegemony enjoyed by northern Congregationalists. In the South, the colonial Anglican Church remained hegemonic, but its power had been compromised because of its British loyalism during the revolution. In neither region was there a group of clergymen "even remotely comparable to the Congregational clergy in numbers, social prestige, education, and the ability to dominate public speech in local settings." Congregationalism's potential expansion however was in the process of being checked by the movement toward church-state disestablishment. "Other, more powerful voices," Stout argues, "dominated in these regions and called for a complete separation of church and state. Through these cries for the disestablishment of religion, New England's ministers glimpsed a new social system that would deprive them of the exalted position they had hoped to preserve in first counseling resistance and revolution."[9]

As noted earlier, what followed in the cultural field of struggles was the first Great Awakening, in which the new post-Calvinist and post-Congregationalist Protestant sects emerged to instantiate a major wave of post-revolutionary religious populism; as we saw, this had great import for slaves. As they expanded into the middle-state regions hitherto uncaptured by Congregationalism, Baptists and Methodists targeted the social margins where rural, uneducated whites could be proselytized. And Baptists and Methodists also endorsed (unevenly and not without wrenching internal debate) the view that blacks too ought to be proselytized, thus spurring the tepid commitment of owners and overseers to extend the religious franchise.

Here lies one crucial rub in the context of abolitionism and the sectarian struggles over the fragmented cultural field of midcentury Protestantism: the cultural work carried out by the Methodists and Baptists who were cultivating the rise of black Christianity in the South was politically harvested by the radical northern Unitarians. As northerners embraced the renegade black Christian abolitionists who were themselves the products of proselytization, and who had challenged the South's failure to embody the core principles of religious teachings, they skewed their emphasis toward particular black cultural expressions. The result was a mode of cultural reception conflated with their cultural projections—they preferred to hear a spiritualized Negro who, to the convenience of northerners, appeared to prefer to sing Negro spirituals. With such cultural-interpretive velocity behind them, these songs demanded to be heard with the new and deep ethos of pathos. This new hearing took on such urgency because it held tremendous cultural tension.

While Methodists and Baptists worked the largely neglected lower-and middle-class populations on the frontier, Unitarians in the Northeast were formulating their own social critique. Influenced by Enlightenment idealism, both Unitarianism and Transcendentalism promoted, at least at their radical edges, a quest for a sense of selfhood that was not reducible to modern market society as well as a search for social perfection, and these came with a critique of American society and a growing apprehensiveness toward capitalist modernity. The liberal Protestantism that emerged out of the socially oriented strains of Unitarianism proved to be crucial in the abolitionist conjuncture.

Unitarianism's cultural significance was greatly expanded in 1805 when Henry Ware was appointed as Hollis Professor of Divinity at the Harvard Divinity School. (A little more than half century later, two of his grandchildren, William Frances Allen and Charles Pickard Ware, along with Lucy McKim Garrison, who married the third son of William Lloyd Garrison, would compile and publish *Slave Songs of the United States*.)[10] With Ware's appointment, the Divinity School passed into Unitarian control. The institutional ascendancy of Unitarianism, however, was not without opposition, and departing religious intellectuals formed the Andover Theological Seminary. Unitarianism served as the primary font of "moral philosophy" taught at Harvard during the first half of the nineteenth century. Although Unitarianism was a minority plank within American Protestantism, its importance, as Daniel Howe points out, was in its relationship to the training of American cultural elites.[11]

Unitarian theology articulated some of the more elaborate criticisms of market society, and it played a major role in the rise of critical antislavery ideology in the North. As early as the 1820s, Unitarian minister William Ellery Channing had begun to address the difficulties faced by wage workers under the growth of industrialization, challenging in the process the larger quietism of established Protestant churches. Channing's socially engaged theology focused primarily on the individual, but his concerns expanded the moral dialogue on the plight of the "laboring classes."[12] Poorhouses were proliferating on the eve of disestablishment. As Walter Trattner has pointed out, "In 1824 Massachusetts had eighty three almshouses; fifteen years later the number had increased to one hundred eight, and by 1860 the total had risen to two hundred nineteen."[13] Channing insisted that there were direct links between factory expansion and pauperism. This put Unitarianism in general, and Channing in particular, in the forefront of the new strain within Protestant theology that argued that reform of the individual was not enough to bring about a better society. Orestes Brownson, another Unitarian minister, stressed that "the perfection of the social state" was necessary in order to obtain individual perfection.[14] At the edges of Unitarianism, the importance of society had begun to precede the sanctity of the individual.[15]

A younger generation of aspiring Unitarian ministers who studied at the Harvard Divinity School during the 1830s and 1840s were part of the movement to reconcile the growing pressure of the new industrial society with the new religious impulse for social engagement. The pulpit had traditionally been the societal site for collective critical moral reflection. But by the 1830s the established ministerial public sphere was being outstripped by the growth of critical public politics and discourses associated with social movements. As abolitionism and reformism ascended in social importance, the pulpit began to lose some of its traditional grip upon moral issues and had to compete with emerging social movements, particularly those that focused on abolitionism, working-class advocacy, and women's rights. Socially concerned ministers were increasingly compelled to go to the people—to the populist lyceums, the political gatherings, the public assemblies that marked fledgling social movements—rather to than wait for them to clamor for the limited peripheral space beyond the pay-per-pew seating held for church members who supported their ministers.

Important changes in the status of the ministry membership itself also propelled clergymen to engage new publics beyond church congregations. During the last quarter of the eighteenth century ministers experienced declining rates of tenure. By the 1830s and 1840s the effects of professional status erosion were being felt. The average tenure of a minister in New Hampshire in 1790 was thirty years. This declined to twenty-five years in 1804. By the late 1830s, the average stay with a congregation had shrunken to a short four to eight years.[16] The shortening of tenure, however, did not signal an erosion of religious practice—on the contrary, the field of religion was actually expanding, but along lines of fragmentation, competition, and multidenominational segmentation (a classic example of what Emile Durkheim called "moral density" and the resultant "division of—in this case, moral—labor").[17] As a field in great flux, religion became mobile, contentious, and multicultural; let us remember that the second Great Awakening was occurring at this time, elevating emotional intensity as an external sign of a spiritual awakening that was linked to antiinstitutionalism.

To the chagrin of Unitarian traditionalists, Unitarianism was in the process of producing renegade clergy who were not tied to pulpits and who took part in the leadership of new ideologies and social movements. A further rupture within Unitarian orthodoxy emerged when the young minister Ralph Waldo Emerson presented an alternative theological view of miracles. Emerson, who trained at the Harvard Divinity School, argued against the established view which held that miracles were the manifestations or "performances" of rare interventions from God. It was not the divine, rare miracles that ought to really matter, he insisted, but rather those miracles of a common daily "Nature" in which one's life was a part. Emerson's notion of nature was certainly theologically inspired, but his turn to nature earned him the brand of "infidel" by church conservatives.[18] More important, Emerson's argument with the interpretive schemas of Unitarian belief was an indication of the new desire for a deep value orientation that was not shackled by the limits of traditional Christian theology. Emerson also drew ideas from romanticism, Indian philosophy, and eastern religion (Orientalism). He was not alone in his attraction to the "Orient"; his interests were representative of a significant but limited intellectual formation among a small number who kindled theosophic ideas outside of denominationally sanctioned Christian frameworks.

Emerson's particular contribution to the larger blend of ideas may be his impact upon the American notion of radical individualism, or "self-reliance."[19] It is, however, the Emersonian turn to nature that I wish to flag, for it contained a theory as well as an incipient notion of a way to analyze culture that merged romanticism with natural history. As Bruce Mazlish notes, "Natural History" was "quite the rage in mid-nineteenth-century England. On the eve of the Darwinian revolution, it was still the clergyman's pursuit and the amateur's hobby. 'Collections' of sea shells, beetles, birds, and so forth were to be found everywhere, even in poor people's houses. Such collections joined the city to the country. On a more professional level, they represented the classifying stage of biological science, about to become evolutionary in nature."[20] Emerson, too, had become acquainted with natural history. After viewing the cabinets of natural history in the Jardin des Plantes in Paris, Emerson declared, " 'I will be a naturalist.' " According to Mazlish, "By this he meant a naturalist of the soul, and his first public lectures on his return to America were on 'The Use of Natural History,' where he declared, 'It is in my judgment the greatest office of natural science (and one which is as yet only begun to be discharged) to explain man to himself.'"[21]

Emerson's turn toward nature was motivated not by the pressures of the new scientist consciousness. Rather, it was driven by a theophiloso-phical radicalism, which included a distinct emancipatory interest. In his essay "Nature," which he published in 1836, he wrote, "Nature is made to conspire with spirit to emancipate us."[22] The larger romantic discovery of nature as a source of truth—which led to the inner (psychocultural) turn to the nature of the discoverable authentic self—was a key theme in the Transcendentalist revolt against theological traditionalism. Nature offered emancipation, but to explain this natural virtue—to "explain man to himself"—required language. In search of an axiom, Emerson sketched a theory of nature and its relationship to language:

> Language is a third use which Nature subserves to man. Nature is the vehicle of thought, and in a simple, double, and threefold degree.
>
> 1. Words are signs of natural facts.
> 2. Particular natural facts are symbols of particular spiritual facts.
> 3. Nature is the symbol of spirit.[23]

This theory of language, which is more specifically a theory of transcen-dental emancipation *into* and *through* nature, implied a modern theolog-ical redefinition and reappropriation of nature in which the latter was no longer a source of trouble, a danger to be conquered, or a material realm devoid of spirit as it was for Calvinism. Contrary to its place in Calvin-ism, nature was reclassified as intrinsically good. Interestingly, the young Marx, who was in the process of drawing upon and critiquing Fourier, Bauer, and other Christian socialists, would say something similar in less than a decade in his provocative passages on the ontology of human na-ture as "species being."[24]

For Emerson, to study words, signs, and symbols was to read toward the source of all signs: nature. This is one major way in which romantic primitivism shares in a struggle for truth as *natural fact*, and is one of the modern recipes for conjuring authenticity through uncovering it histori-cally or recovering it in the present. "As we go back in history," Emerson argued, "language becomes more picturesque, until its infancy, when it is all poetry; or all spiritual facts are represented by natural symbols."[25] As I shall discuss below, this particular kind of theory of nature, as truth to be accessed through *expressivity*, is kindred to the underlying epistemol-ogy that shaped the less-articulate cultural gropings of Higginson and Allen, and many of the less-reflexive discoverers of the Negro spiritual who carried out this Unitarian-Transcendentalist interpretive impulse as they called on the cultural and racial margins to kindly yield the truths of a nonalienated naturalism that could be used to deal with the problems created by an errant market society.

Henry David Thoreau, another Harvard Divinity School student, turned to nature as well. And his turn was away from not just the pulpit and popular lyceums, but from virtually anything remotely organized or institutionalized. His retreat from civil society to nature was a solitary one (which he did share through his writings and occasional public lectures); such retreat was necessary in order to transcend the inherited fetters of society if one was to achieve a unity with one's consciousness in (and of) nature. Thoreau vehemently rejected market society for its rapacious domination toward nature, and its capacity (following Reverend Channing) to reduce workers to the "wage slaves" that the new business culture seemed to require. In this regard, his concern with what modern society did to workers resonated with the emerging labor movement's deep anxieties over the possibility of "free" white workers slipping into slavelike conditions.[26]

Such concern resonated with core Unitarian beliefs, such as the idea that the perfectibility of the soul ought to be linked to the social world through the perfectibility of society. Unitarianism and its critical-liberal offshoot, Transcendentalism, carried the concepts of perfectionism even further by insisting that individuals were compelled to transcend spiritual as well as social flaws. In being "fundamentally united in condemning formalism in religion and literature, Lockean 'sensationalism' in philosophy, and all that was inhuman or materialistic in the popular social morality,"[27] Transcendentalists supported the idea that the destruction of the oppressive aspects of the social order and the rearrangement of society could enable the individual and the social to blossom. Such a vision was radically reformist in spirit; it was, after all, first concerned with the spiritual realm. However, Transcendentalists, particularly those at the forefront of its philosophical helm, like Emerson and Thoreau, had strong individualistic and antiinstitutional orientations. They were not joiners of movements; they displayed a practiced disdain for organizations and cherished their sense of critical distance. Some tried to engender alternative collective strategies by which to live—such as the Associationists' Brook Farm. By and large, with regard to the sphere of formal politics and social institutions, Transcendentalists preferred disengagement.

The reformist impulse, which preceded and encircled many of the social and political issues during the middle of the nineteenth century and afterward, was powerful. As this impulse moved beyond the inner walls of the new religiously sanctioned solipsism of some hard-core Transcendentalists, it provided an ethos that was brought outward by its more socially oriented carriers into increasingly broader circles of civil society.

Indeed, when we trace the broader idea of self and social perfectibility—as it was manifested in radical evangelicalism, then taken up in the more institutionalized forms of the Baptist and Methodist denominations, and then elaborated by the critical Unitarian cultivation of the ties between the self and social change—we see how an orientation that was initially religious and limited to a primarily internal concept (the autonomous Christian self) was rationalized in progressively external directions, from the sacred to the secular, from inner spiritual crisis to institutional operations. In essence, the humanitarian reformist impulse was a movement—from soul to society, from theology to societal intervention. The modern notion of perfectibility of the self became a way of envisioning social structure.[28]

Social perfectibility is of course a utopian ideal, but this sensibility helped spawn some important utopian experiments. Several decades before the outbreak of the Civil War, disenchanted Transcendentalists and Associationists had launched attempts to resist and reject the dominant culture. In an attempt to avoid the new gesellschaft by returning to gemeinschaft, the Associationists tried in the 1840s to carve out an alternative, autonomous, and rather immediate community in the social experiment of Brook Farm. Through Brook Farm, those who were attracted to Associationism sought to disengage from the dominant trends and ideologies in American society by exploring experimental modes of living.[29] It should be noted, however, that the Associationists did not see themselves as simply seeking spiritual renewal; their project was aimed at personal and social reform. Greatly influenced by the writings of Fourier, a central figure in early-nineteenth-century French social utopianism, the Associationists saw themselves in pursuit of secular renewal.[30] Established in 1840, the Associationists' Brook Farm lasted only seven years. It was more a symbol and symptom of disenchantment with the business ethic than it was a counterinstitutional strategy.

Nonetheless, the idea of perfectibility engendered a profoundly important form of social criticism aimed at industrial modernity. To the Transcendentalists and Associationists, the sense of spiritual bankruptcy and vacuousness that came with market society, the same dispirited ennui that Weber pointed to as one of the major cultural outcomes of the rationalization of Calvinism into bureaucratic capitalism, represented a major modern crisis. The Transcendentalist retreat from mainstream society was to avoid market society. In Perry Miller's words, Transcendentalism grounded a "revolt against the rationalism of their fathers." It also represented an attempt to found a "new religious expression in forms derived from romantic literature and from the philosophical idealism of Germany."[31] This revolt amounted to "the first outcry of the heart against the materialistic pressures of a business civilization." Transcendentalists were "Protestant to the core," but they fostered a "protest against what is customarily called the 'Protestant Ethic': they refuse to labor in a proper calling, conscientiously cultivate the arts of leisure, and strive to avoid making money."[32]

It was thus not so much antislavery sentiment that helped ground Transcendentalism as it was the growing disenchantment with market capitalism and its system of morality and ethics. In their neo-Rousseauian view, Transcendentalists saw modernity as threatening to drive a wedge between the individual (and, by extension, society) and a spiritualized notion of nature. Yet because of its antibusiness attitude, Transcendentalism proved quickly to be a crucial ally to the radical antislavery forces. Slavery was in itself morally repugnant, but it also carried tremendous significance for the most radical abolitionists, who saw the "peculiar institution" as the grand analogy to the tendencies of a runaway system of industrial servitude. Radical labor leaders in the North drew parallels to the "wage slavery" foisted upon them by the new modes of industrial labor.[33] Many sectors of organized labor in the North also feared the flood of black wage earners should slavery be dismantled. The slavery analogy was also central to the emergent concerns of women, who were attempting to secure political rights. The critiques of slavery applied to women, as well; like slaves, white women could not vote. Thus, their capacities for public representation were severely curtailed, and what political rights they had were negligible.[34]

For the radical Unitarians and Transcendentalists, slavery as well as the coming of the machine in the garden were, from their different origins, enterprises that had been erroneously justified within a quasi-Christian ethos. Progress had long been cited as evidence of God's approval of the entrepreneurial and utilitarian self (embodied, as Max Weber described so well, in the figure of Benjamin Franklin), and, by extension, of the nation's religious virtue. But it was precisely this religious nexus, which blended an older traditionalism with the power of capitalism and industrialization, that Thoreau abhorred. Christian logic had produced a Christian nightmare: "Let us consider," wrote Thoreau, "the way in which we spend our lives. This world is a place of business. What an infinite bustle! I am awaked almost every night by the panting of the locomotive. It interrupts my dreams. There is no sabbath. It would be glorious to see mankind at leisure for once."[35] As noted earlier, the Christian nightmare had already surfaced in the slave narratives.

While a significant contingent among disenchanted cultural bourgeoisie in the North had found slavery repulsive, many more among the ascending economic bourgeoisie, the new businessmen of manufacture and trade, were relatively indifferent to slavery. Many had investments in the South. As Ralph Waldo Emerson observed, "though slaveholders are apt to have a bad temper, and vicious politics,—a strong desire to keep the peace, and a good humor with them, is felt not only by the financial authorities in State street and Wall street, but also by the cotton-spinners, the freighter, the shoe-dealers, the cabinet-makers, the printers, the booksellers, and by every description of northern salesmen."[36] For these financial and market players, slavery was not initially an issue, but it became one once there was concerted effort to expand slavery westward in ways that might compromise northern economic hegemony over the larger economy.[37]

The troubling connections between market society and slavery were of deep concern to Theodore Parker, one of the most popular and certainly most radical among Unitarian ministers of the 1840s. Parker's engagement as a public intellectual is important because it is through Parker that our elliptical circuit through Unitarianism and Transcendentalism allows us to return to a deeper appreciation of Thomas Wentworth Higginson and how his engagement in some of the political struggles in the North helped prepare his cultural turn to the racial margins. Parker, who even as a religious radical was able to remain a denominational minister, straddled Unitarianism and Transcendentalism. He preached of the inner goodness of the individual trapped in a society that was increasingly governed by an emergent industrialism. By 1840 Parker's ministerial activism and strong advocacy for reformist causes had brought him into increasingly antagonistic relations with mainstream Unitarians. Ostracized (though not removed) by establishment ministers, Parker took his sermons on the public lecture circuit and plied his activist theology of attacking slavery and industrial servitude. Parker's sermons, which he delivered with intensity and inspiration, were considered events; they frequently drew several thousand audience members during his peak popularity.

Also in Parker's congregation was William Lloyd Garrison, the leader of the most radical abolitionist group in the antebellum era.[38] Garrison and his fellow black and white abolitionist followers, who were able to emerge in the opportunity structure engendered by Protestant schisms, represented an important spin-off of the critical Christian disenchantment with both modern society in the North and slavery in the South. It was through his antislavery work that Garrison befriended Frederick Douglass (Garrison wrote an introduction to the 1845 publication of Douglass's *Narrative*), who joined Garrison's movement until Douglass decided to publish his own antislavery paper, the *North Star*.[39] Another member from Parker's congregation was Franklin Sanborn, who later became the first president of the American Social Science Association, which formed in 1865.[40] Parker practiced what he preached. Along with Sanborn, Higginson, and three others, he helped form the "Secret Six" to provide financial and political support for the white abolitionist John

Brown. In 1859, Brown and fewer than fifty accomplices planned to incite a slave uprising. Their raid upon the federal arsenal at Harpers Ferry, Virginia, failed, and Brown was hanged.[41]

Deep cultural currents cut into the larger socioreligious terrain in both the South and the North, currents that also flowed into the abolitionist conjuncture. Northern liberal Protestants attempted to move from an earlier position of wanting to perfect the soul, to that of perfecting civil society as well as souls. Similar developmental ground was covered with the rise of slave subjectivity within the contours of the religious franchise. For blacks, a critical subjectivity had emerged partly and inadvertently when they were bestowed with salvageable souls. Religion provided a cultural terrain that engendered profoundly important collective forms and stimulated the development of new practices, and these, in turn, expanded social subjectivities that culminated in the slave narratives as well as the Negro spirituals. Development in both cases emerged through those Christian teachings that had the most widespread *social* implications. Such principles included the notion of Christian individualism, of the self as free and equal to all others in the eyes of God, and the rejection of human subjection to unsanctified institutional authority. The desired transcendent social order embodied these core principles, which were consistent with Protestantism's deepest psychotheological assumptions of the sanctity of radical individualism. Nonetheless, the cultural work of the slave narratives and the cultural work taking shape on the critical fringes of Unitarian and Transcendentalist antimodernism spoke a kindred grammar within abolitionist conjuncture. It is not surprising that the slave narratives struck such a chord with Theodore Parker, who viewed them as containing the "original romance of Americans."[42]

It is in this confluence of cultural, political, and economic developments that abolitionism emerged with its sprawling sensibility and many facets. Abolitionism was not merely an irruption of self-willed moral entrepreneurs who quite simply had the fate of enslaved blacks foremost in their hearts and who knew good ideas (abolition, free labor, and in some cases the emancipation of women) and a bad social system (slavery) when they saw them. Nor was the abolitionist conjuncture simply a restricted cultural affair in which slaves were being given—and struggling intensely to remake a broken—subjectivity and sense of place. The reconceptualization of social subjects and collective identities was actually much more widespread; it was part of a social configuration in which multiple and interlocking forces constituted a larger social, political, economic and cultural field that was taking the shape of humanitarian reformism. After all, reformism in general and abolitionism in particular were central to the struggles with which older institutions coped with the pressures of modernity. Reformism provided the social site where moral entrepreneurs fought to maintain as well as radically to alter institutions. Reformist battles were certainly concerned with philosophical, ideological, political, and religious ideals; and when translated into flesh and blood, reform pivoted necessarily upon distinct social subjects—slaves, women, wage laborers, the poor, youth, and the growing mosaic of white ethnic immigrants. Indeed, this panoply of emergent social subjects came to occupy the grammar of social talk.[43] But most pressing was the urgency surrounding the abolition of slavery.

Within the abolitionist conjuncture, the renegade ministers were inadvertently laying the ground for the new protoethnography. They had thematized the problems of modern society and opened the quest for authenticity. And in keeping with the important currents of Orientalism, the search pointed away from sites of industrial as well as western contamination. As I shall suggest, the fusion of naturalism and romanticism pointed the junior Transcendentalist Higginson toward the subjective culture of the black soldiers, but this would take shape only after he took the opportunity to command a black regiment of contrabands.

As former Unitarian ministers, Thomas Wentworth Higginson and William Frances Allen inherited the intellectual ferment created within Unitarianism and Transcendentalism. Higginson, however, embodied more clearly the intellectual and ideological tensions that surfaced within these two cultural fronts. Though certainly a modern reformer, he represented the legacy of an older romanticism, which he connected to the retrieval and interpretation of black song making. And it is Higginson who, in his *Army Life in a Black Regiment*, actually wrote about black song making within the framework of what we today would recognize as the "participant observer" in the context of fieldwork. Allen and his fellow editors, on the other hand, were assemblers. And Allen, who wrote the important and lengthy introduction to *Slave Songs of the United States*, was much more the modern classifier. In comparison to Higginson's poetic flair, Allen's staid writing style fit the new scientistic objectivism, and he pushed his and others' observations toward a more modern mode of analytical description. Allen, too, was a retrievalist. Though he displayed little of the romanticism found in Higginson, he also carried out field work, and gathered the first large collection of black songs that included not just transcribed lyrics but also musical notation. The added dimension of musical notation was another feature that Allen and fellow editors of *Slave Songs* brought to the discovery enterprise; it reflected the coming protoscientific sensibility that stressed the consciousness of objectivity, accurate capture, and classification.

These two figures, along with others, worked together quite collegially. Both were in the Port Royal environs during and after the Civil War. And in their combined sensibilities and orientations, both were central to the quite small number of cultural intellectuals who helped set into motion the early interpretive schemas that fed the new cultural-interpretive work. How it was absorbed by the fledgling black colleges after the Civil War and how it paved important paths to the rise of professional folklore studies in the United States will be discussed in the following chapter. Taken together, the two entwined sensibilities—Higginson's romanticism and Allen's scientism—helped propel the new ethnosympathy and pro-toethnography. I turn now to highlight how the discovery of the spiritual first took on its distinctly modern form in Higginson and Allen.

"Natural Transcendentalists": Black Music as Testimony

Higginson deserves to be considered in relationship to the issues and thinkers central to both Unitarianism and New England Transcendental-ism, for he was party to this cultural sphere. He was influenced by and embraced many of its most critical intellectuals, and he participated in some of the most critical social movements that drew, in part, from the ideological ruptures on the edges of nineteenth-century Protestantism. Higginson's interpretive enterprise connected the particular religious for-mations in the North that produced the new ethnosympathy and the phe-nomenon of black religious subjectivity in both the North and the South, both of which had grown in tandem with the extension of the religious franchise. The new ethnosympathy helped forge the cultural connections within the new conjuncture, and Higginson embodied that ethnosympa-thy. In doing so, he helped ground and institutionalize the interpretive current first sparked by Frederick Douglass. Higginson also best repre-sents the early mode of pathos-oriented hearing that came sharply into being at the very onset of the war.

Higginson's romantic and antimodernist perspectives, nurtured as they were through his exposure to left-Protestantism and Christian socialism, were brought fully into play as he supervised the troops under his com-mand. As commander he could observe, listen to, study, request, catch, and transcribe the words of songs that were sung as a matter of cultural routine. He could also use blacks and their modes of expressivity to frame his larger concerns with market society. His romanticism, however, led him to abandon the most pressing questions of the fate of black people, instead preparing him for his desired career as a man of letters against the fading social movements at the century's end. In this regard, Higginson embodied the very shift away from racial politics and toward the new aestheticized culturalism that triumphed toward the end of the nineteenth century.[44]

Among all the Unitarian ministers and Transcendentalist intellectuals, it was Theodore Parker that Higginson most admired. As far as Higginson was concerned, Parker was "the most eloquent talker living; nobody compares to him in that; some are more *original*, perhaps, in talking; but he knows everything, and pours it out in the most simple and delightful way." Compared to other oratorical luminaries, Parker was "wonderful as a specimen of popularizing information and thought, in this he has no equal in this country; he is far before H. W. Beecher as a stump orator. It is a treat to see how people listen to him."[45] Higginson certainly admired Emerson and Thoreau, and he embraced much of Transcendentalist thought; but he was much more like Parker in that he was too strongly attracted to social causes to find the hermetical and utopianist retreats viable. It was perhaps easier in the 1840s for Transcendentalists to simply disengage from political institutions and revel in self-righteous withdrawal and autonomy. Critical Protestants engaged in the utopian projects on the margins of society would later become more involved in the antislavery crusade, but it took the exhaustion of utopian communitarianism to deliver them to the abolitionist ranks.[46] As this intellectual strata—this increasingly "dominated fraction of the dominant class" (to use Pierre Bourdieu's phrase)—and its ideologies of civic reform were squeezed and restricted even more by the new forces of market society, their moral spirit took some of them to the protoethnographic field, where they sought out the important symbolic capital provided by the Negro spiritual.

Like Emerson, Thoreau, and Parker, Higginson sought a career in the ministry and completed his training at the Harvard Divinity School. But it was a career cut short. His radical positions on issues of social reform, particularly workers' and women's rights, and his stance against slavery drew the ire of businessmen in his congregation. Shortly after he began as a minister, Higginson was edged out of his place behind the pulpit by a handful of influential business leaders who had vested interests in maintaining slavery and who found his liberal reformism distasteful.[47] Rather than muzzle his political sentiments, Higginson left the ministry in 1850 and took advantage of the emerging crisis-ridden political public sphere.

While still a minister, Higginson had already launched an activist career that would propel him to become something of a who's who within the progressive social movements that spanned the middle decades of the nineteenth century. He was already sympathetic to and involved with the emerging workingmen's associations that were forming in the industrial sectors of the North in the 1840s. And even as the utopianists retreated to their small-scale, short-lived experiments in alternative communitarianism, Higginson, at the request of the abolitionist poet John Greenleaf Whittier, had attempted to win a seat in Congress in 1848 on the Free Soil ticket. Losing—as well as letting go of—the ministry simplified his political leanings and enabled him to continue his political involvement. Working with Lucy Stone and others, Higginson became one of the men important to the women's rights movement. Indeed, he was one of the few men who chastised the male leaders of the World's Temperance Conference, held in New York in 1853. At the conference men not only rejected the proposals that women be installed on committees (women had, after all, played the crucial role in the rise of temperance), but also refused to allow women to address the gathering.[48]

It was with minister and mentor Theodore Parker that Higginson and others took a stand against the passage of the Fugitive Slave Act. The act, passed in 1850, required northerners in the free states to return runaway slaves to their southern masters. Parker viewed the act as politically intolerable and as evidence that the slave codes had penetrated the free North. Urging citizens to resist the unjust law, Parker was instrumental in forming the Boston Vigilance Committee, which he also chaired. The committee attempted, often with force, to rescue fugitive slaves who had been captured and held by authorities. As George Fredrickson notes, Higginson was Parker's "principal lieutenant" and "led the antislavery mob which attempted to free Anthony Burns, a runaway slave being held by Boston authorities, by assaulting the Boston Courthouse in 1854." When Higginson went to Kansas in 1856 to fight against the expansion of slavery into that state, he became, as Fredrickson put it, "the first transcendentalist in arms."[49] Three years later, along with Parker and others, Higginson supported the abolitionist John Brown's failed assault upon the federal arsenal at Harper's Ferry in Virginia. In 1861, two years after John Brown was hanged, Higginson received the invitation to become a colonel and take command of the first all-black regiment for the Union Army.

The chance to command black troops during the Civil War enabled many of the cultural tensions that were operating in Higginson's life to intersect at the point of discovering and writing about black song making. Romanticism, naturalism, antimodernism, Transcendentalism, humanitarian reformism, and ethnosympathy all came into a new constellation in Higginson's book, *Army Life in a Black Regiment*. His various cultural and ideological dispositions culminated with his ability to observe his soldiers in the dark and bring to his tent, "like some captured bird or insect," his scribbled field notes. By blending political and literary sensibilities with the emerging protoethnographic enterprise, Higginson helped funnel and reshape in a modern direction romanticist dispositions toward the use of black culture. He not only demonstrated the cultural and interpretive orientation that was being inaugurated by the new pathos-oriented hearing; he expanded this orientation greatly. As a memoir,

Army Life in a Black Regiment was one of the first book-length documents that presented in a sympathetic framework the printed transcriptions of a large number of black song lyrics that coincide with detailed observations of the troops under his supervision.

Like Emerson and Thoreau, two of his mentors, Higginson drew fondly from the tropes of natural history, which he blended with his admiration for the romantic Sir Walter Scott. In this opening passage to the chapter entitled "Negro Spirituals," Higginson envisioned himself having the opportunity to do for black song making what Scott had done when he found the cultural remnants of an older world with its stories of love, war, and tragedy. "The war brought to some of us many a strange fulfillment of dreams of other days," Higginson wrote.

> The present writer had been a faithful student of the Scottish ballads, and had always envied Sir Walter the delight of tracing them out amid their own heather, and of writing them down piecemeal from the lips of aged crones. It was a strange enjoyment, therefore, to be suddenly brought into the midst of a kindred world of unwritten songs, as simple and indigenous as the Border Minstrelsy, more uniformly plaintive, almost always more quaint, and often as essentially poetic.[50]

With the prose of a natural historian, he referred to the spirituals as "strange plants" which could now be "gather[ed] on their own soil."[51] Listening to the soldiers sing from the "class of songs under the name of 'Negro Spirituals'"[52] provided him the chance to capture and preserve songs that had for posterity a cultural value similar to those recorded and interpretively embellished by Scott.

Such work on the cultural border was deeply consistent with the retrievalist paradigm in which cultures on the margins of modernity were on the verge of slipping irretrievably into historical anonymity. Higginson's pathos-oriented sensibility enabled him to merge the retrievalist paradigm with the more immediate strains of antimodern disenchantment that were also part of the lessons of Transcendentalism. Sympathetic with Transcendentalism, his reception of black songs and black subjects was framed within a notion of a simple, premodern, authentic life that slavery crushed and American modernity was quite likely to banish. For Higginson, the spirituals and the black soldiers who sang them were strategically useful ideal images. They provided a useful place to integrate his romanticism and his desire to locate and pursue authenticity. Like the Scottish ballads, slave songs were conceived as similarly simple and unwritten, homegrown and unpolished, and coming from a people who were on the verge of being absorbed presumably through the benevolence of a rapidly changing modernity. Early founders of the retrievalist paradigm—Rousseau, Herder, Chateaubriand—had long extolled the virtues of common people whose lives were being buried by the inauthenticity of a more modern society.[53] In the spirit of Chateaubriand, who praised the French peasants for their "popular religion" that manifested the "genius of Christianity," or like Herder, who described folk expressions as "national" and "popular" poetry, Higginson could write that the Union-uniformed contrabands' "philosophizing is often the highest form of mysticism; and our dear surgeon declares that they are all natural transcendentalists."[54]

Nonetheless, these natural black Transcendentalists were not absorbed as partners into the institutions of utilitarian liberalism. They were outsiders, and this marginalized status had its antimodern charm. They did not have the "English and European manners and tastes" toward which Thoreau, according to Emerson, felt much "contempt."[55] Nor were they tainted by modernity, or trapped behind the wall of a dispiriting civilization that severed them from the innocence of nature. Consistent with the romanticist constructions of the modern meaning and value of the "noble savage," they were like children—Higginson referred to them as "young barbarians" and "grown up children."[56] They were close to nature; their ascribed virtues hinged not on what they possessed but on what they lacked.[57] They might not have been who Emerson had in mind when he suggested that history rolled backward would yield the ideal point or state of human infancy when all is "poetry," or when spirituality could be stripped back to reveal the essential "natural symbols." But something of this Emersonian imagery seemed to be at work in Higginson's romanticism. His troops (and blacks in general) appeared as "the world's perpetual children, docile, gay, and lovable, in the midst of this war for freedom on which they have intelligently entered."[58] When they worked, they did so with a robust cheerfulness and without lethargy. Having watched many times his troops from a distance and in the cover of dark, Higginson often marveled at their singing, their exchange of stories and personal accounts, their intensity of description, and their social engagement when they were able to interact outside of externally imposed controls (in the absence of white overseers). After such observations he would ponder the fallacy of the dominant view in which these men were held: "Yet to-morrow strangers will remark on the hopeless, impenetrable stupidity in the daylight faces of many of these very men, the solid mask under which Nature has concealed all this wealth of mother-wit."[59] How absurd, he could also point out, was the view that they were "sluggish and inefficient in labor."[60] On the contrary, the soldiers seemed to exercise all the virtues of daily labor that Emerson and Thoreau extolled for the cultivation of self-reliance, qualities sought as well by the Associationists and the Owenites, who believed that the utopian unity of work and life could be attained if one could gain distance and insulation from the dulling and nerve-deadening edges of modern civil society.[61] Interestingly, black troops were compared favorably to white Americans when Higginson raised social issues of American society. When wounded, the black men showed none of the "restless, defiant habit of white invalids."[62] In contrast to white soldiers, Higginson's troops did not have a problem with frequent "inebriation": "I have never heard of a glass of liquor in the camp, nor of any effort either to bring it in or to keep it out."[63]

Childlike—yet they possessed the wisdom of the ages, which made them only remotely connected to anything American. Their novelty, their appeal, rested partly in their disengagement from all of the vices, vulgarity, and banality that the critical Transcendentalists abhorred in American society. Among the uniformed representatives of childlike innocence there were certainly no incendiary Nat Turners or David Walkers; nor were there any learned and articulate politicos like Frederick Douglass. They were wise, likened to the greatness of the sages—Hebrew, Roman, and Greek. It was a great privilege, Higginson writes, to be "dusky soldiers, who based their whole walk and conversation strictly on the ancient Israelites."[64] The experience was like " 'dwelling in tents, with Abraham, Isaac, and Jacob.' This condition is certainly mine,—and with a multitude of patriarchs beside, not to mention Caesar and Pompey, Hercules and Bacchus."[65] The men possessed feminine characteristics too: "Yet their religious spirit grows more beautiful to me in living longer with them; it is certainly far more so than at first, when it seemed rather a matter of phrase and habit. It influences them both in the negative and the positive side. That is, it cultivates the feminine virtues first,—makes them patient, meek, resigned."[66] They could have all the virtues of Oriental wisdom checked by the submissiveness of a premodern model minority:

> Imbued from childhood with the habit of submission, drinking in through every pore that other-world trust which is the one spirit of their songs, they can endure everything. This I expected; but I am relieved to find that their religion strengthens them on the positive side also,—gives zeal, energy, daring. They could easily be made fanatics, if I chose; but I do not choose. Their whole mood is essentially Mohammedan, perhaps, in its strength and its weakness; and I feel the same degree of sympathy that I should if I had a Turkish command,—that is a sort of sympathetic admiration, not tending towards agreement, but towards co-operation.[67]

Such were the individuals from whom Higginson obtained songs.

There is plenty of mid-nineteenth-century Orientalism here. But why did not the evil specter of slavery appear in these written accounts of the troops from whom Higginson logged so many songs? Indeed, throughout Higginson's encounters, the specter had already disappeared. The narratives and the earliest treatments of Negro religious singing were initially embedded, and inextricably so, in slavery—this was Douglass's insistent insight. But during the Civil War, when Higginson brought his Transcendentalist-inspired romantic antimodernist sensibility to the battlefield to collect—like a good protoethnographer that he was—the much-talked-about "songs of the Contrabands," he participated in shifting the meaning of the spirituals to a different register. With (but certainly not only with) Higginson, the exoticization and romanticization of a black essentialism took form. The significance of this would reach forward, where it would be embraced by W. E. B. Du Bois, who singled out Higginson and other white abolitionists as interpretive allies to the humanistic recovery process, and as predecessors, along with Frederick Douglass, who ventured to open up a modern struggle to grasp the "souls of black folk."[68]

Black music and slaves served as interpretive tropes, as quasi-analytical devices, that helped Higginson and others frame their desires for reenchantment in the midst of all the dispiriting and stultifying effects that market modernity had unleashed. Yet as much as Higginson worked the moral reflection side of the discovery process, he did not marshal long-range concern for the social, economic, and political fate of former slaves. Indeed, the waning of slavery as the backdrop to understanding black expressivity coincided with the ascent of romantic and socially detached images. An aesthetic of authenticity and simplicity took the place of broader social conceptions. This shift signaled a culturally specific use, a restricted codification, of black music.

In spite of its romantic qualities, *Army Life* has a distinctly modern feel. It is a remarkable example of what today we would call fieldwork. Higginson lived with his subjects, his troops. As their commander, he was enmeshed in their daily lives. He observed, noted, probed, gathered, and transcribed black song making with the kind of lived proximity to his work and to his subjects that would become important to a professional ethnographer and anthropologist. He carried out what today some call the methodology of "participant observation." Higginson relays how he obtained black songs—how he observed from a distance, how he approached his subjects as unobtrusively as possible while maximizing his closeness to them, how he indulged in small talk to get big answers and insights, or asked straight out how they actually made new songs. He queried singers for their own meanings and interpretations, and juxtaposed black song making to a variety of comparative examples, often waxing romantically and moralistically in ways that quickly abandoned the actual terrain at hand. While he vacillated between seeing his soldiers as adults and as childlike, never did he deprecate the integrity of his soldiers and musical informants. His method is modern, too, in that it reflects an ostensible willingness to let the subjects tell their side of things—even though the new ethnosympathetic mode of hearing operated nonetheless with its own powers of selectivity, with cultural filters shaped by pressures of ideological legitimation and enclosure. Higginson valued the internal ethos of pathos, that inner and earnest interest in wanting to know about "the Other" because such knowledge was humanly valuable and self-edifying, even though fraught with historical, social, and institutional compromises from the outset. Higginson's work was an example of an emerging humanistic ethnography. But it is most fittingly *protoethnographic*, given that such a discipline had not really emerged as an academically recognized intellectual practice.

Army Life exemplifies the sympathetic turn suggested earlier by Frederick Douglass and others who were steeped in the abolitionist movement. But more important, these accomplishments bridged and simultaneously synthesized ethnosympathy and protoethnography. In presenting his forays into black song making as an important act of recording cultural practices that might soon vanish, Higginson shared the sentiments that were being engendered by intellectuals who felt that something of the Old World was disappearing with the encroachment of modernity. In this regard, part of his orientation toward black culture fed the more serious endeavors of collecting and archiving that were first championed by the proponents of natural history and that would soon be fundamental to an emergent cultural anthropology, scientific folklore, and cultural sociology.

What deserves highlighting, however, is how Higginson helped install as well as crystallize a strategy for interpreting black culture at the racial margins. It was a complicated and complex move that drew upon and merged romanticist, political, and literary motivations. In the process, Higginson helped cut a path that led to the modern academic exoneration of black cultural expressions; the latter were practices to be embraced and read as fundamental indicators of hitherto hidden lives, an enterprise that also simultaneously pushed as well as checked insights into larger cultural tensions. In Higginson, black culture helped ground in flesh and blood a romantic naturalism that was less concerned with actual black lives than with a more inchoate feel for finding authenticity on the edges of modernity, even if what he and many of his sensitive peers were up to involved screening black music for its preferred fit within the new interpretive enterprise.

Spiritual Proclivities and Modern Taxonomies: Black Music as Artifact

Developing in tandem with the romantic and nostalgic strains in Higginson's view was a different dimension of discovery, one reflecting the emergent rationalization of scientific observation and classification. It was *Slave Songs of the United States* (1867), the collection of songs compiled by William Frances Allen, Charles Pickard Ware, and Lucy McKim Garrison, that actually prefigured the modern scientific mode of analysis for black music. The compilers and editors of *Slave Songs* were involved primarily in a mission to "collect and preserve" black songs. The presentation of this work, however, did not indulge in the kind of day-to-day intimacy that informed Higginson's accounts. Higginson championed a romantically infused sensibility, but Allen and his fellow editors systematized this sensibility. In doing so, they checked the earlier romanticist strains with a more neutralized and neutralizing grammar of objective description.

Army Life and *Slave Songs* were written only a few years apart. Both publications, however, drew their inspiration from the Port Royal experiment, which enabled collectors to scour the black cultural landscape for songs. Yet the framing of their content as well as their respective prose styles show signs of an emerging *division of interpretive labor* that harbored as well a significant schematic shift. Higginson's *Army Life*, drawn partly from the notebooks and journals he composed while commanding his black soldiers, reads as a personal memoir, a travel narrative, and a political romance. Written in the historical conjuncture, it draws upon multiple genres inasmuch at it seems a prose in search of a new synthetic genre. Higginson imparts to his readers a familiarity with slaves as characters (as nascent persons with incipient selfhood). He writes of people with faces, of individuals with voices, mannerisms, and idiosyncracies, and of black soldiers with names. Black people and black practices become milestones to mark his remarkable voyage made possible by a moral war. Higginson's *Army Life* is, fundamentally, a testimony, as are the songs he hears and transcribes.

In contrast, the lengthy and interpretive introduction to *Slave Songs of the United States* penned by Allen reads like a scientific treatise with a highly focused aim—to provide a new intellectual scaffolding to the first major collection of black songs. A modern taxonomically inflected rationale positions the collection in relationship to a new sort of classificatory knowledge in the making. *Slave Songs* is clearly up to serious and reflexive archival work; it has little of Higginson's literary pretensions and pursuits, and its authors have no need to be recognized as persons of letters. Higginson plotted his work to be read; Allen's introduction aims to be read as a work of knowledge being plotted. Higginson writes with a modest righteousness; Allen seems just to want to bring the hidden into visibility while getting things descriptively right. Allen, like Higginson, accepted the fact that modernity had banishing power as it moved relentlessly along a path of progress.

Allen's introduction to *Slave Songs* addresses the notion that the culture of slaves, a traditional culture of black song making rooted in oral practices, was now subject to the upheaval of social change. In time, all of the social and institutional forms that had hitherto generated and shaped slave culture would disappear. But more than slavery disappeared in this crowning stage of cultural discovery. Soon to disappear was the ethos of pathos that had only recently addressed the social, economic, and political fate of black lives. Black *culture* certainly attracted a new kind of inquisitive gravity, but the attraction came at the expense of a dialogue over the larger political crisis of the future of freed blacks. A symptom of the new cultural enclosure was an urgent concern for the "specimen" collection. *Slave Songs* is fundamentally an assembled collection of artifacts.

In order to produce *Slave Songs*, Allen and associates launched an extensive campaign to collect black songs and to put their words and music into print. They obtained the songs largely through the missionary-teacher-abolitionist network, which was quite extensive; they even published in the *Nation* a request to the larger liberal readership to aid in the collection process.[69] Higginson, who published an essay on black songs the same year *Slave Songs* was published, also supplied a substantial number of songs for the project.

With its publication, *Slave Songs* became the first major compilation of black songs that included not just lyrics, but also professionally transcribed musical notation.[70] Containing 136 songs, it was the most extensive collection of Negro spirituals ever assembled. It was a milestone, not only in the discovery of black music, but in American cultural history. Important essays and articles had appeared during the war years,[71] but the new compilation was unprecedented. In keeping with what I have called "spiritual proclivities," the songs—"spirichils," to use the editor's rendition of dialect—were predominantly religious, and were gathered from former slaves residing in the Port Royal area and surrounding regions, with additional examples from other regions of the South.[72] Many commentators since the publication of *Slave Songs* have singled out various favorites, have highlighted from these their own lists of which are of more or less importance, have added their aesthetic angles of analysis, and have gone to great lengths to interpret the "meanings" of these songs.

My concern, however, is with the new knowledge formation, the new interpretive scaffolding, the intellectual framework that provided the cultural cartography of black music at this particular conjuncture. Allen had posed the question as to why such a well-known body of music had not been approached by any "systematic effort . . . to collect and preserve their melodies." There is an obvious answer to his question: such melo-

dies were not in danger of disappearing while the system of slavery remained intact. But when it appeared that slavery would be abolished, the
issue of cultural loss became evident, and this, in turn, posed the need for
cultural retention and preservation. Allen spoke of "accurate" collections, and of the "difficulty in attaining absolute correctness."[73] However, as I have suggested, the proclivity for hearing the spiritual stemmed
from deeper cultural sources in which the stakes of ideology were higher
and the religious frames of legitimacy were of greater importance. With
the publication of *Slave Songs*, two sensibilities—the particular ideological preferences toward religious singing as "good culture" and the impulse toward cultural preservation—converged to shape and prefigure
the new field of subcultural interpretation. Those attracted to black religious singing were actually fusing two concerns. Religious singing confirmed their belief that the slaves were disposed toward Christianity;
hence it underscored Christian efficacy, particularly the benevolent antislavery dimensions of Protestant virtue. The spirituals also hosted the
desire to archive for posterity "these relics of a state of society which has
passed away."[74]

Allen pointed out that not all black music was religious or fit the category of spirituals; he referred to such music as "intrinsically barbaric."
But such music was presumably dwarfed in comparison to what many
believed were the much more important effects—an idealized "civilizing"
process—rooted ultimately in Christian signification.

> Still, the chief part of the negro music is *civilized* in its character—partly
> composed under the influence of association with the whites, partly actually
> imitated from their music. . . . On the other hand there are very few which
> are of an intrinsically barbaric character, and where this character does ap-
> pear, it is chiefly in short passages, intermingled with others of a different
> character.[75]

As noted earlier, the published reports of the shouts as disturbingly frequent, and as defined by white observers in the language of noise, suggest
that their construction of the preferred Negro involved simultaneous aims
of cultural denial and active repression.

> Indeed, it is very likely that if we had found it possible to get at more of their
> secular music, we should have come to another conclusion as to the propor-
> tion of the barbaric element. A Gentlemen in Delaware writes: "We must
> look among their non-religious songs for the purest specimens of negro min-
> strelsy. It is remarkable that they have themselves transferred the best of
> these to the uses of their churches—I suppose on Mr. Wesley's principle that
> 'it is not right the Devil should have all the good tunes.' Their leaders and
> preachers have not found this change difficult to effect; or at least they have

taken so little pains about it that one often detects the profane *cropping out*, and revealing the origin of their most solemn 'hymns,' in spite of the best intentions of the poet and artist."[76]

Allen concedes the notion that blacks had an extensive repertoire of nonreligious music, but the early discoverers were not interested in this music. Such interest, however, became much more widespread two decades later, and served as the basis for an expanded folkloristic typology that included more refined distinctions between "work songs," "field hollers," and "corn songs" (these last being the ground for the turn-of-the-century "blues"), and it is important to note that *Slave Songs* did contain examples of songs that had no ostensible religious references.

What mattered in this natural-history-turned-ethnological narrative was what was most natural:

> The greater number of the songs which come into *our possession* seem to be the natural and original production of a race of remarkable musical capacity and very teachable, which has been long enough associated with the more cultivated race to have become imbued with the mode and spirit of European music—often, nevertheless, retaining a distinct tinge of the native Africa.[77]

It was thus culturally convenient for the discoverers to focus upon the distinct separation between the "greater number" of admissible songs in comparison to the number of inadmissible songs. William George Hawkins, one of many clergymen working in the Port Royal area during the war, demonstrated how "native songs" that contained religious references but that could not be easily comprehended were taken by northerners as examples of "specimens of Negro ignorance." To remedy this, teachers ought to "endeavor to teach them something better." He provided an example:

> Here is a specimen which should not be tolerated in these schools:

> > "In de mornin' when I rise,
> > Tell my Jesus, Huddy oh? . . ."

> We hope the day may soon come when all such illiterate, we will not say senseless songs will be discouraged by all who wish and are laboring for the true enlightenment of the African race.

For Hawkins, the task of this uplift fell upon the shoulders of "the refined young ladies at Port Royal [who] will substitute others more sensible and elevated in language."[78] Other observers noted that the former slaves were "receiving an education through their songs which is incalculable" with the aid of "teachers [who] discourage the use of their old barbaric chants, and besides *our beautiful, patriotic and religious hymns teach the virtue of industry, truth, honesty and purity* in rhyme and measure."[79]

The missionaries, teachers, and kindred moral entrepreneurs and uplifters who descended upon Port Royal and who helped contribute to the milieu in which the spirituals were edified as the supreme expression of religiously redeemable and savable subjects all knew about the spirituals before they arrived. These songs had already become charged with authenticity (the term "folklore,"[80] which had recently been coined, would soon provide an irresistible pull upon them). Northerners expected to hear them; they searched for them, and they found them. They also encouraged certain songs. As William Allen noted, among the "spirichils" were those "of special merit" that "soon became established favorites among the whites, and hardly a Sunday passed at the church on St. Helena without 'Gabriel's Trumpet,' 'I hear from Heaven to-day,' or 'Jehovah Hallelujah.'"[81]

Slaves were also taught new songs. After hearing a crew of black boatmen sing "Roll, Jordan, Roll," Charlotte Forten wrote in her journal "Their singing impressed me much. It was so sweet and strange and solemn. . . . I want to hear these men sing [John Greenleaf] Whittier's 'Song of the Negro Boatmen.' I am going to see if it can't be brought about in some way."[82] The abolitionist song "John Brown" was also presented as a song to be learned by the recently emancipated black children: "We taught—or rather commenced teaching the children 'John Brown' which they entered into eagerly. I felt to the full the significance of *that* song being sung here in S.[outh] C.[arolina] by little negro children, by those whom he—the glorious old man—died to save."[83]

Despite the spiritual proclivities that governed their schemas for hearing, there was still plenty of black noise. Those involved in the uplift mission heard music that was not part of what had become a cultural expectation. At Port Royal and surrounding environs, Higginson, Laura Towne, Harriet Ware, Lucy McKim, Lucy's father James McKim Miller, and many other witnessed what were called shouts. This practice involved people gathered in a circle and moving in a circular direction by sliding rather than crossing or lifting their feet. It was a practice accompanied by singing chants, repetitive lines, or more elaborate songs, with words and lyrics ranging (according to various observers) from totally unintelligible to recognizable references to religious figures, events, and desires.[84] The difficulty in distinguishing between shouts and religious singing was captured by Charlotte Forten.

> This eve. our boys and girls with others from across the creek came in and sang a long time for us. Of course we had the old favorites "Down in the Lonesome Valley," and "Roll, Jordan, Roll," and "No Man Can Hender

Me," and beside those several shouting tunes that we had not heard before; they are very wild and strange. It was impossible for me to understand many of the words although I asked them to repeat them for me. Only know that one had something about "De Nell Am Ringing." I think that was the refrain; and of another, some of the words were "Christ build the church widout no hammer nor nail," "Jehovah Halleluhiah," which is a grand thing, and "Hold the light," an especial favorite of mine—they sang also with great spirit.[85]

Forten's account raises the likelihood that white listeners who could not readily recognize black song making as religious were perhaps quick in categorizing such singing as nonreligious.

Interestingly, while the consensus was that blacks sang mostly spirituals, many visitors to Port Royal heard the shouts, and in some cases much to their displeasure. From accounts compiled by Epstein it is clear that such sounds fell outside the schemas of preference. Higginson described these "half powwow, half prayer meeting[s]," with their mixture of "piety and polka," as "always within hearing"[86] and almost of nightly frequency. William Allen, who was always a careful chronicler, and who seldom added moralizing commentary to his ostensibly scientized prose, viewed them as "of African origin, with Christianity engrafted upon [them] just as it was upon the ancient Roman ritual." Others, however, were much less tolerant or accommodating. One unidentified visitor viewed the "little barbarians" in their "African rite" with discouragement at how much would have to be done to educate them. Laura Towne saw "old idol worship" at work, and had "never [seen] anything so savage." "The better persons," she insisted, "go to the praise house." Others complained that the shouts were better attended than the white-supervised praise house meetings. After seeing a shout, Reuben Tomlinson argued for "some regulation [to] be adopted here with reference to the . . . Church organizations of these people, the limits within which they should enjoy them, ought to be rigorously defined." Other reports describe attempts to intervene and stop the practice.[87] Tomlinson's suggestion seems to have held sway. As the instruction of former slaves became more established and routinized, teachers, ministers, and military personnel acknowledged that black practices that fell beyond the boundaries of appropriate culture were discouraged. The effects of disapproval were quickly registered upon the younger black population. Teacher James B. Black noticed the desirable effect: "I have seen them, when requested to sing some of their grotesque hymns, which were great favorites in slave-times, hide their heads while singing, and seem heartily ashamed of them."[88] We would expect northern Protestants who were not the religious offspring of the Baptist and Methodist-inspired revivals to be somewhat uncomfortable with the intense collective emotionality of black song making, regardless of its religious or nonreligious content. For those who sought to intervene, the challenge was to shape black songs to fit the mold of the emerging ideal new Negro who came into view as a spiritualized (e.g., Christianized) and a spiritual-singing subject. Interestingly, Allen had observed that the same song could be sung at the "praise meeting" and then outside of white purview as a shout—an indication of the much more important fact that the actual songs were less an issue than were their conditions of production, and that *white-sanctioned supervision* was the ultimate issue at stake.

The Cultural Enclosure

Higginson wrote of capturing black songs as if he were a natural historian sampling esoteric climes; recall the epigraph at the opening of this chapter. Such imagery and description of the way he "collected" samples of black songs were quite in keeping with the mid-nineteenth-century vogue of natural history. But it was Allen rather than Higginson who actually wrote in the scientized genre of natural history. In thinking of Allen's prose, I have in mind that of Charles Darwin, with his penchant for minute detail, exquisite subdivisions, and typologies and classifications within a general schema, all the while holding in check emotional and value-laden comments. After all, it was Darwin who provided the ideal-type narrative that scientized the older genre of natural history. Allen's introduction to *Slave Songs* approximated the form of a natural history insofar as it lent itself to the quasi-scientized discussion of human cultural practices. Higginson, in Emersonian fashion, pulled black music toward a romanticized natural history. What Allen accomplished, however, was to aim newer interpretive tropes of scientized natural history at black song making. The result was a mode of writing about black song making that represented the first "systematic" assessment of black songs to an educated reading public.

As publications concerned with black culture in the United States, both *Slave Songs* and *Army Life* entered on the eve of modern ethnology's ascendancy within the context of an industrially accelerating society. But it is with *Slave Songs* that the fully modern mode of scientific taxonomy begins to be applied to black music; the study thus capped one important line of development along which black culture was being discovered and mapped. Allen's mode of capturing black music was through a language and an explanatory structure that we would associate with a modern social-scientific approach to cultural classification. The romanticist and humanistic-reformist sensibilities that informed the views of Higginson were not entirely eclipsed. They remained vital and resilient to modern ethnosympathy, though they were increasingly checked as the century came to a close. Allen's more measured prose would prove to set the coming professional tone. Higginson's romanticism had already separated black culture from black fate. Allen's scientific repositioning of black music, along the lines of classification and taxonomy, quickened and deepened this breach by introducing a way to speak more systematically about the cultural operations within the new cultural enclosure: testimonies could reclassified as artifacts.

The developments I have been charting harbor, I believe, the kernel of an emergent interpretive logic that began to link the powerful currents of romantic and reformist ethnosympathy to a sensibility critical of American modernity. This critical sensibility, however, was weak and easily compromised. Market society and industrialization were eroding the older orders of traditional authority, and the landed gentry and cultural elites, who were not the champions of the new industrialization, could not automatically take for granted their positions at the moral and intellectual helms of American institutions. New economic elites were being ushered in by modernity, and it was their pragmatic, fiscal, and technological prowess that grew increasingly more central to the functioning of American society. Older cultural elites had to scramble to maintain their importance; they did so by accommodating the larger pressures of a modernity that was captialist-driven and based on racial hierarchies. Rent with inequalities, the new market society absorbed the seamy problems surrounding the fate of blacks as well as of Indians, women, wage laborers, the poor, and the increasing waves of immigrant groups whose identities were embedded in the triumph of market society. The panoply of social subjects who emerged to make claims for a better place within market society, and whose emergence was coterminous with the very rise of reformism, were greeted by an increasingly modern managerial rather than democratic discourse. This new managerial discourse was aided by the rise of a professional social science that could house (and attempt to tame) the antimodern apprehensiveness toward market society. In its best posture, it would embrace and even celebrate modern society.[89]

The spiritual proclivities of the most radical abolitionists shaped their proclivities to hear spirituals, but not much else. Their limited orientations toward blacks had a peculiar self-confirming dimension. By capturing and classifying black culture, and by refining their discovery of the Negro spiritual, they were casting an interpretive net that *caught* what had (presumably) been *taught* by the hegemonic culture—the performative, singing, and spiritualized subject.[90] In this way, the discovery process that was carried out by the former ministers and others who brought black song making into such critical and appreciative reflection was part of a distinct and complex knowledge formation that contained its own self-flattery by marking the virtues of the modern while simultaneously recognizing what modernity had increasingly little room for—the actual peoples and forms of culture that progress was in danger of (presumably) banishing to history.

The abolitionists' process, then, of preferring to comprehend the social and cultural meanings in black music in a framework of discovery, functioned also like a mirror held up to reflect a preferred image. The process was kindred to the ideological reorientation of culture and education that Matthew Arnold would soon sum up as the "sweetness and light" that a naturally endowed dominant class, in fulfilling its moral obligations of stewardship, ought to radiate to its social and cultural wards, those lower classes and castes who, in turn, were to be guided and educated so that they might internalize through cultural trickle-down "the best which has been thought and said in the world." As a cultural disposition, the discoverer's preference for the Negro spiritual prefigured Arnold's class aesthetic. In his book, *Culture and Anarchy*, Arnold provided the following definition of culture: "culture being a pursuit of our total perfection by means of getting to know, on all the matters which most concern us, *the best which has been thought and said* in the world. . . . Culture, which is the study of perfection, leads us . . . to conceive of true human perfection, as a *harmonious* perfection, developing all sides of our humanity; and as a *general* perfection, developing all parts of our society."[91] Culture was thus always subjected to stewardship. The spiritual was the "best" of what the slave and even the freed Negro could produce, either as testimony or artifact, to complement the kind of class stewardship that was presupposed in this aesthetic and moral recognition and knowledge of the world of lesser men and women. In this regard, the spiritual represented what the civilizing process had bequeathed to the racial margins. In relation to the spiritual, all other black musical noise—and black literature as well as voices striving to address broader and certainly more crucial social, economic, and political aspirations—could be ignored, discounted, and dismissed, at least for a while. The spiritual—as practice, as phenomenon, as spectacle, and as cultural performance—served as a major element in the modern, end-of-century cartography of black expressivity.

The interpretive impulses that pulled upon black song making and caught cherished Christian fragments of culture, caught other entwined things as well. Not only did the new interpretation of black music produce the ideologically preferred black performative subject, a critical-intellectual, pathos-driven parallel to minstrelsy (but without the latter's class-rooted vicious vulgarity and deprecation); it also confirmed the legitimacy of seeing, understanding, and appreciating the very *activity* of cultural capture, which included the modern orientation to the margins and the triumph of the modern protoscientific framework itself. The new interpretive formation was a way of knitting together ideas of how to represent the conjuncture of race, culture, and modernity as a form of managerially empathic representations.

Transcendentalist idealism was weakened and dissipated by the 1860s. It did not survive the upheavals of the Civil War. But as I have argued, its benevolent and theologically driven naturalism fueled the early modern protoethnographic forays into black culture. While the Transcendentalist-inspired mode of interpretation was largely overwhelmed by modern social science, it managed to exert influence. Consider that in the 1888 roster of names of founding members of the American Folk-Lore Society, there appeared the names of four individuals: Thomas Wentworth Higginson, Moncur Conway, Samuel Longfellow, and Caleb Stetson. Two years later, the society's annual roster included these four in addition to the Transcendentalist historian Octavius B. Frothingham. A half century earlier, on September 19, 1836, these five individuals had joined with twenty-five others and formed the Transcendental Club. All of the club members who convened in 1836 were New Englanders, Unitarians, or neo-Unitarian rebels, and for the most part had attended Harvard at least for work in divinity.[92] Only thirteen of the original club members remained alive in 1888, when the professional folklorists launched their national organization. That five managed to be engaged in the founding of the new scholarly body is indicative of the affinities Transcendentalist-inspired philosophy had with the most modern and organized embodiment of ethnosympathy. One might speculate that many of the founding members would have joined the intellectual project of collecting and interpreting culture on the margins had there been an earlier quasi-professional body to do such work in the 1840s.

. . . . .

We can now appreciate how Allen's *Slave Songs* represents much more than what it purports to be, and more than what the received interpretive tradition attributes to this classic text. Far more than just a work of cultural preservation and early musicology, it refracts older lines of thought and prefigures new lines of analysis by anticipating the formation of modern and increasingly more legitimate (e.g., institutionally sanctioned) forms of professional knowledge that draw their contours from a larger and more nebulous notion of *ethnoscience*. *Slave Songs* is a cultural work that recognizes the act of song collection as an important step in preserving for posterity a culture on the wane—it is *natural history*; it speaks of examples of music that highlight "feelings, opinions, and habits of the slaves"—it is psychological and cultural anthropology, or perhaps a nascent sociology of emotions; it traces the lyrical semiotics from the small texts of the song to the big father-text of Christianity—it is a particularly American version of Protestant hermeneutics; it follows the influence of song styles and content across a larger dispersion—it approaches a peculiar kind of moral ecology and certainly a thesis of cultural diffusion; it compares the interpretive preferences of white ministers with those of the black song makers who sometimes insisted on giving meanings to their music in ways that differed from the imputed meanings of white observers—it is comparative religion; it details the internal practices of blacks conducting their prayers and making songs, describes the decor of the rooms in which they assemble, comments on the nature and quality of black interaction and behavior, and strives to produce an interpretive depth out of the surface of the mundane—it is ethnography; it is challenged to record as precisely as possible the musical production of a subcultural group with the procedures of technical notation, scoring, and transcription—it is ethnomusicology; it is reflexive in detailing its own method of categorical accounts, the principles involved in putting musical notation to lyrics, and the search for material while being reflexive with regard to the accuracy as well as limits of the study—it is paradigmatic knowledge maintenance.

Most important, the emerging interpretive formation works with the unquestioned dominant categories of interpretation that have been unleashed by Protestant schisms and social and institutional tensions. The interpretive work, however, is carried out partly through a New World romanticism that must accommodate the onslaught of capitalism and market society. In the wake of slavery's demise and the triumph of capitalist modernity, the critical abolitionist spirit enabled as well as displayed a wide-eyed and passionate look at the cultures of people—in this case former American slaves—found at the edges of the color line. Like many of their counterparts who trafficked in the politics of redemption, who discovered and tried to grasp the fate of women, white wage laborers, the poor, and sometimes Native American peoples, the critical abolitionists tried to see the larger contours of their social moment.

In a fundamental sense, ethnosympathy enabled a new social vision. For the first time, culture on the margins came more fully into view; this was one of the victories of a critical modernity that had begun to probe the very idea of society as an object of investigation while it pondered the hitherto unconscious complicity of human deeds in the shaping of society. Slaves could be seen as human victims and subjects rather than primarily as natural objects in service to an Old World utility. The cultural challenge, which was endemic to romanticism in general and inherited by reformers throughout the nineteenth century, was to salvage forms of authenticity perceived to be under siege. Those on the edge of furthering the new ethnosympathy were thus compelled to extend their redemptive reach toward groups—former slaves, particularly singing ones, in this case—whose fate signaled not so much the peculiar identity but the unchosen and unjustified social position of those groups.

But ethnosympathy was also checked by a glaucoma-glazed vision that was both modern and historically compromised. Even the most critical ethnosympathizers seem to have accommodated themselves to the new rationalism and scientism; these modern forces were quickly annexing the older romantic and religious impulses and restructuring the entire terrain of modern knowledge. Slave music—as cultural practice, as discoverable object, as new intellectual subject matter—played early host to these developments.

By the early 1870s Reconstruction was being rapidly dismantled. As the national abandonment of freed blacks became the evident social and political backdrop, there were new pressures to accommodate the larger political context. Those who championed the new ethnosympathy also registered the compromise. Allen's *Slave Songs* embodied this accommodation. As we have seen in Allen's study, it became sufficiently benevolent for ethnosympathizers to simply place intellectual value upon the *cultural features* of the lives of former slaves—to the extent that they continued to yield cultural objects to the new professional interpreters. Soon a modern cultural analysis would arise and demonstrate an increasingly unconscious and dehistoricized form of knowledge as it sidled up to the managerial challenges of a multiracial and multiethnic society headed by industrial corporate prowess.

Between Higginson's *Army Life in a Black Regiment* and Allen's *Slave Songs in the United States* there was a shift in analytic emphasis. Higginson had managed to retain some of Frederick Douglass's concern to connect music with the human and institutional determinants of social fate and social structure. His primary contribution was his interest in reading culture (romantically and politically) as the embodiment of social testimonies. Allen and his fellow editors, however, captured the dominant direction of the shift in which culture was to be read increasingly as a taxonomical index of artifacts. In the process, the new knowledge—geared to capture pieces of lives through fragments of cultural expressivity—could take shape. Fractured, dissected, sorted, and reclassified into more discrete and knowable parcels, black expressivity was objectified and pulled into modern rationalized interpretation. Along with other artifacts gleaned from other peoples and cultures, it took its new place in the various ethnosciences bent on interpreting domains of culture, each moving forward along distinct paths of cultural annexation, and each providing elements of interpretation for an increasingly culture-hungry modern intelligentsia torn by a nostalgia for, yet gripped too frequently by a hostility toward, socially marginalized peoples. Through the edification of the new and relatively autonomous system of knowledge placed over black music's embeddedness in history and social relations, black song making began to lose what it was once considered to be: "testimonies" to black lives, fragments from voiced subjects, external indicators of hitherto veiled worlds, prisms refracting struggles over authenticity and subjectivity, oral cultural passages through which slaves struggled to negotiate the forces of slavery, signifying strategies that rooted a people in time and space.

Black music on American soil was constituted in response to the systematic pulverization of a captured people who had imposed upon them the culture of their captors. Its forms reflect both the determinant and untranscendable relationship and the resultant nuances of black American cultural production. As a social text embedded in a social context, black song making spoke from and to the indomitable; Frederick Douglass brought this aspect sharply into view in 1845. Even the Reverend Lockwood, who brought the first "spiritual," "Go Down, Moses," into print in 1861, retained in his discussion the crucial sociological connections that linked black lives, and social relations.

But these connections frayed rather quickly. Ironically, the ascendancy of the spirituals and their central place on the new interpretive maps signaled both the new ethnosympathy's highest aesthetic praise as well as the unraveling of the sociological ties between culture, society, and history. The edification of black song making appeared to be a long overdue embrace of culture on the margins. But the process of edifying black culture also charts how the study of black music began to be severed from its crucial social domain. How the spirituals became "specimens" and "relics," defined as eligible for professional appropriation, is explored in the following chapter.

SIX

INSTITUTIONALIZING ETHNOSYMPATHY

Even now the younger generation of colored singers do not
give them with the effectiveness that the "old timers" did, and
the reason, of course, is that the old people made them the
expression of their joys and sorrows, their hopes and fears, and
these hymns or spirituals were a part of their very being. Their
children know or remember nothing of those "dark days," and
the songs do not mean what they did to the parents, so the life
of the rendering isn't there. As [Hampton Institute founder]
General Armstrong truly said, "The more civilized you make
them the more valueless you make them . . ."
(F. G. Rathbun, Director of Music, Hampton Institute, 1893)

BLACK MUSIC MAKING, "discovered" or not, continued to flour-
ish as a popular vernacular, a sphere of cultural work, a situated
grammar, and an arena of social perceptions of everyday life.
Nonetheless, it was being mapped by the new appropriators, who, in
turn, were producing a new cultural knowledge. Higginson and Allen,
along with others who shared their frameworks, may or may not have
understood black music. There are plenty of arguments to pursue, which
are supported by a large body of scholarship, with regard to their "mis-
readings." However, I do not wish to concentrate on whether the appropriators got things right. I wish instead to focus on the interpretive effects
that their new analysis had upon cultural practices at the social margins.
Higginson and Allen both responded to, as well as embellished, the new
interpretive enterprise. Their writings expressed the central tendencies
that were bringing black music making into alignment with an interpretive formation that was consolidating earlier as well as emergent orientations. What is important is that their *understanding* was based on
capturing black music within a framework of preferred identifications:
Higginson managed to create a cultural space for the continuation and
maintenance of ethnosympathy and the emerging hermeneutics of subjectivity. Allen's key contribution was to scientize and legitimize the older
ethos of pathos.

Though both helped install the modern interest in black music, neither could have anticipated how their frameworks of appropriation would feed into and be adopted by and adapted to the rise of professional folklore studies of black music. It is not surprising that both were founding members of the American Folk-Lore Society, and their names appear as supporters of the society in the latter's first published volume of the *American Journal of Folk-Lore* in 1888. Shortly after the turn of the century, when W. E. B. Du Bois reached back to the sorrow songs (as he called them), he noted the important humanistic impulses championed by radical abolitionists like Higginson and Allen.

Interestingly, as unusual and pathbreaking as they were, neither *Army Life in a Black Regiment* nor *Slave Songs of the United States* was met with great enthusiasm. As Dena Epstein points out, only one edition of *Slave Songs* was published, and it fell quickly into oblivion. It was not until 1929 that a second edition was printed.[1] The withering interest was due to a number of important factors. Both works came into print at the end of a long half century of social turmoil capped by a bloody civil war. The critical white reading public for antislavery literature was always small, and the postwar climate of exhaustion appears to have checked its growth. Moreover, the social movement that had created the cultural space for such reception politics dissipated with the ending of slavery. Sea changes were taking place that added to the complex cultural juncture. The institutional interventions attempted during Reconstruction were never popular and were unraveling by the early 1870s; a massive influx of European ethnic immigrants altered the entire social, political, and economic fabric; and labor strife intensified in unprecedented ways. These factors certainly helped derail Reconstruction, but the blame cannot be placed on them.

Given the context, it is not surprising that the empathy of the small critical readership in the North appears to have evaporated. Empathy was, after all, a fragile and underdeveloped sensibility from the beginning. It is well known that the northerners' strong feelings against slavery actually coexisted with an intractable racism. The antislavery movement was never motivated by widespread endearment toward blacks, enslaved or free (outside of the "parlor book" images of Negroes found in the more sentimental genres of antislavery literature).[2] The fact that only a decade was allotted to implement southern Reconstruction was symptomatic of the larger lack of will to confront the dilemma of racial inequality. The withdrawal of national governmental involvement from the South's massive racial problems went hand in glove with the resurgence of the South's landowning power structure, and after the mid-1870s, political leadership in the North did little to challenge the "white redeemers" whose "states' rights" politics quickly resubordinated former slaves to wholesale disenfranchisement. The result was the new institutional form of debt peonage that marginalized the black populations across the South, and the retreat from even the most tepid overtures to egalitarianism was insured by the rapid expansion of violence against blacks that was routine, unbridled, and even highly organized. The new situation was acceptable to cultural analysts who came to acknowledge intransigent southern "folkways."[3] However, the marginalization of and violence against blacks was too widespread to be just a southern phenomenon.

Focusing, however, on the disappearance of white abolitionist sympathizers takes us away from the cultural dynamics that continued to kindle interest in the spirituals. The significance of the cultural turn did not depend upon a waning abolitionist movement and the relative absence of a critical white readership for transcribed black songs. Indeed, the importance of the new paradigm soon acquired an unexpected and crucially important institutional home: the black colleges and universities that were created during the war and in its aftermath. In 1867, William Allen, his fellow collectors, and his kindred colleagues had raised the concern that there was no "systematic effort . . . [t]o collect and preserve [Negro] melodies." Two decades later this challenge was being met through the development of an academically based professional folklore and the formation of an intellectual discipline organized around an intensive search for *folk* culture. The discovery of slave music would become quickly systematized once it was caught up in the larger ethos of professionalization.[4] But in between the war's end and the rise of professional folklore came the emergent black educational institutions.

If any social body or institution inherited the cultural turn and preserved the interpretive velocity unleashed in the abolitionist conjuncture, it was the black schools. The black schools kept alive the vibrant interest in black song making; they held on to the function of music as a marker of interpretive value; they took up and continued the cultural work of musical retrieval and retention. As I shall argue, the schools absorbed many of the issues that concerned the critical abolitionists and the earlier discoverers like Higginson and Allen. These included the growing contradiction between the older romantic and antimodernist sensibilities that championed the search for cultural authenticity and the emerging pressures of the new scientistic orientation—the very tensions we saw emerging in the interpretive schemas of Higginson and Allen. The black colleges actually served as the cultural links between the interpretive sensibilities that took shape in the abolitionist conjuncture and the rise of modern professional folklore. I turn, then, to examine ethnosympathy as it developed along the front of black music after the Civil War to form at century's end a modern interpretive orientation toward culture at the racial margins.

Schooling the Spiritual

We have already established how Unitarianism fostered a broad sense of social crisis that prepared, in turn, a small but significant number of cultural entrepreneurs who turned a sympathetic ear to black music making. The result was a cottage industry of cultural production that served as an intersection for shifting intellectual appraisals of black culture (including cultivating caricaturizations of the latter). A major cultural transposition stemmed from this: what had been an oral tradition was selectively transcribed, and the *written* songs were launched into the world of written texts, where they joined the abolitionist's field of kindred literary objects. What remains to be examined is how the small number of black schools functioned as mechanisms of interpretative continuity by bridging ethnosympathy with ethnoscience.

The black colleges and universities in the South, which were organized to educate and train the new freedpersons, mark the first *formal-institutional* incorporation of black music that grew from the discovery process.[5] And what is important to consider here is that this took place *before* the professional folklorists seized upon black music in particular and black culture more generally. The black schools were pivotal in maintaining—and thus linking as well as mediating the process of transcribing the spirituals to—the emergent folkloristic interest in black songs. Most of the major schools—Fisk University, Hampton Institute, Tuskegee Institute—engaged wholeheartedly in the intellectual and analytical appropriation of black music. They did this building upon the already established practice of producing transcriptions of spirituals and merging this enterprise with the musical pedagogy of black students.

One major outcome of this institutional work was the establishment of student singing groups, some of which became immensely popular performers of Negro spirituals. The earliest and most famous of these school-based groups was the Fisk Jubilee Singers. Fisk University was established in 1865, and by the early 1870s the Jubilee Singers had become something of a cultural spectacle. Their fund-raising performances in cities in the North were met with astonishing success, and they toured and performed in England, Wales, Scotland, Holland, and Germany, earning the school more than $150,000. So unexpected was the reception of the performances and the funds garnered that the cultural capital of the spirituals was again reassessed. What the Jubilee Singers brought into view was the tremendous positive reception from sectors of the white

world for "authentic slave songs." The postwar interest in black performances of religious songs encouraged more institution-based collection,
transcription, and publication. Higginson's and Allen's work may have
waned, but the schools continued the textual production and literary doc-
umentation. The songs that the Fisk Jubilee Singers sang were printed in
Gustavus Pike's *Jubilee Songs* (1872). This collection presented a series of
revised, expanded, and updated compilations that included newly discovered and transcribed materials.[6]

The success of the Jubilee Singers appears to have spurred many of the
black schools to cultivate black singing. As Alain Locke noted, by
"spread[ing] the knowledge of these songs far and wide in their concert
campaigns," the schools saved the older forms of black music perma-
nently by recording and publishing "collection after collection." Black
religious songs were thus "saved during that critical period in which any
folk product is likely to be snuffed out by the false pride of the second
generation. . . . This [was] a service worth much more to the race and the
nation than the considerable sums of money brought to these struggling
schools. Indeed it saved a folk art, preserved the most perfect registration
of the Negro folk temperament and the most unique embodiment of its
folk experience."[7] This was not an act of tradition; there was no school-
based tradition of Negro spiritual choirs. Rather, it was in response to the
entwined issues of the discovery of an *authenticity* in the eroding wake of
social transformations and the phenomenon of audience development
that had come about through the interplay of increasingly available literary transcriptions of black songs, concerts, and touring.

Funds generated by black singing groups were certainly a welcome
fringe benefit, and the accounts of the rise of such singing groups took
note of fund-raising. But the process of incorporating black musical production within the new educational context was not simply motivated by
pecuniary interests. What was taking hold was the more complicated
spirit of preservation, of salvaging black "folk culture." Hampton Institute, which was established in 1868, pushed even farther the emergent
collection-oriented approach toward professional folklore. Shortly after
its inception, Hampton began cultivating singing groups. By the 1890s,
its musical teachers were actively engaged in the professionalization of
black folk studies. Hampton's musical personnel also expressed the tensions between meaning-oriented and objectivist-orientated approaches.

Fourteen years before the professional folklorists emerged under the
auspices of the American Folk-Lore Society, Hampton Institute was rais-
ing the concern for "folk songs." Hampton's director of music, Thomas
P. Fenner, reiterated the concerns that William Allen had raised in 1867.
In keeping with the general practice of organizing student singing groups,
Fenner had trained the first choir of the Hampton Student Singers. In the

preface to his *Religious Folk Songs of the Negro* (1874), Fenner wrote: "The slave music of the South presents a field for research and study very extensive and rich, and one which has been scarcely more than entered upon." He also noted how difficult it was to grasp the full meaning of songs when they were pulled out of their collective, socially embedded practices. Songs, argued Fenner, ought be recognized as activities and practices. Dislodging songs from their context and transporting them through musical transcription invariably resulted in the loss of meaning.

Fenner was probing the distinction between testimonies and artifacts, lived lives and caricaturizing snapshots. He raised the concern that "slave music" was "rapidly passing away. . . . The freedmen have an unfortunate inclination to despise it as a vestige of slavery; those who learned it in the old time, when it was the natural outpouring of their sorrows and longings, are dying off; and if efforts are not made for its preservation the country will soon have lost this wonderful music of bondage."[8] The concern that a vital aspect of black culture was in danger of disappearing was indeed deepening, at the same time it was motivating intellectuals to capture, collect, transcribe, and then reteach the songs to younger black students. What was presumably at stake was the loss of connectedness, of tradition, of lived historical memory. Fenner sensed as well the erosion of a social, cultural, and political consciousness that had been central to the earlier function of black culture as testimony. And this function was not reducible to a notion of an idealized religiosity disconnected from the "sorrows and longings" of people in socially embedded lives.

The retrieval of music continued as a crucial response to the sense of a waning black authenticity. In 1893, Hampton Institute's director of music, Frederick Rathbun, noted in the institution's own publication, the *Southern Workman*, that Hampton had collected "over one hundred different songs" with "many more in manuscript as taken down from the lips of our students from various parts of the South year after year."[9] The desire to retain the spirituals did not originate with former slaves; rather, it came from educators who continued to prefer religious song making as the venerable dimension of black culture. Students were as likely to abandon cultural forms that no longer resonated with their social context.[10] Caught, however, in postslavery social transformations, they became resources for those who were collecting songs. They were also expected, under tutelage, to learn and perform them.

As academics brought an increasing professionalism to the retrieval of spirituals, their interest merged with the already articulated desire to preserve a cultural arena modern social change threatened to banish. Problems of judgment and evaluation invariably surfaced. What methods of collection and retention were best? What material best warranted such efforts? In 1897, a decade after the American Folk-Lore Society had emerged, the Hampton leaders who were involved in song preservation retained their formative concerns regarding the fragile line between testimonies and artifacts. The discovery process was well on its way to becoming scientistically rationalized; it could possibly, through its own professional development, lose the meanings of the songs that it sought to capture. On December 29, 1897, Hampton representative Alice Mabel Bacon attended the annual meeting of the American Folk-Lore Society in Baltimore, where she presented a paper outlining the work that was being carried out by the Hampton Folk-Lore Society. Bacon and others at Hampton shared the worry that aspects of black culture, especially the spirituals, might disappear. Bacon's paper opened with some preliminary remarks about the obstacles in retrieving materials by relying upon students who no longer took such songs seriously. She also extended the Institute's thanks to individuals like William Wells Newell, Booker T. Washington, Reverend Alexander Crummel (one of W. E. B. Du Bois's mentors), and Thomas Wentworth Higginson, "who so helped forward the work at the beginning." Higginson, not surprisingly, continued after the war to aid the Hampton Institute's attempts to retrieve and retain black folk music, and the institute's important publication, the *Southern Workman*, recorded many of these endeavors.

Speaking as a layperson before a professional audience, Bacon defined her notion of authenticity in relation to the collecting process. "Our methods as a society," Bacon stated, "have been, as a rule, altogether lacking in originality. We have gathered in for our own use all things relating to negro folk-lore that we could find, with this single exception,—*nothing must come in that we have ever seen in print.*"[11] Bacon also reiterated the problems that arose when the testimonies of black music were overtaken by collection efforts that lead to reification and caricaturization, the very concerns that Thomas Fenner had raised twenty-three years earlier. But this time the problem was associated with the new institutional context of black education.

> The Hampton School has already done much work in the line of collecting, arranging for our system of musical notation, and publishing, the negro spirituals, but that is not the kind of work that [the Hampton Folk-Lore] Society wishes to do. Our desire is, not to obtain any song in a more or less *changed or mangled conditions*, as you surely do when you take it out of its foreordained and appropriate setting in some part of the *complicated* negro religious ritual, and adapt it to be sung as a regular four-part song by a choir or congregation, either white or black.[12]

Bacon continued to argue before the professional gathering that each song "has its place and its history, and the work of our Society must be to find the place and the history of each song." An all-too-common practice—"beautiful new plantation song" is found, the music teacher transcribes it, then drills the student choir to learn it—was to be avoided. The results, Bacon insisted, were twofold. Ripped from context, the song "becomes a totally different thing," and the process undermined what she believed was the authenticity of the spiritual. She drew this argument toward the larger debate as to whether black song making was autonomous and original or simply a mimetic response to white culture. The reason why there was "so much doubt to-day in the minds of so many of the best authorities, as to whether the negro spirituals are the product of the negroes, is because they have been subjected to this *process of civilizing* into regular written forms."[13] Bacon was indicting the practices of the black schools and other musically invested bodies who were not after authenticity or historical memory; the new cultural production was too satisfied with "mangled" representations.

Bacon's criticism could have just as well been applied to the contemporary surge of interest that the new professional folklorists were bringing to black expressions. As an enterprise birthed by science, the capture of artifacts as an end in itself was leading to the eclipse of black meaning. And in this very problem was an echo of the deeper historical crisis of slavery itself, a repetition of the tragic. It was black individuals who had been snared by slave catchers and pulled from their social contexts; now the technicians of cultural study were engaged in a similar strategy to capture the collective expressions of slaves and former slaves.

Ironic, however, are Bacon's concluding remarks before the professional organization. She did not offer a critique of objectivism as one might expect, but ended with a deferential tone toward the assembled professionals. More and better science was the solution: "There is not in [the Hampton Folk-Lore Society's] membership a single scientific folklorist, although we hope that when our material is published it may serve as one additional stepping-stone for the advancement of the science of folk-lore."[14] Moreover, the greatest obstacle that stood in the way of professional folklore study was black education. "Folk-lore," Bacon insisted, "has no greater enemy than the common school, and more than one half of the Negro children of the country are now enrolled in the public schools."[15] Bacon's end-of-century view of the way the education process was impeding the work of gathering authentic artifacts from black students bears an uncanny echo of the passage that Hampton musical director Frederick Rathbun had attributed to Hampton founder General Samuel Armstrong, who, in speaking of black song making, had said, "The more civilized you make them the more valueless you make them."[16]

Alice Mabel Bacon was involved in the difficult cultural work of trying to hold together the conflict inherent within a new interpretive formation that tried to grasp testimonies and artifacts in the same wide reach. Her address before the American Folk-Lore Society displayed as well the tensions that shaped the evolving career of ethnosympathy. She was insistent that the work to be carried out needed to avoid conflating cultural preservation and retention with mere pedagogical routines; this only culminated in banal performativity at the expense of cultural authenticity. In this regard she was negotiating the conflict between two sensibilities. On the one hand was the desire to locate black authenticity, not only for its value in grounding romanticist and antimodern ideologies, but also for its function in enabling a view of social histories and group fate; on the other were the larger pressures that were eclipsing from view the raging problem of politics and the crucial struggles over substantive egalitarianism for former slaves. This negotiation and resolution—resulting in the culturalist eclipse of politics—had already been foreshadowed in the writings of Higginson, Allen, and others.

Bacon was also acknowledging publicly what Hampton did not have—scientific legitimacy. And scientific legitimacy was required if she and fellow institutionally based retrievalists were to remain in good standing with the new professional gatekeepers of cultural interpretation. Bacon rightly questioned the gap that was emerging between testimonies and artifacts, but she embraced even more strongly the scientistic filters that enabled the latter to be considered at the expense of the former. Like many of the professionals who followed, Bacon showed no recognition of how the sheer cultural turn might also maintain a larger blind spot.

Consistent with the larger cultural eclipse, the musical directors and well-intentioned administrators at Hampton were not likely to question General Armstrong, Hampton's founder. Armstrong had his own ideas of what function a school under his supervision would fulfill in the context of Reconstruction and beyond. Hampton was, after all, formally known as Hampton Normal and Agricultural Institute, and its official publication, the *Southern Workman*, carried on its front-page banner the slogan: "Devoted to the Industrial Classes of the South." As a title, *Southern Workman* fit the school's emphasis on preparing laborers for nonunionized service jobs—which is what Republican virtue would come to mean for those racialized groups that stood distinctly untouched by, and excluded from, the touted virtues of the new Republicanism's "free men, free soil, and free labor."

Nor were the cultural retrievers there to question Armstrong's educational philosophy. In Armstrong's view, "What the colored people need is not Greek culture of the head, not chiefly a knowledge of history and literature, but enough training of the brain to make them think well, control their lower desires, and love their fellow-men, but mainly industrial training steadiness and mastery of trades, loving skillful use of hands and eyes and voice."[17]

This was a blueprint for the *training* of a black servicing class, one that would soon trouble W. E. B. Du Bois and set him on a collision course with the accommodationist leader Booker T. Washington. At the end of the nineteenth century Du Bois observed that the black common schools were "knitting . . . the Negro to the great industrial possibilities of the South." But for Du Bois the ensuing subordination was "not enough." Du Bois's vision of education for black people was a radically socialized Arnoldian view. Black Americans, too, ought to have the best of, rather than just the meager trickle-down from, what the great western cultural tradition promised to its most privileged. And this, of course, contrasted sharply with—indeed, it was a rebuke of—the policies inaugurated by Armstrong. It was not just "discipline" to achieve "industrial training" that Du Bois envisioned; black inclusion also ought to bring about kultur, that "culture of the head" that Armstrong insisted blacks did not need.

> I sit with Shakespeare and he winces not. Across the color line I move arm in arm with Balzac and Dumas, where smiling men and welcoming women glide in gilded halls. . . . I summon Aristotle and Aurelius and what soul I will, and they come all graciously with no scorn nor condescension. So, wed with Truth, I dwell above the Veil. Is this the life you grudge us, O knightly America? Is this the life you long to change into the dull red hideousness of Georgia? Are you so afraid lest peering from this high Pisgah, between Philistine and Amalekite, we sight the Promised Land?[18]

But Armstrong's earlier vision of black education was shaped by the formation of a contained black laboring class whose entrance into the new society was to begin and end at the margins—at the marginalized jobs in the new industrial and service sectors. It was based on a view of black and Indian[19] admission to civility through servility.[20] As James Anderson points out, the Hampton model was based on an alignment with the "conservative wing of southern reconstructionists who supported new forms of external control over blacks, including disfranchisement, segregation, and civil inequality." The "Hampton idea," which served as Armstrong's philosophy of "black Reconstruction," insisted on rescinding black voting privileges and relegating "black workers to the lowest forms of labor in the southern economy, and the establishment of a general southern racial hierarchy."[21] Indeed, the political gains that were made by blacks in the early years of Reconstruction, as reflected in black voting rights and office holding, were vehemently opposed by Armstrong, who campaigned against black political rights.[22]

Armstrong's political philosophy, brokered through the careful management of Negro education, had prevailed. Thus, by the time Alice Mabel Bacon confessed before the gathering of the American Folk-Lore Society that the Hampton Folk-Lore Society had no professionally trained folklorist, all of the gains established during the decade-long experiment of Reconstruction had been reversed, and blacks in the South had been thoroughly disenfranchised. And now, as Bacon argued, even the schooling of blacks had become an obstacle to recovering black authenticity.

The tension (as well as progressive separation) between testimony and artifact, and the troubled discourses surrounding the retrieval and retention of black songs, thus underscored a much larger social and political problem—the growing disjunction between moral and political reflection, and the role of the new scientized culturalism that appeared fascinated (if not enamored) with black *culture*. Moreover, the new culturalism that inherited the ethos of pathos was tragically speechless with regard to black *fate*. Bacon's presentation before the professional folklorists emblematized the capitulation of an early humanistic hermeneutics and the politics of subjects in crisis to the new wave of knowledge makers and knowledge making. What was taking shape between testimonies and artifacts was a growing chasm between a politics for subjects and a science for cultural objects. Being installed in the process was a form of cultural interpretation that posited a new field of study at the racial margins.

Like other smaller voluntary intellectual societies, the Hampton Folk-Lore Society was not in the position to avoid the process of scientific rationalization. In 1895, two years before Bacon's presentation, the *American Journal of Folk-Lore* published an article that probed the role of folklore and the relationship between professionals and amateurs. The article, entitled "Folk-Lore Study and Folk-Lore Societies," noted the importance of the amateur groups in gathering materials that were threatened by extinction. But it also emphasized the emerging hierarchical relations of professionalism: the smaller societies needed to become more rationalized in their work, tighten up their membership, and begin formal presentations before the professional body at the national level. In pointing out the "possible utility of subordinate societies," the author wrote, "in advancing this important cause, it is not intended to depreciate their independent usefulness, but to indicate that by performing this function alone they are accomplishing a sufficient work to justify their existence."[23] With such a tone coming from the national organization barely a decade old but now fully established at the helm, amateur folklorists like Bacon working within the context of the black schools were put in a double bind. They had to operate with the new objectivistic currents from establishment intellectuals in order to strengthen their cultural work, but within a schooling process that was meant to train a black underclass rather than promote a black sphere of musical aesthetics.

The Lore of Professional Folk

By the 1880s the notion of *folk* had permeated many of the issues that were nascent in the cultural turn. As was the case with the idealized trope of the black singing subject, *folk* signified multiple tensions. It harbored the ongoing search for authenticity while marking anxiety-ridden responses to modernity and social change. It also offered an intellectual perspective in which the cultural products (but not the subjects who produced them) could be envisioned as salvageable and redeemable. Indeed the salvaging of black culture rather than black fate seems to have had the upper hand when cultural intellectuals paid attention to the plight of blacks after the Civil War.

Yet one of the operating premises of the professional folklorists was the belief that the new science could finally get inside the culture of its subjects. As we have seen, this "inside," this orientation to the subjective interior, had its own particular history. It was first problematized with the idea of blacks having salvageable souls that could be redeemed through religious instruction, and thus traceable through the phenomenon of observable religious activity, particularly the singing of religious songs—hence the interplay of the spiritual proclivities of white ministers and their proclivities for the Negro spirituals. It is this history—of problematizing, discovering, marking, and tracking a comprehensible black interior—that was being annexed and rationalized by the coming of an ethnoscience attuned to the racial margins. As one commentator wrote in the *Journal of American Folk-Lore*, "The true character of the plantation negro, a mystery to his former masters, who viewed him only from the outside, is to be found in his folk-lore."[24] In the pursuit of scientistic legitimacy *and* the inner culture, folklore objectified the notion of "folk" in a great range of forms. Virtually every sphere of premodern life could be grasped within a folk studies framework. Consistent with the historical-interpretive reliance upon natural history as the initial explanatory framework, folklorist Otis T. Mason could claim: "Without doubt, there is also a folk-speech, folk-trades and practices, folk fine art, folk-amusement, folk-festival, folk-ceremonies, folk-customs, folk-government, folk-society, folk-history, folk-poetry, folk-maxims, folk-philosophy, folk-science, and myths or folk-theology. Everything that we have, they have,—they are the back numbers of us."[25]

Passionate as the early folklore enterprise was, what stands out within the quite remarkable interest in black expressivity is how any sustained concern for the political and economic well-being of blacks (and Indians) withered in contrast to the ascending value placed on their cultural expressions. The growing interest in black culture functioned more as a kind of enclosure in which the promotion of "preferred" representations was exemplified. The spirituals had served to map the highest *acceptable* virtue of a black presence and a black expressivity. In the case of Native Americans, the retrieval process was also in full operation, but language studies were the primary interest. Franz Boas, a founding officer of the American Folk-Lore Society, was instrumental in shaping the folkloristic orientation toward Native Americans. Professional folklore study came into being during a period in which the American political economy was exercising its most relentless push to conquer and consolidate nature within a nationalist space. Policy makers set a course bent on dominating rather than interacting with the nature and inhabitants of the western region of the continent. National expansionism coincided with the full-scale militarization of the relationship between Native Americans and the U.S. government. The almost total decimation of Native Americans was the result. Prior to the Civil War the federal government had worked out separate legal agreements with individual Indian tribes, but after the war this practice ceased. Native Americans were continually pushed farther west, to the Great Plains. In 1887 Congress passed the Dawes Act, which recognized not tribes but "individuals." Land allotments were designed to dismantle tribal solidarity as well as tribal land claims. The result was that two thirds of the hitherto tribal and reservation lands were annexed by white settlers and homesteaders. With the coinciding slaughter of over 13 million buffalo in a twenty-year period and the penetration of the transregional and transcontinental railroads, the material conditions for the earlier reservation inhabitants were destroyed.

The Native American's only hope for survival rested with their willingness to let white society convert them to white ways. In the crudest terms this meant imposing the Bible, the schoolbook, and the plow on Native Americans. Thus, after wholesale ethnic cleansing, language erosion was the next crucial loss—hence, the modus operandi of the linguistically oriented anthropologists who rose to ply their skills to the retrieval of "folklore." Retaining Indian languages, not as lived systems, but as artifacts, remained a central goal in Indian-oriented folklore study. The editors of the *Journal of American Folk-Lore* put their task bluntly: "A great change is about to take place in the condition of the Indian tribes, and what is to be done must be done quickly. For the sake of the Indians themselves, it is necessary that they should be allowed opportunities for civilization; for our sake and for the future, it is desirable that a complete history should remain of what they have been, since their picturesque and wonderful life will soon be absorbed and lost in the uniformity of the modern world."[26]

In comparison to black spirituals, Indian languages were to be salvaged precisely because social policies and practices required Indians to lose their languages and adopt English. But slaves and the post-slavery African Americans had long lost their original languages and had taken on English. And slaves were not targets of removal; they were too vital to the economy. The fetish for the spiritual, however, represented a cultural good that was distinct from all other cultural practices. The spiritual was thus the preferred example of a slave culture to be salvaged from the uprooting of the social conditions that had produced such expressions.

In essence, the edification of black cultural expressions coincided with the politics of an aborted Reconstruction. Professional folklore emerged to make a benevolent place for black culture after the collapse of Reconstruction. In the context of the larger dismantling and abandonment of any substantial commitment to recently freed blacks, the edification of black culture in the hands of new cultural experts amounted to an *imaginary relationship of intellectuals to the real conditions of black existence.*[27] Put another way, the White Redeemer culture in the South, with the aid of its silent and acquiescent allies in the North, regained control over the political economy while the cultural intellectuals in the North— or, more precisely, a dominated fraction among the dominant class— annexed black culture as part of a new grammar for a modernity sanctioned by, while quarantined within, the growing parameters of late-nineteenth-century academic social science.[28]

Nonetheless, the two parallel sensibilities we have traced through Higginson and Allen, which culminate in different yet overlapping orientations toward testimonies and artifacts, continued to run in tandem. However, the tension between testimonies and artifacts was increasingly compromised by a triumphant objectivism. The interplay was evident in the early professional treatments of black music in the 1880s and after. As a new cultural science, folklore was certainly attuned to the already strong disenchantment with modernization. Folklore was, after all, one of the key social-intellectual mechanisms that blended the older strains of romantic disenchantment and nostalgia with the promise of science's ultimate capacity to adjudicate the anxieties that were produced by modern market society. Thus in early folklore we find tensions between interpretations disposed toward the humanistic-testimonial and the taxonomic-artifactual. Yet, both of these orientations still attempt to carry out their interpretive work within the framework of a benevolent ethnosympathy that is busy being transformed into modern cultural interpretation.

Professional folklore inherited from its intellectual parents—romanticism and humanitarian reformism—the concern for cultural authenticity, as did the entire range of modern social theory and social science, or at least those aspects of the new enterprise that were ostensibly concerned with culture and interpretation. Folklore, however, extended in a more systematic manner many of the same sentiments launched by the initial discoverers of the Negro spiritual. As I have argued, the modern ethnosympathetic imagination and the ensuing protoethnographic work of the earlier discoverers of black culture paved the way. But the new enterprise took on scientistic accents that marked a significant shift in interpretation.

Traversed as it was by sentimentality and science, testimony and artifact, folklore was born with congenital ambivalence. Nonetheless, the rationalist dispositions came to outweigh antimodern disenchantment. By the turn of the century, folklore was resigned to the triumph of modernization and market society. Unlike mid-nineteenth-century romanticism in general, and American Transcendentalism in particular, scientific folklore was not designed to battle modernization. As noted, Transcendentalism had served as a rejection of modernization. Professional folklore, however, aided capitalist modernity by providing a partial map of its own sense of cultural superiority. If anything, folklore largely mitigated modernity's harsh edges by lobbying the intellectual world not to forget its benevolent responsibilities toward the racial and cultural margins. For folklore this came to mean archiving the objects and texts of cultural practices and cultural production. In this regard, professional folklore, along with much of the enterprise of social science, was symptomatic of an intellectual and cultural concession. Industrialization was here to stay. The pressures upon modern cultural interpretation would have to adjudicate this bald social fact. There would likely be no more Brook Farms on the urban outskirts; the centripetal forces of industrialization would soon favor the coming of Taylorized wage labor. Black sharecroppers in the South would also disappear from national intellectual concern and reflection.

As we trace the transformation of the reception of black music from the abolitionists to the professional folklorists, what comes into view is the process in which nineteenth-century romanticism and reformist politics were being rationalized. Abolitionists relied, in part, on the expressive practices of slaves for purposes of engendering a social, cultural, and political critique of American society—this was the critical facet of the emergence and reception of the slave narratives and, later, the Negro spiritual. Folklore however, compelled as it was by the new scientism, managed to transform some of the romantic recognition of critical social visions and cultural loss into a systematic and objectified inventory of cultural activities, beliefs, products, and practices. In the process, the political thrust of romanticist antimodernism acquiesced to, because it had to live within, the new and increasingly powerful accents of scientific knowledge. Primitivism, which at the turn of the century functioned as an orientation that straddled and even conflated aesthetic and ethnological modes of knowledge, would draw a peculiar nurturance from this troubled marriage.[29]

With a concern to retrieve aspects of culture on the verge of being overshadowed by modern industrial society, the editors of the first volume of the *Journal of American Folk-Lore* announced the "scientific character" of the professional mission as it pursued its "principle object"—to collect "the fast vanishing remains of folk-lore in America." The stated goals of the American Folk-lore Society were to obtain the "relics of Old English folk-lore," the "lore of Negroes in the southern states of the Union," and the "lore of the Indian tribes of North America."[30] From its inception in 1888 until 1914, the journal published over one hundred entries on African Americans, many containing treatments of music. The cultural turn that had emerged with the abolitionist movement was now being fully rationalized and institutionalized with the work of the American Folklore Society, and the interest in the racial margins played a central role in launching folklore into its development within the academy. The interest in the cultural—and especially the racial—margins vis-à-vis professional folklore had its highbrow corollary in the concern to identify, produce, legitimize, and institutionalize a genuine American high culture.[31]

In perusing the early pages of the *Journal of American Folk-Lore* one encounters what could be expected in an interpretive formation that worked the tensions between testimonies and artifacts: a neoromantic and sentimentalized framework that operated in tandem with an increasingly dominant as well as dry, matter-of-fact, category-driven, and taxonomically inspired spirit. Both sensibilities could claim the task of capturing the remnants of cultural practices disappearing in the march of progress. In this regard, the journal mediated between the older romanticism and the newer scientism. Yet, on closer examination the newer language could display, indeed boast, a presumed maturity. It had abandoned its ostensibly moral tongue, had discarded the "feminine" dimension, had traded sentimentalism for facticity, and had trimmed back to a mere acknowledgment the earlier fervor—the ethos of pathos—that had helped bring it into being. What triumphed behind the language shift was a profoundly important ideological shift in the wake of modernity—a shift from romanticism to realism. This shift, as Dorothy Ross has documented, had begun as early as 1868 with Frances Walker's call for a new, hard-nosed version of Republican virtue. Ross's comment on Walker: "'The world has lost its taste for a priori politics.' The postwar world required 'stern and practical inquiry into the workings of government' and 'the facts of society.' Indeed, 'We must regard liberty no longer as a female, but as a fact,' hence not as a romantic ideal to be wooed, but as something concrete, to be seized in particular pieces."[32] As George Fredrickson has pointed out, numerous influential New Englanders like Charles Eliot Norton, Oliver Wendell Holmes, Sr., and Francis Parkman distrusted, even detested, the Transcendentalism of Emerson. William Ellery Channing, the Unitarian minister that Emerson had found so influential, was despised by Parkman, who equated the Transcendentalist spirit with emasculation and fanaticism.[33] Higginson and Allen were negotiating this juncture. Recall how Higginson had attributed as endearing and positive the "feminine" qualities to his black troops, those "natural transcendentalists,": recall also how Allen's staid description was comparatively empty of any such attributes that extolled the virtues of emotional depth.

As it progressed in the second half of the nineteenth century, scientific realism also shed (at least linguistically) its earlier religious roots. These developments were also expressed in professional folklore. Even with its humanistically benevolent phrases, the new folklore embodied a depoliticized, morally tepid scientism. Writing in the *Forum* for a more general middle-class readership, folklorist Lee J. Vance summed up the new science's mission: "folk-lore is concerned more particularly with the survival of primitive or ancient ideas and customs in modern civilization."[34] It was not the meaning of the expressions that motivated this view of folklore; it was the concern over the very survival of culture itself. Vance was pleased with the new science of which he was a practitioner:

> the end of the nineteenth century [was] remarkable for the immense number of books devoted to the Folk—to people who have shared . . . least in the general advance. These people are, first, the backward races, as the natives of Australia and our Indian tribes; then the European peasantry, Southern negroes, and others out of touch with towns and schools and railroads.[35]

If the cultures of those "least in the general advance" were under threat of destruction, folklore's role was to intervene and its task was to *preserve*— to salvage remnants, specimens, and artifacts before they were banished by history. In the early-twentieth century, the "salvage paradigm," pursued by anthropologists like Franz Boas and Alfred Kroeber, "reflected," as James Clifford notes, "a desire to rescue 'authenticity' out of destructive historical change." But this process of salvaging is much older, and is rooted in a much earlier confrontation with modernity. It is envisioned early with Rousseau's trope of the "disappearing" subject, the "noble savage" (which marks a very important social critique of existing institutions as well as of the new directions emerging within eighteenth-century civil society). As a sprawling ideology, romanticism developed as a crisis response to early modernity. But as Virginia Dominguez notes, it is only after the subjugation of particular subjects that romanticism is fully carried out.

> The emergence of anthropology did not come about in the 19th century by accident. The expansion of European colonialism, the growth of an almost unbending faith in science, the combined condescension and universalization inherent in global, all-encompassing theories of biological and social evolution, and the successful domination of much of the world's political economy by 19th-century European and American capitalism made the emergence of academic anthropology not only possible but highly likely.[36]

Triumph of the Taxonomic

Nonetheless, in the new folklore no longer was the testimonial function of the spirituals most salient. Largely gone from the early pages of the *Journal of American Folk-Lore* was the expression of the capacity for the spirituals to reverberate across a range of anxieties, tensions, and problems that accompanied the history of the breaking of sound barriers and the rise of the critical reflections of pathos-oriented hearers; and gone was the initial and very short-lived, morally inspired mode of appropriation that had taken place a mere three decades earlier. The spiritual had once been the site of vibrant testimony to the burden of slavery, a social marker of the peculiar institution, the expressive property of an otherwise propertyless people, and a sign of an emergent yet largely elusive and clandestine black public sphere. But in the shadow of the new folklorist's professional acts, the older moral-political imperatives were being overtaken by the cultural-categorical imperatives of a modern, more exacting knowledge.

In keeping with the new proclivities toward more exact observation, Hampton music director Frederick Rathbun offered the following musicologically and aesthetically informed approach to the spirituals:

> The most striking attribute of the genuine "spirituals" is their utter simplicity, being based entirely on three chords, or the tonic, sub-dominant and the dominant of the key, and I have yet to find one containing a modulation, either forward or backward; and as originally sung the harmony is often confined to open fifths and octaves, the third often being absent; but in rhythm they are especially rich.[37]

In the mid 1890s, Hampton started a "Department of Folk-Lore and Ethnology" section as part of the institution's monthly publication, the *Southern Workman*. In a discussion reflecting the new interest in taxon-

omy, an article printed in 1895 in the journal drew a distinction among
"Corn-Songs," "Dance-Songs," and "Shouts or Spirituals": "Words may
differ, terms may differ in different localities or in the same locality from
year to year, but the Negro must sing as he works, as he plays, and as he
worships, and so these three classes of songs are always found."[38] The
following song was published for analysis:

> What in de worl' is de marter here
>   Oh. . . .oh, ho
> What in de worl' is de marter here
>   Oh. . . .oh, ho
> Fall out here and shuck dis corn
>   Oh. . . .oh, ho
> Bigges pil ever see sence I was born
>   Oh. . . .oh, ho
> Marster's niggers is fat and slick,
>   Oh. . . .oh, ho
> Case dey gits enough to eat
>   Oh. . . .oh, ho
> Joneses niggers is mighty po,'
>   Oh. . . .oh, ho
> Don't know whedder dey gets enough er no,
>   Oh. . . .oh, ho
> I loves ol' marster an' mistis too,
>   Oh. . . .oh, ho
> Case deys rich an' kin an' true,
>   Oh. . . .oh, ho
> Po white trash I does despise . . .

What does not appear—indeed, what had already begun to disappear
with Higginson and Allen years earlier—is any sustained discussion of
what the words might mean, what they might be addressing, and what
might matter socially and culturally for the singers of such lyrics. The
social categories of the song's main subjects, "Marster" and "I," address
the context of slavery—of owners and the owned, of the distribution of
the products of labor, and of strong social sentiments behind despising
"Po white trash." What underwrites this historically embedded text's social reference—the social relations of slavery—is eclipsed by a budding
ethnomusicology. In the new scientistic view, the song took on significance through—indeed, it was resignified within—the framework of
the taxonomy that gave it a new place within folklore: this song was a
work song, and more specifically a *corn song*.

Examples like the one above, with their clarity in addressing the relationships of slavery, are quite numerous, and many scholars have pointed

them out. But the new analytical and taxonomic template made painful histories and the social, economic, and political culpabilities to the constitution of such pain vanish.[39] In place of historical testimonies of lived relationships triumphed a new and improved technical description that spoke in a proper new grammar of knowledge—a fledgling ethnomusicology. "The rhythm sets the time of the work on which all are engaged, and the beating of the feet, the swaying of the body or the movement of the arm may be retarded or accelerated at will by the leader."[40] The song "Run, Nigger, Run," presented as a corn song, is given similar treatment. But the song's content—with lines like "Run, nigger, run patteroler'll ketch yer / Hit yer thirty-nine and ware 'e didn' tech yer"—engenders no reflection in the discussant, but is simply another example of "rhythmical combinations."[41] A similar technical neutrality, under which the social disappears, is blended with an interpretive aesthetic regarding the mechanics of form in Rathbun's discussions of dance songs.[42]

These interpretative shifts feature the displacement of one set of symbols by another that are ostensibly more refined because they draw more consciously on the logic of objectivism and scientific classification. More important, the shift illustrates how the ties between music and social and institutional conditions of slavery, which were never fully fathomed by those who followed Frederick Douglass's hermeneutic invitation, were so vulnerable to, and so quickly overtaken by, a new interpretive aesthetic. This new aesthetic was authorized and legitimized by science; its legitimacy, its self-referential and methodological virtue, rested upon its own formalism, a formalism carried out by the canonization of methodologies over interpretive orientations, a process that reworked the ground upon which authenticity could be reconfigured and given a new legitimacy. "Folk" had become an objective, scientific category.

Although artifacts were more likely to be discussed in the vocabulary of the new grammar, it was still permissible to nod to testimonies. There remained one dialect (though increasingly obscure) that spoke of the earlier moral and political impulses formed at the more radical edges of abolitionism. In keeping with the legacy that put black religious singing on the cultural map a few decades earlier, the shouts and spirituals could still be acknowledged as content rich. But such treatment was often reserved for the preface to or conclusion of an otherwise taxonomically informed article. When sympathy appears in just the conclusion of an otherwise scientistic discussion, it demonstrates the larger evolution of the narrative: the older ethos of pathos served no longer as a code for fathoming culture and the situated lives of people, but rather as a coda placed at the end of a musical score, as an afterthought to the cultural turn, or as homage to intellectual ancestors respected but whose wisdom now seemed out of date.

Consider the following example. After deciphering the artifactual value of black songs, the scholarly article can afford the brief conclusion (one not preceded by analysis) that in the spirituals

> the emotional expression of the Negro reach[es] its highest development. In the Spirituals the length and breadth and depth and height of the American slave's religious and historical experience are laid bare. . . . There is real poetry in the rude words, and harmony in the wild strains. . . . It is not art, it is life,—the life of the human soul itself, manifest in music and in words. . . . No truer folk-music can be found in this or any other country, than the religious song of the black peasantry of the South.[43]

Toward the end of the century such analytical descriptions were becoming formalized. Mainly, they featured major taxonomic treatments of black music and other forms of black cultural expression as artifacts, but could conclude with a tip of the hat to testimonies. It was a pattern of professional writing that now appeared somewhat routine, part of the new disposition of the trained modern cultural interpreter.

Both the presentation of desubjectivized cultural forms and the acknowledgment of black culture's intrinsic spiritualism had a double function: they bestowed upon black culture the attributes of categorical quaintness while demonstrating a benevolent and condescending appreciation. In the ever-broadening shadow of contract peonage in the South, racial segregation in the North, and racial strife always ready to explode into violence, disengaged engagement had only come of (a rationalized) age—it could disregard the festering crisis of race relations and yet patronizingly imbue black culture with pathos-dripping sweetness and light. The latter did not trickle down from above in the manner that so enthralled the cultural stewards who saw themselves at the helm of civilization. It instead rose up from a romantic subterranean innocence, emerging as an objectified essence and finding its proper place within the scientized salvaging operations of interpretive work at the racial margins.

From the vantage point of the new ethnosciences, the sites of folk life and popular culture offered remnants of a quaint irrationality. What folklore marked as objects of knowledge were cultural forms noted for their *absence of fit*; and, correspondingly, the people with which such forms were associated were, by definition, *fit for absence* within modern industrial culture (or, if present, understandably marginalized). Such objects—and even such people—could be displayed in museums, galleries, and world's fairs. Many folklorists framed their observations in ways that avoided blatantly reducing folk practices of presumably waning cultures to perspectives that assumed their Darwinistic disappearance.

Yet the notion of "survivals" that appeared in late-nineteenth-century social science writing was largely derived from Edward Burnett Tylor's study, *Primitive Cultures* (1874). Tylor had first employed the notion of "survivals" within an evolutionary stage theory, and the term was associated with the residues of premodern cultural practices. In Tylor's view, the presence of survivals functioned juxtapositionally to mark the contrast between primitive culture and civilized progress. The study of primitive culture was motivated, especially in Tylor's paradigm, to ferret out just those elements of modern culture that were remnants of a less civilized age. Tylor put the task quite bluntly: "It is a harsher, and at times even painful, office of ethnography to expose the remains of crude old culture which have passed into harmful superstition, and to *mark these out for destruction*. Yet this work, if less genial, is not less urgently needful for the good of mankind. Thus, active at once in aiding progress and in removing hindrance, the science of culture is essentially a reformer's science."[44] Survivals represented cultural lag. Such traits of primitivism would inevitably be purged by the progress of modernity. Reform meant extirpation. In this view, "culture" could be separated from life; artifacts could be saved, but practices that involved practitioners—"primitive peoples," in this case—were dispensable. In this regard, the social Darwinistic strains that were woven into the entire field of ethnoscience helped the new objectivism manage the distinction. Culture could be separated from life precisely because the lives of people on the receiving end of an imperial knowledge and an imperial power mattered only insofar as they could be absorbed and reshaped in the molds of cultural domination and subjugation.

Folklorist William Wells Newell, another founder of the American Folk-lore Society, who also assisted the early efforts at Hampton, stated the parameters of the ultimate relationship that professional folklore was to have between *its* dominant culture and the culture of others. "In folklore as in civilization diffusion takes place from the higher culture to the lower; whenever two races are in culture-contact, the more civilized, itself comparatively unaffected, bestows on its neighbor the entirety of its ideas and customs. The valve is open in the flow of information from the superior to the inferior, but (with rare exception) closed in the reverse direction."[45]

Like the earliest observers of black expressivity who heard only noise, the neo Darwinists also (again) heard only noise. Like the early, pre-pathos modes of hearing discussed in Chapter 2, this noise was sound out of order. Such noisy survivals did have a preferred place within the desire (again) for sound management—in collections where the problem of the music's meaning could be truncated and ultimately managed. As pieces in a collection (and thus, by definition, firmly captured), musical artifacts could not serve as socially embedded practices, humanly embodied testimonies, and knowledge-filled signifiers for the society in which they were

constituted. Disembodied, decontextualized, and depoliticized, the taxonomic enterprise, when applied to black culture, exemplified the modernization of an older disengaged engagement, and the ultimate intellectual
practicing of "safe race." One would never really need to know much
about historical subjects who were displaced and rendered invisible by
the triumph of their artifacts.

．　．　．　．　．

Of course the ambivalence between the humanistic and scientistic pressures persisted and the tension between testimonies and artifacts had become endemic to the modern interpretive enterprise at century's end. Indeed they became symbiotically linked in a competitive manner, with the
one helping to define the other. Those folklorists with an interest in black
music in particular, and in the expressive cultural forms of many other
groups identified through racial, ethnic, and class attributes, continued to
pursue the older testimonial thematics. Their desire to recover the problem of lived meanings and inner culture remained intractable. This was
especially the case as the pace of modernity quickened, for subjects became necessary for critical intellectuals who invoked them as signifying
figures against ever-shifting ground. Collective groups—workers,
women, immigrants, deviants, youth, ethnic enclaves, racial minorities,
subcultures—serviced the rise of a critical intelligentsia and the latter's
capacity to bring modernity and its relentless transformations into some
kind of understandable focus. This enterprise was often presented in the
language of social and humanitarian reform, and such struggles also invited the much larger hegemonic interests of sheer managerialism.

Though the political urgency that had once been associated with the
discovery of the slave narrative and the spiritual had largely evaporated,
the currents were still felt. Folklore, cultural anthropology, ethnography,
and cultural sociology all maintained some interest in testimonies, though
in the new century these enterprises were not ostensibly engaged in the
kind of inquiry that had drawn its charge in the context of the nineteenth
century's most powerful social movement. With W. E. B. Du Bois the
meaning of "survivals" was reversed and resignified. Neither "cultural
lag" nor "cultural residuals," folk practices represented a crucial retention of solidarity in the face of dehumanization and marginalization. Du
Bois referred instead to the resilience of psychic survival. In his book *The
Souls of Black Folk*, he acknowledged the retention of Africanist orientations that had been renegotiated in the American context, and that had
resulted in a unique cultural response—an African American sensibility.
William Allen had pointed this syncretism out as well.

Contrary to the professional view that black education snuffed the life out of slave culture, Du Bois would also point out in his massive study of Reconstruction a quite different function of the black schools. Regardless of their design to incorporate and resubjugate, the educational opportunities were of great historical importance to blacks. True, they provided the barest mechanisms of integration; but under slavery such educational opportunities did not even exist, and were indeed illegal in many contexts. Four decades after Alice Mabel Bacon indicted the black schools, with the likely approval of folk purists, for purging cultural authenticity, Du Bois would revise the historical significance of the schools. The fledgling schools, he argued, had been crucial in preventing the South from slipping back into a slavery worse than the existing dead end of sharecropping. What the new schools enabled was a political and cultural bulkhead for freedpersons. "Had it not been for the Negro school and college," Du Bois wrote,

> the Negro would, to all intents and purposes, have been driven back to slavery. His economic foothold in land and capital was too slight in ten years of turmoil to effect any defense or stability. His reconstruction leadership had come from Negroes educated in the North, and white politics, capitalists and philanthropic teachers. The counter-revolution of 1876 drove most of these, save the teachers, away. But already, through establishing public schools and private colleges, and by organizing the Negro church, the Negro had acquired enough leadership and knowledge to thwart the worst designs of the new slave drivers. They avoided the mistake of trying to meet force by force. They bent to the storm of beating, lynching and murder, and kept their souls in spite of public and private insult of every description; they built an *inner culture* which the world recognized in spite of the fact that it is still half-strangled and inarticulate.[46]

Du Bois referred to something entirely different when he noted the existence of a resilient "inner culture" that had withstood the storm of slavery, murder, beatings, and lynchings. This inner culture was certainly not a reference to the presumably disappearing rituals at which modernity's new folklorists and kindred social scientists could nod through methodologies that, in effect, bestowed the last rites of a people banished for their lack of fit in the New World. Nor was it simply the great resolve that blacks displayed in the face of the collapse of Reconstruction. Rather, it was a cultural fortitude that had long been shaped in the confrontation between Africanist cultural dispositions and the insertion of blacks into slavery, that had set flowing the rivers of music making, that had given slaves their grammar of solidarity, their "hidden transcripts" that nurtured their clandestine discourses and their symbolic constructs that made possible their fledgling but always policed public spheres.[47] Such cultural production within the social rigidities of slavery enabled slaves to assemble in order to practice (as well as to assemble in the guise of practicing) sanctioned religion and to forge the sensibilities that surfaced in the critical elaborations of the slave narratives. Music making certainly had a religious dimension. But it was also much more than any reflection of doctrine—it was the *psychic property* of subjects who themselves were the objects of property. For overseers who were primarily interested in maximizing labor, for neo-Transcendentalists in search of reenchantment, and for protoscientific taxonomists eager to draw up the new objective maps of black culture, it was this psychic property that the discovery process tried to tap.

SEVEN

CONCLUSION

AS WE HAVE SEEN, it was within the cultural conjuncture of what Max Weber called "elective affinities"—the historically specific and strategic integration of ideas and interests—that troubled cultural entrepreneurs from the North were able to turn their gaze to the South's and the nation's moral and social crisis. In the North they could read as well as hear what the radical black and white abolitionists had to say. In the South they could hear black song making. It was Frederick Douglass who first bridged the thick descriptive power of the slave narratives to the subterranean and clandestine world of black music making. Douglass opened black music to external examination; from this moment discoverers and appropriators sought to inhabit this expressive domain. Black song making was actually a large cultural terrain, but it was the spiritual that became the most prized symbolic real estate. The spiritual was discovered as a black cultural good, but in the process it quickly became good black culture. There was, then, a deeper and more profoundly important cultural dialectic at work in the shifting meanings attributed to black song making. The value of the spiritual as a cultural practice was transformed through the historical transformation of the practices of its being discovered by those who were most vested in bringing back religious singing into its edified position. Such shifts, when contextualized—that is, when pushed back into the most important social relations responsible for giving them their lived urgency—invariably involved social conflicts and antagonisms over cultural actions and practices because they involved struggles over meanings, definitions, and interpretations that conditioned the very schemas of appropriation.

As I have argued, those who invested in the edification of the spirituals were propelled by individual and collective responses to social crises. Outsiders, of course, could never inhabit this musical terrain; they could squat here and there, drive claim stakes into some of the surface features, even encircle parts of this cultural productivity with institutional powers—which was necessary for launching an interpretive formation that could accommodate the larger and often contradictory pressures to establish critical accounts of modernity as well as of forms of knowledge amenable to social management. But they could not annex the vitality of the cultural infrastructure. And it would soon shift from under their feet as the spirituals gave birth to new and increasingly myriad forms of expressivity (such as blues and jazz). Besides, the new cultural entrepreneurs shared little with the economic bourgeoisie, and even less with the lowest classes and castes from whom they sought authentic cultural goods. The renegade religious intellectuals and cultural entrepreneurs saw themselves in much the same way as did other autonomous intelligentsia in the mid-nineteenth century. According to Arnold Hauser, autonomus intellectuals were a social strata losing "the feeling of having a mission to fulfill in society. [They] saw [themselves] cut off from the social class of which [they] had hitherto been the mouthpiece" and were feeling "completely isolated between the uneducated classes and the bourgeoisie."[1] Though they heard black soundings with new ears, a managerial aesthetic none-theless governed the new schemas for hearing.

As I have argued, the filters that determined what was culturally acceptable were initially, and largely, religious. Certainly Unitarian-Transcendentalist theosophy played a major role in breaking the old sound barriers that had maintained black music as sheer noise. Shaped by the entwined crises of an emerging industrialized market society and the moral, political, and economic pressures to abolish slavery, this religion spawned at its most radical edges the small number of individuals who became strategically positioned to hear the black subjects who also had emerged from the terrain of religious and ideological struggles over slavery. Most of the white collectors, certainly the noteworthy ones, had religious affiliations with Unitarianism. As we have seen, their attraction to black religious song making flowed from a cultural logic. The radicals of that denomination, who drew much of their inspiration from the religious crisis that engendered Transcendentalism and nudged the ministry toward questions of social engagement, were some of the clearest expositors of the new disenchantment with modernity. What the racial and cultural margins offered to them was a site where disenchanted intellectuals could visit to refresh their half-critical, half-romantic sensibilities of why market society had lost its capacity for human authenticity. Black culture helped them sharpen and recenter their identities. In this regard the discovery process was itself symptomatic of a legitimation crisis and a cultural struggle within a larger but deeply embattled paternalism. We could perhaps just as meaningfully envision the discovery process as one of the fronts of battle being waged in the great paternalistic suit over which form—slavery or Republicanism—would manage civil society and its complex racial, gendered, and classed dynamics.

With the rise of social science, the interest in black music shifted in place, tone, and function. First, abolitionists were eclipsed, displaced, and superseded by folklorists and social scientists, consistent with the fact that humanitarian reformism helped give birth to modern social science. The ascendancy of social science did not obliterate the cultural sensibility of the earlier radical abolitionists, but it did modify and realign the latter with the former. Secondly, the interpretive tone changed from a concern with what was ostensibly moral and political to a preoccupation with what could best be grasped descriptively, taxonomically, and analytically within the larger intellectual schemas of objectification and classification. What resulted was a functional separation between an earlier *politics of subjects* and a new *science of objects*. Thirdly, the uncoupling of moral-political discourse from African American music in particular (and African Americans in general) helped service the much larger institutional uncoupling of the state from southern Reconstruction. The debated "failure" of Reconstruction has been well told. What I wish to underscore here are the cultural links between an earlier period during which blacks seemed to represent a greater moral value for northern liberals than they did after their status as slaves had been legally changed.[2]

The earlier interpretive sentiments had politically sharp edges that had been honed all the way back to the social movements surrounding abolitionism. However, professionalism did much to purge such sentiments from the entire field of humanitarian reformism. The earlier testimonial orientation toward black song making did not disappear, but it began to wither and atrophy under the new science's attempt to avoid the contamination of sentiment. As Dorothy Ross has shown, the new social sciences were engaged deeply in the politics of late-nineteenth-century social transformation. As new forms of knowledge, the social sciences were fed by every major institutional pressure and every current of social, economic, and political change that unfolded in the late nineteenth century.[3] Despite their rhetorical overtures to objectivism, the social sciences were central players in adjudicating the installation of the modern corporate-industrial society. At the edges of social science were the debates about people on the margins. In addition to women, these certainly included now free African Americans, but also Native Americans, Mexicans, Asians, and problematic and under-Americanized white ethnic immigrants. It is upon these groups that ascendant neo-Darwinists and the now fractured and beleaguered humanists would continue to battle over modes of interpretation.

The largely scientific discourses of early folklorists still managed to praise the spiritual as sanctified culture, as beyond "art," as tantamount to "life" itself. Such a framework invoked the intuitive idealism of Transcendentalism, but more as afterthought. It might appear, at first pass, that this was the height of pathos, and it actually was at the time. But it was a peculiar kind of pathos—one that had no distinct subject because it celebrated and embraced, through disengaged engagement, a disembodied "soul" and a Negro-in-general. This pathos embraced a cultural form that appeared to be uninhabited by any particular and discernable subject. It celebrated a caricaturization. What triumphed was a cultural trope that invoked a generic Negro reduced to a generic genre. Within the new interpretive formation, social acceptability thus took place through a cultural form. The culturalist move avoided (as well as voided) through aestheticism any substantive dialogue with the people who actually lived in what Du Bois and others would soon call the "black belt" and the "black metropolis." In a way, the disengaged engagement of Mary Boykin Chestnut—who wrote in 1861 that "the best way to take Negroes to your heart is to get as far away from them as possible"—was being rearticulated at the center of the new ethnoscience.[4]

Let us recall that it was the slave narratives rather than black song making that articulated the broader, elaborate, and critical logic. After all, Frederick Douglass's narrative did not pivot mainly upon song making, but used music as one of several ways to grasp the ties between collective histories and collective biographies. Their immanent critiques drew upon the religious imagination to pose the rottenness beneath the religious halo worn by the advocates of slavery. The Civil War, however, engendered an even more fervent interest in black testimonies that compressed them into black song making. And from this moment there arose something equivalent to a moral and political enclosure around the symbolic terrain of musical and cultural production. As Pierre Bourdieu has pointed out, "Struggles over the appropriation of economic or cultural goods are, simultaneously, symbolic struggles to appropriate distinctive signs in the form of classified, classifying goods or practices, or to *conserve or subvert the principles of classification* of these distinctive properties."[5] It appears to be the case that the critical intellectual impulses that fueled both the narratives and their critical receptive publics were subverted and evicted (along with the larger and common set of shared uses and practices of music) from the intellectual enclosure around cultural valuation and interpretation. What was permitted to remain, what was conserved, was the spiritual embodied in the idealized singing subject.[6] Singing subjects, unequivocally spiritualized, could now be heard.

But the new ears that adored the rehabilitated Negro as a signifying *folk object* were deaf when it came to hearing the voices critical of the massive backslide trapping blacks into poverty and marginality, and managing the boundaries with brutality. Georg Lukacs's assessment of romanticism seems to apply. As Lukacs argued, romanticism's "subjectively lyrical attitude toward events" in the form of a "flight from the present" was carried out with a mood of "disillusioned romanticism, an over-intensified, over-determined desire for an ideal life as opposed to the real one, a desperate recognition of the fact that this desire is doomed to . . . an uneasy conscience and the certainty of defeat." A corresponding sense of resignation thus took the form of an "immoderate elation of the subject" coupled with "the abandonment of any claim to participation in the shaping of the outside world."[7]

The shift from viewing the crisis of black subjects through a moral and political lens to the treatment of blacks through cultural artifacts was also symptomatic of the modern separation between *moral reflection* (new cultural politics) and *knowledge management* (new ethnoscience). Black music and black subjects could be embraced for their aesthetic virtue, for their preferred performative selves. Yet such an embrace of disembodied symbolism would remain thoroughly disconnected from the flesh-and-blood fate of black people. In the years surrounding World War I, the cultural turn hinged even more on the focus upon an exoticized singing subject and on the attitude fostering an aestheticized obliviousness to the deeply marginalized and institutionally sanctioned exclusion of African Americans from the full benefits of civil society. The narrowing cultural-ism also placed social limits on ethnosympathy. Taken to extremes, aes-theticized sentimentality nurtured social blindness.

Consider the conflation of Transcendentalist notions of intuition with primitivism in the following comment: "With the Negro, it would seem that the further back one traces the current of musical inspiration that runs through the race (that is, the more primitive the people and thus the more instinctive the gift), the nearer does one come to the divine source of song,—intuition, which is in turn the well-spring of all genius."[8] This, of course, is one way the legacy of Transcendentalism could be *remembered*, shorn of its criticisms of capitalism and market domination. We see some-thing of preferred memory-making continuing in an observation made in 1925 by the amateur folklore collector Dorothy Scarborough: "DuBose Heywood tells of the work that the Charleston group is doing, in teaching the Negro children their racial songs. The white people go to the planta-tions, where they learn the authentic songs, and then teach them orally to the colored children—not writing them down at all, for they feel that oral transmission is the true method for folk-songs."[9] The deeper tragedy in this particular juncture of disengaged engagement is that romanticist im-ages helped perpetuate a social system in which the black possessors of the Emersonian *over soul* would continue to bear the repression that came with their status as a racialized *underclass*, while the new academic culturalism enabled so many to wallow in a sentimentalism that remained largely silent about lynching.

Black singing subjects were still capable of representing Transcenden-talist ideals as they did in 1919: "Is it not in the Song of the Negro that we glimpse the spirit of the race reaching forward toward development and eventual unfolding? And when we see that song illuminating with an in-ner light multitudes of otherwise darkly inarticulate and groping, we think of Emerson and ponder: 'The Negro "Over-Soul"—is it Music?' "[10] This romantic association linking black song makers with Emersonian Transcendentalism could still be invoked in the context of a larger setting that was not able to transcend the legacy of a populist racial hatred fixed psychically and institutionally in what Du Bois called the "color line." Indeed, the cultural turn could even embrace the color line by cultivating a romantic and pathos-oriented appreciation for black culture that relied simultaneously upon a deeply racialized modern ethnology.

Behind the irony is the function of disengaged engagement. In the cultural turn, symbolic blacks and actual blacks did not have to coexist— either in the cultural imagination of the new interpreters of black culture or in their actual historical and social relationships. Some of the most virulent attacks on black communities in the North and South were being carried out as blacks were being praised for their Transcendentalist and spiritual virtues. In 1917, thirty-eight African Americans were lynched; the number doubled the following year. Spurred by the Ku Klux Klan, the interracial conflict was so intense during the summer of 1919 that James Weldon Johnson called it the "Red Summer."[11]

Thomas Wentworth Higginson's troops, those black "natural Transcendentalists," donned Union uniforms and marched on battlefields in the service of securing Republican virtue, only to return to an American society that wanted just their docile servitude. This new place was more characteristic of feudal society: high on duties, low on rights. The black troops who returned home from the European battlefields of World War I did not do much better. It is with painful irony that intellectuals within the dominated fraction of the dominant class could with good intentions practice the disconnected aesthetic praise of African Americans for their musically anchored spiritualism while black civilians were being killed in urban racial conflagrations. At the war's end W. E. B. Du Bois summarized the key terms facing blacks when he announced, "Make way for Democracy! We Saved it in France, and by the great Jehovah, we will save it in the United States of America, or know the reason why."[12] In this context Du Bois's words signal the disenchantment and emergent political anger that was to simmer until the period of World War II. It is also in this context that Marcus Garvey's emphasis on racial pride and negritude found fertile ground among blacks who lived out the bitter meaning of fighting to save the democratic principles that the larger society refused to extend to them.

As Roland Barthes observed, "A text's [social] unity lies not in its origin but in its destination."[13] In a way, the destination I have sketched is the complex career of noise. But I have also sketched part of the career of a modern mode of hearing. Throughout the eighteenth century, slavers and their associates wrote of the "crude," "barbaric" noise that their human commodities emitted. In the early-twentieth century W. E. B. Du Bois wrote, in words that inflected Transcendentalist-inspired theories of nature, authenticity, and truth, that "there are to-day no truer exponents of the pure human spirit of the Declaration of Independence than the American Negroes; there is no true American music but the wild sweet melodies of the Negro slave; the American fairy tales and folklore are Indian and African; and, all in all, we black men seem the sole oasis of simple faith and reverence in a dusty desert of dollars and smartness."[14] An enormous cultural as well as historical transformation marks the distance between these two sensibilities.[15] The transformation is capped by the rise of a modern mode of interpreting the culture of groups whose practices function as ways of marking and critiquing the coming of a modernity that also created the new interpretation. As I have suggested, black music making was central to this interpretive transformation.

Modern cultural interpretation is, of course, not reducible to the discovery of black music, the conflicted attention it received, and the various appropriations to which it was subjected; such a reductionistic view would grant a cultural arena and cultural forms too much autonomy. Moreover, there are many additional factors that could be brought into the nexus between black music and cultural interpretations, which would exceed and complicate (probably rightly) the restricted threads that I have tried to trace in this study. Nonetheless, the discovery of the spiritual, and the preferred frameworks the key discoverers deployed, demonstrate how crucial the spiritual was in serving as a pivoting point that connected modern ethnosympathy to the cultural expressions of racial and marginal peoples.

The rise of modern social science certainly fed the process. But upon closer examination, we have seen how interpretive struggles surrounded black music making quite some time before the rise of modern social science. We might say that black music served a kind of midwifery function, helping to birth the modern orientation toward culture on the margins. We could also argue as well that the abolitionist movement was actually the midwife of modern American cultural interpretation. Either way, it is clear that black American music had a very significant, perhaps even a mediating, position in the birthing of American cultural interpretation, particularly in relationship to what we moderns would call "subcultures." But to take one lesson from this study, there is an irony lodged in the misplaced concreteness of inherited terminology, for if black music is considered (as it is) an expression of subculture, then why was it so central in shaping of the larger struggle to launch modern strategies of interpretation? Clearly, there are serious problems and limits that surround the evolution and use of this term, but to further clarify this warrants another study.

The discovery process was inaugurated by multiple lines of development. I have discussed some of these in terms of consequences, and among them I have given general emphasis to two that are entwined but also distinct: the turn toward meaning and the turn toward taxonomic categorization. The cultural turn sprang from, as well as fostered, the interest and appreciation in, the inner life, the realm(s) of meaning, and the purposive dimensions behind cultural expressions. In tandem with this was a new sensitivity to the realm of subjectivity (individual as well as collective) in relationship to objective culture.[16] But the cultural turn also accommodated the new scientistic impulses that pushed some of the earlier ethnosympathetic impulses toward positivist and objectivist dimension. The tension between these two impulses, which I have described as testimonies versus artifacts, has remained a part of the modern intellectual infrastructure, and continues to condition the inquiry into cultural practices.

The rationalization and professionalization of ethnosympathy may have eclipsed the problem of collective groups and their social fate, but this is understandable insofar as professionalism's primary function was (and remains) managerial rather than critical. Certainly, within the work of professional students of culture during the early decades of the twentieth century, the substantive ties between music making and social fate may have largely disappeared. But the function of music to chart social fate did not disappear. Indeed, music making continued as a vibrant vernacular, and as a dimension of a larger public sphere. This dimension was not central to the new professionals and was seemingly not conducive to—indeed, it was incompatible with—the pressures of rationalization.

Yet something urgent and vital seems to have disappeared toward the end of the century that investigators over our century have tried to retrieve. In the early years of the twentieth century Du Bois looked at the social rubble of an aborted Reconstruction and took stock of a civil society deeply divided by the color line. And it was Du Bois who remembered something of the urgency that Frederick Douglass had introduced in his narrative of more than a half century earlier. It fell upon Du Bois to retrieve the unique sociology of music that Douglass and the most critical moments of abolitionism had bequeathed. The difficulty in recuperating the moments of critical vision involved the fact that the cultural turn that opened up the chance for modern intellectuals to envision the deeper ties between social fate, cultural practices, and history also turned away from the opportunities of such broader envision. The tensions and contradictions between the view of black music as either testimony or artifact, as well as the desires to hold these two orientations together in relationships that connected an emergent science of objects and a politics of subjects, were nonetheless major currents within the rise of modern cultural interpretation. These analytical strands continue as part of the weave of our modern orientation toward cultural analysis. In the American case, they belong to a larger juncture in which the meanings of culture, race, and modernity have become inescapably refracted in one another. Du Bois's call in 1903 to rediscover the spirituals included recognition and gratitude for the white discoverers of the spirituals during the Civil War years, though he said nothing of the rise of professional folklore studies, which was one of the outgrowths of the new knowledge formation that had already emerged to annex the study of black culture. Du Bois listed ten "master songs" that were, for him, the quintessential examples of the phenomenon he called the sorrow songs.[17] Many of these had appeared in William Allen's 1867 compilation. Du Bois and others would soon reopen the pursuit of testimonies, of situated vocabularies embedded in lived histories that demanded to be retrieved, not for romantic or nostalgic purposes, but because the historical memory of the political moment that had produced a potentially more critical redemptive politics was now being purged by the brazen disregard for the fate of black lives.

We might now wonder, given the analysis provide here, how to position the crucial retrieval of black culture by African American intellectuals, writers, and artists in the 1920s. Certainly the celebrated cultural (re)turn during the 1920s that is associated with the "Harlem Renaissance" helped restore what had been severed by the rationalization of the earlier cultural turn. Renaissance intellectuals and artists pushed open wider the doors of black culture with an emphasis on performativity and aesthetics as points of entry into black life. As a cultural development, it also came on the historical heels of an already well established turn toward "folk," and in this regard it shared aspects of the older retrievalist framework that had, in the wake of Reconstruction's demise, been driven underground. Moreover, the intellectual contours of this cultural turn had ties to the earlier cultural conjuncture in which the spiritual had been discovered. The rise of the Renaissance and the emergence of the (second) "New Negro" movement in part amplified the (inherited) aestheticism, but Renaissance intellectuals also attempted to reappropriate the entire sphere of black cultural production that had been partially and selectively appropriated by attending to the wide range of vernacular including blues, jazz, and literature. This enterprise rehearsed and renewed the older and deeper schisms between testimonies and artifacts and the bifurcation between a politics for subjects and a science of objects. Renaissance illuminations would soon dim under the ravaging forces of the Great Depression, but the retrievalist ethos would flare again during the Civil Rights movement of the 1960s and become an important impetus for reinstalling a critical humanist and social scientific revisionism.

.   .   .   .   .

We have traced the transformation of hearing black music by examining the shifting schemas of perception among important moral, political, and cultural entrepreneurs, and we have tracked important strands of development within the social career of musical soundings. In following the appropriation of black music, we have charted its earliest roots as noise, initially barbaric, grotesque, aberrant, and certainly irreverent, to its culmination as meaningful sound, civilized, beautiful, indeed spiritual. We have examined the rise of a pathos that began as a kind of crude perplexity, but that slowly evolved and transformed into ethnosympathy—a cultural complex and a complex cultural development that centered progressively upon the recognition of meanings and the psychic interiors that became accessible behind the cultural expressions of a subordinate group. We noted the emergence of sociocultural opportunities that were of use to slaves within the cultural contradictions of an extended religious franchise that simultaneously granted yet denied the cultural grounds that fostered modern subjectivity. We followed the "discovery" of black music and the rationalization of this discovery, first as a new politics of subjects during the height of the abolitionist movement, then as a restricted and increasingly enclosed domain that centered upon the preferred religious expressivity of blacks, and then as its culmination in the modern bifurcation between inner knowledge and objective classifications. And we have observed the always ambivalent ethos of pathos, seeing it unfold in the abolitionist conjuncture, take root after the Civil War in the fledgling black schools, and become both an impetus for and a thing to be partially annexed by the rise of early folklore. What began with the emergence of pathos-oriented hearing and an ethnosympathetic disposition on the fringes of Protestantism was progressively transformed into the testimonial schemas of abolitionist representations; these, in turn, were transformed again into cultural artifacts. From this perspective we can see how the serializing of slave narratives in the early abolitionist papers could culminate fifty years later in the professional article on subcultural practices published in the new professional publications exemplified by the *Journal of American Folk-Lore*.

The interpretive formation operated with historically bequeathed schisms. On the one hand, there remained the earlier idea, forged in the interplay of romanticist and humanitarian reformist sensibilities, that the inner life of subjects could be discovered, fathomed, and apprehended through their cultural testimonies. This was a new and benevolent view of the cultural interior of groups (and, more broadly, as Michel Foucault has shown, this finding and making of the interiority of subjects had ties to strategies of normalization).[18] On the other hand, the scientistic impulse, which brokered and partially usurped this earlier hermeneutical interest, legitimized its investigatory and interpretive spirit within the framework of objectivism. Both orientations remained vibrant and were never mutually exclusive. The benevolent attitude could blend with the managerial attitude to limit the value of cultural expressivity within larger structures of subjugation.

The legacy of moral reflection and knowledge management, or politics and science, took its most modern seat in the burgeoning (and returning) interest in the fate and identity, as well as the social and political struggles, of groups on the racial, cultural, and gendered margins of American society. This has opened wide the entire problem of cultural representation. Once opaque, the questions of cultural interpretation have become increasingly transparent. As Raymond Williams has argued, *interpretation* is no longer an idea marking reified modes of knowing, let alone a skill or practice; it is a *problem*.[19] In the American context, the crisis of modernity, the legacy of politics, the conundrum of race, the interpretation of *cultures*, and the manner in which these transect one another developed from their inception in the nineteenth century. Black song making, particularly the spiritual, was at the very core of the rise of the cultural interpretations that grew from that juncture.

EPILOGUE

WRITING IN 1977, Lawrence Levine put the modern redemptive mission most succinctly: "It is time," he wrote, "for historians to expand their own consciousness by examining the consciousness of those they have hitherto ignored or neglected. . . . The problem is that historians have tended to spend too much of their time in the company of the 'movers and shakers' and too little in the universe of the mass of mankind." What was at stake in Levine's view was the redemptive project: "Even in the midst of the brutalities and injustices of the antebellum and postbellum racial systems black men and women were able to find the means to sustain a far greater degree of self-pride and group cohesion that the system they lived under ever intended for them to be able to do."[1] Levine's call to take the cultural turn to common lives was meant to rectify the eclipse of common people.[2]

Levine's challenge to cultural historians and social scientists was part of a larger critical revisionism that played a central role in relaunching the modern retrievalist orientation toward cultural analysis. It helped return to black music the kind of thick description that had been first advocated by Frederick Douglass in 1845. Music could again be understood with regard to how it helped create and maintain solidarity amidst the pulverizing forces that turned human beings into property, how it cultivated a sense of place in a world full of displacement. It could be appreciated for its capacity to forge collective expressions that enabled its practitioners to make meanings that could squeeze past the repressive guard of overseers, and to take on the power to frame, comprehend, and speak to others and back to the world. Revisionist social scientists sought to rectify the blind spots that had eclipsed the lives of people whose ticket to obscurity was their lowly social status. They took to task the kind of intellectual enterprise that had largely ignored, dismissed, or buried subjects simply because they were on the receiving rather than the delivering end of power and wealth.

I hold such retrievalist work in esteem and value its deep commitment to ensure that the richness of all voices is freed from the poverty of imposed silence. I believe that there is always a need for such redemptive work. Bringing social subjects into relief against the backdrop of modernity enables us to grasp what modern society actually means with regard to the fate of distinct social groups. The problem of modernity (and now "postmodernity") means nothing unless we can measure it in relation to the lives of individuals, groups, and peoples. Careful retrievalist work bypasses and thus undermines the dominant knowledge formations that work to eclipse significant groups from our critical social view.

I trust that my intellectual debts and analytical inspiration, which I owe to post-sixties cultural studies and sociohistorical revisionism, are evident. However, I have not reworked the grooves that have been cut by those who have interpreted the interior of common or populist culture. I instead chose to look at the productive interplay between black music making and the relatively small number of ethnosympathetic cultural entrepreneurs who appropriated black music, precisely those social types that Levine insisted had already received the lion's share of attention. I took this route because I believe it can contribute to the reflection at this century's end upon the historical legacy behind the critical post-1960s revisionist scholarship and particularly upon the emphases given to subject-centered social analyses. As I have suggested, the recent intellectual spirit with which such scholarship works is not new. Rather, it is, in itself, a retrieval of sorts, and functions as an important critical and an indispensable continuation of an older, deeper, more sedimented approach that was actually quite vibrant in the second half of the nineteenth century. This was the era when slaves and former slaves, women, wage workers, the poor, Native Americans (and to a much lesser extent Mexicans and Asians) were being discovered and attributed (always unevenly) with some kind of new subjectivity, and in the context of much larger forces that were inimical toward the welfare of such social subjects.

The fate of these marginalized subjects hinged (and in many cases continues to hinge) on just how the forces within civil society could bury them, and how, they, in turn, could be exonerated as historically embedded and socially situated human beings who desired (and desire) inclusion within a larger and different definition of civil society. To say, then, that the post-1960s revisionism, identified as it is today with critical interpretive scholarship, is not new, but is instead tied to older historical developments, is to also suggest a deeper lesson. How do interpretive sensibilities that try to see and hear voices, cultures, and peoples on the margins come into being? How and why do they fall into disrepair? What social and cultural mechanisms work to promote as well as eclipse the larger struggles of inclusion? The double-edged complexity of modern ethnosympathy requires confrontation by such questions. Cultural complexities have long surrounded black culture and the relationships that other groups bring to it. As George Lipsitz has pointed out, "White Americans may have turned to black culture for guidance because black culture contains the most sophisticated strategies of signification and the richest grammar of opposition available to aggrieved populations." But the propensities for culturalism to eclipse politics is a problem that continues to trouble. As Hazel Carby suggests, "The publishing explosion of the fiction of black women has been a major influence in the development of the multicultural curriculum," but the unprecedented assimilation of black fiction appears to take place in ways in which "the texts of black women and men sit uneasily in a discourse that seems to act as a substitute for the political activity of desegregation."[3]

There are of course many factors and forces that help to account for the eclipse of the critical impulses of ethnosympathy. Such sensibilities become dulled today, as they did in the nineteenth century, by an American civil religion of utilitarianism and individualism that shrivels the capacity for people to think in social and historical frameworks; by the absorption and political placation of a middle class tamed by the security of a relatively efficient and always promising consumer society; and by wars of national engagement abroad, and by domestic wars at home devoted to smoking out and purging enemies within, both goading a populist nationalism and a sordid but politically expedient solidarity that silences voices on the margins. Such forces make it difficult for a critical ethnosympathy to emerge in the first place, and even harder for it to forge a deeper, institutionally engaged, and critical grammar. As did the era of post-Reconstruction and all of its "unfinished business," our "post-civil rights" era is again struggling at this century's end with repair work, and under the shadow of forces antagonistic to such work.

Difficulties notwithstanding, my focus upon the emergence of an interpretive formation that took shape at the racial margins of American society underscores what I believe to be one of the important intellectual victories of modernity and within the academy: the culmination of the indispensable insight that the people on the so-called margins of society can actually tell us much about the fateful, disastrous, or promising directions of the center. This is the premise as well as the promise of ethnic and women's studies and the kindred strains found in interpretive sociology and the humanities in the academy today. Indeed, American ethnic studies appears to have taken root in the abolitionist conjuncture. As heirs of this history, we can see that it has been long in the making; it did not pop out of nowhere, or emerge simply as a strategic concession to activists in the post-sixties era, or as a modern victory of a cultural liberalism that is being battered by the twin pressures of the centrifugal forces of global capitalism and the centripetal forces of domestic cultural crises. The concern to give different social groups a place within American civil society is indebted to the egalitarian ethos, perpetually stymied as it is. It runs deep in the larger struggles over how to put a human face on not only the dehumanization of racial and gender domination, but also on the defacing forces of modernity.

This study has sketched only some of the lines of development that have contributed to our modern forms of cultural interpretation. As a sketch there is much that has been omitted, some things by design, many things by my own limitations. What I have tried to do in this study is to stay on the sociological edges of black music, not in the center of it. By "center" I refer to the important kind of work that has grown from the very cultural terrain that I have presented here—work that has been concerned explicitly with highlighting the problem of cultural meanings and *inner* meanings, of the *purposive* schemas of song makers and song making, and of the mapping of cultural practices. Such work, with its aims to decipher the cultural interiority of black and other culture, has given us extremely valuable knowledge. From such work we know that the social, cultural, economic, and political history of black music in America is a complex one. Indeed, today there are many studies that mine the testimonial dimension of music; that highlight the ways slaves maintained and cultivated cultural practices even under the pulverizing conditions of slavery; that show how, in the face of the atrophy of mother tongues, the persistent will that enabled people to generate new forms and new discourses; that demonstrate how despite massive cultural repression and retribution, their musical practices remained crucial in maintaining cohesive identities and collective memories. This process entailed an elaborate mode of communication that created as well as drew from deep reservoirs of renewable symbols, sensibilities, and histories. Such reservoirs—which were never fully plumbed by the centuries of overseers, and by the great variety of moral, political, and economic entrepreneurs who sought (and still seek) some kind of entry into this symbolic traffic—are richly documented in the work of more recent revisionist historians and social scientists like John Blassingame, Eugene Genovese, Lawrence Levine, Sterling Stuckey, and Angela Davis. They, in turn, draw upon the black and white humanists and social scientists who first brought such music making into visibility, who thematized and analyzed the content of black culture during the first half of the twentieth century, and whose earlier work championed the resurgent redemptive and interpretive spirit. These and other American critical revisionists retrieved black agency in relationship to cultural practice. In ways similar to the recent constitution of cultural studies,[4] American revisionists have provided an account of how hitherto ignored peoples were present in their own making. They helped restore to them their intentionality and resilience in the face of domination, and they brought to light the cultural strategies that enabled them to retain a sense of place and purpose.[5]

My shift away from traveling the inside tracks of modern ethnos-centered analysis and moving toward an attempt to track the trackers, to uncover the "discoverers," and to describe the development of interpretive developments is thus not meant to cede the larger issue of agency or collective subjectivity. The latter kind of analyses represents a hard-won development that marks the coming into being of peoples and groups whose lives are deeply woven into the fabric of American history. In this regard, my study offers no substantial break from the interpretive mold. Rather, I have embraced it in order to revisit one of the sites of its very formation. However, rather than inhabit and celebrate the new culturalism, I have instead tried to bring into focus cultural forces that worked (and continue to work) to blind social insight, vision, and criticism. I believe this kind of critical appraisal is needed. As I hope I have shown, modern ethnosympathy is complex and contradictory and comes with a twin-edged thrust. It presents a way of rectifying blindness, but it also so easily courts a reified culturalism that can exacerbate social blindness. Culturalism can simultaneously open up the lives of subjects and close down the critical dialogue on their larger social fate.

Today the complex history of ethnosympathy is in the pores of what we call cultural interpretation. It is central to interpretive sociology and cultural studies, particularly in the areas that maintain strong interest in subcultures and the interior meanings and expressive dimensions of cultural practices. It is also core to much of the humanities, and fully expressive within—and as—ethnic and women's studies. But to put things this way is to acknowledge the historical developments of the nineteenth century that feed into the now wide and indispensable parameters of cultural interpretation.

The consideration of such historical ties might appear inconsistent in an era in which intellectuals at this century's end talk of postmodernity as if "it" represented a massive rupture from some past. The latter perspective may actually be symptomatic of amnesia (which seems to perpetually inflict the sense of history in America). The suggestion in this study, however, is that the interpretive formations that emerged in the nineteenth century reach from the past to the present, and tie us to a modernity that continues to register symptomatically as problems of culture and interpretation. In all of this there is the peculiar sense that cultural tensions and struggles over representation, rapidly shifting identity formations, the expansion and contraction of race as a lens through which to view the larger society—things supposedly new and arguments supposedly fresh— seem strangely familiar.

·   ·   ·   ·   ·

Artifacts sit in silence. Even when imbued with glory, when severed from life, they are at best obituaries. They become meaningful only when they are redefined by being rejoined with, and serve as accounts for, the lives of particular individuals and groups. Artifacts return as testimonies when they again speak back to the society in which they are shaped, when they are inhabited by peoples whose lives are intersected by the social forces that such testimonies attempt to comprehend and confront. Comprehending this dynamic enables us to resist the pressures, benevolent as they might appear, that maintain and manage *people* on the margins.

NOTES

INTRODUCTION

1. See Norbert Elias, *The Court Society*, trans. Edmund Jephcoot (New York: Pantheon Books, 1983), 208.

2. See H. H. Gerth and C. Wright Mills, *From Max Weber: Essays in Sociology* (New York: Oxford University Press, 1946), 55.

3. See Fernand Braudel, *The Mediterranean and the Mediterranean World in the Age of Philip II*, vol. 2 (1949; reprint, New York: Harper and Row, 1973), 899.

4. Gramsci's theoretical statements on intellectuals are scattered across his writings, many of which were composed while he was incarcerated during Mussolini's reign. See Antonio Gramsci, *Selections from the Prison Notebooks of Antonio Gramsci*, trans. and ed. Quintin Hoare and Geoffrey Nowell Smith (New York: International Publishers, 1971). Many of Gramsci's central statements on intellectuals have been gathered in David Forgacs, ed., *An Antonio Gramsci Reader: Selected Writings, 1916–1935* (New York: Schocken Books, 1988), 300–322.

5. See Raymond Williams, *Marxism and Literature* (Oxford: Oxford University Press, 1977), 119; Raymond Williams, *The Sociology of Culture* (New York: Schocken Books, 1982), 57–86.

6. Cf. Lawrence Levine, *Highbrow/Lowbrow: The Emergence of Cultural Hierarchy in America* (Cambridge: Harvard University Press, 1988), 8.

7. This nexus has been explored by Ronald Takaki, *Iron cages: Race and Culture in Nineteenth-Century America* (New York: Oxford University Press, 1990); Richard R. Slotkin, *Regeneration through Violence: The Mythology of the American Frontier* (Middletown, Conn.: Wesleyan University Press, 1973); Richard R. Slotkin, *The Fatal Environment: The Myth of the Frontier in the Age of Industrialization, 1800–1890* (New York: Atheneum, 1985); Richard R. Slotkin, *Gunfighter Nation: The Mythology of the Frontier in Twentieth-Century America* (New York: Atheneum, 1992); Alexander Saxton, *The Rise and Fall of the White Republic: Class Politics and Mass Culture in Nineteenth-Century America* (London: Verso, 1990); and Paul Gilroy, *The Black Atlantic: Modernity and Double Consciousness* (Cambridge: Harvard University Press, 1993).

CHAPTER ONE
THE CONUNDRUM OF AUTHENTICITY

1. In Giddens's words, "Social science is concerned with concept-bearing and concept-inventing agents, who theorize about what they do as well as the conditions of doing it. . . . Natural science . . . in the 'newer philosophy of science,' involves a hermeneutic. Science is an interpretative endeavor, in which the theories comprise meaning-frames. Unlike natural science, however, the social sciences involve a double hermeneutic, since the concepts and theories developed

therein apply to a world constituted of the activities of conceptualizing and theorizing agents." See "The Social Sciences and Philosophy—Trends in Recent Social Theory," in Anthony Giddens, *Social Theory and Modern Sociology* (Stanford, Calif.: Stanford University Press, 1987), 70. Cf. also Anthony Giddens, *New Rules of Sociological Method* (New York: Basic Books, 1976), 146.

2. Frederick F. Douglass, *Narrative of the Life of Frederick Douglass, an American Slave, Written by Himself* (1845; reprint, New York: Penguin Books, 1982), 58.

3. Ibid., 57–58.

4. W. E. B. Du Bois, *The Souls of Black Folk* (1903; reprint, New York: NAL Penguin, 1969), 52.

5. Du Bois, *Souls*, 270. Shortly after the turn of the century, the "coon songs" to which Du Bois refers were central commodities in the fledgling recording industry. As one historian of recording technology observed, in the late 1890s "Columbia and Edison had made a few tentative infiltrations into the giant domain of great music that was supposed to envelop the American home in an aura of uplifting art, but the bulk of their efforts pointed in the direction of pure home-grown 'corn.'" By the turn of the century Victor was placing its market bets on the opera singer Caruso while Edison was gambling on coon songs. See Roland Gelatt, *The Fabulous Phonograph: From Tin Foil to High Fidelity* (Philadelphia: J. B. Lippincott Co., 1954), 73, 158.

6. Alain Locke, *The Negro and His Music* (1939; reprint, New York: Arno Press, 1969), 4.

7. Adorno's notion of criticism has ties to particular critical-philosophical traditions that culminate in western Marxism, but it also shapes the apprehension that conservatives like Ortega y Gasset felt with regard to society. See also Andreas Huyssen, "Adorno in Reverse: From Hollywood to Richard Wagner," *New German Critique* 29 (spring/summer 1983): 8–38; Theodore Adorno and Max Horkheimer, *Dialectic of Enlightenment*, trans. John Cumming (1944; reprint, New York: Seabury Press, 1972); and Martin Jay, *The Dialectical Imagination: A History of the Frankfurt School and the Institute for Social Research, 1923–1950* (Boston: Little Brown and Co., 1973).

8. See Steve Chapple and Reebee Garofalo, *Rock 'n' Roll Is Here to Pay: The History and Politics of the Music Industry* (Chicago: Nelson-Hall, 1977).

9. Frances Anne Kemble, *Journal of a Residence on a Georgia Plantation, 1838–1839* (New York: Harper and Bros., 1863), 218.

10. The complexity of minstrelsy as a system of cultural representations becomes glaring when we consider that Irish immigrants were subjected to being "negroized"—they were targets of the same deprecatory descriptions leveled at blacks—yet played a significant role in producing minstrelsy. Exploited by nativists, the Irish working class was incorporated in the context of the twin pressures of industrial expansion and the possibility that abolitionism would unleash a large former-slave proletariat. Cf. Christopher Small, *Music of the Common Tongue: Survival and Celebration in Afro-American Music* (New York: Riverrun Press, 1987), chap. 5; Eric Lott, *Love and Theft: Blackface Minstrelsy and the American Working Class* (New York: Oxford University Press, 1993); David Roediger, *The Wages of Whiteness: Race and the Making of the American Work-*

ing Class (London: Verso, 1991); Alexander Saxton, *The Indispensable Enemy: Labor and the Anti-Chinese Movement in California* (1971; reprint, Berkeley: University of California Press, 1995); and Noel Ignatiev, *How the Irish Became White* (New York: Routledge, 1995).

11. Cf. Robert Toll, *Blacking Up: The Minstrel Show in Nineteenth-Century America* (London: Oxford University Press, 1974); Henry T. Sampson, *Blacks in Blackface* (Metuchen, N.J.: Scarecrow Press, 1980); Sam Dennison, *Scandalize My Name: Black Imagery in American Popular Music* (New York: Garland Publishing, 1982); Joseph Boskin, *Sambo: The Rise and Demise of an American Jester* (New York: Oxford University Press, 1986). In analytical contrast to Lott's study, see Michael Paul Rogin, *Blackface, White Noise: Jewish Immigrants in the Hollywood Melting Pot* (Berkeley: University of California Press, 1996).

12. Dvořák is quoted in John Lovell, *Black Song: The Forge and the Flame* (New York: Macmillan, 1972), 10. Eight years later, W. E. B. Du Bois would reiterate this thesis in the closing chapter to *The Souls of Black Folk*. On the struggle to forge an distinct American high culture see Paul DiMaggio, "Cultural Entrepreneurship in Nineteenth-Century Boston: The Creation of an Organizational Base for High Culture in America" and "Cultural Entrepreneurship in Nineteenth-Century Boston, Part II: The Classification and Framing of American Art," *Media, Culture, and Society* 4 (1982): 33–50 and 303–22; Levine, *Highbrow/Lowbrow*. See also Peter Dobkin Hall, *The Organization of American Culture, 1700–1900: Private Institutions, Elites, and the Origins of American Nationality* (New York: New York University Press, 1982).

13. See the important discussion between *kultur* and *zivilization* in Norbert Elias, *The Civilizing Process*, vol. 1, trans. Edmund Jephcoot (1939; reprint, New York: Urizen Books, 1978).

14. Mary Boykin Chestnut, *A Diary from Dixie*. Ed. by Ben Ames Williams (Boston: Houghton Mifflin, 1949), 148–49. Cf. Dena J. Epstein, *Sinful Tunes and Spirituals: Black Folk Music to the Civil War* (Urbana: University of Illinois Press, 1977), 225–26.

15. This point is amply illustrated in Elaine Scarry's study of human pain. Something as fundamentally human and meaningful as excruciating bodily pain is not devoid of meaning, but as Scarry argues, even the best and most exact language cannot capture and represent it. See Elaine Scarry, *The Body in Pain: The Making and Unmaking of the World* (New York: Oxford University Press, 1985).

16. Chestnut, *A Diary From Dixie*, 199.

17. See Marion Wilson Starling, *The Slave Narrative: Its Place in American History* (Boston: G. K. Hall and Co., 1981). William Appleman Williams suggests that *Uncle Tom's Cabin* was the first "dime novel," even though the form is commonly attributed to Erastus Beadle's publications, which did not emerge until 1860. Williams also argues that as a cultural work, Stowe's novel represented a pro-laissez faire ideology. See Williams, *The Contours of American History* (New York: New Viewpoints, 1973), 287.

18. As Leon Litwack has pointed out, most northerners detested slaves as well as slavery. See Leon Litwack, *North of Slavery: The Negro in the Free States, 1790–1860* (Chicago: University of Chicago Press, 1961). Ann Douglas's study of

the role sentimentality played as a cultural script given to women in the nineteenth century is relevant. See *The Feminization of American Culture* (New York: Avon Books, 1977).

19. Quoted in J. B. T. Marsh, *The Story of the Fisk Jubilee Singers* (1881; reprint, New York: Negro Universities Press, 1960), 80. See also Gilroy, *Black Atlantic*, 87–93.

20. See the historical assessment of the concept of the "noble savage" in Hoxie Neale Fairchild, *The Noble Savage: A Study in Romantic Naturalism* (New York: Columbia University Press, 1928). Also valuable is Marianna Torgovnick, *Gone Primitive: Savage Intellects, Modern Lives* (Chicago: University of Chicago Press, 1990).

21. The idea of minstrelsy as a white voyage into blackness is treated quite provocatively in Lott, *Love and Theft*.

22. Du Bois, *Souls*, 271.

23. Cf. Suzanne Keller, *Beyond the Ruling Class: Strategic Elites in Modern Society* (New York: Random House, 1963).

24. Mezzrow quoted in Levine, *Black Culture and Black Consciousness*, 295.

25. Thomas Wentworth Higginson, *Army Life in a Black Regiment and Other Writings* (1870; reprint, New York: Penguin, 1997); Thomas Wentworth Higginson, "Negro Spirituals," *Atlantic Monthly* 19 (June 7, 1867): 684–94; William Frances Allen, Charles Pickard Ware, and Lucy McKim Garrison, *Slave Songs of the United States* (New York: A. Simpson and Co., 1867).

26. W. E. B. Du Bois's appeal to "gentle readers" functions as a call to salvage not just the black subjects that had been cast aside by the abandonment of Reconstruction, but also as a call to retrieve the dying cultural spirit that had given black culture a place within modern cultural interpretation. Du Bois echoes—as well as laments the loss of—the abolitionist's humanistic turn that facilitated the reception of black culture. But as he came of age at century's end, the battle for humanitarian reform for African Americans had turned into an eerie silence punctuated by ostensibly isolated lynchings and the collective violence of "race riots." The war for a greater political and economic egalitarianism had receded to sheer culturalism, and Du Bois emerged as one of the last self-authenticating troops of that earlier fight. This is the nagging problem that moves Du Bois from the half romantic–half social science perspective of *The Souls of Black Folk* to become the incensed historian of Reconstruction. See W. E. B. Du Bois, *Black Reconstruction in America, 1860–1880* (1935; reprint, New York: Atheneum, 1969).

27. In addition to Christopher Small's already noted study, examples of recent musicological approaches that demonstrate the importance of incorporating social frameworks in music analysis include Susan McClary, *Feminine Endings: Music, Gender, and Sexuality* (Minneapolis: University of Minneapolis Press, 1991); and Robert Walser, *Running with the Devil: Power, Gender, and Madness in Heavy Metal Music* (Hanover, N.H.: University Press of New England, 1993).

28. I thank Troy Duster for bringing this analogue and its illustrative possibilities for social phenomena to my attention.

29. Metaphors and analogues have their limits. The metaphor used here is not meant to suggest biological reductionism. I use it to suggest conceptual methods that are not found in readily recognized methodologies. In praise of metaphor, it

is worth considering how much metaphoric thought is, arguably, the font of representation. Metaphors organize complex thought. Theoretical work in the natural and social sciences are full of metaphoric employment, often in early work of intellectual inception, and certainly in pedagogical dissemination. For an early contribution to this perspective see Susanne K. Langer, *Philosophy in a New Key: A Study in the Symbolism of Reason, Rite, and Art* (Cambridge: Harvard University Press, 1942). The classic statement of this kind of semiological analysis in sociological theory is presented in Emile Durkheim's *Elementary Forms of the Religious Life*, trans. Joseph Ward Swain (London: Allen and Unwin, 1915); and extended in Roland Barthes, *Image, Music, Text*, trans. Stephen Heath (New York: Hill and Wang, 1977).

30. Nomothetic analysis (causality extending over time) is thus facilitated. However, the ideographic approach (emphasizing the historical specificity and uniqueness of a particular thing) eludes us, for social contexts and historically specific moments, which are fixed only as intellectual acts of abstraction facilitated by categorical imposition, are not fixed. Rather, they are processes moving forward in time, only to bequeath new conditions and developments that must accommodate to, or alter, social relations. Both nomothetic and ideographic approaches are conceptual ideals that are comprehensible only by blocking out the messiness of society and history. The trade-off cannot be avoided; it is the deal cut by social science in order to operate as such. This problem occupied much of Max Weber's deepest conceptualizations of sociology. H. Stuart Hughes's *Consciousness and Society: The Reorientation of European Social Thought, 1890–1930* (New York: Vintage Books, 1958) provides a useful assessment of the tension that Weber posed between "individual" and "historical" frameworks.

31. C. Wright Mills, *The Sociological Imagination* (London: Oxford University Press, 1959). V. N. Volosinov's theory of the sign is relevant on this issue. According to Volosinov, signs are embedded in a context of multiple appropriations. Signification is constituted within a field of social interests. Rather than being fixed, signs thus take on a weakened "multiaccentuality." Volosinov, however, limits this provocative theory by reducing the field of multiaccentuality to a mechanistic notion of class, rendering the sign a site ultimately of class struggle. The theory of multiaccentuality, however, is a socially productive one, especially if it is not hampered by class reductionism. See V. N. Volosinov, *Marxism and the Philosophy of Language*; trans. Ladislave Matejka and I. R. Titunik (New York: Seminar Press, 1973).

Pierre Bourdieu's concepts of *habitus* and *disposition*, which map individual, group, class, or ideological features as they are situated in arenas of cultural struggles, captures some of Volosinov's model, but without the latter's simple version of class reductionism. Bourdieu, however, substitutes a milder version of class structuration that is mediated by education. Bourdieu adopts Louis Althusser's theoretical form of the overdetermination of the "ideological state apparatuses" when he elevates the educational dimension as the key matrix for reproducing cultural as well as economic capital, resulting in a model that hinges on something like an "ideological schooling apparatuses." Cf. Louis Althusser, "Ideology and Ideological State Apparatuses," in *"Lenin and Philosophy" and Other Essays*, trans. Ben Brewster, 127–86 (New York: Monthly Review Press,

1971); Pierre Bourdieu and Jean-Claude Passeron, *Reproduction in Education, Society, and Culture*, trans. Richard Nice (London: Sage Publications, 1977); and Pierre Bourdieu, *Distinction: A Social Critique of the Judgement of Taste* (Cambridge: Harvard University Press, 1984). Both Volosinov and Bourdieu provide models that invoke but do not explicate the historical dimension. In Volosinov's case signs and class intersect in a framework of cultural materialism without history. Habitus, practice, language, and symbols operate in Bourdieu's schemas as forms that articulate an underlying structure of cultural and class distributions, which in turn represent a slice in time. In this regard, Bourdieu's model, derived in part from the suggestiveness of Saussure's structural theory of language, emphasizes the *synchronic* at the expense of the *diachronic*. At best, these models provide powerful ways to image social reproduction, but against a rather rigid, presupposed, and dehistoricized cultural moment—in essence, they are dynamic models trapped in stasis. The functions of symbolic and cultural capital within the context of social and historical change lack conceptualization.

32. I agree with Christopher Small's notion of "musicking" for the conceptual advantages it gives to our ability to grasp music as social process. "Music," Small argues, "is not primarily a thing or a collection of things, but an activity in which we engage." Meaning in music "is to be found in the act rather than in the actual works themselves." To restore the social dimension requires that we try to understand why a particular music takes place at a particular time and place and for particular audiences. See *Music of the Common Tongue*.

33. The classic expression of this problem is actually found in Max Weber's notion of "concept formation." See Thomas Burger, *Max Weber's Theory of Concept Formation: History, Laws, and Ideal Types* (Durham, N.C.: Duke University Press, 1976). Cf. also Hughes, *Consciousness and Society*. Not only did pure objectivism elude the social sciences; the enterprise of interpretation—cultural interpretation in particular—was from the outset symptomatic of the modernity it sought to grasp. This very problem also serves as one of the formative concerns of modern phenomenology.

But there is ample room for modesty, for it is not just the social sciences that enter modernity with this troubled epistemological shadow. Modern physics confronted this problem as well. I have in mind Neils Bohr's "complementarity principle," in which electrons could be considered "particles" or "waves" depending upon the kind of instrumentality one used for observation. Werner Heisenberg's "indeterminacy principle" raised a similar problem with regard to our limits of knowing the physical world. The issues raised by Bohr and Heisenberg were of some interest to reflexive humanists and social scientists with regard to questions of epistemology in the early 1960s. William Barrett's important study, *Irrational Man: A Study in Existential Philosophy* (New York: Doubleday Anchor Books, 1962) captured well the largely unexplored nexus between intellectual disciplines lined along the hard science versus humanities dichotomy. While epistemological doubt has never been a popular position among most practitioners of any modern discipline, there has remained nonetheless a growing discourse on what could loosely be called constructionism. To some extent, it would appear that critical epistemology in the social sciences has unwittingly adopted some of the concerns raised by epistemological reflections taking place with the advent of relativity theory in physics. Addressing the epistemological core of modern physics, Percy Bridgman suggested that the physicist "has learned the object of knowledge is not to be separated from the instrument of knowledge. We can no longer think of the object of knowledge as constituting a reality which is revealed to us by the instrument of knowledge, but the two together, object and instrument, constitute a whole so intimately knit that it is meaningless to talk of object and instrument separately." Bridgman, who championed the concept of "operationalism," suggested that what we take to be "knowledge" is the *function of operations* that are inextricably tied to tools and techniques of knowing through the instruments of framing and appropriation. The implication was that the neutrality of natural objects cannot be known (as Kant would say) as a "thing in itself." See Bridgman's quote in Arthur March and Ira Freeman, *The New World of Physics* (New York: Random Hourse, 1962), 161. Cf. the more recent discussion on the affinity between relativity theory and the social sciences in Peter Novick, *That Noble Dream: The "Objectivity Question" and the American Historical Profession* (Cambridge: Cambridge University Press, 1988), 133–50. In this regard, Anthony Giddens's distinction between the natural and the social sciences is not clear-cut.

And the beat goes on. Consider how kindred "operationalism" in physics is with Michel Foucault's notion of discourses and their resultant "truth effects" and Pierre Bourdieu's notion of objectivism. But it is not relativity physics or operationalism of the 1930s or more recent poststructuralist theory that provided the first important so-called epistemological break. Rather, it is with the classical social theorists—Marx, Durkheim, and Weber—and Nietzsche who first attempted to make visible and transparent the social origins (including the technical origins) of the production of knowledge formations. Their ability to see this problem constitutes an important framework for the newer developments of "poststructuralism," though many who embrace the latter appear not able to acknowledge, nor do they feel compelled to even read, classical sociology's struggle with, while being a symptom of, modernity.

34. See Karl Mannheim, *Ideology and Utopia: An Introduction to the Sociology of Knowledge*, trans. Louis Wirth and Edward Shils (New York: Harcourt, Brace and World, 1936).

35. The dominant contours of ethnoscience, which were shaped by nationalist currents and colonial relations, have been well documented by the historical reflexivity of the social sciences since the 1960s. My concern is not with the dominant forms that drew upon and fed strategies of racialization, but with the smaller window through which the attempt to fathom black cultural production as a realm of meaning emerged. I explore the framework and legacy of romanticist and humanitarian reformist currents that shape some of the terrain of modern cultural interpretation in "Subject Crises and Subject Work: Repositioning Du Bois," in *From Sociology to Cultural Studies: New Perspectives*, ed. Elizabeth Long (Oxford: Blackwell Publishers, 1997), 92–122.

36. See Antonio Gramsci, *Selections from the Prison Notebooks*, trans. and ed. Quentin Hoare (New York: International Publishers, 1971), 8, emphasis added. Cf. also 83–89.

Gramsci's approach has much in common with historian Roger Chartier's conceptualization of *appropriation*. Drawing on Norbert Elias and Pierre Bourdieu, Chartier suggests that

> ... appropriation really concerns a social history of the various interpretations, brought back to their fundamental determinants (which are social, institutional and cultural) and lodged in the specific practices that produce them. . . . Structures of the social world are not an object given. . . . They are all produced historically by the interconnected practices—political, social and discursive—that construct their figures.

See Roger Chartier, *Cultural History: Between Practices and Representations*, trans. Lydia G. Cochrane (Ithaca: Cornell University Press, 1988), 13–14.

Chartier's neo-Bourdieuian notion of appropriation suggests that a number of analytical merits. Rather than proceeding with already objectified "things in themselves" (where cultural objects such as African American music appear already formed), Chartier's approach first considers the question of what an object *is* to those who find it useful. The challenge is to understand what kinds of meanings help *make* objects *knowable*, how they become part of the constitution of cultural realities, and thus worthy of appropriation. A culture's appropriation of objects thus refracts culture as practice rather than culture as already embodied in material things. This critical approach to appropriation, which tries to avoid reification, is necessary to bring into focus the cultural sensibilities, strategies, and practices—the common sense—that groups use to objectify and construct their social world.

Second, by emphasizing the historically specific cultural fields in which appropriations take place, the problem of power and unequal access to goods as well as the uneven consequences unleashed by struggles over appropriation come into view. Orientations toward the world are organized schemas, *forms of attention*; and the forms of attention that groups bring to objects and social relations differ greatly. The neutrality of sheer utilitarianism, found in numerous considerations of appropriation, fades against the social backdrop of groups that converge within a cultural field who are also not commensurate in their institutional locations, their resources, and their abilities to unleash larger effects upon other groups (e.g., cultural practices are much more than the production of meaning, or "tool kits," or navigational aids through the social milieu).

Third, this approach is highly suggestive for the process of grasping the connections between *cultural forms* and *cultural formations* without indulging in ahistorical presuppositions of the existence of some essential, transcendental, and underlying or immutable structure. It is a transformative approach (one that shares theoretical features similar to what Jean Piaget and Lucien Goldmann called "genetic epistemology"). It thus enables us to avoid the pitfalls of determinism on the one hand (which poststructuralism brings so acutely to our attention) and of the evacuation of historically and institutionally embedded social relations on the other (which poststructuralism plunges toward so easily). These perspectives allow us to heed Raymond Williams's advice to be wary of *determinism* without abandoning the critical notion of *determinations*. See Roger Chartier, *The Cultural Uses of Print in Early Modern France* (Princeton: Princeton University Press, 1987); Roger Chartier, "Texts, Printing, Readings," in *The New Cultural History*, ed. Lynn Hunt (Berkeley: University of California Press, 1989), 154–75; Jean Piaget, *Genetic Epistemology*, trans. Eleanor Duckworth (New York: W. W. Norton and Co., 1970); Lucien Goldmann, *Essays on Method in the Sociology of Literature*, trans. and ed. William Q. Boelhower (St. Louis: Telos Press, 1980); Lucien Goldmann, *Cultural Creation in Modern Society*, trans. Bart Grahl (St. Louis: Telos Press, 1976); and R. Williams, *Marxism and Literature*, 83–89.

37. Pierre Bourdieu, *The Logic of Practice*, trans. Richard Nice (Stanford, Calif.: Stanford University Press, 1990), 291 n. 5.

38. As Foucault has pointed out, there are different modes by which human beings are made into "subjects." The notion of "subjects," however, has a number of important facets. It refers to "individuals" in the phenomenological sense (Cartesianism and its psychological refinements culminating in neo-Kantian frameworks of the self or person). Subjectivization is also more than a reference to the social instantiation of the individual and his or her attributes. "Individuals" are produced through societally situated processes and practices (here we should acknowledge the Durkheimian legacy, mediated by Althusser's influential notion of "interpellation," that underwrites important aspects of Foucault's analytical model). Foucault's accomplishment was to pitch the problem of ideology and interpellation to a much larger historical level, where the whole notion of subjectification could be repositioned in the wake of the "linguistic turn" associated with Saussure and Levi-Strauss. Subjectivization is thus transformed in this deepening critical reflexivity—away from its earlier religious and philosophical essentialism (e.g., from "soul" to "self"), and toward reconceptualization as a historically specific construction or formation maintained by institutional spheres. The latter can then be understood as both the outcome of, as well as the constitutive conditions for, the reproduction of discursive practices. From these developments, subjectivization takes on great social complexity.

"Subjects" thus produced are crucial cultural demarcations. Subjects are certainly individuals; but they are also arenas of knowledge (as in knowing a subject matter) made possible by fixing and grouping objects, practices, and activities according to systems of categories and classification. This process can—and often does—include culturally subjectivized human groups and the practices and attributes that render such groups "knowable" to others.

The process, then, of coming to "know" something is fundamentally related to the problem of epistemology. However, in the Foucauldian view, the problem of knowledge is not based on the search for an increasingly abstract plane of Truth, which, in turn, will function as a reference for an empirical universe antedated and presupposed by an unproblematic human cognition. Knowing is a determinate condition, shaped by discursive relations and constituted through the historically specific combinations of material and institutional practices (which cannot be simply reduced to discursivity). It is in this sense that I refer to the "discovery" of African American music from the "outside." The installing work is Emile Durkheim's *The Division of Labor in Society*, trans. George Simpson (New York: Free Press, 1933). Michel Foucault's most central work on this problem can be found in *The Archaeology of Knowledge* (New York: Harper and Row, 1972); in

The Order of Things: An Archaeology of the Human Sciences (New York: Vintage Books, 1973); and in *Discipline and Punish: The Birth of the Prison* (New York: Vintage Books, 1979). Cf. also "The Subject and Power," in *Michel Foucault: Beyond Structuralism and Hermeneutics*, ed. Herbert L. Dreyfus and Paul Rabinow (Chicago: University of Chicago, 1982).

CHAPTER TWO
SOUND BARRIERS AND SOUND MANAGEMENT

1. I am indebted to Dena Epstein's assembly of many of the earliest statements on black music by Europeans. See *Sinful Tunes*, 3–17.

2. Ibid., 3.

3. Great Britain, House of Commons, *Minutes of Evidence Taken Before a Committee of the House of Commons, Being a Select Committee, Appointed to Take Examination of Witnesses Respecting the African Slave Trade, Sessional Papers*, 1731–1800, 34:14, 20–22. Cf. Epstein, *Sinful Tunes*, 8–9.

4. Falconbridge quoted in Epstein, *Sinful Tunes*, 3, 8–9.

5. Eugene D. Genovese, *Roll, Jordan, Roll: The World the Slaves Made* (New York: Pantheon, 1974), 37.

6. Frederick Law Olmsted, *A Journey in the Seaboard Slave States in the Years 1853–1854*, vol. 1 (1856; reprint, New York: G. P. Putnam's Sons, 1904), 26–29; Epstein, *Sinful Tunes*, 236–37.

7. Coxe quoted in Epstein, *Sinful Tunes*, 130.

8. Allen, Ware, and Garrison, *Slave Songs*, vii.

9. *The Journals of Charlotte Forten Grimke*, ed. Brenda Stevenson (New York: Oxford University Press, 1988), 441. Such examples of a critical romanticism lapsing into sentimental caricature are frequent among many radical white abolitionists.

10. For the most sustained anthropologically based discussion on the continuation of Africanist practices in the context of black diaspora see Melville J. Herskovits, *The Myth of the Negro Past* (Boston: Beacon Press, 1958). See also Epstein, *Sinful Tunes*, 127–38.

11. John Riland's observations, published in *Memoirs of a West-India Planter* (London: Hamilton, Adams, 1828), are quoted in Epstein, *Sinful Tunes*, 11.

12. See Douglass, *Narrative of the Life*, 87–88.

13. Sally Bradford, *Harriet, Moses of Her People* (New York: George Lockwood, 1886), 27.

14. Kemble, *Journal of a Residence*, 129.

15. Eileen Southern, *The Music of Black Americans: A History* (New York: W. W. Norton, 1971), 153.

16. Agricola [pseud.], "Management of Negroes," *De Bow's Review* 19 (September 1855), 361; quoted in Epstein, *Sinful Tunes*, 162.

17. Genovese, *Roll, Jordan, Roll*, 324. See also Raymond Bauer and Alice Bauer, "Day to Day Resistance," *Journal of Negro History* 27 (October 1942): 388–419; and Miles Mark Fisher, *Negro Slave Songs in the United States* (New York: Russell and Russell, 1953), 21. On the ties between work, tempo, and the

incorporation of traditional African practices, cf. Levine, *Black Culture and Black Consciousness*, 7; Lovell, *Black Song*, 161–62.

18. McKim's quote is in Allen, Ware, and Garrison, *Slave Songs of the United States*, xviii.

19. Quoted in Giles Oakley, *The Devil's Music: A History of the Blues* (New York: Harcourt Brace Jovanovich, Harvest, 1976), 15.

20. Allen, Ware, and Garrison, *Slaves Songs*, vii–viii.

21. Higginson, *Army Life in a Black Regiment*, 11. As Levine notes, slaves often used music to shame or ridicule a fellow slave for inappropriate behavior or to criticize one for "not pulling his weight." See Levine, *Black Culture and Black Consciousness*, 10–11.

22. "Negro Folk Songs," *Southern Workman* 24 (February 1895): 30–32. Reprinted in *The Black Perspective in Music* 4, no. 2 (July 1976): 145–51 (quotation on 150–51).

23. Ibid.

24. Washington is quoted in Henry Edward Krehbiel, *Afro-American Folk Songs; A Study in Racial and National Music* (New York and London: G. Schirmer, 1914), 47.

25. Charles Peabody, "Notes on Negro Music," *Journal of American Folk-Lore* 16 (July 1903): 148–52. Reprinted in *The Black Perspective in Music* 4, no. 2 (July 1976), 133–37 (quotation on 133).

26. Newman I. White, *American Negro Folk-Songs* (Cambridge: Harvard University Press, 1928), 7.

27. Southern, *Readings in Black American Music*, 31, 15–16. Many of the advertisements for runaway slaves that were published in southern newspapers highlighted the musical skills of the slaves being sought (31–35); Epstein, *Sinful Tunes*, 80, 112–14; "Eighteenth-Century Slaves as Advertised by Their Masters," *Journal of Negro History* 1 (April 1916): 163–216.

28. Levine, *Black Culture*, 16; Epstein, *Sinful Tunes*, 150.

29. Solomon Northup, *Twelve Years a Slave: The Narrative of Solomon Northup, a Citizen of New York, Kidnaped in Washington City in 1841 and Rescued in 1853, from a Cotton Plantation near the Red River in Louisiana* (Auburn, N.Y.: Derby and Miler, 1853), 216–17; Epstein, *Sinful Tunes*, 150.

30. Genovese, *Roll, Jordan, Roll*, 315–24. See also Fredrika Bremer, *Homes of the New World: Impressions of America*, trans. Mary Howitt (New York: Harper and Brothers, 1853), 1:370.

31. Quoted in Southern, *Readings*, 88–89. Cf. also Genovese, *Roll, Jordan, Roll*, 315–19. An early important discussion of the corn shucking songs as they begin to appear after the postspiritual fixation in early folklore can be found in "Negro Folk Songs," 30–32.

32. Southern, *Readings*, 89 (emphasis added).

33. Ibid.

34. In this regard corn-shucking festivals like the one described by Paine functioned as a strategic release of societal tension in the context of extremely repressive class hierarchies. The function of tension dissipation is reminiscent of the cultural routines of carnival in early modern Europe, at least up until the com-

bined developments of the Protestant Reformation and the eclipse of market society eroded its older institutional framework. Cf. LeRoy Ladurie, *Carnival in Romans* (New York: George Braziller, 1979); Peter Burke, *Popular Culture in Early Modern Europe* (New York: Harper Torchbooks, 1978).

35. Max Weber has done much to clarify the historical constellation of cultural orientations and how they culminate in the realm of "action." The strength of Weber's approach lies in his historical sweep, but his actual treatment of concrete action is somewhat anemic. Though from a distinctly structuralist rather than historical perspective, Pierre Bourdieu's important concepts of *habitus* and *disposition* continue the kind of analysis suggested by Weber's historical approach by rooting action in precise ethnographic contexts. Bourdieu's strengths reside in the concrete details of class actors whose day-to-day practices, as well as lived ideas and ideologies, are accounted for. Bourdieu's actors, however, operate largely within a general concept of society treated within a historical vacuum. When brought in dialogue and considered together, Weber and Bourdieu suggest important ways to integrate historical forces and historically specific practices— that is, how to conceptualize and analyze cultural sensibilities and distinct practices as they are related to deeper historical and cultural ties. Cf. Max Weber, *The Protestant Ethic and the Spirit of Capitalism* (1905; reprint, New York: Charles Scribner's Sons, 1950); Bourdieu, *Distinction*.

36. Black music historian Eileen Southern wrote in 1971 that Frances Ann Kemble's and Fredrika Bremer's narratives were the ones that researchers ought to pay attention to, for these works "reveal the most about the musical practices of the slaves" in the antebellum period. Southern, *The Music of Black Americans*, 150. To these two we need to add Frederick Law Olmsted's important narrative. These three writers appear the most important, insofar as they are the most frequently cited by analysts interested in black music during the antebellum era. Cf. Bremer, *Homes of the New World*; Kemble, *Journal of a Residence*; and Olmsted, *Journey in the Seaboard Slave States*.

37. Benjamin Henry Boneval Latrobe, *Impressions Respecting New Orleans: Diary and Sketches, 1818–1820*, ed. Samuel Wilson, Jr. (New York: Columbia University Press, 1951), 49–51. Quoted in Epstein, *Sinful Tunes*, 97.

38. See Charles Taylor, *Sources of the Self: The Making of the Modern Identity* (Cambridge: Harvard University Press, 1989), 368–69. As Wolfgang Schluchter points out, the modern development of subjective interiorization becomes increasingly linked to religion and secularization. Building on Weber, Schluchter argues that "secular humanism, with the support of some sectors of theology, helps to make religion subjective through its idea of a world that can in principle be controlled through calculation and is thus without surprises. Religion is translated from an external fact into a component of individual consciousness." Wolfgang Schluchter, "The Future of Religion," in *Religion and America*, ed. Mary Douglas and Steven M. Tipton (Boston: Beacon Press, 1982), quoted in Jeffrey C. Alexander and Steven Seidman, eds. *Culture and Society: Contemporary Debates* (Cambridge: Cambridge University Press, 1990), 253.

39. The idea of "practice" as a distinct domain is thus much older than a post–1960s analytical development, though as Sherry Ortner had noted, it was greatly refined after the 1960s. Cf. Ortner's assessment of the important transfor-

mations that took place in anthropology after the 1960s in "Theory in Anthropology since the Sixties," in *Culture/Power/History: A Reader in Contemporary Social Theory*, ed. Nicholas B. Dirks, Geoff Eley, and Sherry B. Ortner (Princeton: Princeton University Press, 1994).

The concern with language as practice representing not just semiotic or semantic content through linguistic forms, but also as an objective domain (a material form of practice) to be ascertained analytically came into being in the seventeenth century. As Michel Foucault points out, by the end of the eighteenth century language had emerged as distinct domain. "In the sixteenth century" it was "possible to know that a sign did in fact designate what it signified"—in other words, language was inextricably tied to an irreducible operation of signification, with no painstaking probes into the links between signifiers and the signified. Language as pure representation was not problematic. But in the seventeenth century, as a more reflexive hermeneuticism took shape, it became increasingly possible "to ask how a sign could be linked to what it signified." The move, Foucault argues, was crucial in that it separated "things and words." This disjunction paved the way for more refined orientations toward language as a system that could be analytically penetrated, broken down, and investigated in order to grasp language operations as modes of classification and representation. See Foucault, *Order of Things*, 42–43, cf. also 217–300.

This transformation takes us to the threshold of early modern social theory. By the mid-nineteenth century Marx was working simultaneously with the old and the new conceptualizations of practice. On the one hand the older indivisibility of language and the world was still operative in the claim that "life-activity" was indissoluble, and that "thinking and being," though distinct, were "at the same time . . . in *unity* with each other." Thus, "the element of thought itself—the element of thought's living expression—*language*—is of a sensuous nature. The *social* reality of nature, and *human* natural science, or the *natural science about man*, are identical terms." In sum, language "is as old as consciousness, language *is* practical consciousness." See Karl Marx, *The Marx-Engels Reader*, ed. Robert C. Tucker, 2d ed. (New York: W. W. Norton and Co., 1978), 86, 92, 158. This older, unconscious identitarian view is what was being challenged by the conscious treatment of language as distinct practice, a newly autonomous practice that was not identical with so-called nature (whether materially, historically, socially, or scientifically conceived).

The separation between language as identity and language as the artifice behind representation that was noted by Foucault was also being worked out by Marx as well on numerous fronts, but most importantly as a critical theory of ideology in which the "ruling ideas" of an epoch could be ascertained as class-governed representations passing as universal and identitarian. Most crucial, at least for Marx, this breaking and rendering visible the ruling class's alienation-producing shams of representation could only be fully realized (through the ultimate practice-driven reflexive activity) by the most important social subject, the proletariat, whose fate rested on being able to see itself as a socially constructed object (constituted in the social processes that expressed "historical materialism"). In this regard, Marx straddles the peculiar juncture in which the old and new notions of practice are held conjointly (in both an older idealism as well as with a new radical approach to epistemology). Their rationalized separation, of course, is achieved by the triumph of modern science, with the latter presuming to have championed the methods of sheer and pure objectivism.

It is in this larger conjuncture, then, that a score of language mappers emerge in the 1880s, such as Franz Boas, who initiated paradigm-setting taxonomic studies of the languages of the Indians in the northwestern region of the North American continent. But even with modern folklore the older notion of a buried meaning continues to coexist in the tenuous ties between scientism and humanism, with the former deployed as either a new tool to get better at, or to distance modern rationality from, the latter. As I shall suggest in the last two chapters, this tension pulses through the modern modes of cultural interpretation as they are installed in modern folklore at the end of the nineteenth century.

40. Jacques Attali, *Noise: The Political Economy of Music*, trans. Brian Massumi (Minneapolis: University of Minnesota Press, 1985, 11.

41. The criticism of black music as falling beyond the bounds of acceptability continues like clockwork and can be found applied to every genre and style shift in the history of black music—from early blues to jazz, up to rap and hip-hop. The negative reaction to black music occurs most consistently when moral gatekeepers hear "noise" and their younger wards—especially "youth"—hear "music." This was the case when white youth were attracted to early jazz during the so-called dance craze in the 1920s, during the rise of rock 'n' roll in the 1950s, and with rap and hip-hop in the late 1980s and throughout the 1990s. Such persistent evaluations, however, have been greatly marginalized by the sheer force of market society and the progressive transformation of black music into a major cultural cash crop with a tremendous harvest at the register. Music, particularly popular music, is, after all, a major staple in the commodification of culture.

Today, the market annexation of black music has largely muted the ostensibly moral criticisms of what is now popular culture. The kinds of articles that appeared in the popular press in the early 1920s lambasting jazz for its power to engender unwanted cultural miscegenation can be readily found today. But any sustained criticism must take on the deeper and powerful normative and institutional corporate logic of market society—e.g., free-market capitalism.

In the second half of the nineteenth century, the spheres of discourse were largely moral and political, and increasingly scientific rather than economic and market driven. This is not to say that commodification of black culture was not present; we can observe commodification taking place with the first endeavors by black authors to sell their slave narratives to raise money to purchase the freedom of their loved ones. Frederick Douglass's autobiography, first published in 1845, was enormously popular. But deeply organized commodification of black culture began to take its *modern* form shortly after the rise of the modern recording industry, the discovery of black markets for "race records," and the ensuing spread of black culture beyond black consumption in the early 1920s. Important treatments of white uses of black music are found in Kathy Peiss, *Cheap Amusements: Working Women and Leisure in New York City, 1880–1920* (Philadelphia: Temple University Press, 1985); Lewis A. Erenberg, *Steppin' Out: New York Nightlife and the Transformation of American Culture, 1890–1930* (Chicago: University of Chicago Press, 1981). For an account of the rise of race records see Paul Oliver, *Songsters and Saints: Vocal Traditions on Race Records* (Cambridge: Cambridge University Press, 1984). On the significance of black religious music recorded on race records see Evelyn Brooks Higginbotham's important study "Rethinking Vernacular Culture: Black Religion and Race Records in the 1920s and 1930s," in *The House the Race Built: Black Americans, U.S. Terrain*, ed. Wahneema Lubiano (New York: Pantheon Books, 1997), 157–77. For early critical treatments of jazz see A. S. Faulkner, "Does Jazz Put the Sin in Syncopation?" *Ladies' Home Journal* (August 1921); R. McMahon, "Unspeakable Jazz Must Go!" *Ladies' Home Journal* (December 1921); "Jazz Path of Degradation," *Ladies' Home Journal* (January 1922). Tricia Rose's *Black Noise: Rap Music and Black Culture in Contemporary America* (Hanover, N.H.: Wesleyan University Press, 1994) is an excellent work that socially contextualizes rap and hip-hop music in the late-twentieth century.

CHAPTER THREE
FROM OBJECTS TO SUBJECTS

1. See Starling, *Slave Narrative*, 294.

2. See Lucky McKim, "Songs of the Port Royal 'Contrabands,'" *Dwight's Journal of Music* 21 (November 8, 1862): 254–55; Henry George Spaulding, "Under the Palmetto," *Continental Monthly* 4 (August 1863); Higginson, "Negro Spirituals"; Higginson, *Army Life in a Black Regiment*; Allen, Ware, and Garrison, *Slave Songs*. Spaulding, Higginson, Allen, and Ware all had strong Unitarian ties. The first three were trained as Unitarian ministers at the Harvard Divinity School. Allen and Ware were the grandchildren of Henry Ware, who was appointed in 1805 as Hollis Professor of Divinity at the Harvard Divinity School. I will return to the significance of Unitarianism and its role in helping shape the appreciation of black song making in chapter 5. Cf. also Thomas Riis, "The Cultivated White Tradition and Black Music in Nineteenth-Century America: A Discussion of Some Articles in *J. S. Dwight's Journal of Music*" *Black Perspective in Music* 4, no. 2 (July 1976): 156–76. All of these writers, including John Dwight, who founded *Dwight's Journal of Music*, were Unitarians, an important cultural connection I will explore later. While *Dwight's Journal* did acknowledge black music in its earlier years, its cultural significance as a publication was in helping establish a sense of high culture that could claim to be distinctly American, and thus autonomous from the pressures to emulate European forms. As Lawrence Levine has recently pointed out, *Dwight's Journal* was one of the key sites in which the struggle to forge a distinction between high and popular culture was unfolding. The journal played a central role in institutionalizing the emergent highbrow perspective: "real culture" could find its "pure" expression in and through "the great masterworks of men of genius." What was afoot in *Dwight's Journal* as a whole was the struggle to install a cultural hierarchy of taste. See Levine, *Highbrow/Lowbrow*, 121.

3. As James Scott so keenly argues, "Every subordinate group creates, out of its ordeal, a 'hidden transcript' that represents a critique of power spoken behind the back of the dominant. The powerful, for their part, also develop a hidden transcript representing the practices and claims of their rule that cannot be

openly avowed. A comparison of the hidden transcript of the weak with that of the powerful and of *both* hidden transcripts to the public transcript of power relations offers a substantially new way of understanding resistance to domination." See James C. Scott, *Domination and the Arts of Resistance: Hidden Transcripts* (New Haven: Yale University Press, 1990), xii. Most of the important attempts to retrieve the inner meanings of black music, from W. E. B. Du Bois's closing essay in *The Souls of Black Folk* to contemporary studies associated with "cultural studies" and with a concern for "oppositional cultures" or notions of "cultural resistance," are highly attentive to elucidating this dimension of cultural practice.

4. See Althusser, "Ideology and Ideological State Apparatuses," 127–86.

5. See Albert J. Raboteau, *Slave Religion: The "Invisible Institution" in the Antebellum South* (New York: Oxford University Press, 1978), 101–2; also 96–150. The belief that extending Christianity to slaves would make slaves proud, ungovernable, and rebellious was debated throughout the eighteenth century, but especially with greatest intensity during the Great Awakening. See ibid., 128. The contemporary discussions on blacks lacking souls is noted on 220.

6. Masters who teach their slaves Christian piety would be compensated by God; their slaves would be "better servants" for being made "Christian Servants," and would be dutiful, patient, and filled with goodness. Mather admitted the deeper logic: slaves possessed "reason," and reason revealed God's "Design" given to "Men" and not to beasts. How could slaves be Christianized and still remain enslaved? Mather addressed this fundamental concern:

> But if the *Negroes* are *Christianized*, they will be *Baptized*; and their *Baptism* will presently entitle them to their Freedom; so our Money is thrown away.
>
> Man, If this were true; that a *Slave* bought with thy *Money*, were by thy means brought unto the *Things that accompany Salvation*, and thou shouldest from this time have no more Service from him, yet their *Money* were not thrown away. That Mans *Money will perish with him,* who had rather the Souls in his Family should *Perish*, than that he should lose a little *Money*.

The solution stemming from the implication of carrying out religious duty was solved, in Mather's view, by the existing worldly—that is colonial—laws:

> Suppose it were so, that *Baptism* gave a legal Title to *Freedom*. Is there no guarding against this Inconvenience? You may be sufficient *Indentures*, keep off the things that you reckon so Inconvenient. But it is all a Mistake. There is no such thing. What *Law* is it, that Sets the *Baptised Slave at Liberty*? Not the *Law of Christianity*: that allows of *Slavery*. . . . [Christianity] supposes, That there are *Bond* as well as *Free*, among those that have been *Renewed in the Knowledge and Image of Jesus Christ*. . . . The *Canons* of Numberless *Councils*, mention, the *Slaves of Christians*, without any contradiction. . . . The way is now cleared, for the work that is proposed: that excellent *WORK, THE INSTRUCTION OF THE NEGROES IN THE CHRISTIAN RELIGION*.

See Cotton Mather, *The Negro Christianized: An Essay to Excite and Assist that Good Work, the Instruction of Negro Servants in Christianity* (Boston B. Green, 1706), 18–27.

7. With regard to the role of religion as source of strength, the modern statement is W. E. B. Du Bois's *The Souls of Black Folk*, which contains insights that have since been amplified by many. Cf. Carter G. Woodson, *The History of the Negro Church* (1921; reprint, Washington, D.C.: Associated Publishers, 1972); E. Franklin Frazier, *The Negro Church in America* (New York, Schocken, 1963); Milton C. Sernett, *Black Religion and American Evangelicalism: White Protestants, Plantation Missions, and the Flowering of Negro Christianity, 1787–1865* (Metuchen, N.J.: Scarecrow Press, 1975); Timothy L. Smith, "Slavery and Theology: The Emergence of Black Christian Consciousness in Nineteenth-Century America," *Church History* 41, no. 4 (December 1972); and Raboteau, *Slave Religion*. Cf. also Levine, *Black Culture and Black Consciousness*, 3–80; and Genovese, *Roll, Jordan, Roll*, 161–284.

8. At the dawn of the Civil Rights movement that unfolded during the 1950s and 1960s, the Swedish social scientist Gunnar Myrdal wrote of this deeply structured cultural and political legacy, the rhetoric of egalitarianism and racial repression, as the "American dilemma." See Gunnar Myrdal, *An American Dilemma: The Negro Problem and Modern Democracy* (New York: Harper and Brothers, 1944).

9. That Christianity could be so plastic, so flexible, in its use to support warring social interests appears to have deepened the sense of its rhetorical rather than ontological power. This seems especially the case resulting from the profound division of labor that Christianity underwent as Catholicism was challenged by the Protestant Reformation. Protestantism has generated, in turn, a host of sectarian subdivisions (mainline as well as marginal) that irrupted in the late-eighteenth and throughout the nineteenth century. With the rise of the abolitionist movement (and humanitarian reformism in general), religious tension intersected the multiculturalism of Protestant subdivisions and facilitated continued argumentation to the extent that every denomination could have its intellectual piece of the slavery issue.

10. Selfhood as a modern notion was still emerging in the late-eighteenth century, but primarily within the higher domains of intellectual reflection in philosophy and hermeneutics, both of which had deep roots in religious discourses. Cartesianism, which assimilated religious discourse, is perhaps the best early form of this kind of cultural work and marks its modern profile. Such intellectual developments represented class as well as cultural hierarchies. But this does not mean that selves emerged only within the high culture of philosophical discourses. The subjectivization process was much more pervasive and cannot be reduced to such sophisticated intellectual codifications. The process of addressing subjects is, after all, as fundamental as coming into birth and being given a name by a clan, a village, a tribe, or bourgeois nuclear family. Certainly the elevation of selfhood as a philosophical problem (one tied to shifting developments of modern epistemology) is another matter, and the two should not be conflated (though they interpenetrate during the process of the rationalization of modern institutions). But masters' identification of their slaves as chattel, and later as possessors of souls, did not require the reading of Aquinas, Descartes, or Kant; it did require the diffusion of religious ideologies in general, and such ideologies provided the ground upon which more secular philosophical reflection could emerge. Michel Foucault and Charles Taylor, each in quite different ways, trace how the modern notion of

selfhood takes on institutional manifestation and seeps downward into more popular levels in the eighteenth century. Cf. Foucault, *The Archaeology of Knowledge*; Foucault, "Subject and Power"; cf. also 102–204; and Taylor, *Sources of the Self*.

11. Cf. Epstein, *Sinful Tunes*, 101. I rely upon Epstein's research for my discussion of how blacks were viewed by representatives of the Society for the Propagation of the Gospel in Foreign Parts in their visits to the American colonies.

12. These tensions within the division of cultural and political labor are consistent with the general features of religious proselytization coupled with racial domination. Catholicism's spread in the fifteenth through the eighteenth centuries, for example, proceeded with the constitution of large land-bases *encomiendas* (estates) that relied upon subjugating indigenous populations and transforming them into conscripted labor. This relationship forced landlords to rely upon the clergy to explain the fit between the former's frequently rapacious treatment of the people and the latter's role, which, in Friedrich Engels's words, amounted to "surround[ing] [its] feudal institutions with the halo of divine consecration." See Friedrich Engels, *Socialism, Utopian and Scientific* (New York: International Publishers, 1935), 16. Cf. also Magali Sarfatti's discussion of how members of the clergy functioned as the "spiritual arm" to provide the "ideological justification of the conquest" in "Spanish Bureaucratic-Patrimonialism in America" in Politics of Modernization Series, no. 1 (Berkeley: Institute of International Studies, 1966). The role of the clergy in the southern slave system was similarly ridden with contradiction. Their task over time amounted to granting souls and, by modern extension, selfhood and subjecthood to black individuals who were still encircled by a social system that reduced them to objects of property relations.

13. The society evidently continued to send Bibles for distribution among slaves. Eileen Southern has compiled a number of letters written in the mid-eighteenth century from colonial clergymen who note their work of cultivating religious singing while thanking the society for Bibles and other religious materials for slave instruction. See Southern, *Readings*, 27–30.

14. Quoted in Epstein, *Sinful Tunes*, 101–2.

15. Ibid.

16. Ibid.

17. Quoted ibid., 103. See also Raboteau, *Slave Religion*, 220.

18. Zephaniah Kingsley, *Treatise on the Patriarchal or Cooperative System of Society as it Exists in Some Governments, and Colonies in America, and in the United States, under the Name of Slavery, with its Necessity and Advantages. By an Inhabitant of Florida*, 2d ed. (n.p., 1829, 14–15; N. White, *American Negro Folk-Songs*, 6; Epstein, *Sinful Tunes*, 194.

19. On the reluctance to convert slaves, see Raboteau, *Slave Religion*, 66, 98–108.

20. Mechal Sobel, *Trabelin' On: The Slave Journey to an Afro-Baptist Faith* (Princeton: Princeton University Press, 1988), 158. See also 158–73 for Sobel's discussion of religion and slave revolts.

21. Herbert Aptheker, *American Negro Slave Revolts* (New York: Columbia University Press, 1943).

22. For important treatments of slave preachers and their ties to slave resistance, rebellion and revolt, see Joseph R. Washington, Jr. *Black Religion: The Negro and Christianity in the United States* (Boston: Beacon Press, 1964), 202–4; Raboteau, *Slave Religion*, 163, 318; Vincent Harding, "Religion and Resistance among Ante-Bellum Negroes, 1800–1860," in *The Making of Black America: Essays in Negro Life and History*, ed. August Meier and Elliot Rudwick (New York, 1969), 179–97; William C. Suttles, "African Religious Survivals as Factors in American Slave Revolts," *Journal of Negro History* 56 (1971): 97–104.

23. See John Hope Franklin, *From Slavery to Freedom: A History of Negro Americans* (New York: McGraw-Hill Publishing Co., 1988), 131–35.

24. Holland quoted in Epstein, *Sinful Tunes*, 195.

25. William W. Freehling, *Prelude to Civil War: The Nullification Controversy in South Carolina, 1816–1836* (New York: Harper and Row, 1965), 72–73.

26. Ibid., 75.

27. Cf. [Frederick Dalcho], *Practical Considerations*, 33–36, quoted at length in Epstein, *Sinful Tunes*, 196.

28. After the series of slave conflagrations culminating in the Nat Turner revolt, religious practices came under tighter scrutiny, and in some cases the opportunities to indulge in such practices were withdrawn. See Sernett, *Black Religion and American Evangelicalism*, 46; Donald G. Mathews, "Religion and Slavery: The Case of the American South," in *Anti-Slavery, Religion, and Reform: Essays in Memory of Roger Anstey*, ed. Christine Bolt and Seymour Drescher (Hamden, Conn.: Archon Books, 1980), 207–32; and Raboteau, *Slave Religion*, 163–64.

29. Lydia Maria Child, "Charity Bowery," in *The Liberty Bell. By Friends of Freedom*, ed. Maria W. Chapman (Boston: American Anti-Slavery Society, 1839), 26–43, quote from 42–43.

30. Cf. Hugo James Johnston, *Race Relations in Virginia and Miscegenation in the South, 1776–1860* (Amherst: University of Massachusetts Press, 1970), 135–36; Epstein, *Sinful Tunes*, 229; Genovese, *Roll, Jordan, Roll*, 186.

31. Freehling, *Prelude*, 73.

32. Genovese, *Roll, Jordan, Roll*, 186. Genovese argues that in spite of the laws passed to suppress black religious practices, they were strictly enforced "only during insurrection scares or tense moments occasioned by political turmoil. . . . Too many planters," he suggests, "did not want them enforced. They regarded their slaves as peaceful, respected their religious sensibilities, and considered such interference dangerous to plantation morale and productivity" (236).

33. See Sernett, *Black Religion*, 36–81. For general studies on historical aspects of the Negro church, see W. E. B. Du Bois, *The Negro Church* (Atlanta, Ga.: Atlanta Press, 1903); Woodson, *History of the Negro Church*; Frazier, *Negro Church in America*; and W. D. Weatherford, *American Churches and the Negro: An Historical Study from Early Slave Days to the Present* (Boston: Christopher Publishing House, 1957).

34. See Timothy Smith, *Revivalism and Social Reform: American Protestantism on the Eve of the Civil War* (New York: Harper Torchbooks, 1965), 45–62; Henry F. May, *Protestant Churches and Industrial America* (New York: Harper and Row, 1967); and Perry Miller, *The Life of the Mind in America from the*

Revolution to the Civil War (New York: Harcourt, Brace and World, 1965), 3–35.

35. See Smith, *Revivalism*, 20–21.

36. As Raboteau notes, "among other denominations in the antebellum South—Presbyterian, Lutheran, Disciples, Episcopalian, Moravian—black ministers were extremely rare or nonexistent." See *Slave Religion*, 207. See also Joseph R. Washington, Jr., *Black Sects and Cults* (New York: Doubleday, 1972), 36–57. Cf. also Sobel, *Trabelin' On*. Sobel gives Presbyterians a greater role.

37. See David Brion Davis, "The Emergence of Immediatism in British and American Antislavery Thought," *Mississippi Valley Historical Review* 49, no. 2 (September 1962); and George M. Fredrickson, *The Black Image in the White Mind: The Debate on Afro-American Character and Destiny, 1817–1914* (New York: Harper and Row, 1971), 29.

38. This ideological and demographic conjuncture in the South did not spawn radical abolitionism, nor was this social sector full of people who took quick to the book counters to buy the latest slave narrative. That kind of cultural purchase took place in cities like Boston and New York. The expanding Methodist and Baptist denominations fostered a middle-class ideology that was distinctly antiintellectual as well as antiinstitutional and easily aligned with Jacksonian democratic populism.

On the important ties to racial politics see Saxon, *Rise and Fall*; and Roediger, *Wages of Whiteness*, on Jacksonian politics, see Arthur M. Schlesinger, Jr., *The Age of Jackson* (Boston: Little, Brown, and Co., 1953).

39. Washington, *Black Sects and Cults*, 37–38. E. Franklin Frazier suggest that the uninhibited emotionalism encouraged by Baptists and Methodists offered blacks a more accessible form of Christianity. Important is the fact that these two sects had rejected slavery as early as the second half of the eighteenth century. See Luther P. Jackson, "Religious Development of the Negro in Virginia from 1760 to 1860," *Journal of Negro History* 16 (April 1931): 168–239. Cf. Genovese's important discussion of the appeal of Baptist and Methodist denominations, as well as of the modifications slaves made of these orientations in *Roll, Jordan, Roll*, 232–33.

40. Charles Colcock Jones, *The Religious Instruction of the Negroes in the Southern States* (New York: Negro Universities Press, 1969), 39–40.

41. This form of dance was called a "shout," and the slapping of the body, "pattin," or "pattin juba." See Southern, *Readings*, 62. Harold Courlander provides an extensive description of the shout in *Negro Folk Music, U.S.A.* (New York: Columbia University Press, 1963), 194–200. Sterling Stuckey treats the ring shout as the prototypical Africanist cultural practice maintained by blacks throughout slavery, and argues that it played an important role in maintaining a sense of black nationalism. See *Slave Culture: Nationalist Theory and the Foundations of Black America* (New York: Oxford University Press, 1987). Stuckey's emphasis on very specific Africanist practices represents a refinement of Eugene Genovese's suggestion that Protestantism, "diluted and perverted" through its reappropriations, modifications, and transformations to fit the slave's needs, helped create "a protonational black consciousness." *Roll, Jordan, Roll*, 168, but see especially his provocative discussion on the role of Christianity in slave relations and the cultural complexities this engendered, 161–68.

42. John F. Watson, *Methodist Error; or, Friendly Christian Advice to Those Methodists Who Indulge in Extravagant Religious Emotions and Bodily Exercises* (Trenton, N.J.: D. and E. Fenton, 1819). Quoted in Eileen Southern, *Readings*, 62–63.

43. Southern, *Readings*, 62.

44. Quoted ibid., 63–64. Emphasis added.

45. Cf. George P. Rawick, *The American Slave: A Composite Autobiography*, vol. 1, *From Sundown to Sunup: The Making of the Black Community* (Westport, Conn.: Greenwood Publishing, 1972); Raboteau, *Slave Religion*; Stuckey, *Slave Culture*; and Sobel, *Trabelin' On*.

46. Freehling, *Prelude to Civil War*, 73.

47. Levine, *Black Culture and Black Consciousness*, 46. These cultural contradictions of slavery had to be adjudicated. Black religious *church* autonomy was one major accommodation.

48. The slave narratives and their crucial importance will be discussed later.

49. Charles Ball, *Slavery in the United States: A Narrative of the Life and Adventures of Charles Ball, a Black Man, Who Lived forty Years in Maryland, South Carolina, and Georgia, as a Slave* (New York: J. S. Taylor, 1837), 164.

50. See Small, *Music of the Common Tongue*, 81–115.

51. See Sobel, *Trabelin' On*, 97–98. On camp meeting racial segregation see Dickson D. Bruce, Jr., *And They All Sang Hallelujah: Plain-Folk Camp-Meeting Religion, 1800–1845* (Knoxville: University of Tennessee Press, 1974), 73, 86, 89. See also Levine, *Black Culture and Black Consciousness*, 21–22; Epstein, *Sinful Tunes*, 197–99.

The extension of Evangelical outreach to blacks did not make Evangelicalism antislavery or abolitionist. Evangelicalism cannot be said to have produced or to have resisted abolitionism. How, then, did Evangelicalism exert a productive and endorsing effect upon antislavery? According to Donald Mathews, abolitionism emerged as the cultural beneficiary of Evangelicalism's failures to deliver on some of its implied promises.

If "conversion to evangelicalism frequently crystallized vague reformist and humanitarian conviction," it could and did lead ironically to rejection of an evangelicalism unable to transform a "vague . . . conviction" into an absolute commitment to fight slavery. The result was that *abolitionism itself became a "surrogate religion" to replace an evangelicalism* which by 1830s had declined into "hollow ritual."

Popular piety reflected the "American obsession with the superficial forms of religious life rather than its inner meaning." The entwining of slavery and religion came to be a moral judgement on both.

See Mathews, "Religion and Slavery," 207–32, quotation from 209–10. The quotations that Mathews cites are from Ronald G. Walters, *The Anti-Slavery Appeal: American Abolitionism after 1830* (Baltimore: Johns Hopkins University Press, 1976), 44 (italics added). Henry James, Sr., made a similar indictment against Unitarianism as a "feeble" form of "sentimentality" that had arisen in the very decline of an earlier "virile" Protestantism. See F. W. Dupee, *Henry James: His Life and Writings* (New York: Doubleday and Co., 1956), 11. Cf. Douglas, *Feminization of American Culture*, 17.

What inherits this increasingly "hollow ritual" created by a religious movement that could not deliver the goods? It would appear that the larger beneficiary was the burgeoning humanitarian reform movement (which encompassed abolitionism) that was gaining in political and cultural importance during the middle decades of the nineteenth century. In this regard, as a populist social movement, Evangelicalism's infectious, part-romantic, deeply antiinstitutional, antimodern, and antirational charisma was soon to be rationalized by the social engagement of reformism. As Max Weber argued, "charismatic authority is specifically unstable." And extreme instability was such the case with Evangelicalism and the premium it placed upon immediate emotional catharsis. See Max Weber's discussion of charisma in Gerth and Mills, *From Max Weber*, 245–52; Weber's passage is found on 248. On the instability of Protestantism in general in the context of Congregationalism's waning hegemony see Harry S. Stout, *The New England Soul: Preaching and Religious Culture in Colonial New England* (New York: Oxford University Press, 1986), 133, 312–16.

52. Genovese, *Roll, Jordan, Roll*, 283.

53. See Marx's discussion on how the critique of philosophy, ideology, and religion requires material "realization" in "Contribution to the Critique of Hegel's Philosophy of Right: Introduction," in *The Marx-Engels Reader*, 2d ed,. Robert C. Tucker (New York: W. W. Norton and Co., 1978), 53–65.

54. That religious principles could be so flexible and open to new combinations of "ideas" and "interests" is a point Max Weber argued in showing (through the concept of *elective affinities*) how dominant ideas can be reinterpreted to fit changing historical interests. Cf. Weber, *Protestant Ethic*.

55. See Starling, *Slave Narrative*, 15, 19.

56. Marx, "Contribution to the Critique," 54.

57. Gustavus Vassa, *The Interesting Narrative of the Life of Oloudah Equiano, or Gustavus Vassa, the African* (1789; reprint, Leeds: James Nichols, 1814). The quotation is taken from the reprint of Vassa's narrative in Henry Louis Gates, Jr., ed., *The Classic Slave Narratives* (New York: Mentor, 1987), 38. According to Gates, Vassa's narrative is the prototype of the nineteenth-century slave narrative (xiv).

58. Franklin and Moss, *From Slavery to Freedom*, 159–61. See also Washington, *Black Sects and Cults*, 104–5; Sobel, *Trabelin' On*, 156–57; and Raboteau, *Slave Religion*, 158–59.

59. David Walker, *Appeal in Four Articles, Together with a Preamble to the Coloured Citizens of the World, But in Particular, and very Expressly, to those of the United States of America* (Boston, 1830), 68; Franklin, and Moss, *From Slavery to Freedom*, 161; Stuckey, *Slave Culture*, 98–137.

60. Washington, *Black Sects and Cults*, 105. See also Litwack, *North of Slavery*, 232–34.

61. See Washington's discussion of Nat Turner as a "Christian mystic" in *Black Sects and Cults*, 105.

62. According to Marion Wilson Starling, when William Lloyd Garrison launched *Liberator*, "he singlehandedly fastened the romantic movement to the institution of slavery." See *Slave Narrative*, 19. Relevant also is George Fredrickson's discussion of the importance of the Great Awakening as the source of

Garrison's earlier millennialism. See *The Inner Civil War: Northern Intellectuals and the Crisis of the Union* (New York: Harper and Row, 1965), 4–5. Yet, more crucial was the earlier mobilization of free blacks who, in 1816, formed the important Negro Convention movement to oppose the American Colonization movement's advocacy to solve race relations by the expulsion of blacks through forced repatriation to Africa. Led largely by black ministers (one of the few professions generally open to free blacks), over three thousand blacks gathered in the cities of Richmond and Philadelphia to oppose colonization. The Negro Convention movement constituted the first important organized body of black abolitionists. William Lloyd Garrison initially favored the colonization solution, but during his attendance at the Negro Convention's national meeting in 1831 he was swayed to support the black abolitionists' position rejecting colonization in favor of domestic freedom. Cf. Robert Allen, *Reluctant Reformers: Racism and Social Reform Movements in the United States* (Garden City, N.Y.: Doubleday, Anchor Press, 1975), 9–49; and Franklin and Moss, *From Slavery to Freedom*, 164–67.

63. Franklin and Moss, *From Slavery to Freedom*, 165; Litwack, *North of Slavery*, 236. The rise of publishing for an increasingly growing reading public as well as the internal divisions of literary commodities for more distinct readership was taking place from the 1830s on. As Michael Denning argues, the practice of serializing stories in general was part of the larger development of the dime novels, whose precursor was the penny press of the 1830s. The penny press helped to spin off serialized narratives in the form of "story papers," pamphlet novels of cheap and sensational fiction emerging as early as 1842, which were also the immediate forerunners to the successful series of Beadle's Dime Novels, which appeared in 1860 and culminated in the "cheap library" of nickel and dime pamphlets in the 1870s. These publications, read by the working class, were culturally distinct from those middle-class periodicals Victorians read, like *Century*, *Scribners*, *Harpers*, and *Atlantic*. Within the various burgeoning reading publics Garrison's *Liberator* emerged as one of the most important antislavery publications of the 1830s. The *Liberator* was involved as well in serializing slave narratives. On the rise of working-class literary forms, especially the dime novels, see Michael Denning, *Mechanical Accents: Dime Novels and Working-Class Culture in America* (London: Verso, 1987), 9–16. On the rise of the penny press see Michael Schudson, *Discovering the News: A Social History of American Newspapers* (New York: Basic Books, 1978).

64. Starling, *Slave Narrative*, 295.

65. See ibid., 19.

66. Harriet Jacobs [Linda Brent], *Incidents in the Life of a Slave Girl* (Boston, 1861). The quote is from the reprint of Jacob's narrative in Gates, *Classic Slave Narratives*, 402.

67. Ephriam Peabody, "Narratives of Fugitive Slaves," *Christian Examiner* 47 (July 1849): 63. Peabody is quoted in Charles H. Nichols, "Who Read the Slave Narratives?" *Phylon*, no. 20 (1959): 149–62.

68. Quoted in the *Leeds Anti-Slavery Series*, no. 34, (1853): 12. William Andrews notes that "after the Civil War, few ex-slave autobiographers recounted their lives in the manner of Douglass." Douglass and Henry Bibb stand out, according to Andrews, in that they "trace their salvation back to an intuition of

individual uniqueness and a sense of special destiny which they claim has inspired them since their early youth." See "The Representation of Slavery and the Rise of Afro-American Literary Realism, 1865–1920," in *Slavery and the Literary Imagination*, ed. Deborah E. McDowell and Arnold Rampersad (Baltimore: Johns Hopkins University Press, 1989), 62–80, quotation on 64–65. As I suggest here, the sense of individuality is largely the result of the cultural efficacy of the religious franchise, which highlighted individuality in the concept of the salvageable, redemptive soul.

69. On Douglass's break with Garrison, see Litwack, *North of Slavery*, 240–44; Allen, *Reluctant Reformers*, 39–42. Douglass chose to recognize the radical egalitarianist ideology behind the bourgeois social contract. Cf. also Jurgen Habermas's argument with regard to the critical kernel in the bourgeois revolution in Jurgen Habermas, *The Structural Transformation of the Public Sphere* (1962; reprint, Cambridge: MIT Press, 1989).

70. Douglass quoted in Franklin and Moss, *From Slavery to Freedom*, 167.

71. Theodore Adorno and Max Horkheimer called this kind of thought "immanent critique." Cf. Andrew Arato and Eike Gebhardt, eds., *The Essential Frankfurt School Reader* (New York: Urizen Books, 1978), 197–207; Martin Jay, *Adorno* (Cambridge: Harvard University Press, 1884), 115–17; and Gillian Rose, *The Melancholy Science: An Introduction to the Thought of Theodor W. Adorno* (New York: Columbia University Press, 1978), 17–18, 51. Immanent critique involves the critical reflection upon the very categories of the system of rules to show how social relations configured in forms of domination produce appearances that "explain" and justify reality.

On this very point, Critical Theory overlaps with the important and equally provocative theoretical perspectives of the American sociologist W. I. Thomas, poststructuralist Michel Foucault, and the social reproduction theorist Pierre Bourdieu. Thomas raised the argument that when people believe things to be true, things become true "in their consequences." This is quite similar to Michel Foucault's insistence that we need to distinguish between the concept of "Truth" and the "truth effects," and by effects he meant the actual results that follow when people pursue Truth as a concept or ideal. Similarly, Pierre Bourdieu suggests that people are likely to misrecognize as normal and natural the actual relations of domination by confusing surface features of canons, laws, and norms of orthodoxy and heterodoxy with the more nebulous cultural *doxa* that makes such social surfaces possible. Bourdieu uses the notion of doxa as a way to conceptualize and account for the (impugned) deepest, unconscious, taken-for-granted assumptions operating within a society—how the world "works." Doxa, as underlying assumptions, as unquestioned epistemology, is thus always operating within a society and to a large extent it underscores and makes possible and logical the more visible activities within both orthodoxy and heterodoxy. All of these writers' views, in their very formulation, enlarged the capacity to expose the constructed dimension of domination by grasping both the rules or the dominant principles of an ethical system and the social manipulation of such rules. The slave narratives approached this kind of critical reflexivity. Cf. Michel Foucault, *The History of Sexuality* (New York: Vintage Books, 1980); Pierre Bourdieu, *Outline of a Theory of Practice* (London: Cambridge University Press, 1977).

72. This, of course, is precisely the major accomplishment of modern social theory—making the social an object available to critical contemplation.

73. See Takaki, *Iron Cages*, 156–60.

74. The passage quoted is from the *Liberator* 5 (August 29, 1835): 140. Ball's narrative was published the following year. See Ball, *Slavery in the United States*.

75. The sociocultural production of representation outlined above can be grasped only by recognizing its cultural roots in the antinomies and contradictions that were played out through the extension of the religious franchise, which was itself caught in profound struggles over economic and moral schisms. This sociocultural development constitutes and conditions the modern interpretive scaffolding upon which much of modern cultural criticism stands and begins its work.

This developmental outcome appears to be related to an important starting point for literary criticism. In his assessment of the slave narratives, Henry Louis Gates, Jr. notes how they embody a "rhetorical movement" that proceeds "from institution and property to the shaping of the human subject." See *Figures in Black: Words, Signs, and the "Racial" Self* (Oxford: Oxford University Press, 1987), 22. Houston Baker proceeds from the developments of this cultural conjuncture to seek the origins of an emergent *national* identity. Baker refers to this kind of cultural practice as "spirit work," an apt term for this kind of enterprise. As a conceptual framework, the term is designed to grasp the inner logic of how Douglass and W. E. B. Du Bois, for example, deploy common struggles to map a sense of a past, and to claim stakes and to stake claims for a critically reflective sense of a place in the present. In exploring the black subject and the struggle for self-, collective, and racial location, Houston Baker puts the problem of contention over *national* imagery as unfolding on cultural terrain. "Black expressive culture [served] as a reservoir from which a quintessentially Afro-American spirit flowed. No matter how ineffable the source of this spirit or elusive its precise contours, it was a national spirit—an impulse, that is to say, which argued the birth of a nation perceptibly different from the one conceived [in *Birth of a Nation*] by D. W. Griffith." For Baker, the "national impulse valorized by Locke, Du Bois, and Washington is best described . . . as Afro-American spirit work." This angle of analysis and interpretation comprises a "critical model" and "a kind of racial poetics." See Houston A. Baker, Jr., *Afro-American Poetics: Revisions of Harlem and the Black Aesthetic* (Madison: University of Wisconsin Press, 1988), 5.

As starting points, the "racial self" and the "nationalist spirit work" are already the product of cultural struggles structured (loosely) within discrepant modes of interpreting a hegemonic ideology (Christianity and modern subjectivity) and the bequeathed "selfhood" engendered by the religious franchise. These moves are central to the redemptive cultural work that was engendered during the mid-nineteenth century and core to humanitarian reformism as the latter bequeathed new modes of *reading culture*.

76. As Jurgen Habermas has shown, the significance of the Enlightenment was its initial capacity to thematize the rise of a critical subjectivity (which happened to be bourgeois subjectivity). This new subjectivity fostered the critique of traditionalism but culminated in the new forms of social, political, economic, and

ideological enclosure favoring the rise of bourgeois society. This development, Habermas suggests, was convened with the emergence of a critical "bourgeois public sphere" and its progressive transformation to a "liberal public sphere." Yet, it was in this historical nexus of ideological irruptions that new subjectivities first gained their modern and contestatorial significance. See Habermas, *Structural Transformation*. The current search for viable subjectivity within the contemporary context of "post-Enlightenment" and "antifoundationalist" theorizing has not been able to shed the significance of this historical irruption, and to this day inherits the framework of the historically shifting pressure to identify and exonerate social subjects. See Cruz, "Subject Crises and Subject Work," 92–122.

77. Jurgen Habermas discusses how these issues were surfacing in western Europe in the late-eighteenth and early-nineteenth centuries. See *Structural Transformation*. See also Gilroy, *The Black Atlantic*.

78. Quoted in Gates, *Classic Slave Narratives*, 335–36. See also William Andrews's valuable discussion on the role of evangelicalism in facilitating black subjecthood in his introduction to *Six Women's Slave Narratives*, ed. Henry Louis Gates, Jr. (New York: Oxford University Press, 1988).

79. In his provocative essay, Timothy Smith suggests a point that numerous historians have echoed. According to Smith, "slaves and freedmen received the Christian faith with a keener sense of some of its enduring meanings than many of their white teachers." However, this was not necessarily the result of an underlying and imputed black theology. Rather, the value that slaves and freedpersons found in Christian principles has a simpler psychosocial explanation. Africans, notes Smith,

> were pressed up against the wall by American slavery's vast assault upon their humanity. This tragic circumstance compelled them to discover in the religion of their white oppressors a faith whose depths few of the latter had even suspected, enabling the Black Christians to reconcile suffering and hope, guilt and forgiveness, tyranny and spiritual freedom, self-hate and divine acceptance. In that faith some of them found the strength to throw off their bonds, and many others the dignity, when once emancipated, to stand up free.

See Timothy L. Smith, "Slavery and Theology: The Emergence of Black Christian Consciousness in Nineteenth-Century America," *Church History* 41, no. 4 (December 1972), 512. The concern here is not to fathom the relative autonomy of black religious practices, but to examine the interpretative orientation toward black cultural expressions that emerged out of antislavery sensibilities, and with particular regard to practices associated with religious song making.

CHAPTER FOUR
FROM AUTHENTIC SUBJECTS TO AUTHENTIC CULTURE

1. The problem of politics was never fully absent from the protoethnographic interests even though concern with the fate of black Americans was being profoundly muted and even rendered invisible precisely as black culture became visible. The return of such problems characterizes certain modern refinements in

anthropology and critical ethnography. These interpretive enterprises appear (belatedly) to wrestle with the legacy that informed them—the discovery of social groups as ways in which larger social issues, concerns, problems, and even crises invariably come into play and how such discoveries serve to grasp, understand, and broker social relations. One need only look at the so-called new ethnography of the 1980s to see how contemporary intellectuals struggle over the question of social inquiry and ideological investments that come inadvertently when social scientists turn to the study of groups, subcultures, and "whole" cultures, only to confront not just an objective world but their own reflections in the subjects their methods hope to capture. Certainly the process of cultural interpretation has shifted increasingly with greater reflexivity since the probes of the mid-nineteenth century. Cf. James Clifford and George E. Marcus, eds., *Writing Culture: The Poetics and Politics of Ethnography* (Berkeley: University of California Press, 1986); James Clifford, *The Predicament of Culture: Twentieth-Century Ethnography, Literature, and Art* (Cambridge: Harvard University Press, 1988); and George E. Marcus and Michael M. J. Fischer, *Anthropology as Cultural Critique: An Experimental Movement in the Human Sciences* (Chicago: University of Chicago Press, 1986).

2. The mutually interdependent poles of externality and internality have an even more important sociohistorical source: the crisis of modernity in the nineteenth century. In the North this was registered strongly in the transition from a predominantly agrarian to an increasingly industrial society. The case discussed here, along with its racial lines, is only one strand of this, but nonetheless linked more deeply and broadly to this crisis. To understand the constant dislocation that modernity invariably brings, we are required to define social groups as indices of such forces. This process takes place and is actually quite pervasive within the domestic talk of nations having crossed the bridge from feudalism to capitalism and from agrarianism to industrialism. Whole lexicons of compressed terms have arisen, aided of course by the talk of modern social science. But it is not the sociological abstractions such as industrialization, capitalism, market society, urbanization, consumer society, globalization, and so forth that enable us to understand modernity. We grasp the meaning of these abstractions only through the way in which they can be grounded in the context of concrete social subjects (such as slaves or the poor under the impending industrial revolution of the nineteenth century). Social subjects are our measurement of what we come to know about the social meaning of modernity.

What comes with this framework is an inescapable logic: we can only gauge change by first assuming that social groups and collective subjects have some kind of distinct and relatively fixed identity—and the precursor to this modern construct of identity is *authenticity*, which, in turn, has roots in older religious constructs. The "fixing" of social subjects enables us to speak of *place* and *displacement*. In this way we grasp the forces of modernity that dislocate what we presume to be fixed. The *recognition* of social crises is thereby registered as subject crisis, and is thus legitimated in the process and proceeds as the justification for addressing groups. The histories of romantic, reformist, social scientific as well as revolutionary forms tap into this cultural logic of measuring and mediating social change. The example being discussed in these pages traces how this process works in one domain—how religiously inclined overseers ascribed souls and, by extension, subjectivity to slaves, and how this culminates in not just the rise of recognizing and exonerating black spirits shackled as slaves, but also in the growing recognition of a *reinterpretive crisis* taking place within the liberal wings of a deeply troubled Protestantism that has the engines of a dispiriting industrialization running over its back. In other words, the problem of authenticity, with its historically specific forms of subject crises, necessarily entails struggles that involve attempts to reenchant a cultural terrain that has been simultaneously disenchanted by modernity. See Cruz, "Subject Crises and Subject Work," 92–122.

3. See Raymond Williams, *Culture and Society, 1780–1950* (New York: Harper and Row), 1958; and R. Williams, *Marxism and Literature*.

4. The double function of authenticity as the identification of essential attributes and as a marker of the legitimacy of the identifiers themselves is not simply a practice of deception or a sham behind which simple utilitarian strategies of power and domination are exercised (which is what both Marx and Nietzsche labored to make transparent). It is not so conscious. It operates more fundamentally in the deeper strategies of social reproduction, and is thus rudimentary to how power and domination are normalized (Durkheim), routinized (Weber), and organized into discursive forms (Foucault) that are always enforced by the institutional forms that must be present in order to make such effective and shared expressions possible. Cultural efficacy and institutionalization are thus coterminous in social reproduction. In this regard the double function of authenticity (seeking the object in ways that confirm the purposes of the seeker) enables the cultural achievement of what Bourdieu calls *doxa*—the confirmation of social and historical hierarchies that do not themselves have to be brought into visibility (*misrecognition*). Having put domination and its opacity into this kind of sociologism is not meant to sum up culture and domination as if they were a brick-and-mortar couplet and thus impenetrable. As noted in the previous chapter, these constructs were rendered visible in the slave narratives (immanent critique), an important moment in the ideological ruptures of domination that Bourdieuian theory seems to evade. Nonetheless, as noted, those critiques embraced the doxa, the core values, the central principles. They did not call for the abandonment of core religious values, but instead represented struggles over preferred interpretations. As such, they are symptomatic of the struggles *inside* the so-called hermeneutic circle rather than attempts to abandon the dominant principles of hegemony.

5. Quoted in Epstein, *Sinful Tunes*, 105.

6. This ideal separation of external behavior from reflexive values became increasingly untenable once the religious franchise was put into operation.

7. Quoted in Epstein, *Sinful Tunes*, 108.

8. See the important and highly influential discussion of "African survivals" in Herskovits, *Myth of the Negro Past*.

9. The strategy is somewhat reminiscent of Martin Luther's recognition that it would be unwise to repress heathen folk songs since they were to important to their originators, but they could be commandeered by keeping the form and melody while purging their lyrics and replacing them with acceptable Christian text. On Luther, see Burke, *Popular Culture*, 223.

10. C. Jones, *Religious Instruction*, 266.

11. Quoted in Epstein, *Sinful Tunes*, 164. See also Levine, *Black Culture*, 17.

12. Bremer, *Homes of the New World* 2:509–10.

13. Ibid., 442–44. Cf. Epstein, *Sinful Tunes*, 90–91.

14. Marion Wilson Starling makes this argument in *The Slave Narrative*.

15. On studies of the slave narratives, see Benjamin A. Botkin, *Lay My Burden Down: A Folk History of Slavery* (Chicago: University of Chicago Press, 1945); Starling, *Slave Narrative*; Frances Smith Foster, *Witnessing Slavery: The Development of Ante-Bellum Slave Narratives* (Westport, Conn.: Greenwood Press, 1979); Charles H. Nichols, *Many Thousand Gone: The Ex-Slaves' Account of Their Bondage and Freedom* (Leidan, Netherlands: E.J. Brill, 1963); William L. Andrews *To Tell a Free Story: The First Century of Afro-American Autobiography, 1760–1865* (Urbana and Chicago: University of Illinois Press, 1986); Hazel Carby, *Reconstructing Motherhood: The Emergence of the Afro-American Woman Novelist* (New York: Oxford University Press, 1987); and Valerie Smith, *Self-Discovery and Authority in Afro-American Narrative* (Cambridge: Harvard University Press, 1987). See also Rawick, *The American Slave*; and Norman Yetman, "The Background of the Slave Narrative Collection," *American Quarterly* 19 (1967): 534–53.

16. Ball is quoted in *The Liberator* 5 (August 29, 1835): 140.

17. Douglass, *Narrative of the Life*, 58.

18. Ibid., 58.

19. Ibid., *Narrative*, 57.

20. Douglass wrote three versions: *Narrative of the Life of Frederick Douglass, an American Slave, Written by Himself* (1845); *My Bondage and My Freedom* (1855); and *Life and Times of Frederick Douglass* (1881). For an analysis of how Douglass's sense of his emergent self shifted in the sequence of these three autobiographies, cf. Gates, *Figures in Black*, 98–124; Andrews, "Representation of Slavery"; and David Leverenz, *Manhood and the American Renaissance* (Ithaca: Cornell University Press, 1989), 108–34.

21. Garrison's passage is found in Douglass, *Narrative of the Life*, 38.

22. On this point we can appreciate the emotional yoke that actually binds the lower-class populism of Evangelicalism and the Great Awakenings (including all of the importance given to emotionalism as the affect most suitable for spiritual conversion), with the disenchantment and the outrage of the neo-Unitarians of the New England gentry. Both religious developments, though quite different, were busy shifting the cultural map upon which emotionalism played a significant role in the recognition of black expressivity. Evangelicalism exonerated emotions as the language of truth; radical abolitionists championed their incense and outrage at slavery. Both were strategies of an unleashed emotionalism that served to ground a sense of truth.

23. Frederick Douglass, *My Bondage and My Freedom* (New York, 1855), 97–100, 251–56. These lines are from the song "Run to Jesus," which is printed as one of the spirituals sung by the Fisk Jubilee Singers. The song, printed as no. 69 in the 1881 publication *The Story of the Fisk Jubilee Singers* is prefaced by the following words: "This song was given to the Jubilee Singers by Hon. Frederick Douglass, at Washington, D.C., with the interesting statement, that it first sug-

gested to him the thought of escaping from slavery." See J. B. T. Marsh, *The Story of the Fisk Jubilee Singers* (1981; reprint, New York: Negro Universities Press, 1960), 188.

24. Douglass, *Bondage and Freedom*. In discussing the "worldly" dimensions of the early spirituals, Le Roi Jones [Amiri Baraka] offers an interesting account which seems to elide the observation made by Douglass:

> The religious imagery of the Negro's Christianity is full of references to the suffering and hopes of the oppressed Jews of Biblical times. Many of the Negro spirituals reflect this identification: *Go Down, Moses, I'm to Zion, Walk Into Jerusalem Just Like John*, etc. "Crossing the river Jordan" meant not only death but also the entrance into the very real heaven and a release from an earthly bondage; it came to represent all the slave's yearnings to be freed from the inhuman yoke of slavery. But at the time, at least for the early black Christian, this freedom was one that could only be reached through death. The later secular music protested conditions *here*, in America. No longer was the great majority of slaves concerned with leaving this country (except, perhaps, the old folks who sat around and, I suppose, remembered). *This* was their country, and they became interested in merely living in it a little better and a little longer.

See Le Roi Jones, *Blues People: The Negro Experience in White America and the Music That Developed from It* (New York: Morrow Quill Paperbacks, 1963), 40. Douglass, however, argued that the songs of sorrow could also serve as codes to help evade the social death of slavery. The otherworldly was not death but a "speedy pilgrimage toward a free state" and a life in the North free of shackles.

25. Douglass, *Bondage and Freedom*.

26. See the helpful discussion of these issues in Lovell, *Black Song*, 198.

27. Genovese, *Roll, Jordan, Roll*, 236.

28. Lawrence Levine makes the following important point: "It is possible that a greater number of religious than nonreligious songs have survived because slaves were more willing to sing these ostensibly innocent songs to white collectors who in turn were more eager to record them since they fit easily with their positive and negative images of the Negro. But I would argue that the vast preponderance of spirituals over any other sort of slave music rather than being merely the result of accident or error is instead an accurate reflection of slave culture during the antebellum period."

Levine attributes this to the "widespread conversion of slaves to Christianity and the impact of the revivals." See *Black Culture and Black Consciousness*, 18. This argument illustrates, I believe, the example of ideological and cultural miscegenation between Africanist "survivals" and American white Protestantism's peculiar institutions through slavery. And this is what constitutes the broader meaning of "slave culture" as an expression of social relationships rather than of a racial essence. When read together, Levine's study, along with the studies by Eugene Genovese, Dena Epstein, and Sterling Stuckey, demonstrates how profoundly infused slave culture is with the hegemonic and institutional formations of slave-based civil society. Cf. Genovese, *Roll, Jordan, Roll*; Epstein, *Sinful Tunes*; and Stuckey, *Slave Culture*.

29. See Child, "Charity Bowery," 43.

30. James Scott's distinction between "hidden transcripts" and "public transcripts" is helpful in thinking about this matter. According to Scott, hidden transcripts enable individuals to pursue a "realm of relative discursive freedom, outside the earshot of powerholders." Public transcripts, on the other hand, instantiate the more or less official and "open interactions between subordinates and those who dominate." However, in the case of particular spirituals, we have a case of slaves presenting hidden transcripts in the form of public presentations. According to Scott,

> Every subordinate group creates, out of its ordeal, a "hidden transcript" that represents a critique of power spoken behind the back of the dominant. The powerful, for their part, also develop a hidden transcript representing the practices and claims of their rule that cannot be openly avowed. A comparison of the hidden transcript of the weak with that of the powerful and of *both* hidden transcripts to the public transcript of power relations offers a substantially new way of understanding resistance to domination.

See *Domination*, 2, 23, xii. The distinction, however, between the hidden and the public is not at all neat—which is precisely why black song making functioned in what I call a *clandestine public sphere* that forced the expression of restricted messages through public presentations.

31. The clandestine culture of slaves has been noted by many. See especially Raboteau, *Slave Religion*; and Stuckey, *Slave Culture*. The classic study of slave strategies to maximize a sense of cultural integrity or solidarity is Bauer and Bauer's "Day to Day Resistance," 388–419. James Scott draws upon examples from slavery, serfdom, caste subordination, colonialism, racism, and other forms of domination that generate hidden transcripts that in turn enable groups of unequal power to talk in the presence as well as absence of one another. See Scott, *Domination*.

32. See Theodore Parker, "The American Scholar," in *The American Scholar*, vol. 8. of *Centenary Edition of Theodore Parker's Writings*, ed. George Willis Cooke (Boston: American Unitarian Association, 1907), 37.

33. Olmsted, *Journey in the Seaboard Slave States*, 1:148.

34. Douglass, *Narrative of the Life*, 104. As Leon Litwack points out, black abolitionists were yoked with stereotypes, and their attempt to free themselves from the pervasive influences of minstrelsy proved difficult. While a formidable orator, Douglass's acumen, self-presentation, and polish raised concerns among some of his closest white abolitionist allies, who thought that he might not be believed to have ever been a slave. Douglass was advised by white abolitionist John Collins: "People won't believe that you were ever a slave, Frederick, if you keep on in this way." It was suggested that it would be "better [to] have a little of the plantation speech than not; it is not best that you seem too learned." See Litwack, *North of Slavery*, 225; quote from Douglass, *Life and Times*, 269–70. Cf. also Boskin, *Sambo*, 124.

35. Douglass, *Narrative of the Life*, 58.

36. See Kemble, *Journal of a Residence*, 129.

37. See Rawick, *American Slave*, 138. Such notions of paternalistic benevolence and slave gratitude, widespread among apologists in the antebellum era, and fundamental to minstrelsy, managed to find their modern expression in rigorous

scholarship well into the twentieth century. In a classic study of African American music published in 1928, Newman White demonstrated the tenacity of this view:

> Of course the Negro laborer is sometimes surly; of course, he sometimes growls and is dissatisfied with his lot. But the real significance of his songs expressing race-consciousness is the fact that they show so little of this mood. Fundamentally they are striking evidence of the deep conservatism, humor, patience, and sense of present realities with which the Negro has contributed probably more than his full share to the concord of the two races in the South.

White's view fits squarely within an interpretive tradition that could not recognize that the South had a "racial problem." In this passage, the social conservatism of the southern social system is projected onto African Americans through the analysis of songs. See White, *American Negro Folk-Songs*, 378.

38. Douglass, *Narrative of the Life*, 58. While the happy slave is a massive distortion, Douglass's claim that the slaves "sing most when they are most unhappy" is also hyperbolic. The emotional limit of song that Douglass describes may very well be true of his personal experience. But the extensive compilations of interviews from former slaves and many other black accounts show music to have an extremely wide range of emotion. Douglass, however, was concerned with countering the pervasive view of slaves as "happy." A half century later W. E. B. Du Bois pointed out the disparity between the popular view of the contented slave fully embellished in the mythology of "Sambo," and the demeanor of blacks who lived under great repression. Regarding the black tenant farmers who lived in the "black belt" he noted the same seemingly intractable and preferred interpretation: "They are not happy, these black men whom we meet throughout this region. There is little of the joyous abandon and playfulness which we are wont to associate with the plantation Negro." See Du Bois, *Souls*, xlii.

39. "Music," *Atlantic Monthly*, no. 1 (November 1857): 125.

40. Cf. "Music," *Atlantic Monthly* 1, no. 5 (March 1858): 636.

41. Raymond Williams points out the parallel case in the British cultural context:

> The idea of such an *elite*, for the common good of society, has not been lost sight of, down to our own day. All that now needs emphasis, with Carlyle as with Coleridge, and as with Matthew Arnold after them is that the then existing organization of society, as they understood it, offered no actual basis for the maintenance of such a class. The *separation* of the activities grouped as "culture" from the main purposes of the new kind of society was the ground of complaint.

See R. Williams, *Culture and Society*, 85. Carlyle, whom Williams goes on to quote, summed up the new purpose and drive for an increasingly autonomous notion of culture governed by intellectuals.

> Never, till about a hundred years ago, was there seen any figure of a Great Soul living apart in that anomalous manner; endeavoring to speak forth the

inspiration that was in him by Printed Books, and find place and subsistence by what the world would please to give him for doing that. Much had been sold and bought, and left to make its own bargain in the market place; but the inspired wisdom of a Heroic Soul never till then, in that naked manner.(85)

Carlyle's statement, according to Williams, represented

the immediate criterion by which the faulty organization, the narrow purposes, of the new society might be perceived. It is in these terms, reinforced by more general conclusions, that Culture came to be defined as separate entity and a critical idea. (85–86)

The efforts of the literary-minded Transcendentalists do not appear to have accomplished their deepest desires for a cultural shift significantly distinct to overcome the Europe envy among significant American cultural elites. In Henry James's view, America remained a barren setting for a writer in contrast to the "denser, richer, warmer European spectacle." Henry James, *Hawthorne* (London: Macmillan, 1879), 42.

42. Cf. Levine, *Highbrow/Lowbrow,* 85–168; and DiMaggio, "Cultural Entrepreneurship," 33–50.

43. See Clarence L. F. Gohdes, *The Periodicals of American Transcendentalism* (Durham, N.C.: Duke University Press, 1931).

44. See Alexander Kern, "The Rise of Transcendentalism, 1815–1860," in *Transitions in American Literary History* ed. Harry Hayden Clark (Durham, N.C.: Duke University Press, 1953), 311–12.

45. Cf. Riis, "Cultivated White Tradition," 156–76.

46. See Daniel Walker Howe, *The Unitarian Conscience: Harvard Moral Philosophy, 1805–1861* (Cambridge: Harvard University Press, 1970). Howe's work provides an important study of Unitarianism's major role in the abolitionist movement. See also William R. Hutchinson, *The Transcendentalist Ministers: Church Reform in the New England Renaissance* (New Haven: Yale University Press, 1959); and Lawrence Buell, "The Unitarian Movement and the Art of Preaching in the Nineteenth Century" *American Quarterly* 24 (May 1972): 166–90.

47. See David Montejano, *Anglos and Mexicans in the Making of Texas, 1836–1986* (Austin: University of Texas, 1987).

48. The contrast with regard to the treatment of Indians is provided in Slotkin, *Regeneration through Violence*; Richard Drinnon, *Facing West: The Metaphysics of Indian-Hating and Empire-Building* (New York: New American Library, Meridian, 1980); and Thomas Almaguer, *Racial Fault Lines: The Historical Origins of White Supremacy in California* (Berkeley: University of California Press, 1994).

49. The extent to which "culturalism" trumps black political expressivity (e.g., the spiritual rather than the slave narratives) within a larger American public sphere is the much larger problem that follows from the "cultural turn." The tension between culture and critical intellectual issues is treated in David Levering Lewis's critical study, *When Harlem Was in Vogue* (New York: Knopf, 1981); and Harold Cruse, *The Crisis of the Negro Intellectual* (New York: Morrow,

1967). Valuable also are Alain Locke's jointly published studies, *The Negro and His Music and Negro Art*. Cf. also Claude McKay, *Harlem: Negro Metropolis* (New York: Harcourt Brace Jovanovich, 1940); Arna Bontemps, ed., *The Harlem Renaissance Remembered* (New York: Dodd, Mead and Co., 1972); Jervis Anderson, *This Was Harlem: A Cultural Portrait, 1900–1950* (New York: Farrar Strauss Giroux, 1981); and Houston Baker, *Modernism and the Harlem Renaissance* (Chicago: University of Chicago Press, 1987). Hazel Carby's important study of black women writers in the last two decades of the nineteenth century raises similar problems of the cultural eclipse of politics. Cf. *Reconstructing Womanhood*.

50. For a discussion of how Stowe's novel along with Theodore Weld's *American Slavery as It Is* helped put slavery on trial, see Fredrickson, *Inner Civil War*, 81.

51. Epstein, *Sinful Tunes*, 100.

52. Gramsci, *Selections from the Prison Notebooks*, 8.

CHAPTER FIVE
FROM TESTIMONIES TO ARTIFACTS

1. On the role of cultural activities at Port Royal and the coming of Reconstruction, see Willie L. Rose, *Rehearsal for Reconstruction: The Port Royal Experiment* (New York: Vintage, 1967).

2. Allen, Ware, and Garrison, *Slave Songs*, i–ii.

3. The political and institutional backdrop to this eclipse was critically reassessed by W. E. B. Du Bois, first in the form of several eloquent and interlocking sketches that were published as *The Souls of Black Folk* (1903) and then in his magnum opus, *Black Reconstruction in America, 1860–1880* (1935).

4. I draw from Epstein's discussion of Lockwood. See Epstein, *Sinful Tunes*, 243–48.

5. Ibid., 245.

6. *American Missionary*, 6 (February 1862): 30; Epstein, *Sinful Tunes*, 248.

7. This song appears to be the first Negro spiritual to be commodified, though the commodification of antislavery songs had already occurred when the black novelist and compiler William Wells Brown published *The Anti-Slavery Harp: A Collection of Songs for Anti-Slavery Meetings* (Boston: B. March, 1849). These songs were popular airs and melodies with antislavery lyrics set to them. The commodification of black writings, however, was actually well established. Slave narratives were serialized in William Lloyd Garrison's *Liberator*, and the practice of serialization, as Michael Denning has noted, was common in mid-nineteenth-century popular culture. See Denning, *Mechanical Accents*. Some former slaves sold their narratives to help pay for the freedom of loved ones, and the musical skills of a slave were widely recognized to earn a seller of an individual with such talents a higher price. What is fundamental is not when commodification annexed black expressivity, but rather the recognition that the slave was by definition a commodity from the outset.

8. Drawing upon Thorstein Veblen, Alexander Kern suggests that "the Transcendentalists of the clerical group . . . a sort of vicarious leisure class attached to

the older aristocracy, opposed Jacksonianism . . . because they unconsciously recognized the threat to their previous position of dominance." "The Rise of Transcendentalism," 313.

9. Stout, *The New England Soul*, 313.

10. See the valuable discussion of the role the Ware family played in discovering, transcribing, and publishing black music in the aftermath of the Civil War in Epstein, *Sinful Tunes*, 252–358.

11. See Howe, *Unitarian Conscience*. Cf. also Harold Clarke Goddard, *Studies in New England Transcendentalism* (New York: Hillary House Publishers, 1960), 23; Douglas, *Feminization of American Culture*, 47–48, 174, 277; May, *Protestant Churches*.

12. Channing's sermons, many of which contain references to the "laboring classes," are compiled. *The Complete Works of William Ellery Channing, D.D.* (London: "Christian Life" Publishing Company, 1884). See also Kern, "Rise of Transcendentalism," 250; and Hutchinson, *Transcendentalist Ministers"*.

13. See Walter I. Trattner, *From Poor Law to Welfare State: A History of Social Welfare in America* (New York: Free Press, 1974), 53.

14. William R. Hutchinson, *The Modernist Impulse in American Protestantism* (Oxford: Oxford University Press, 1982), 161. This problem is certainly not peculiar to the field of American religion. It is actually symptomatic of larger transformations in the West, and linked to a more general attempt to adjudicate tensions between older cultural orientations toward individuals, society, and social redemption engendered by the deepened sense of crisis and the loss of control. This, of course, is the very problem that stimulated the origins of Durkheimian sociology a half century later. The rise of modern sociological theory in general expresses this very transformation of the coming of modernity. What Karl Marx did (through his critical-hermeneutic reading of Hegel's preoccupation with spirit and consciousness) when he turned Hegel "on his head" was to "realize" through flesh-and-blood social categories what was being thought out in the farthest reaches of a critical philosophical modernity. My point here is that the modern attempts to think through these intertwined issues, which we traditionally associate with European intellectual formations, ought to be grasped as ideologically kindred to developments that were taking place in the deepest and most troubled trenches of American Protestantism at precisely the same time. Hegel's influence was being negotiated by more than the young Hegelians in the young Marx's Germany; it also touched the critical margins of an uneasy American Protestantism. See D. Lloyd Easton, *Hegel's First American Followers* (Athens: Ohio University Press, 1966).

Max Weber's *Protestant Ethic and the Spirit of Capitalism* bears mentioning in this vein. The line of development from inner tension to worldly operations is thematized by Weber. The crisis that Weber highlights hinges on the thesis that Calvinism's puritanical perspective prevented individuals from ever having knowledge of their fate. This condition was psychologically intolerable; hence the progressive shift toward a series of (re)searches for the external signs of salvation through works, ultimately culminating in rational capitalistic acquisition. Weber's study, however, does not treat the side route that also developed out of the crisis of Calvinism, which unfolded between the era of Benjamin Franklin and the rise of capitalist magnates, the so-called captains of industry, at the end of the nineteenth century. *The Protestant Ethic* makes no mention of any antimodernist responses; there is no treatment of Transcendentalism, Thoreau, Emerson, or like company, or discussion of the utopian reactions expressed, for example, in the seven-year experiment of Brook Farm, all of which signify important antirational-ist tendencies in revolt against the coming of the cultural "iron cage" of capital-ism. This line signaled a deep religious disenchantment with capitalism. And such disenchantment had a focus; it was not just an unspecified malaise. Ironically, this development is just as much a route of rationalization that can be traced through, for example, the romanticist literature that raises the love-hate-and-annihilation of the Indian and the thematization of the American version of the noble savage (James Fenimore Cooper), to the dimensions of Evangelicalism that turned to the marginalized classes as well as to blacks (the Great Awakenings), and to the im-portant concerted efforts to turn the negative legacy of Calvinist individualistic depravity into the sprawling forms of humanitarian and social reform in the mid-to-late nineteenth century. This series of developments is just as much a rational-izing path as is the one Weber charts. It has overlapping dimensions with the rise of capitalism (as might be summed up by what I believe is the hasty argument that would reduce humanitarian reformism to nothing but the dirty work of capitalist domination), but it also has a more complex, troubled, and, in many ways, a competitively antagonistic relationship to the strand of rationalization champi-oned by Weber. It is this *other* strand, a parallel and contentious one, that con-cerns me in this study.

15. The emphasis on changing society to improve the individual was clearly a more liberal orientation. The conservative orientation, which also drew its roots from romanticism-inflected religious notions of perfectionism, was much more prevalent. John Thomas argues that after the American revolution and the rise democratic politics, "egalitarianism and rising demands for church disestablish-ment suddenly appeared to threaten an inherited Christian order and along with it the preferred status of the clergy." Key clergymen like Lyman Beecher spoke of the new anxiety, warning that Americans were fast becoming "another people." When it appeared that disestablishment could not be stopped, "the evangelicals, assuming a defensive posture, organized voluntary benevolent associations to strengthen the Christian character of Americans and save the country from in-fidelity and ruin. Between 1815 and 1830 nearly a dozen moral reform societies were established to counter the threats to social equilibrium posed by irreligious democrats." The American Bible Society, the American Sunday School Union, the American Home Missionary Society, and the American Tract Society sprang from these Evangelical societies. By the mid-1830s, these associations "formed a vast if loosely coordinated network of conservative reform enterprises staffed with clergy and wealthy laymen who served as self-appointed guardians of American morals." See John L. Thomas, "Romantic Reform in America, 1815–1865," *American Quarterly* 17 (winter 1965): 656–81, quotation on p. 657. Cf. also John R. Bodo, *The Protestant Clergy and Public Issues, 1812–1848* (Princeton: Princeton University Press, 1954); and Clifford S. Griffin, *Their Brothers' Keepers* (New Brunswick, N.J.: Rutgers University Press, 1960).

16. See Daniel Calhoun, *Professional Lives in America: Structure and Aspiration, 1750–1850* (Cambridge: Harvard University Press, 1965), 120–21; Douglas, *Feminization of American Culture*, 32, but see also 17–49.

17. Durkheim, *Division of Labor*.

18. See Howe, *Unitarian Conscience*, 87–90.

19. On the importance of and interests in eastern religions, see Arthur Christy, *The Orient in American Transcendentalism: A Study of Emerson, Thoreau, and Alcott* (1932; reprint, New York: Octagon Books, 1963). The writings of Octavius Brooks Frothingham, himself a Transcendentalist as well as self-appointed historian of the school, also document the quite remarkable intellectual gropings for inspiration far outside the established Protestant American canons. See especially his *Transcendentalism in New England: A History* (New York: G. P. Putnam's Sons, 1880); and *The Religion of Humanity: An Essay* (New York: G. P. Putnam's Sons, 1875). As Howe points out, "Emerson, Thoreau, George Ripley, Bronson Alcott—such Transcendentalists as these could never have written their splendid paeans to individualism if the Unitarians had not paved the way for them by destroying Calvinist doctrines of original sin." See Howe, *Unitarian Conscience*. On Emerson's larger and deeper significance within modern American ideology see the important study by Christopher Newfield, *The Emerson Effect: Individualism and Submission in America* (Chicago: University of Chicago Press, 1996). The deeply structured ties between even the most radical abolitionists and the frameworks of individualistic atomism have been noted by many historians. Cf. Eric Foner, *Politics and Ideology in the Age of the Civil War* (New York: Oxford University Press, 1980), 23.

20. Bruce Mazlish, *A New Science: The Breakdown of Connections and the Birth of Sociology* (New York: Oxford University Press, 1989), 102.

21. Ibid., 102–3.

22. Ralph Waldo Emerson, *Selections from Ralph Waldo Emerson*, ed. Stephen E. Whicher (Boston: Houghton Mifflin Co., 1960), 43.

23. Ibid., 31. For a broader historical and cultural contextualization of this new synthesis of self and nature, see the important discussion of what Charles Taylor calls the "expressive turn" in *Sources of the Self*, 368–90.

24. As Marx wrote,

The animal is immediately identical with its life-activity. It does not distinguish itself from it. It is *its life activity*. Man makes his life-activity itself the *object of his will and of his consciousness*. He has conscious life-activity. It is not a determination with which he directly merges. Conscious life-activity directly distinguishes man from animal life-activity. It is just because of this that he is a species being. Or it is only because he is a species being that he is a conscious being, i.e., That his own life is an object for him. Only because of that is his activity *free* activity. Estranged labour reverses this relationship, so that it is just because man is a conscious being that he makes his life-activity, his *essential* being, a mere means to his *existence*.

Estranged labor turns "man's species being, both nature and his spiritual species property, into a being *alien* to him, into a *means* to his *individual existence*. It estranges man's own body from him, as it does external nature and his spiritual essence, his *human* being." Robert Tucker, ed., *The Marx-Engels Reader*, 2d ed. (New York: W. W. Norton and Co. 1978), 76–77.

25. Emerson, *Selections*, 31. This passage of Emerson's is particularly interesting in that its modern and systematic fulfillment as social theory did not emerge from American Transcendentalism but rather in French sociology, and specifically in Emile Durkheim's *Elementary Forms of the Religious Life* (1915). It is not the case that French sociology learned anything from Transcendentalism, but rather that both had roots in Kantianism. Kant's *Critique of Pure Reason* (1781) gave the problem of the "transcendental" a central place in philosophical studies.

26. See also Roediger, *The Wages of Whiteness*; Eric Foner, *Free Soil, Free Labor, Free Men: The Ideology of the Republican Party before the Civil War* (New York: Oxford University Press, 1970); John Mayfield, *Rehearsal for Republicanism: Free Soil and the Politics of Anti-Slavery* (Port Washington, N.Y.: Kennikat Press, 1980).

27. Quoted in Hutchinson, *Transcendentalist Ministers*. 30. Cf. Howe, *Unitarian Conscience*.

28. This, of course, opens up to the massive discourses within the entire field of modern social theorizing in which the problem of the subject and the self, remapped as an effect of history and social structure is grappled with in writings that range from Marx to Foucault—but only after the notion of "the social" had become itself something of an empirical object and was operationalized in some form of materialization (modes of production, modes of discourse, etc.).

29. In this regard, the utopian radicals, who disdained the mass populism taking place within Evangelicalism, shared the sense of "immediatism"—the doctrine of immediate transformation of the soul, the possibility of erasing of one's spiritual history (specifically sin), and the possibility of starting anew (being "saved"). This doctrine of immediate repentance and salvation thus had its societal corollaries. One was in the notion of immediate community, pursued by retreat from civil society, as did the Transcendentalist-inspired Associationists and the Quaker-supported Owenites. Another was the notion of immediate and total abolition, which radical social reform promised. Whether retreat from or engagement in political struggle, immediatism had a radical transcending dimension.

The fact that Unitarianism was itself caught up in a process of disestablishment from Protestant orthodoxy gave it some important ideological parallels with the larger mass-based and antiinstitutional orientations taking place within Evangelicalism and the Great Awakenings. Though the middle- and lower-class populist religious sphere associated with Baptist and Methodist sects was certainly not attractive to elite Boston Brahmins, Unitarian elites, and the highly educated. Radical northerners nonetheless had their religious struggles against orthodoxy and, like the Evangelicals, pursued their notions of perfectibility. See Davis, "Emergence of Immediatism." For a perceptive discussion on disestablishment, see Douglas, *Feminization of American Culture*; Hutchinson, *Modernist Impulse*, 12–40; and Howe, *Unitarian Conscience*.

30. But in some cases utopian communitarianism went too far into retreat for some of its important benefactors. The abolitionist Quaker William Allen sup-

ported financially Robert Owen's New Lanark community. Allen, however, threatened to withdraw his support when it became evident that Owen was far too secular and a "determined enemy" of religion. As Davis points out, Owen was "bent on proving that human happiness required emancipation from the belief in the divinity of the Bible." See David Brion Davis, "Quaker Ethic and Antislavery International," in *The Antislavery Debate: Capitalism and Abolitionism as a Problem in Historical Interpretation,* ed. Thomas Bender (Berkeley: University of California Press, 1992), 59. Allen was successful in forcing Owen to introduce the Bible. On the influence of French Utopianism on the New England renaissance, see V. L. Parrington, *The Romantic Revolution in American, 1800–1860* (1927; reprint, Norman: University of Oklahoma Press, 1987), 379.

31. Miller, *Life of the Mind,* ix.

32. Ibid., ix–x.

33. See also Roediger, *Wages of Whiteness.*

34. Upon marriage, women's property was transferred to the husband. When abolitionist and women's rights advocate Lucy Stone married Henry Blackwell, she requested the former Unitarian minister Thomas Wentworth Higginson to perform the ceremony. Higginson's presence was also for the "prearranged propaganda feature"—the couple read aloud a "Protest" that Higginson mailed with his own introductory remarks, to Worcester and Boston newspapers, as well as to Garrison's *Liberator.* The protest read:

> While we acknowledge our mutual affection by publicly assuming the relationship of husband and wife, yet, in justice to ourselves and a great principle, we deem it a duty to declare that this act on our part implies no sanction of, nor promise of voluntary obedience to, such of the present laws of marriage as refuse to recognize the wife as an independent, rational being. . . .
>
> We believe that personal independence and equal human rights can never be forfeited, except for crime; that marriage should be an equal and permanent partnership, and so recognized by law; that until it is so recognized, married partners should provide against the radical injustice of present laws by every means in their power.

See Elinor Rice Hays, *Morning Star: A Biography of Lucy Stone, 1818–1893* (New York: Harcourt, Brace and World, 1961), 128–29.

35. See Henry David Thoreau, "Life without Principle," in *The American Transcendentalists: Their Prose and Poetry,* ed. Perry Miller (Garden City, N.Y.: Doubleday Anchor Books, 1957), 308–29; quotation is on 309. I draw the phrase "machine in the garden" from Leo Marx's study of the coming of industrialization as it was refracted through literature. See Leo Marx, *The Machine in the Garden: Technology and the Pastoral Ideal in America* (Oxford: Oxford University Press, 1964).

36. Emerson quoted in Len Gougeon and Joel Myerson, eds., *Emerson's Antislavery Writings* (New Haven and London: Yale University Press, 1995), 42.

37. See Mayfield, *Rehearsal for Republicanism;* Foner, *Free Soil, Free Labor;* Foner, *Politics and Ideology;* Eric Foner, "Abolitionism and the Labor Movement in Antebellum America," in *Anti-Slavery, Religion, and Reform: Essays in Memory of Roger Anstey,* ed. Christine Bolt and Seymour Drescher (Hamden, Conn.:

Archon Books, 1980), 254–71; Litwack, *North of Slavery*; and Eric J. Sundquist, "Slavery, Revolution, and the American Renaissance," in *The American Renaissance Reconsidered*, ed. by Walter Benn Michaels and Donald E. Pease (Baltimore: Johns Hopkins University Press, 1985), 1–33.

38. There were an estimated two hundred "paying members" of the Twenty-Eighth Congregational Society to which Theodore Parker preached. See Hutchinson, *Transcendentalist Ministers*, 183 n. 113.

39. Garrison, with whom Douglass had joined forces in the early 1840s, believed adamantly that moral suasion alone was adequate to the abolitionist struggle, and that the Constitution was flawed because it was a proslavery document. Having spent a good part of the decade as a spokesperson for the Garrisonian abolitionists, Douglass developed his own critical differences, and by the late 1840s, he was coming to reject both of these views. By 1851 he broke with the Garrisonian agenda. As Douglass saw the situation, rhetoric alone would not secure an interpretation of the Constitution as a document unequivocally in opposition to slavery. His impatience with these abolitonists' insistence that Christian rhetoric would win over the hearts and minds of overseers was registered in caustic wit. In 1853 Douglass listened to clergyman Henry Ward Beecher address a meeting sponsored by the American Anti-Slavery Society and tell those assembled that it would be better to wait seventy-five years for Christian faith to overcome the evils of slavery. Douglass followed Beecher with his own speech, during which he replied: "If the reverend gentleman had worked on plantations where I have been, he would have met overseers who would have whipped him in five minutes out of his willingness to wait for liberty." The comments by Beecher and Douglass are reported in the *Annual Report of the American Anti-Slavery Society for 1853* (New York, 1853), 51–55. This exchange can be found in Benjamin Quarles, "Abolition's Different Drummer: Frederick Douglass," in *The Antislavery Vanguard: New Essays on the Abolitionists*, ed. Martin Duberman (Princeton: Princeton University Press, 1965), 123–34. On Douglass's rejection of Garrison's support for the dissolution of the Union and on his insistence that the Constitution was to be preserved by struggling over its interpretation rather than abandoning it, see his *Life and Times*, 322; Fredrickson, *Inner Civil War*, 17; Leon F. Litwack, "The Emancipation of the Negro Abolitionist," in *The Antislavery Vanguard: New Essays on the Abolitionists*, ed. Martin Duberman (Princeton: Princeton University Press, 1965), 147–50.

40. Hutchinson, *Transcendentalist Ministers*, 183 n. 113; Sanborn's importance in the rise of American social science is treated in Thomas Haskell, *The Emergence of Professional Social Science: The American Social Science Association and the Nineteenth Century Crisis of Authority* (Urbana: University of Illinois Press, 1977).

41. Haskell, *Emergence of Social Science*, 49; Howe, *Unitarian Conscience*, 1970. Both Emerson and Thoreau publicly supported John Brown, who exemplified Transcendentalism's belief that actions must be true to a person's innermost political beliefs. Thoreau stated that Brown was "a transcendentalist, above all, a man of ideas and principles" and that Brown's actions represented "the best news America has ever had." See Fredrickson, *The Inner Civil War*, 40. Thoreau

is quoted from *The Writings of Henry David Thoreau: Journal*, ed. Bradford Torrey (Boston and New York, 1906), xii, 420, 408, 438–39.

42. Parker, "American Scholar," 37.

43. Beyond this complex multiracial, gendered, and multiclassed cartography were Indians, Mexicans, and the Chinese. These groups remained even more marginalized and were not central to the discourses on reformism that emerged in the second half of the nineteenth century. Indeed, Indians were being driven from or quarantined upon "reservations" within civil society. Some were partially incorporated in the attempts to provide schooling, in some cases along with recently emancipated blacks. Hampton Institute, founded in 1868, was designed to provide "industrial training" for both blacks and Indians.

44. The background of class tensions surrounding the emergence of a distinctly elite cultural struggle over American aesthetics and the withdrawal of upper classes from "popular" culture in the latter part of the nineteenth century is treated in Levine, *Highbrow/Lowbrow*.

45. Thomas Wentworth Higginson, *Letters and Journals of Thomas Wentworth Higginson, 1846–1906*, ed. Mary Thatcher Higginson (1921; reprint, New York: Da Capo Press, 1969), 53.

46. Transcendentalists, however, were not a unified group, nor did Transcendentalism reflect a unified philosophy. This feature showed up in their views toward slavery. Individual orientations toward slavery varied among individuals, and this was in keeping with a doctrine that placed emphasis on radical individuality rather than on collective moral or political action. See Gougeon and Myerson, *Emerson's Antislavery Writings*, xi–lvi, 205, n. 40.

47. Cf. Howard N. Meyer, *Colonel of the Black Regiment: The Life of Thomas Wentworth Higginson* (New York: W. W. Norton, 1967), 56–58.

48. See Hays, *Morning Star*, 98–99.

49. Fredrickson, *Inner Civil War*, 37. The crisis in Kansas was rooted in the 1850 Compromise, which granted the settlers of the new Kansas territory, once it was populated sufficiently, to vote on whether their region would allow slavery or not. On Transcendentalist reactions to the Fugitive Slave Act see also Litwack, *North of Slavery*, 248–52; Harold Schwartz, "Fugitive Slave Days in Boston," *New England Quarterly* 27 (March 1954): 191–212; Kern, "Rise of Transcendentalism," 306–7; and James Brewer Steward, *Holy Warriors: The Abolitionists and American Slavery* (New York: Hill and Wang, 1996), 151–80.

50. Higginson, *Army Life*, 149. See also Meyer, *Colonel of the Black Regiment*, 232.

51. Higginson, *Army Life*, 149. Unitarian minister George Spaulding, who published one of the first important articles on black religious singing, used another analogy that promoted the idea that value was to be retrieved out of black music. "The music of the negro shouts," he wrote, "opens a new and rich field of melody–a mine in which there is many rough quartz, but also many veins of sparkling ore." See Spaulding, "Under the Palmetto," 198.

52. Ibid.

53. For an excellent overview of the discovery of popular culture in early modern Europe, see Burke, *Popular Culture*.

54. Higginson, *Army Life*, 41.

55. The quote from Emerson is found in Perry Miller, *The American Transcendentalists* (New York: Doubleday Anchor Books, 1957), 371.

56. Higginson, *Army Life*, 6, 13.

57. Higginson's reasoning reflects ties to a larger set of discourses on modern cultural distinctions that equate various races with states of nature and the relationship between race and civilization. On the complex ties between racialization and civilization see Thomas F. Gosset, *Race: The History of an Idea in America* (Dallas: Southern Methodist University Press, 1963); Winthrop D. Jordan, *White over Black: American Attitudes toward the Negro, 1550–1872* (Chapel Hill: University of North Carolina Press, 1968). Fredrickson, *Black Image,* 1971; Takaki, *Iron Cages,* 1990.

58. Higginson, *Army Life*, 22.

59. Ibid., 10.

60. Ibid., 11.

61. See especially the highly reflective discussions of the philosophies of work compiled in the letters and correspondences of members affiliated with Brook Farm in Henry W. Sams, *Autobiography of Brook Farm* (Englewood Cliffs, N.J.: Prentice-Hall, 1958).

62. Higginson, *Army Life*, 41.

63. Ibid., 29.

64. Ibid., 99.

65. Ibid., 15. In his address to the Harvard Divinity School in 1838, Ralph Waldo Emerson said that he

> look[ed] for the hour when that supreme Beauty which ravished the souls of those Eastern men, and chiefly of those Hebrews, and through their lips spoke oracles to all time, shall speak in the West also. The Hebrew and Greek Scriptures contain immortal sentences, that have been bread of life to millions. But they have no epical integrity; are fragmentary; are not shown in their order to the intellect. I look for the new Teacher that shall follow so far those shining laws that he shall see them come full circle; shall see their rounding complete grace; shall see the world to be the mirror of the soul.

It would appear that the junior Transcendentalist Higginson saw through his romanticist eyes the "new Teacher" that Emerson longed to see—an Orientalized, yet humbly mundane subject in the form of recently emancipated slaves. Emerson's quote can be found in his *Selections,* 115–16.

66. Higginson, *Army Life*, 41. Romanticism is not a sensibility cut out of whole cloth; it has great variation. The Unitarians, according to Howe, preferred "the delicate, escapist, and artificial emotions of Walter Scott and the female sentimentalists," but were "frightened and repelled" by "Faustian, rebellious romanticism" and the "titanic, untamed romantics like Goethe and Byron." See Howe, *Unitarian Conscience,* 200–201.

67. Higginson, *Army Life*, 41. As he sat in his tent Higginson often watched the troops move by: "In all pleasant weather the outer 'fly' is open, and men pass and repass, a chattering throng. I think of Emerson's Saadi, 'As thou sittest at thy

door, on the desert's yellow floor,'—for these bare sand-plains, gray above, are always yellow when upturned, and there seems a tinge of Orientalism in all our life."(16) Higginson's nod toward Orientalism is not surprising. As Edward Said has pointed out, Orientalism was a rather elaborate form of imagery that enabled the modern West to conceptualize itself as distinct. The Transcendentalists had already cultivated a strong interest in particular Eastern religious texts, and both Emerson and Thoreau made use of them to ground their own critiques of market society. As Alexander Kern notes, "The Oriental scriptures had some effect on the Transcendentalist, though this appeared less in the ideas specifically supplied than in the imagery furnished. The impact of the Hindu and Persian writings was not in any case made very early. For Emerson, at least, though he had read scattered bits earlier, it was first outlined in De Gerando's *Histoire Comparee des Systemes de Philosophie* which he began to read in 1830. . . . The emphasis upon Asia in *Representative Men* and works like 'Hamatraya,' 'Brahma,' and 'Illusions' shows the depth and extent of the influence on Emerson." See Kern, "Rise of Transcendentalism," 247–314, quote is on 270–71. Thoreau's translations appear in *Dial*, 3 (1843): 493–94; 4 (1843), 59–62, 205–10, and 402–4. See also Christy, *Orient in American Transcendentalism*. Edward Said's *Orientalism* (New York: Vintage Books, 1979) provides a most valuable study of "Orientalism" as a construction central to the very meaning of modern Western identity.

68. See the last chapter in Du Bois, *Souls*.

69. *Nation* (May 30, 1867): 428.

70. Lucy McKim Garrison played the major professional role due to her extensive musical training. See Dena Epstein, "Lucy McKim Garrison, American Musician," *New York Public Library Bulletin* 67 (October 1963): 529–46.

71. Spaulding, "Under the Palmetto"; Higginson, "Negro Spirituals," 684–94; L. McKim, "Songs of the Port Royal 'Contrabands,'" 254–55; James McKim, "Negro Songs," *Dwight's Journal of Music* 21 (1862): 148–49. Cf. also Charlotte Forten, "Life on the Sea Islands," *Atlantic Monthly* 13 (May 1864): 666–76; and Riis, "Cultivated White Tradition," 156–76.

72. Both Higginson (*Army Life*) and Allen, Ware, and Garrison (*Slave Songs*) in their respective books point out songs they think are local favorites.

73. Allen, Ware, and Garrison, *Slave Songs*, iv.

74. Ibid., iii.

75. Ibid., vi.

76. Ibid., vii–viii.

77. Ibid., viii, emphasis added. In a passage that clearly anticipated some of William Allen's remarks, Charlotte Forten had noted the debate with regard to the religious identity of the "shouts." "We cannot determine," she wrote, "whether it has a religious character or not. Some of the people tell us that it has, others that it has not. But the shouts of the grown people are always in connection with their religious meetings, it is probable that they are the barbarous expression of religion, handed down to them from their African ancestors, and destined to pass away under the influence of Christian teachings." See Forten, "Life on the Sea Islands," 594. For an excellent discussion on the disapproval of "native songs," the approval of unequivocally spiritual songs, and the introduction of songs, see Epstein, *Sinful Tunes*, 274–300.

78. William George Hawkins, *Lunsford Lane; or, Another Helper from North Carolina* (Boston: Crosby and Nichols, 1863), 294. Quoted in Epstein, *Sinful Tunes*, 275.

79. Epstein, *Sinful Tunes*, 275.

80. Richard M. Dorson notes that the term "folklore" was coined in England in 1846. Cf. Dorson, *American Folklore* (Chicago: University of Chicago Press, 1959), 168.

81. Allen, Ware, and Garrison, *Slave Songs*, ii.

82. Grimke, *Journals*, 389–90.

83. Ibid., 397

84. Cf. Courlander, *Negro Folk Music*, 194–200; Southern, *Readings in Black American Music*, 62. Sterling Stuckey offers an extended discussion of the ring shout as a deep structure of Africanist practices retained over the long history of slavery and to which he attributes the origins of black nationalist culture. Cf. *Slave Culture*, passim.

85. Grimke, *Journals*, 402.

86. Higginson, *Army Life*, 13, 18. Higginson's reference to "pow wow" seems somewhat mimetic of an observation made in Frederick Law Olmsted's widely read travel narrative. Describing a religious gathering of slaves Olmsted wrote:

> The negroes kept their place during all of the tumult; there may have been a sympathetic groan or exclamation uttered by one or two of them, but generally they expressed only the interest of curiosity in the proceedings, such as Europeans might at a performance of the dancing dervishes, an Indian pow-wow, or an exhibition of "psychological" or "spiritual" phenomena.

See Olmsted, *A Journal in the Seaboard Slave States*, 2:92.

87. See Epstein, *Sinful Tunes*, 280–87.

88. Ibid., 275.

89. This larger problem is analyzed in Dorothy Ross, *The Origins of American Social Science* (Cambridge: Cambridge University Press, 1991). See also James Weinstein, *The Corporate Ideal in the Liberal State, 1900–1918* (Boston: Beacon Press, 1968).

90. The importance of proselytization and its connection to black song making, particularly with regard to the "spirituals," has spawned contentious arguments about black authorship. Numerous articles in the *Journal of American Folk-Lore* that were written after the turn of the century took the position that black song making was simply cultural mimicry. Cf. for example E. C. Perrow, "Songs and Rhymes from the South," *Journal of American Folk-Lore* 26 (1913): 145–46. Folklorist Newman White is the most notable for furthering such interpretations of what has been called the "white-to-black" thesis, which fostered the assumption that black spirituals were simply gleaned from white "primitive religion." Presumably, as whites began to shed some of these earlier practices, slaves maintained and continued to cultivate them. According to White, the "Negro's religious primitivism" is "last year's clothes," and "simply a continuation and development of the white spiritual." See White, *American Negro Folk-Songs*, 50. The white-to-black cultural paradigm is continued in Guy B. Johnson, *Folk Cul-*

ture on St. Helena Island (Chapel Hill: University of North Carolina Press, 1930); and George Pullen Jackson, *White and Negro Spirituals: Their Life Span and Kinship* (New York: J. J. Augustin, 1944).

Extensive historical research carried out over the last fifty years has shown this thesis to be wrong, and has demonstrated the rich realm of cultural production that had Africanist roots and that could not be reduced to simply being "taught"—regardless of how pulverizing slavery was from a cultural standpoint. W. E. B. Du Bois and Carter Woodson first raised the arguments that black song making had Africanist roots as well as reflecting cultural influences stemming from enslavement. Melville Herskovits and Mark Miles Fisher opened up the problem of Africanist "survivals" more systematically. Cf. Herskovits, *Myth of the Negro Past*; and Fisher, *Negro Slave Songs*. More recent studies have expanded our understanding of the relative autonomy of black culture. Cf. Genovese, *Roll, Jordan, Roll*; Levine, *Black Culture and Black Consciousness*; Raboteau, *Slave Religion*; Epstein, *Sinful Tunes*; and Stuckey, *Slave Culture*. The ethnomusicological debate between the white-to-black school and the survivalist school in early folklore and cultural sociology is discussed in George L. Starks, Jr., "Salt and Pepper in Your Shoe: Afro-American Song Tradition on the South Carolina Sea Islands," in *More Than Dancing: Essays on Afro-American Music and Musicians*, ed. Irene V. Jackson (Westport, Conn.: Greenwood Press, 1985), 59–80.

91. Arnold's quote is found in R. Williams, *Culture and Society*, 115. Emphasis added.

92. See Kern, "The Rise of Transcendentalism," 249–50.

CHAPTER SIX
INSTITUTIONALIZING ETHNOSYMPATHY

1. Epstein, *Sinful Tunes*, 336–41.

2. For a discussion of northern racial attitudes during the abolitionist era, see Foner, *Free Soil, Free Labor*; and Foner, *Politics and Ideology*.

3. See William Graham Sumner, *Folkways: A Study of the Sociological Importance of Usages, Manners, Customs, Mores, and Morals* (Boston: Ginn and Company, 1906).

4. On the rise of professional social science, see L. L. Bernard and Jessie Bernard, *Origins of American Sociology: The Social Science Movement in the United States* (New York: Russell and Russell, 1965); Haskell, *Emergence of Professional Social Science*; Ross, *Origins of American Social Science*.

5. One might argue that earlier discoverers like William Lloyd Garrison, Thomas Wentworth Higginson, and William Frances Allen provided an institutional base: Unitarianism. But this would be to conflate institutional affiliations with formal institutionalization. As noted, these figures were former ministers and cultural renegades; they were not mainstream even to Unitarianism, and their work was certainly not fronted by any formal institution. Nor was abolitionism an institutional phenomenon; on the contrary, and particularly at its more radical edges, it was one of numerous cultural symptoms of a much wider antiinstitution-

alism. Drawing upon Stanley Elkins, George Fredrickson has pointed out that "anti-institutionalism was more than a vague and utopian way of thinking. It was also an adaptation to what was actually happening in America. Traditional forms of social control were in fact breaking down, not so much from the trumpet blasts of reformers as from the natural conditions of a capitalistic society in the state of rapid economic and geographical expansion." Garrison's burning of the Constitution expressed the most extreme forms of antiinstitutionalism. Cf. Fredrickson, *Inner Civil War,* 9, 17.

One also might argue that the institutionalization of the spirituals was already lodged first and foremost in the formation of black churches. To this argument I would strongly agree. However, my focus from the outset has not been upon the *internal* meanings and histories of black cultural expressivity but rather upon the emergence of the larger societal modes of appropriation that culminate in modern institutionalized and somewhat canonized forms of interpretation, particularly those that precede yet become traversed by the rise of modern ethnoscience.

6. Cf. Gustavus D. Pike, *The Jubilee Singers and Their Campaign for Twenty Thousand Dollars* (Boston: Lee and Shepherd Publishers, 1872). An 1875 edition, *The Singing Campaign for Ten Thousand Pounds,* reported on the actual experiences of the singers during their English tour. As John Lovell notes, by the 1880s the Reverend J. B. T. Marsh was writing about the Jubilee singers, and his book had sold over 180,000 copies. Cf. Lovell, *Black Song,* 407. For a contemporary example of missionary interest in the spirituals see George H. Griffin, "The Slave Music of the South," *American Missionary Magazine* 36 (1882): 70–72.

7. See Locke, *Negro and His Music,* 19.

8. Thomas P. Fenner, *Religious Folk Songs of the Negro* (1874; reprint, New York: AMS Press, 1973), iii–iv. Cf. also *Hampton and its Students By Two of Its Teachers, Mrs. M. F. Armstrong and Helen W. Ludlow. With Fifty Cabin and Plantation Songs*; arr. Thomas P. Fenner (New York: G. P. Putnam's Sons, 1874). Fenner, then director of the music department at Hampton, noted that the lyrics were "common property throughout the South." (iv). See ed., R. Nathaniel Dett, *Religious Folk-Songs of the Negro as Sung at Hampton Institute* (Hampton, Va.: Hampton Institute Press, 1927), which is another revision of the earlier Hampton-based collection.

9. Rathbun, "Negro Music of the South," 174.

10. The reluctance of recently freed slaves to sing older songs was noted earlier. A similar dynamic took place with black students. In 1909 Howard University students rebelled against being asked to sing spirituals. The incident was reported in the student *Howard University Journal,* and was followed up as a front-page story in the *Washington Post,* and later treated in the *New York Sun.* See Lovell, *Black Song,* 416.

11. Alice Mabel Bacon, "Work and Methods of the Hampton Folk-Lore Society," *Journal of American Folk-Lore* 11, no. 40 (1897): 17–21, quote is from p. 18.

12. Ibid., 19.

13. Ibid., 19–20, emphasis added.

14. Ibid., 21.

15. Ibid.

16. Rathbun's quote of Armstrong is found in "The Negro Music of the South," *Southern Workman*, 22 (November 1893): 174.

17. Armstrong is quoted in W. N. Hartshorn, ed., *An Era of Progress and Promise, 1863–1910* (Boston: Priscilla Publishing Co., 1910), 314.

18. Du Bois, *Souls*, 137, 139.

19. *Southern Workman* also was devoted to "the current literature of the Negro and Indian races." Hampton also enrolled Native Americans.

20. Cf. James D. Anderson, *The Education of Blacks in the South, 1860–1935* (Chapel Hill: University of North Carolina Press, 1988), 33–78.

21. Ibid., 36. Such a desired strategy would help produce the entrenched relations of "caste" that reached well into the twentieth century and were so acutely observed by Charles S. Johnson, W. E. B. Du Bois, Arthur Raper, and John Dollard. See Charles S. Johnson, *Shadow of the Plantation* (Chicago: University of Chicago Press, 1934); Du Bois, *Black Reconstruction*; Arthur Raper, *Preface to Peasantry: A Tale of Two Black Belt Counties* (1936; reprint, New York: Atheneum, 1974); and John Dollard, *Caste and Class in a Southern Town* (London: Oxford University Press, 1937).

22. Anderson, *Education of Blacks*, chap. 2.

23. "Folk-Lore Study and Folk-Lore Societies," *Journal of American Folk-Lore* 8, no. 30 (July–September 1895): 237.

24. Ibid., 233.

25. Otis T. Mason, "The Natural History of Folklore," *Journal of American Folk-Lore* 4 (1891): 97–105, quote from p. 103.

26. *Journal of American Folk-Lore* 1, no. 1 (April–June 1888): 6.

27. Here I am taking liberties with Louis Althusser's well-known definition of ideology as "an imaginary relationship of individuals to their real conditions of existence." See his essay, "Ideology and Ideological State Apparatuses," 36. In this case the intellectuals salvaged symbols for symbolic consumption, and left the people to whom these symbols had long been attributed stranded on the other side of the color chasm. It would be a few years before W. E. B. Du Bois, in *The Souls of Black Folk*, would try to make sense of this process and address fellow "gentle readers" to remember the not so distant times when sympathy connected people in ways that envisioned a larger, promising society.

28. As Alan Trachtenberg notes, "Republicans were willing, in 1877, to barter Reconstruction and the federal occupation of the South, with its military protection of blacks, in exchange for the Presidency. Through the Compromise of 1877, the House of Representatives settled the disputed electoral count between Republican Rutherford Hayes and Democrat Samuel Tilden by declaring Hayes the victor by a single vote." See Alan Trachtenberg, *The Incorporation of America: Culture and Society in the Gilded Age* (New York: Hill and Wang, 1982), 76. For a full treatment of the political juncture involving the Reconstruction-busting alliance between southern Democrats and northern Republicans see C. Vann Woodward, *Reunion and Reaction: The Compromise of 1877 and the End of Reconstruction* (Boston: Little, Brown, 1951).

29. See Torgovnick, *Gone Primitive*.

30. See the introductory statement of intent in the first issue of the *Journal of American Folk-Lore* 1, no. 1 (April–June 1888).

31. Cf. John Henry Raleigh, *Matthew Arnold and America* (Berkeley: University of California Press, 1961); DiMaggio, "Cultural Entrepreneurship," 33–50 and 303–22; and Levine, *Highbrow/Lowbrow*.

32. Walker is quoted in Ross, *Origins of American Social Science,* 59. See also pp. 53–97 for an important assessment of the shift from an earlier romanticism to a nationalist-inflected sense of realism.

33. Fredrickson, *Inner Civil War*, 33. Parkman and others, Fredrickson argues, "devoted at least part of their energies to lashing out against the unwashed democracy that was stripping the old families of their political and social influence"(31). Charles Norton's belief that "that the cultivated class must seize control of society and give it practical direction"(32) found its modern academic expression in the professionalization of the social sciences. Cf. Haskell, *Emergence of Professional Social Science*; and Ross, *Origins of American Social Science*. It is against the larger backdrop of professionalism that the corollary interest in the problem of an American "highbrow" culture took form in a publication like *Dwight's Journal of Music*. For an elaboration of this cultural juncture, see Levine's *Highbrow/Lowbrow*.

34. Lee J. Vance, "The Study of Folk-Lore," *Forum* 22 (1896–97): 249–56, quote from p. 249.

35. Ibid., 249.

36. Both James Clifford and Virginia Dominguez are quoted in Hal Foster, ed., *Discussions in Contemporary Culture* (Seattle: Bay Press, 1987), on 121 and 133.

37. Rathbun, "Negro Music of the South," 174.

38. Cf. "Negro Folk Songs," 30–32.

39. For an exceptionally lucid study of the social and cultural symptoms that manifest the process of rendering the social invisible, see Avery F. Gordon, *Ghostly Matters: Haunting and the Sociological Imagination* (Minneapolis: University of Minnesota Press, 1997).

40. "Negro Folk Songs," 31.

41. Ibid.

42. The distinctions being made between spirituals, corn songs, dance songs, and other genres appear matter-of-fact in the new penchant for taxonomy. These categories, however, appear more reified to social scientific outsiders. As Lawrence Levine points out, slave song making did not operate with a fixed or rigid distinction between sacred and secular. In a comment on the meaning of the blues, pianist Eubie Blake captured well the distinction between a musical genre and music's sociocultural and material embeddedness in everyday life. When asked about his thoughts regarding the blues in Baltimore, Blake replied: "Blues in Baltimore? Why, Baltimore is the blues!" See Levine, "Slave Songs and Slave Consciousness," 114, 99–130. Blake is quoted in Southern, *Music of Black Americans*," 332–33.

43. "Negro Folk Songs," 32.

44. Edward Burnett Tylor, *Primitive Culture*, vol. 2 (Boston: Estes and Lauriat, 1874), 453, emphasis added. Cf. also Morton White, *Social Thought in America: The Revolt against Formalism* (Boston: Beacon Press, 1957), 18.

45. William Wells Newell, "Individual and Collective Characteristics in Folk-

Lore," *Journal of American Folk-Lore*, 19, no. 4 (January–March 1906): 1–15, quote from p. 4.

46. Du Bois, *Black Reconstruction*, 667, emphasis added.

47. The analogue of black music as a "river" is eloquently described by Thomas L. Webber, *Deep Like the Rivers: Education in the Slave Quarter Community, 1831–1865* (New York: Norton, 1978). The term "hidden transcripts" is James Scott's. See his *Domination and the Arts of Resistance*.

It was not until Melville Herskovits's book, *The Myth of the Negro Past*, which appeared in 1941, that the modern counterformulation, which retrieved and argued for the fundamental importance of Africanist cultural practices, was carried out somewhat systematically in the social sciences. Herskovits's use of *survivals* actually represented the important reappropriation of the term within a modern social scientific framework. Survivals, as redefined, were exonerated and restored as features of a group's capacity to maintain cultural integrity, identity, and solidarity. The notion of survivals, when traced from Tylor's framework to Herskovits's, represents a modern *culturalist transvaluation* of the term's meaning. Important works on this subject include Small, *Music of the Common Tongue*; and Stuckey, *Slave Culture*.

CHAPTER SEVEN
CONCLUSION

1. Arnold Hauser, quoted in Jurgen Habermas, *The Structural Transformation of the Public Sphere*, trans. Thomas Burger (1962; reprint, Cambridge: MIT Press, 1989), 174.

2. Free blacks could now gather as free laborers, but outside the walls of white organized labor. As Philip Foner has shown, the terrain of organized labor serves as a crucial indicator of the fundamental historical relations between black and white workers, as the former are systematically excluded. The complex politics of exclusion was a cultural cornerstone in the larger "success" of Republican virtue. On black and white labor relations after the failure of Reconstruction, Philip S. Foner, *Organized Labor and the Black Worker, 1619–1981* (New York: International Publishers, 1981), 17–102.

3. Ross, *Origins of American Social Science*.

4. Chestnut, *Diary from Dixie*, 199.

5. Pierre Bourdieu, *Distinction: A Social Critique of the Judgment of Taste* (Cambridge: Harvard University Press, 1984), 249. Emphasis added.

6. An adequate treatment of the cultural logic of minstrelsy, which exceeds the scope of this study, would greatly complement this juncture in my argument. But there are many valuable studies that examine the massive popular ideology around imagining blacks in the antebellum and postbellum era. See chap. 1 n. 11.

7. Georg Lukacs, *The Theory of the Novel*, trans. Anna Bostock (1920; reprint, Cambridge: MIT Press, 1971), 116–17.

8. "Negro Music at Birth," *Musical Quarterly*, 15, no. 1 (January 1919): 88–89.

9. See Dorothy Scarborough, *On the Trail of Negro Folk-Songs* (Cambridge: Harvard University Press, 1925), 282.

10. "Negro Music at Birth," 88–89.

11. See Franklin and Moss, *From Slavery to Freedom*, 307–18.

12. Du Bois's quote is found in the *Crisis*, 18 (May 1919): 13–14.

13. Barthes, *Image, Music, Text*, 145–46.

14. Du Bois, *Souls*, 52.

15. Let us not lose sight of the fact that old, deeply racialized modes of hearing the music of African Americans as noise remains very much a part of modern culture. Animosity toward the cultural expressions of groups is alive and well. One need only, for example, trace the debates that have invariably surrounded the entire history of black music making—from blues to ragtime, jazz, rhythm and blues, soul, rap, and hip-hop—to find the thread of racist continuity. As discussed in chapter 2, noise is sound out of place; when applied to the sociology of music, it reflects the perceptions of some people who believe that other people are either out of place or in need of having their places routinely redefined.

16. The idea of modernity producing an expansion of both subjective and objective culture would be championed by the German sociologist Georg Simmel. But of course, a small number of moral, political, cultural, spiritual, and intellectual entrepreneurs preceded Simmelian sociology. The gap that is much more perplexing is the fact that one can read a vast number of books on social theory and the transformation to modernity and come away quite empty-handed with regard to any substantive discussion on the abolitionist movement. For brief but valuable excerpts of Simmel's ideas, see his *On Individuality and Social Forms*, ed. Donald N. Levine (Chicago: University of Chicago Press, 1971). On "subjective culture," see 227–34; on "objective culture" see the essay "The Metropolis and Mental Life," 324–39.

17. Du Bois, *Souls*, 268–69.

18. Cf. Foucault, *Discipline and Punish"; The History of Sexuality*.

19. Williams, *Culture and Society, 1780–1950* (New York: Columbia University Press, 1958). This "problem" has become the alpha and omega of much of contemporary cultural theory, especially in the areas of the latter that have been deeply influenced by poststructuralism.

EPILOGUE

1. Levine, *Black Culture and Black Consciousness*, ix–xi.

2. Levine's intervention was not meant as a recipe for all cultural analysis. See his provocative study of elites and the construction of an American "high" culture in *Highbrow/Lowbrow*.

3. See George Lipsitz, *Rainbow over Midnight: Labor and Culture in the 1940s* (Urbana: University of Illinois Press, 1994), 305; Hazel V. Carby, "The Multicultural Wars" in *Black Popular Culture*, ed. Gina Dent (Seattle: Bay Press, 1992), 197.

4. I have in mind here E. P. Thompson, Richard Hoggart, and Raymond Williams. See Edward P. Thompson, *The Making of the English Working Class* (New York: Vintage Books, 1963); Richard Hoggart, *The Uses of Literacy* (New York: Oxford University Press, 1970); and R. Williams, *Marxism and Literature* (Oxford: Oxford University Press, 1977). These three are often credited with creating

the more contemporary intellectual juncture for British cultural studies. Their contributions were crucial in reestablishing a more historically grounded and subject-sympathetic orientation to social studies that contrasted with the desubjectivized models championed by the legacies of economistic Marxism, midcentury functionalism, and a relatively subjectless structuralism. There were also parallel developments. In France, Jean-Paul Sartre's reworking of Marxian phenomenology helped shape what came to be the French contributions to so-called everyday life. Henri Lefebvre's *Everyday Life in the Modern World* (New York: Harper and Row, 1971) encapsulated many of the intellectual currents in French Marxism's retrieval of phenomenology. Cf. also Mark Poster, *Existential Marxism in Postwar France: From Sartre to Althusser* (Princeton: Princeton University Press, 1975). In Germany, Jurgen Habermas's work on the rise and fall of the classical bourgeois public sphere—in addition to being an attempt to provide a needed historicization of the Frankfurt School's explanation of where modernity took the wrong turn—also tried to show how a critical agency was (at one time) operative. Cf. his *Structural Transformation*. In their combination these British, French, German, and American intellectual developments were crucial in retrieving the critical orientation toward social subjects.

5. In the American context the intellectual spirit of revisionism was and remains much more complicated. The sociocultural retrieval of subjects long ignored by historiography had its important intellectual and analytical corollary in the critique of corporate liberalism. Within sociology the debt here is to C. Wright Mills, who interrogated like few others the cozy fit between liberalism and cold-war technicism. Cf. C. Wright Mills, *The New Men of Power: America's Labor Leaders* (New York: Harcourt, Brace, 1948); *White Collar: The American Middle Classes* (New York: Oxford University Press, 1951); *The Power Elite* (New York: Oxford University Press, 1956); *The Causes of World War Three* (New York: Simon and Schuster, 1958); *Listen, Yankee: The Revolution in Cuba* (New York: Ballantine Books, 1960); and *Power, Politics and People: The Collected Essays of C. Wright Mills*, ed. Irving L. Horowitz, (New York: Oxford University Press, 1963). Mills's studies stand in sharp contrast to the majority of sociological writings that were caught in the seductive grip of 1950s and early 1960s structural functionalism. His studies also helped install a critical sensibility among younger intellectuals who, in turn, fueled the new social criticism and retrievalist agendas that emerged in the 1970s. Similarly, historians John Higham, Robert Weibe, James Weinstein, William Appleman Williams, Gabriel Kolko, and Herbert Gutman did much to problematize historiography during as well as after the cold war context of intellectual conformity. Cf. John Higham, *Strangers in the Land: Patterns of American Nativism, 1860–1925* (New Brunswick, N.J.: Rutgers University Press, 1955); *From Boundlessness to Consolidation: The Transformation of American Culture, 1848–1860* (Ann Arbor, Mich.: William L. Clements Library, 1969); "The Re-orientation of American Culture in the 1890s," in *Writing American History: Essays on Modern Scholarship* (Bloomington: Indiana University Press, 1970); Robert H. Weibe *The Search for Order, 1877–1920* (New York: Hill and Wang, 1967); Weinstein, *Corporate Ideal*; W. Williams, *Contours of American History*; Gabriel Kolko, *Main Currents in Modern American History* (New York: Harper and Row, 1976); and Herbert Gutman, *Work, Culture, and*

Society in Industrializing America: Essays in American Working-Class and Social History (New York: Vintage Books, 1977). The sociology of C. Wright Mills, consciously alienated as it was from the complicity of accommodation and silence, and the new historical revisionists did much to create the sense of intellectual crisis that was simultaneously being underwritten by the Civil Rights movement. This conjuncture (much like the abolitionist conjuncture) laid the ground for the post-1960s cultural (re)turn within American scholarship.

BIBLIOGRAPHY

Adorno, Theodore, and Max Horkheimer. *Dialectic of Enlightenment*. Translated by John Cumming. 1944. Reprint, New York: Seabury Press, 1972.

Agricola [pseud.]. "Management of Negroes." *De Bow's Review* 19 (September 1855): 361.

Alexander, Jeffrey C., and Steven Seidman, eds. *Culture and Society: Contemporary Debates*. Cambridge: Cambridge University Press, 1990.

Allen, Robert. *Reluctant Reformers: Racism and Social Reform Movements in the United States*. Garden City, N.Y.: Doubleday, Anchor Press, 1975.

Allen, William Francis, Charles Pickard Ware, and Lucy McKim Garrison. *Slave Songs of the United States*. New York: A. Simpson and Co., 1867.

Almaguer, Thomas. *Racial Fault Lines: The Historical Origins of White Supremacy in California*. Berkeley: University of California Press, 1994.

Althusser, Louis. "Ideology and Ideological State Apparatuses." In *"Lenin and Philosophy" and Other Essays*, translated by Ben Brewster, 127–86. New York: Monthly Review Press, 1971.

American Missionary 6 (February 1862).

Anderson, James D. *The Education of Blacks in the South, 1860–1935*. Chapel Hill: University of North Carolina Press, 1988.

Anderson, Jervis. *This Was Harlem: A Cultural Portrait, 1900–1950*. New York: Farrar Strauss and Giroux, 1981.

Andrews, William L. "The Representation of Slavery and the Rise of Afro-American Literary Realism, 1865–1920." In *Slavery and the Literary Imagination*, edited by Deborah E. McDowell and Arnold Rampersad, 62–80. Baltimore: Johns Hopkins University Press, 1989.

———. *To Tell a Free Story: The First Century of Afro-American Autobiography, 1760–1865*. Urbana and Chicago: University of Illinois Press, 1986.

Annual Report of the American Anti-Slavery Society for 1853. New York: Anti-Slavery Society, 1853.

Aptheker, Herbert. *American Negro Slave Revolts*. New York: Columbia University Press, 1943.

Arato, Andrew, and Eike Gebhardt, eds. *The Essential Frankfurt School Reader*. New York: Urizen Books, 1978.

Attali, Jacques. *Noise: The Political Economy of Music*. Translated by Brian Massumi. Minneapolis: University of Minnesota Press, 1985.

Bacon, Alice Mabel. "Work and Methods of the Hampton Folk-Lore Society." *Journal of American Folk-Lore* 11, no. 40 (1897): 17–21.

Baker, Houston A., Jr. *Afro-American Poetics: Revisions of Harlem and the Black Aesthetic*. Madison: University of Wisconsin Press, 1988.

———. *Modernism and the Harlem Renaissance*. Chicago: University of Chicago Press, 1987.

Ball, Charles. *Slavery in the United States: A Narrative of the Life and Adventures of Charles Ball, a Black Man, Who Lived forty Years in Maryland, South Carolina, and Georgia, as a Slave*. New York: J. S. Taylor, 1837.

Barrett, William. *Irrational Man: A Study in Existential Philosophy*. New York: Doubleday Anchor Books, 1962.

Barthes, Roland. *Image, Music, Text*. Translated by Stephen Heath. New York: Hill and Wang, 1977.

Bauer, Raymond, and Alice Bauer. "Day to Day Resistance." *Journal of Negro History* 27 (October 1942): 388–419.

Bender, Thomas, ed. *The Antislavery Debate: Capitalism and Abolitionism as a Problem in Historical Interpretation*. Berkeley: University of California Press, 1992.

Bernard, L. L., and Jessie Bernard. *Origins of American Sociology: The Social Science Movement in the United States*. New York: Russell and Russell, 1965.

Bodo, John R. *The Protestant Clergy and Public Issues, 1812–1848*. Princeton: Princeton University Press, 1954.

Bontemps, Arna, ed. *The Harlem Renaissance Remembered*. New York: Dodd, Mead and Co., 1972.

Boskin, Joseph. *Sambo: The Rise and Demise of an American Jester*. New York: Oxford University Press, 1986.

Botkin, Benjamin A. *Lay My Burden Down: A Folk History of Slavery*. Chicago: University of Chicago Press, 1945.

Bourdieu, Pierre. *Distinction: A Social Critique of the Judgement of Taste*. Cambridge: Harvard University Press, 1984.

———. *The Logic of Practice*. Translated by Richard Nice. Stanford, Calif.: Stanford University Press, 1990.

———. *Outline of a Theory of Practice*. London: Cambridge University Press, 1977.

Bourdieu, Pierre, and Jean-Claude Passeron. *Reproduction in Education, Society, and Culture*. Translated by Richard Nice. London: Sage Publications, 1977.

Bradford, Sally. *Harriet, Moses of Her People*. New York: George Lockwood, 1886.

Braudel, Fernand. *The Mediterranean and the Mediterranean World in the Age of Philip II*. vol. 2. Reprint, New York: Harper and Row, 1973.

Bremer, Fredrika. *Homes of the New World; Impressions of America*. Translated by Mary Howitt. New York: Harper and Brothers, 1853.

Brown, William Wells. *The Anti-Slavery Harp: A Collection of Songs for Anti-Slavery Meetings*. Boston: B. March, 1849.

Bruce, Dickson D., Jr. *And They All Sang Hallelujah: Plain-Folk Camp-Meeting Religion, 1800–1845*. Knoxville: University of Tennessee Press, 1974.

Buell, Lawrence. "The Unitarian Movement and the Art of Preaching in the Nineteenth Century." *American Quarterly* 24 (May 1972): 166–90.

Burger, Thomas. *Max Weber's Theory of Concept Formation: History, Laws, and Ideal Types*. Durham, N.C.: Duke University Press, 1976.

Burke, Peter. *Popular Culture in Early Modern Europe*. New York: Harper Torchbooks, 1978.

Calhoun, Daniel. *Professional Lives in America: Structure and Aspiration, 1750–1850*. Cambridge: Harvard University Press, 1965.

Carby, Hazel V. "The Multicultural Wars." In *Black Popular Culture*, edited by Gina Dent, 187–99. Seattle: Bay Press, 1992.

————. *Reconstructing Motherhood: The Emergence of the Afro-American Woman Novelist*. New York: Oxford University Press, 1987.

Channing, William Ellery. *The Complete Works of William Ellery Channing, D.D.* London: Christian Life Publishing Co., 1884.

Chapple, Steve, and Reebee Garofalo. *Rock 'n' Roll Is Here to Pay: The History and Politics of the Music Industry*. Chicago: Nelson-Hall, 1977.

Chartier, Roger. *Cultural History: Between Practices and Representations*. Translated by Lydia G. Cochrane. Ithaca: Cornell University Press, 1988.

————. *The Cultural Uses of Print in Early Modern France*. Princeton: Princeton University Press, 1987.

————. "Texts, Printing, Readings," in *The New Cultural History*, edited by Lynn Hunt, 154–75. Berkeley: University of California Press, 1989.

Chestnut, Mary Boykin. *A Diary From Dixie*. Edited by Ben Ames Williams. Boston: Houghton Mifflin, 1949.

Child, Lydia Maria. "Charlty Bowery." In *The Liberty Bell. By Friends of Freedom*, edited by Maria W. Chapman, 26–43. Boston: American Anti-Slavery Society, 1839.

Christy, Arthur. *The Orient in American Transcendentalism: A Study of Emerson, Thoreau, and Alcott*. Reprint, New York: Octagon Books, Inc. 1963.

Clark, Harry Hayden, ed. *Transitions in American Literary History*. Durham, N.C.: Duke University Press, 1953.

Clifford, James. *The Predicament of Culture: Twentieth-Century Ethnography, Literature, and Art*. Cambridge: Harvard University Press, 1988.

Clifford, James, and George E. Marcus, eds. *Writing Culture: The Poetics and Politics of Ethnography*. Berkeley: University of California Press, 1986.

Courlander, Harold. *Negro Folk Music, U.S.A.*. New York: Columbia University Press, 1963.

Cruse, Harold. *The Crisis of the Negro Intellectual*. New York: Morrow, 1967.

Cruz, Jon D. "Subject Crises and Subject Work: Repositioning Du Bois." In *From Sociology to Cultural Studies: New Perspectives*, edited by Elizabeth Long, 92–122. Oxford: Blackwell Publishers, 1997.

————. "Testimonies and Artifacts: Elite Appropriations of African American Music in the Nineteenth Century." In *Viewing, Reading, Listening: Audiences and Cultural Reception*, edited by Jon D. Cruz and Justin Lewis, 125–50. Boulder, Colo.: Westview Press, 1994.

Davis, David Brion. "The Emergence of Immediatism in British and American Antislavery Thought," *Mississippi Valley Historical Review* 49, no. 2 (September 1962): 209–30.

————. "Quaker Ethic and Antislavery International." In *The Antislavery Debate: Capitalism and Abolitionism as a Problem in Historical Interpretation*, edited by Thomas Bender, 27–64. Berkeley: University of California Press, 1992.

Denning, Michael. *Mechanical Accents: Dime Novels and Working-Class Culture in America*. London: Verso, 1987.

Dennison, Sam. *Scandalize My Name: Black Imagery in American Popular Music*. New York: Garland Publishing, 1982.

Dett, R. Nathaniel, ed. *Religious Folk-Songs of the Negro as Sung at Hampton Institute*. Hampton, Va.: Hampton Institute Press, 1927.

DiMaggio, Paul. "Cultural Entrepreneurship in Nineteenth-Century Boston: The Creation of an Organizational Base for High Culture in America" and "Cultural Entrepreneurship in Nineteenth-Century Boston, Part II: The Classification and Framing of American Art." *Media, Culture, and Society* 4 (1982): 33–50, 303–22.

Dollard, John. *Caste and Class in a Southern Town*. London: Oxford University Press, 1937.

Dorson, Richard. *American Folklore*. Chicago: University of Chicago Press, 1959.

Douglas, Ann. *The Feminization of American Culture*. New York: Avon Books, 1977.

Douglass, Frederick. *My Bondage and My Freedom*. New York: Miller, Orton and Mulligan, 1855.

———. *The Life and Times of Frederick Douglass*. Hartford, Conn.: Park Publishing, 1884.

———. *Narrative of the Life of Frederick Douglass, an American Slave, Written by Himself*. 1845. Reprint, New York: Penguin Books, 1982.

Dreyfus, Herbert L., and Paul Rabinow. *Michel Foucault: Beyond Structuralism and Hermeneutics*. Chicago: University of Chicago, 1982.

Drinnon, Richard. *Facing West: The Metaphysics of Indian-Hating and Empire-Building*. New York: New American Library, Meridian, 1980.

Du Bois, W. E. B. *Black Reconstruction in America, 1860–1880*. 1935. Reprint, New York: Simon and Schuster, Touchstone Edition, 1995.

———. *The Negro Church*. Atlanta, Ga.: Atlanta Press, 1903.

———. *The Souls of Black Folk*. 1903. Reprint, New York: NAL Penguin, 1969.

Duberman, Martin, ed. *The Antislavery Vanguard: New Essays on the Abolitionists*. Princeton: Princeton University Press, 1965.

Dupee, F. W. *Henry James: His Life and Writings*. New York: Doubleday and Co., 1956.

Durkheim, Emile. *The Division of Labor in Society*. Translated by George Simpson. New York: Free Press, 1933.

———. *The Elementary Forms of the Religious Life*. Translated by Joseph Ward Swain. London: Allen and Unwin, 1915.

Easton, D. Lloyd. *Hegel's First American Followers*. Athens: Ohio University Press, 1966.

"Eighteenth-Century Slaves as Advertised by Their Masters." *Journal of Negro History* 1 (April 1916): 163–216.

Elias, Norbert. *The Civilizing Process*. Translated by Edmund Jephcoot. 1939. Reprint, New York: Urizen Books, 1978.

———. *The Court Society*. Translated by Edmund Jephcoot. New York: Pantheon Books, 1983.

Emerson, Ralph Waldo. *Selections from Ralph Waldo Emerson*. Edited by Stephen E. Whicher. Boston: Houghton Mifflin Co., 1960.

Engels, Friedrich. *Socialism, Utopian and Scientific*. New York: International Publishers, 1935.

Epstein, Dena. "Lucy McKim Garrison, American Musician." *New York Public Library Bulletin* 67 (October 1963): 529–46.

———. *Sinful Tunes and Spirituals: Black Folk Music to the Civil War*. Urbana: University of Illinois Press, 1977.

Erenberg, Lewis A. *Steppin' Out: New York Nightlife and the Transformation of American Culture, 1890–1930*. Chicago: University of Chicago Press, 1981.

Fairchild, Hoxie Neale. *The Noble Savage: A Study in Romantic Naturalism*. New York: Columbia University Press, 1928.

Faulkner, A. S. "Does Jazz Put the Sin in Syncopation?" *Ladies' Home Journal* 38 (August 1921): 16.

Fenner, Thomas P. *Religious Folk Songs of the Negro*. 1874. Reprint, New York: AMS Press, 1973.

Fisher, Miles Mark. *Negro Slave Songs in the United States*. New York: Russell and Russell, 1953.

"Folk-Lore Study and Folk-Lore Societies." *Journal of American Folk-Lore* 8, no. 30 (July–September 1895): 231–42.

Foner, Eric. "Abolitionism and the Labor Movement in Antebellum America." In *Anti-Slavery, Religion, and Reform: Essays in Memory of Roger Anstey*, edited by Christine Bolt and Seymour Drescher, 254–71. Hamden, Conn.: Archon Books, 1980.

———. *Free Soil, Free Labor, Free Men: The Ideology of the Republican Party before the Civil War*. New York: Oxford University Press, 1970.

———. *Politics and Ideology in the Age of the Civil War*. New York: Oxford University Press, 1980.

Foner, Philip S. *Organized Labor and the Black Worker, 1619–1981*. New York: International Publishers, 1981.

Forgacs, David, ed. *An Antonio Gramsci Reader: Selected Writings, 1916–1935*. New York: Schocken Books, 1988.

Forten, Charlotte. "Life on the Sea Islands," *Atlantic Monthly* 13 (May 1864): 666–76.

Foster, Frances Smith. *Witnessing Slavery: The Development of Ante-Bellum Slave Narratives*. Westport, Conn.: Greenwood Press, 1979.

Foster, Hal, ed. *Discussions in Contemporary Culture*. Seattle: Bay Press, 1987.

Foucault, Michel. *The Archaeology of Knowledge*. New York: Harper and Row, 1972.

———. *Discipline and Punish: The Birth of the Prison*. New York: Vintage Books, 1979.

———*The History of Sexuality*. Vol. 1, *An Introduction*. New York: Vintage Books, 1980.

———. *The Order of Things: An Archaeology of the Human Sciences*. New York: Vintage Books, 1973.

———. "The Subject and Power." In *Michel Foucault: Beyond Structuralism and Hermeneutics* edited by Herbert L. Dreyfus and Paul Rabinow, 208–26. Chicago: University of Chicago, 1982.

Franklin, John Hope, and Alfred A. Moss, Jr. *From Slavery to Freedom: A History of Negro Americans*. New York: McGraw-Hill Publishing Company, 1988.

Frazier, E. Franklin. *The Negro Church in America*. New York: Schocken Books, 1964.

Fredrickson, George M. *The Black Image in the White Mind: The Debate on Afro-American Character and Destiny, 1817–1914*. New York: Harper and Row, 1971.

———. *The Inner Civil War: Northern Intellectuals and the Crisis of the Union*. New York: Harper and Row, 1965.

Freehling, William W. *Prelude to Civil War: The Nullification Controversy in South Carolina, 1816–1836*. New York: Harper and Row, 1965.

Frothingham, Octavius Brooks. *The Religion of Humanity: An Essay*. New York: G. P. Putnam's Sons, 1875.

———. *Transcendentalism in New England: A History*. New York: G. P. Putnam's Sons, 1880.

Gates, Henry Louis, Jr. *Figures in Black: Words, Signs, and the "Racial" Self*. New York: Oxford University Press, 1987.

———. *Six Women's Slave Narratives*. New York: Oxford University Press, 1988.

———. *The Classic Slave Narratives*. New York: Mentor, 1987.

Gelatt, Roland. *The Fabulous Phonograph: From Tin Foil to High Fidelity*. Philadelphia: J. B. Lippincott Co., 1954.

Genovese, Eugene D. *Roll, Jordan, Roll: The World the Slaves Made*. New York: Pantheon, 1974.

Gerth, H. H., and C. Wright Mills. *From Max Weber: Essays in Sociology*. New York: Oxford University Press, 1946.

Giddens, Anthony. *New Rules of Sociological Method*. New York: Basic Books, 1976.

———. *Social Theory and Modern Sociology*. Stanford, Calif.: Stanford University Press, 1987.

Gilroy, Paul. *The Black Atlantic: Modernity and Double Consciousness*. Cambridge: Harvard University Press, 1993.

Goddard, Harold Clarke. *Studies in New England Transcendentalism*. New York: Hillary House Publishers, 1960.

Gohdes, Clarence L. F. *The Periodicals of American Transcendentalism*. Durham, N.C.: Duke University Press, 1931.

Goldmann, Lucien. *Cultural Creation in Modern Society*. Translated by Bart Grahl. St. Louis: Telos Press, 1976.

———. *Essays on Method in the Sociology of Literature*. Translated and edited by William Q. Boelhower. St. Louis: Telos Press, 1980.

Gordon, Avery F. *Ghostly Matters: Haunting and the Sociological Imagination*. Minneapolis: University of Minnesota Press, 1997.

Gosset, Thomas F. *Race: The History of an Idea in America*. Dallas: Southern Methodist University Press, 1963.

Gougeon, Len, and Joel Myerson, eds. *Emerson's Antislavery Writings*. New Haven and London: Yale University Press, 1995.

Gramsci, Antonio. *Selections from the Prison Notebooks*. Translated and edited by Quentin Hoare. New York: International Publishers, 1971.

Great Britain, House of Commons. *Minutes of Evidence Taken Before a Committee of the House of Commons, Being a Select Committee, Appointed to Take Examination of Witnesses Respecting the African Slave Trade. Sessional Papers*, vol. 34, 1731–1800.

Griffin, Clifford S. *Their Brothers' Keepers*. New Brunswick, N.J.: Rutgers University Press, 1960.

Griffin, George H. "The Slave Music of the South." *American Missionary Magazine* 36 (1882): 70–72.

Grimke, Charlotte Forten. *The Journals of Charlotte Forten Grimke*. Edited by Brenda Stevenson. New York: Oxford University Press, 1988.

Gutman, Herbert. *Work, Culture, and Society in Industrializing America: Essays in American Working-Class and Social History*. New York: Vintage Books, 1977.

Habermas, Jurgen. *The Structural Transformation of the Public Sphere*. 1962. Reprint, Cambridge: MIT Press, 1989.

Hall, Peter Dobkin. *The Organization of American Culture, 1700–1900: Private Institutions, Elites, and the Origins of American Nationality*. New York: New York University Press, 1982.

Hampton and its Students By Two of Its Teachers, Mrs. M. F. Armstrong and Helen W. Ludlow. With Fifty Cabin and Plantation Songs. Arranged by Thomas P. Fenner. New York: G. P. Putnam's Sons, 1874.

Harding, Vincent. "Religion and Resistance among Ante-Bellum Negroes, 1800–1860." In *The Making of Black America: Essays in Negro Life and History*, ed. August Meier and Elliot Rudwick, 179–97. New York, Atheneum, 1969.

Hareven, Tamara K., ed. *Anonymous Americans: Explorations in Nineteenth-Century Social History*. Englewood Cliffs, N.J.: Prentice-Hall, 1971.

Hartshorn, W. N., ed. *An Era of Progress and Promise, 1863–1910*. Boston: Priscilla Publishing Co., 1910.

Haskell, Thomas. *The Emergence of Professional Social Science: The American Social Science Association and the Nineteenth-Century Crisis of Authority*. Urbana: University of Illinois Press, 1977.

Hawkins, William George. *Lunsford Lane; or, Another Helper from North Carolina*. Boston: Crosby and Nichols, 1863.

Hays, Elinor Rice. *Morning Star: A Biography of Lucy Stone, 1818–1893*. New York: Harcourt, Brace and World, 1961.

Herskovits, Melville J. *The Myth of the Negro Past*. Boston: Beacon Press, 1958.

Higginbotham, Evelyn Brooks. "Rethinking Vernacular Culture: Black Religion and Race Records in the 1920s and 1930s." In *The House the Race Built: Black Americans, U.S. Terrain*, edited by Wahneema Lubiano, 157–77. New York: Pantheon Books, 1997.

Higginson, Thomas Wentworth. *Army Life in a Black Regiment and Other Writings*. 1870. Reprint, New York: Penguin, 1997.

———. *Letters and Journals of Thomas Wentworth Higginson, 1846–1906*. Edited by Mary Thatcher Higginson. 1921. Reprint, New York: Da Capo Press, 1969.

Higginson, Thomas Wentworth. "Negro Spirituals." *Atlantic Monthly* 19 (June 7, 1867):684–94.

Higham, John. *From Boundlessness to Consolidation: The Transformation of American Culture, 1848–1860*. Ann Arbor, Mich.: William L. Clements Library, 1969.

———. "The Re-Orientation of American Culture in the 1890s." In *Writing American History: Essays on Modern Scholarship*. Bloomington: Indiana University Press, 1970.

———. *Strangers in the Land: Patterns of American Nativism, 1860–1925*. New Brunswick, N.J.: Rutgers University Press, 1955.

Hoggart, Richard. *The Uses of Literacy*. New York: Oxford University Press, 1970.

Howe, Daniel Walker. *The Unitarian Conscience: Harvard Moral Philosophy, 1805–1861*. Cambridge: Harvard University Press, 1970.

Hughes, H. Stuart. *Consciousness and Society: The Reorientation of European Social Thought, 1890–1930*. New York: Vintage Books, 1958.

Hutchinson, William R. *The Modernist Impulse in American Protestantism*. Oxford: Oxford University Press, 1982.

———. *The Transcendentalist Ministers: Church Reform in the New England Renaissance*. New Haven: Yale University Press, 1959.

Huyssen, Andreas. "Adorno in Reverse: From Hollywood to Richard Wagner," *New German Critique* 29 (spring/summer 1983): 8–38.

Ignatiev, Noel. *How the Irish Became White*. New York: Routledge, 1995.

Jackson, George Pullen. *White and Negro Spirituals, Their Life Span and Kinship*. New York: J.J. Augustin, 1944.

Jackson, Luther P. "Religious Development of the Negro in Virginia from 1760 to 1860," *Journal of Negro History* 16 (April 1931): 168–239.

Jacobs, Harriet [Linda Brent]. *Incidents in the Life of a Slave Girl* (Boston, 1861). Reprinted in *The Classic Slave Narratives*, ed. Henry Louis Gates, Jr., 333–515. New York: Mentor, 1987.

James, Henry. *Hawthorne*. London: Macmillan, 1879.

Jay, Martin. *Adorno*. Cambridge: Harvard University Press, 1984.

———. *The Dialectical Imagination: A History of the Frankfurt School and the Institute for Social Research, 1923–1950*. Boston: Little Brown and Co., 1973.

"Jazz Path of Degradation," *Ladies' Home Journal* (January 1922).

Johnson, Charles S. *Shadow of the Plantation*. Chicago: University of Chicago Press, 1934.

Johnson, Guy B. *Folk Culture on St. Helena Island*. Chapel Hill: University of North Carolina Press, 1930.

Johnston, Hugo James. *Race Relations in Virginia and Miscegenation in the South, 1776–1860*. Amherst: University of Massachusetts Press, 1970.

Jones, Charles Colcock *The Religious Instruction of the Negroes in the United States*. 1842. Reprint, New York: Negro Universities Press, 1969.

Jones, Le Roi. *Blues People: The Negro Experience in White America and the Music That Developed from It*. New York: Morrow Quill Paperbacks, 1963.

Jordan, Winthrop D. *White over Black: American Attitudes toward the Negro, 1550–1872.* Chapel Hill: University of North Carolina Press, 1968.

Journal of American Folk-Lore, 1, no. 1 (April–June 1888).

Keller, Suzanne. *Beyond the Ruling Class: Strategic Elites in Modern Society.* New York: Random House, 1963.

Kemble, Frances Anne. *Journal of a Residence on a Georgia Plantation, 1838–1839.* New York: Harper and Brothers, Publishers, 1863.

Kern, Alexander. "The Rise of Transcendentalism 1815–1860." In *Transitions in American Literary History,* edited by Harry Hayden Clark. Durham: Duke University Press, 1953.

Kingsley, Zephaniah. *Treatise on the Patriarchal or Cooperative System of Society as it Exists in Some Governments, and Colonies in America, and in the United States, under the Name of Slavery, with its Necessity and Advantages. By an Inhabitant of Florida.* 2d ed. (n.p., 1829).

Kolko, Gabriel. *Main Currents in Modern American History.* New York: Harper and Row, 1976.

Krehbiel, Henry Edward. *Afro-American Folk Songs: A Study in Racial and National Music.* New York and London: G. Schirmer, 1914.

Ladurie, LeRoy. *Carnival in Romans.* New York: George Braziller, 1979.

Langer, Susanne K. *Philosophy in a New Key: A Study in the Symbolism of Reason, Rite, and Art.* Cambridge: Harvard University Press, 1942.

Latrobe, Benjamin Henry Boneval. *Impressions Respecting New Orleans: Diary and Sketches, 1818–1820.* Edited by Samuel Wilson, Jr. New York: Columbia University Press, 1951.

Lefebvre, Henri. *Everyday Life in the Modern World.* Translated by Sacha Rabinovitch. New York: Harper and Row, 1971.

Leverenz, David. *Manhood and the American Renaissance.* Ithaca: Cornell University Press, 1989.

Levine, Lawrence. *Black Culture and Black Consciousness: Afro-American Folk Thought from Slavery to Freedom.* New York: Oxford University Press, 1977.

———. *Highbrow/Lowbrow: The Emergence of Cultural Hierarchy in America.* Cambridge: Harvard University Press, 1988.

———. "Slave Songs and Slave Consciousness: An Exploration in Nineteenth-Century Social History." In *Anonymous Americans: Explorations in Nineteenth-Century Social History,* edited by Tamara K. Hareven, 99–130. Englewood Cliffs, N.J.: Prentice-Hall, 1971.

Lewis, David Levering. *When Harlem Was in Vogue.* New York: Knopf, 1981.

Lipsitz, George. *Rainbow over Midnight: Labor and Culture in the 1940s.* Urbana: University of Illinois Press, 1994.

Litwack, Leon F. "The Emancipation of the Negro Abolitionist." In *The Antislavery Vanguard: New Essays on the Abolitionists,* edited by Martin Duberman. Princeton: Princeton University Press, 1965.

———. *North of Slavery: The Negro in the Free States, 1790–1860.* Chicago: University of Chicago Press, 1961.

Locke, Alain. *The Negro and His Music and Negro Art: Past and Present.* 1936. Reprint, New York: Arno Press, 1969.

Long, Elizabeth, ed. *From Sociology to Cultural Studies: New Perspectives*. Oxford: Blackwell Publishers, 1997.

Lott, Eric. *Love and Theft: Blackface Minstrelsy and the American Working Class*. New York: Oxford University Press, 1993.

Lovell, John. *Black Song: The Forge and the Flame*. New York: Macmillan, 1972.

Lubiano, Wahneema, ed., *The House the Race Built: Black Americans, U.S. Terrain*. New York: Pantheon Books, 1997.

Lukacs, Georg. *The Theory of the Novel*. Translated by Anna Bostock. 1920. Reprint, Cambridge: MIT Press, 1971.

Mannheim, Karl. *Ideology and Utopia: An Introduction to the Sociology of Knowledge*. Translated by Louis Wirth and Edward Shils. New York: Harcourt, Brace and World, 1936.

March, Arthur, and Ira Freeman. *The New World of Physics*. New York: Random House, 1962.

Marcus, George E., and Michael M. J. Fischer. *Anthropology as Cultural Critique: An Experimental Movement in the Human Sciences*. Chicago: University of Chicago Press, 1986.

Marsh, J. B. T. *The Story of the Fisk Jubilee Singers*. 1881. Reprint, New York: Negro Universities Press, 1960.

Marx, Leo. *The Machine in the Garden: Technology and the Pastoral Ideal in America*. Oxford: Oxford University Press, 1964.

Mason, Otis T. "The Natural History of Folklore." *Journal of American Folk-Lore* 4 (1891): 97–105.

Mather, Cotton. *The Negro Christianized: An Essay to Excite and Assist that Good Work, the Instruction of Negro Servants in Christianity*. Boston: B. Green, 1706.

Mathews, Donald G. "Religion and Slavery: The Case of the American South." In *Anti-Slavery, Religion, and Reform: Essays in Memory of Roger Anstey*, edited by Christine Bolt and Seymour Drescher, 207–32. Hamden, Conn.: Archon Books, 1980.

May, Henry F. *Protestant Churches and Industrial America*. New York: Harper and Row, 1967.

Mayfield, John. *Rehearsal for Republicanism: Free Soil and the Politics of Anti-Slavery*. Port Washington, N.Y.: Kennikat Press, 1980.

Mazlish, Bruce. *A New Science: The Breakdown of Connections and the Birth of Sociology*. New York: Oxford University Press, 1989.

McClary, Susan. *Feminine Endings: Music, Gender, and Sexuality*. Minneapolis: University of Minnesota Press, 1991.

McDowell, Deborah E., and Arnold Rampersad, eds. *Slavery and the Literary Imagination*. Baltimore: Johns Hopkins University Press, 1989.

McKay, Claude. *Harlem: Negro Metropolis*. New York: Harcourt Brace Jovanovich, 1940.

McKim, James. "Negro Songs." *Dwight's Journal of Music* 21 (1862): 148–49.

McKim, Lucy. "Songs of the Port Royal 'Contrabands.' " *Dwight's Journal of Music*, 21 (November 8, 1862): 254–55.

McMahon, R. "Unspeakable Jazz Must Go!" *Ladies' Home Journal* 38 (December 1921): 34.

Meier, August, and Elliot Rudwick, eds. *The Making of Black America*. New York: Atheneum, 1969.

Meyer, Howard N. *Colonel of the Black Regiment: The Life of Thomas Wentworth Higginson*. New York: W. W. Norton, 1967.

Miller, Perry. *The American Transcendentalists*. New York: Doubleday Anchor Books, 1957.

———. *The Life of the Mind in America, from the Revolution to the Civil War*. New York: Harcourt, Brace and World, 1965.

Mills, C. Wright. *The Causes of World War Three*. New York: Simon and Schuster, 1958.

———. *Listen, Yankee: The Revolution in Cuba*. New York: Ballantine Books, 1960.

———. *The New Men of Power: America's Labor Leaders*. New York: Harcourt, Brace, 1948.

———. *The Power Elite*. New York: Oxford University Press, 1956.

———. *Power, Politics, and People: The Collected Essays of C. Wright Mills*. Edited by Irving L. Horowitz. New York: Oxford University Press, 1963.

———. *The Sociological Imagination*. London: Oxford University Press, 1959.

———. *White Collar: The American Middle Classes*. New York: Oxford University Press, 1951.

Montejano, David. *Anglos and Mexicans in the Making of Texas, 1836–1986*. Austin: University of Texas, 1987.

"Music," *Atlantic Monthly* 1, no. 1 (November 1857): 125–28.

"Music," *Atlantic Monthly* 1, no. 5 (March 1858): 534–36.

Myrdal, Gunnar. *An American Dilemma: The Negro Problem and Modern Democracy*. New York: Harper and Brothers, 1944.

"Negro Folk Songs," *Southern Workman* 24 (February 1895): 30–32.

"Negro Music at Birth," *Musical Quarterly* 15, no. 1 (January 1919): 88–89.

Newell, William Wells. "Individual and Collective Characteristics in Folk-Lore." *Journal of American Folk-Lore* 19, no. 4 (January–March 1906): 1–15.

Newfield, Christopher. *The Emerson Effect: Individualism and Submission in America*. Chicago: University of Chicago Press, 1996.

Nichols, Charles H. *Many Thousand Gone: The Ex-Slaves' Account of Their Bondage and Freedom*. Leidan, Netherlands: E. J. Brill, 1963.

———. "Who Read the Slave Narratives?" *Phylon* no. 20 (1959): 149–62.

Northup, Solomon. *Twelve Years a Slave: The Narrative of Solomon Northup, a Citizen of New York, Kidnaped in Washington City in 1841 and Rescued in 1853, from a Cotton Plantation near the Red River in Louisiana*. Auburn, N.Y.: Derby and Miler, 1853.

Novick, Peter. *That Noble Dream: The "Objectivity Question" and the American Historical Profession*. Cambridge: Cambridge University Press, 1988.

Oakley, Giles. *The Devil's Music: A History of the Blues*. New York: Harcourt Brace Jovanovich, Harvest, 1976.

Oliver, Paul. *Songsters and Saints: Vocal Traditions on Race Records*. Cambridge: Cambridge University Press, 1984.

Olmsted, Frederick Law. *A Journey in the Seaboard Slave States in the Years 1853–1854*. 2 vols. 1904. Reprint, New York: G. P. Putnam's Sons, 1856.

Ortner, Sherry B. "Theory in Anthropology since the Sixties." In *Culture/Power/ History: A Reader in Contemporary Social Theory*, edited by Nicholas B. Dirks, Geoff Eley, and Sherry B. Ortner. Princeton: Princeton University Press, 1994.

Parker, Theodore. "The American Scholar." In *The American Scholar*, edited by George Willis Cooke. Vol 8. of *Centenary Edition of Theodore Parker's Writings*. Boston: American Unitarian Association, 1907.

Parrington, V. L. *The Romantic Revolution in American, 1800–1860*. 1927. Reprint, Norman: University of Oklahoma Press 1987.

Peabody, Charles. "Notes on Negro Music." *Journal of American Folk-Lore* 16 (July 1903): 148–52.

Peabody, Ephriam. "Narratives of Fugitive Slaves." *Christian Examiner* 47 (July 1849), 61–93.

Peiss, Kathy. *Cheap Amusements: Working Women and Leisure in New York City, 1880–1920*. Philadelphia: Temple University Press, 1985.

Perrow, E. C. "Songs and Rhymes from the South." *Journal of American Folklore* 26 (1913): 145–46.

Piaget, Jean. *Genetic Epistemology*. Translated by Eleanor Duckworth. New York: W. W. Norton and Co., 1970.

Pike, Gustavus D. *The Jubilee Singers and Their Campaign for Twenty Thousand Dollars*. Boston: Lee and Shepherd Publishers, 1872.

Poster, Mark. *Existential Marxism in Postwar France: From Sartre to Althusser*. Princeton: Princeton University Press, 1975.

Quarles, Benjamin. "Abolition's Different Drummer: Frederick Douglass." In *The Antislavery Vanguard: New Essays on the Abolitionists,* edited by Martin Duberman, 123–34. Princeton: Princeton University Press, 1965.

Raboteau, Albert J. *Slave Religion: The "Invisible Institution" in the Antebellum South*. New York: Oxford University Press, 1978.

Raleigh, John Henry. *Matthew Arnold and America*. Berkeley: University of California Press, 1961.

Raper, Arthur. *Preface to Peasantry: A Tale of Two Black Belt Counties*. 1936. Reprint, New York: Atheneum, 1974.

Rathbun, Frederick G. "The Negro Music of the South." In *Southern Workman* 22 (November 1893):174.

Rawick, George P. *The American Slave: A Composite Autobiography*. Vol. 1, *From Sundown to Sunup: The Making of the Black Community*. Westport, Conn.: Greenwood Publishing, 1972.

Riis, Thomas. "The Cultivated White Tradition and Black Music in Nineteenth-Century America: A Discussion of Some Articles in J. S. Dwight's *Journal of Music*." *Black Perspective in Music* 4, no. 2 (July 1976): 156–76.

Riland, John. *Memoirs of a West-India Planter*. London: Hamilton, Adams, 1828.

Roediger, David R. *The Wages of Whiteness: Race and the Making of the American Working Class*. London: Verso, 1991.

Rogin, Michael Paul. *Blackface, White Noise: Jewish Immigrants in the Hollywood Melting Pot*. Berkeley: University of California Press, 1996.

Rose, Gillian. *The Melancholy Science: An Introduction to the Thought of Theodor W. Adorno*. New York: Columbia University Press, 1978.

Rose, Tricia. *Black Noise: Rap Music and Black Culture in Contemporary America*. Hanover, N.H.: Wesleyan University Press, 1994.

Rose, Willie L. *Rehearsal for Reconstruction: The Port Royal Experiment*. New York: Vintage, 1967.

Ross, Dorothy. *The Origins of American Social Science*. Cambridge: Cambridge University Press, 1991.

Said, Edward. *Orientalism*. New York: Vintage Books, 1979.

Sampson, Henry T. *Blacks in Blackface*. Metuchen, N.J.: Scarecrow Press, 1980.

Sams, Henry W. *Autobiography of Brook Farm*. Englewood Cliffs, N.J.: Prentice-Hall, 1958.

Sarfatti, Magali. "Spanish Bureaucratic-Patrimonialism in America." Politics of Modernization Series, no. 1. Berkeley: Institute of International Studies, 1966.

Saxon, Alexander. *The Indispensable Enemy: Labor and the Anti-Chinese Movement in California*. 1971. Reprint, Berkeley: University of California Press, 1995.

———. *The Rise and Fall of the White Republic: Class Politics and Mass Culture in Nineteenth-Century America*. London: Verso, 1990.

Scarborough, Dorothy. *On the Trail of Negro Folk-Songs*. Cambridge: Harvard University Press, 1925.

Scarry, Elaine. *The Body in Pain: The Making and Unmaking of the World*. New York: Oxford University Press, 1985.

Schlesinger, Arthur M., Jr. *The Age of Jackson*. Boston: Little, Brown, and Co., 1953.

Schluchter, Wolfgang. "The Future of Religion." In *Religion and America*, edited by Mary Douglas and Steven M. Tipton. Boston: Beacon Press, 1982.

Schudson, Michael. *Discovering the News: A Social History of American Newspapers*. New York: Basic Books, 1978.

Schwartz, Harold. "Fugitive Slave Days in Boston." *New England Quarterly* 27 (March 1954): 191–212.

Scott, James C. *Domination and the Arts of Resistance: Hidden Transcripts*. New Haven: Yale University Press, 1990.

Sernett, Milton C. *Black Religion and American Evangelicalism: White Protestants, Plantation Missions, and the Flowering of Negro Christianity, 1787–1865*. Metuchen, N.J.: Scarecrow Press, 1975.

Simmel, Georg. *On Individuality and Social Forms*. Edited by Donald N. Levine. Chicago: University of Chicago Press, 1971.

Slotkin, Richard R. *The Fatal Environment: The Myth of the Frontier in the Age of Industrialization, 1800–1890*. New York: Atheneum, 1985.

———. *Gunfighter Nation: The Mythology of the Frontier in Twentieth-Century America*. New York: Atheneum, 1992.

———. *Regeneration through Violence: The Mythology of the American Frontier*. Middletown, Conn.: Wesleyan University Press, 1973.

Small, Christopher. *Music of the Common Tongue: Survival and Celebration in Afro-American Music*. New York: Riverrun Press, 1987.

Smith, Timothy L. *Revivalism and Social Reform: American Protestantism on the Eve of the Civil War.* New York: Harper Torchbooks, 1965.

————. "Slavery and Theology: The Emergence of Black Christian Consciousness in Nineteenth-Century America." *Church History*, 41, no. 4 (December 1972): 497–512.

Smith, Valerie. *Self-Discovery and Authority in Afro-American Narrative.* Cambridge: Harvard University Press, 1987.

Sobel, Mechal. *Trabelin' On: The Slave Journey to an Afro-Baptist Faith.* Princeton: Princeton University Press, 1988.

Southern, Eileen. *The Music of Black Americans: A History.* New York: W. W. Norton, 1971.

————. *Readings in Black American Music.* New York: W. W. Norton, 1971.

Spaulding, Henry George. "Under the Palmetto." In *Continental Monthly* 4 (August 1863), 188–203.

Starks, George L., Jr. "Salt and Pepper in Your Shoe: Afro-American Song Tradition on the South Carolina Sea Islands." In *More Than Dancing: Essays on Afro-American Music and Musicians*, edited by Irene V. Jackson, 59–80. Westport, Conn.: Greenwood Press, 1985.

Starling, Marion Wilson. *The Slave Narrative: Its Place in American History.* Boston: G. K. Hall and Co., 1981.

Steward, James Brewer. *Holy Warriors: The Abolitionists and American Slavery.* New York: Hill and Wang, 1996.

Stout, Harry S. *The New England Soul: Preaching and Religious Culture in Colonial New England.* New York: Oxford University Press, 1986.

Stuckey, Sterling. *Slave Culture: Nationalist Theory and the Foundations of Black America.* New York: Oxford University Press, 1987.

Sumner, William Graham. *Folkways: A Study of the Sociological Importance of Usages, Manners, Customs, Mores, and Morals.* Boston: Ginn and Company, 1906.

Sundquist, Eric J. "Slavery, Revolution, and the American Renaissance." In *The American Renaissance Reconsidered*, edited by Walter Benn Michaels and Donald E. Pease, 1–33. Baltimore: Johns Hopkins University Press, 1985.

Suttles, William C. "African Religious Survivals as Factors in American Slave Revolts." *Journal of Negro History* 56 (1971): 97–104.

Takaki, Ronald. *Iron Cages: Race and Culture in Nineteenth-Century America.* New York: Oxford University Press, 1990.

Taylor, Charles. *Sources of the Self: The Making of the Modern Identity.* Cambridge: Harvard University Press, 1989.

Thomas, John L. "Romantic Reform in America, 1815–1865." *American Quarterly* 17 (winter 1965): 656–681.

Thompson, Edward P. *The Making of the English Working Class.* New York: Vintage Books, 1963.

Thoreau, Henry David. "Life without Principle." In *The American Transcendentalists: Their Prose and Poetry*, edited by Perry Miller, 308–29. Garden City, N.Y.: Doubleday Anchor Books, 1957.

————. *The Writings of Henry David Thoreau: Journal.* Edited by Bradford Torrey. Boston and New York, 1906.

Toll, Robert. *Blacking Up: The Minstrel Show in Nineteenth-Century America.* London: Oxford University Press, 1974.

Torgovnick, Marianna. *Gone Primitive: Savage Intellects, Modern Lives.* Chicago: University of Chicago Press, 1990.

Trachtenberg, Alan. *The Incorporation of America: Culture and Society in the Gilded Age.* New York: Hill and Wang, 1982.

Trattner, Walter I. *From Poor Law to Welfare State: A History of Social Welfare in America.* New York: Free Press, 1974.

Tucker, Robert C., ed. *The Marx-Engels Reader.* 2d ed. New York: W. W. Norton and Co., 1978.

Tylor, Edward Burnett. *Primitive Culture.* Vol. 2. Boston: Estes and Lauriat, 1874.

Vance, Lee J. "The Study of Folk-Lore." *Forum* 22 (1896–97): 249–56.

Vassa, Gustavus. *The Interesting Narrative of the Life of Oloudah Equiano, or Gustavus Vassa, the African.* 1789. Reprint, Leeds: James Nichols, 1814.

Volosinov, V. N. *Marxism and the Philosophy of Language.* Translated by Ladislave Matejka and I. R. Titunik. New York: Seminar Press, 1973.

Walker, David. *Appeal in Four Articles, Together with a Preamble to the Coloured Citizens of the World, But in Particular, and very Expressly, to those of the United States of America.* Boston, 1830.

Walser, Robert. *Running with the Devil: Power, Gender, and Madness in Heavy Metal Music.* Hanover, N.H.: University Press of New England, 1993.

Walters, Ronald G. *The Anti-Slavery Appeal: American Abolitionism after 1830.* Baltimore: Johns Hopkins University Press, 1976.

Washington, Joseph R., Jr. *Black Religion: The Negro and Christianity in the United States.* Boston: Beacon Press, 1964.

————. *Black Sects and Cults.* New York: Doubleday and Co. 1972.

Watson, John F. *Methodist Error; or, Friendly Christian Advice to Those Methodists Who Indulge in Extravagant Religious Emotions and Bodily Exercises.* Trenton, N.J.: D. and E. Fenton, 1819.

Weatherford, W. D. *American Churches and the Negro: An Historical Study from Early Slave Days to the Present.* Boston: Christopher Publishing House, 1957.

Webber, Thomas L. *Deep Like the Rivers: Education in the Slave Quarter Community, 1831–1865.* New York: Norton, 1978.

Weber, Max. *From Max Weber: Essays in Sociology.* Edited by Hans Gerth and C. Wright Mills. New York: Oxford University Press, 1946.

————. *The Protestant Ethic and the Spirit of Capitalism.* 1905. Reprint, New York: Charles Scribner's Sons, 1950.

Weibe, Robert H. *The Search for Order, 1877–1920.* New York: Hill and Wang, 1967.

Weinstein, James. *The Corporate Ideal in the Liberal State, 1900–1918.* Boston: Beacon Press, 1968.

White, Newman I. *American Negro Folk-Songs.* Cambridge: Harvard University Press, 1928.

White, Morton. *Social Thought in America: The Revolt against Formalism*. Boston: Beacon Press, 1957.

Williams, Raymond. *Culture and Society, 1780–1950*. New York: Harper and Row, 1958.

———. *Marxism and Literature*. Oxford: Oxford University Press, 1977.

———. *The Sociology of Culture*. New York: Schocken Books, 1982.

Williams, William Appleman. *The Contours of American History*. New York: New Viewpoints, 1973.

Woodson, Carter G. *The History of the Negro Church*. 1921. Reprint, Washington, D.C.: Associated Publishers, 1972.

Woodward, C. Vann. *Reunion and Reaction: The Compromise of 1877 and the End of Reconstruction*. Boston: Little, Brown, 1951.

Yetman, Norman. "The Background of the Slave Narrative Collection." *American Quarterly* 19 (1967): 534–53.

SUBJECT INDEX

abolitionism: and the cultural turn, 23, 131; and ethnosympathy, 6, 69; first probe of black music by, 117; as juncture, 12; racial attitudes during, 251n.2; radical, 88, 118, 120; redemptive politics of, 6; and religion, 134; and religious antagonism, 120; as site for romanticism and disenchantment, 126; as "surrogate religion", 227n.51

abolitionist movement, 13, 43, 82, 97; cultural arsenal of, 99; and cultural authenticity, 27, 82; interpretive benevolence within, 111; and societies, 88

abolitionist press, 88, 90

abolitionists, 4, 11, 59, 106; black, 66, 88; and black song making, 11, 69, 121; hearing schemas of, 43; self- flattery of, 119; white, 13, 17, 19, 36, 109, 121. *See also* critical abolitionists

Adorno, Theodor, 25; and criticism, 208n.7; immanent critique, 230n.71, 234n.4

aestheticism: of black subjects, 31; and social disengagement, 31, 183

aesthetic nationalism, 115. *See also* cultural nationalism.

aesthetics, 17

African-American Methodist Church, 77, 80

Africanist practices, 85, 216n.10

alienation, sense of, 5

Allen, William Frances, 13, 33, 54, 56, 100, 124, 130, 136, 142, 155, 164, 168, 180, 249n.77; compared to Higginson, 151, 162; and cultural interpretation, 123, 126; cultural syncretism noted by, 186; and natural history, 160; and Reconstruction, 162; role in cultural preservation of black songs, 152–53, 166; role in publication of black songs, 33, 49, 125, 128, 133; scientism in, 143, 151–54, 157, 197; and shift away from black music as testimonies, 162–63, 177, 182; on shouts, 156; and *Slave Songs of the United States*, 133, 142, 152–54, 160, 165; ties to Unitarianism, 221n.2

Althusser, Louis, 71; ideological state apparatuses, 211n.31, 253n.27; interpellation of subject, 71, 215n.38

American Anti-Slavery Society, 80, 246n.39

American cultural aesthetic, 102

American culture, 7

American Folk-Lore Society, 55, 160, 165, 185; and Franz Boas, 176; and Hampton Institute, 168–69, 171–72, 174, 185

American Journal of Folk-Lore, 174, 176, 198, 250n.90; abandonment of moral-political imperatives in, 181; professional mission of, 179

American music criticism, 115

American Social Science Association, 140

Anderson, James, 173

Andover Theological Seminary, 133

Andrews, William, 229n.68, 232n.78

antiinstitutionalism, 251–52n.5; convergence of black Christianization and, 82; disenchantment in, 82; and Transcendentalism, 137; and Unitarianism, 82; and Weber, 242n.14

antislavery movement, 67, 117, 165; and Garrison, 6, 90, 112, 118; growth of, 76, 80; literature, 67; propaganda of, 125; white reading public for, 165

Anti-Slavery Standard, 129

Aptheker, Herbert, 77

Aquinas, Thomas, 223n.10

Armistead, Wilson, 91

Armstrong, General Samuel, 164, 171, 174; opposition to black political rights in, 173

Arnold, Matthew, 159; *Culture and Anarchy*, 159

art, 114, and black music, 37

Asians, 191, 201

associationism, 115, 137, 147, 244n.29

Atlantic Monthly, 114–15

Attali, Jacques, 63–65; *Noise: The Political Economy of Music*: 63

authenticity: and American high-brow culture, 29, 114; black, 6; black schools concerned with, 166–75; capturing, 101; conjuring, 42; crisis of, 21, 23–26, 100;

SONGS CITED INDEX